# PERU

## INCIDENTS OF TRAVEL AND EXPLORATION

### IN THE

# LAND OF THE INCAS

GATE-WAY AND VALLEY OF OLLANTAYTAMBO.

# PERU ILLUSTRATED

OR,

## Incidents of Travel and Exploration
## in the Land of the Incas.

BY

### E. GEORGE SQUIER, M.A., F.S.A.,

*LATE U. S. COMMISSIONER TO PERU.*

**Author** of "NICARAUGA," ANCIENT MONUMENTS OF MISSISSIPPI
VALLEY," Etc., Etc.

NEW YORK:
HURST & COMPANY,
PUBLISHERS.

# CONTENTS.

## CHAPTER I.

### INTRODUCTORY.

## CHAPTER II.

### NEW YORK TO LIMA.

## CHAPTER III.

### LIMA—THE CITY OF THE KINGS.

## CHAPTER IV.

### PACHACAMAC.

## CHAPTER V.

### RUINS IN THE VICINITY OF LIMA.

## CHAPTER VI.

### UP THE COAST TO TRUXILLO.

## CHAPTER VII.

### TRUXILLO—RECONNOISSANCE OF GRAND CHIMU.

## CHAPTER VIII.

### THE RUINS AT MOCHE.

## CHAPTER IX.

### EXPLORATIONS AT GRAND CHIMU.

## CHAPTER X.

### LEGENDARY HISTORY OF THE CHIMUS.

## CHAPTER XI.

### THE ART, CUSTOMS, AND RELIGION OF THE CHIMUS.

## CHAPTER XII.

### EXPLORATIONS NEAR THE COAST.

## CHAPTER XIII.

### FROM LIMA TO TACNA.

## CHAPTER XIV.

### OVER THE CORDILLERA TO TIAHUANACO.

## CHAPTER XV.

### TIAHUANACO, THE BAALBEC OF THE NEW WORLD.

## CHAPTER XVI.

### AT TIAHUANACO, AND TO THE SACRED ISLANDS.

## CHAPTER XVII.

### THE SACRED ISLANDS OF TITICACA.

# CHAPTER XXI.

### FROM LAKE TITICACA TO CUZCO.

# CHAPTER XXII.

### CUZCO, THE CITY OF THE SUN.

## CHAPTER XXIII.

### SACSAHUAMAN, THE ANCIENT FORTRESS OF CUZCO.

## CHAPTER XXIV.

### THE VALLEY OF YUCAY.—OLLANTAYTAMBO.

## CHAPTER XXV.

### THE VALLEY OF YUCAY.—PISAC.

## CHAPTER XXVI.

### OVER THE CORDILLERA, FROM CUZCO TO THE COAST.

## CHAPTER XXVII.

### CONCLUSION.

# ILLUSTRATIONS.

1

# INCIDENTS OF TRAVEL AND EXPLORATION

IN

# THE LAND OF THE INCAS.

## CHAPTER I.

### INTRODUCTORY.

MANY years ago, Mr. Prescott, in the Essay on the Civilization of the Incas, prefixed to his "History of the Conquest of Peru," said, in words which were echoed by every thoughtful student of antiquities:

"The hand of the conquerors fell heavily on the venerable monuments of Peru; and, in their blind and superstitious search for hidden treasure, they caused infinitely more ruin than time or the earthquake. Yet enough of the monuments of the Incas remain to invite the researches of the antiquary. Those only in the most conspicuous situations have hitherto been examined. But, by the testimony of travellers, many more are to be found in the less-frequented parts of the country, and we may hope they will one day call forth a kindred spirit of enterprise to that which has so successfully explored the myste.· ous recesses of Central America and Yucatan."

At that time a mere youth, I was engaged, with limited resources but an earnest purpose, in investigating the aboriginal monuments of the Mississippi Valley, and these words of Prescott did not fall on unheedful ears. One of the results of those investigations was the warm, personal friendship of that distinguished historian. It was, in a great degree, through his influence that I was subsequently sent as representative of the United States to Central America, where every interval of leisure was dedicated to the discovery of the resources and the illustration of the ante-Columbian, and as yet imperfectly understood, history of that interesting region. In all my labors I was constantly and earnestly supported by the sympathy, and, so far as my researches deserved it, by the appreciation, of that most estimable man and conscientious student. To visit the land of the Children of the Sun, and to realize, in some degree at least, his aspirations, became a leading purpose of my life.

But inexorable circumstances, distracting occupations, and the thousand vicissitudes which make us what we are, and often prevent us from becoming what we might have been, interfered to defeat my hopes and aspirations; till at length, owing to undue exposure and protracted over-exertion, the light began to fade away before my eyes, and a dark veil fell between them and the bright and moving world without. The skill of eminent oculists was exerted in vain, and I was told that my only alternative lay between absolute mental rest and total blindness. Rest, and an entire change of scene and occupation, might perhaps restore, at least partially, my failing vision.

Then, and not till then, an unexpected concurrence of circumstances enabled me to realize the hope which I had so long cherished. I received the appointment of Commissioner of the

United States to Peru, charged with the settlement of the conflicting claims between the two countries. Away from the rush of business, and the irritation of the morning newspaper; in the cool corridors of the gray old Palace of the Inquisition, in Lima, the city of the kings, which Pizarro founded, and in which he died; listening calmly to quotations from Vattel, Puffendorf, and Wheaton; valuing guano with an indifference that might startle thrifty farmers; and disposing, in a day, of reclamations which had sent more than one war-vessel around the Horn, and had even brought on the direful catastrophe of striking the flag of an envoy extraordinary: here, close by the spot where more than a hundred heretics had been burned alive, and more than three hundred had been beaten with rods—here the day came back to the failing vision, and the glorious light once more vibrated on responsive nerves, and filled the sinking heart with joy and gratitude.

It was on the conclusion of my duties as Commissioner that I commenced my explorations in Peru; explorations directed mainly to the elucidation of its aboriginal monuments, the only positive and reliable witnesses of the true condition of its ancient inhabitants. My travels and investigations occupied me actively for more than a year and a half. During that time I probably went over more ground than any of my predecessors in the same field. I carried with me the compass, the measuring-line, the pencil, and the photographic camera; knowing well that only accurate plans, sections, elevations, drawings, and views can adequately meet the rigorous demands of modern science, and render clear what mere verbal description would fail to make intelligible.

My expeditions carried me first through the coast region of Peru, lying between the Cordillera and the sea, from Tumbez to Cobija, or from latitude 2° to 22° south. Within this region lie the vast ruins of Grand Chimu, Pachacamac, and Cajamarquilla, besides numberless others, less known but equally interesting, in the valleys of Santa, Nepeña, Casma, Chillon, Rimac, Cañete, Pisco, and Arica. From the port of Arica my course

was inland over the Cordillera into Bolivia, where are the remarkable ruins of Tiahuanuco; thence to Lake Titicaca and
its sacred islands, whence the Incas dated their origin. I believe I am the only traveller who ever thoroughly traversed
this great and interesting lake, lying 12,500 feet above the sea;
an undertaking of no little difficulty and danger, when carried
out in a small open boat. From the Titicaca basin my course
was still northward, over the great divide, or water-shed, separating the head-waters of the streams flowing into the grand
basin of Lake Titicaca from the sources of the Amazon; down
the valley of the Vilcanota, which is probably the true parent
stream of the Amazon, to the cluster of mountain-circled *bolsones*, or high valleys, in which the Incas founded the capital
of their mighty empire. From Cuzco my expeditions radiated
for one hundred miles in every direction, and were carried to
the savage frontier, on the Atlantic declivity of the Andes.
Several months were spent in and around the Inca capital, in
many respects the most interesting spot on the continent.
Thence my course was to the north-west, very nearly on the
line of the great interior road of the Incas, which extends from
Cuzco to Quito, crossing the head-waters of the streams which
combine to form the Amazon, through Abancay, the ancient
Guamanga, now called Ayacucho, and thence back to Lima.

With a longer time and more adequate means at my command, I could have greatly extended the field of my explorations; but, so far as my principal object—that of illustrating
Inca civilization from its existing monuments—is concerned, I
believe that the results would have been merely cumulative.
As it was, I brought back with me more than four hundred
plans, sections, and elevations; about as many sketches and
drawings; a large number of photographs, and a considerable
collection of works of art and industry. A selection of the
most important and interesting of these will be embodied in
this volume, leaving little to be desired by the student in respect of Peruvian archæology, so far as its elucidation depends
on the monuments of the country.

These materials will, I think, show not only that there were originally several detached and distinct civilizations in Peru, but that some of them antedated the Incas; while my observations on the geography and topography of the country will show how the Incas were enabled to establish their extensive dominion, and how their expansive and astute policy was suggested and developed. My researches will, I think, correct many mistakes and exaggerations as regards ancient Peru, and enable us to form a rational and just estimate of the power and development of the most thoroughly organized, most wisely administered, and most extensive empire of aboriginal America, concerning which we have hitherto had little for the guidance of our judgment, except the vague traditions of the natives themselves, and the too often partial and distorted chronicles of the conquerors. The absence of written records of the Incas and the tribes consolidated with them unhappily leave us only these traditions and chronicles whence to deduce their character and original condition; and hence researches like those I undertook become invested with a value less to be measured by the capacity of the individual who made them, than by the number and nature of the facts presented by him.

The Inca empire had attained its greatest extension and power precisely at the period of the discovery by Columbus, under the reign of Huayna Capac, who, rather than Huascar or Atahualpa, should be called the last of the Incas. His father, the Inca Tupac Yupanqui, had pushed his conquests on the south, beyond the great desert of Atacama, to the river Maule, in Chili; while, at the same time, Huayna Capac himself had reduced the powerful and refined kingdom of the Sciris of Quito, on the north. From their great dominating central plateau, the Incas had pressed down to the Pacific, on the one hand, and to the dense forests of the Amazonian valleys, on the other. Throughout this wide region, and over all its nations, principalities, and tribes, Huayna Capac at the beginning of the sixteenth century ruled supreme. His empire extended from four degrees above the equator to the thirty-fourth southern parallel of latitude, a distance of not far from three thousand miles; while from east to west it spread, with varying width, from the

Pacific to the valleys of Paucartambo and Chuquisaca, an average distance of not far from four hundred miles, covering an area, therefore, of more than one million square miles, equal to about one-third of the total area of the United States, or to the whole of the United States to the eastward of the Mississippi River.

The geographical and topographical features of this vast region are singularly bold and remarkable, and reacted powerfully on its ancient, as they do on its present, inhabitants. The physical characteristics, the mental and moral traits, the polity and religion, the architecture and arts, the manners, customs, and modes of life of the aboriginal population could not escape being moulded or controlled by natural conditions and circumstances so extraordinary and potential as prevailed throughout the Inca dominions. The empire itself could never have existed, nor the Incas have obtained any extraordinary ascendancy over their neighbors, or have developed a civilization so advanced as theirs, had it not been for exceptional circumstances of position, influencing alike climate and productions, and directing their power and ambition in fixed channels.

In no part of the world does nature assume grander, more imposing, or more varied forms. Deserts as bare and repulsive as those of Sahara alternate with valleys as rich and luxuriant as those of Italy. Lofty mountains, crowned with eternal snow, lift high their rugged sides over broad, bleak *punas*, or tablelands, themselves more elevated than the summits of the White Mountains or of the Alleghanies. Rivers, taking their rise among melting snows, precipitate themselves through deep and rocky gorges into the Pacific, or wind, with swift but gentler current, among the majestic but broken Andes, to swell the flood of the Amazon. There are lakes, ranking in size with those that feed the St. Lawrence, whose surfaces lie almost level with the summit of Mont Blanc; and they are the centres of great terrestrial basins, with river systems of their own, and having no outlet to the sea.

The two great mountain ranges which determine the physical aspect of the South American continent attain their maximum of bulk, and have their most decided features in what was the Inca Empire. The western range, popularly denominated the Cordillera, runs nearly parallel to the coast throughout its whole length, and at such short distance inland that, to the voyager, the ocean seems literally to break at its feet. Even where it recedes farthest from the shore, it throws forward outliers, or spurs, which cease to be imposing only when contrasted with the mighty masses of the mother mountain. There is, nevertheless, a narrow but often interrupted strip of land between the Cordillera and the sea, which, however, from Guayaquil southward is throughout as desert as the flanks of the mountains themselves are bare and repulsive. A waste of sand and rock, it is the domain of death and silence—a silence only broken by the screams of water-birds and the howls of the sealions that throng its frayed and forbidding shore.

Bold men were the *conquistadores*, who coasted slowly along these arid shores in face of the prevailing south wind and against the great Antarctic current. Nothing short of an absorbing love of adventure, and a consuming and quenchless avarice, could have prevented them from putting down their helms and flying shudderingly from the Great Desolation before them.

For the most part the sand is hard, swept smooth by the winds, and unrelieved by anything except an occasional stone and the more frequent skeletons of mules and horses that have perished by the way. In places, however, the traveller comes upon great heaps formed by the drifting sands, called *medanos.* They are all crescent-shaped, with the bow of the crescent towards the wind, and as regular and sharp in outline as the new moon itself. Some, which have a core of rock, are permanent; but most are shifting, varying in shape and position with the varying winds.

This desert strip, averaging perhaps forty miles in width, where rain falls only at rare and uncertain intervals, is nevertheless intersected here and there by valleys of great fertility and beauty, and often of considerable size. They are formed by the streams and torrents from the mountains, which are fed by the melting snows, or by the rains that fall, during a part of the year, in the interior. Some of these streams are swallowed up by the thirsty sands before they reach the sea, and only form oases at the outlets of the gorges whence they emerge. But both oasis and valley, in the ancient time, were densely populated by men who exhausted the utmost capabilities of the narrow valleys, and who have left many monuments of their skill and greatness. Under the pressure of peculiar conditions and limited means, they developed a social and industrial system (as is shown by their remains) that Fourier might have envied, and the apostles of economical organizations may study with profit and admiration.

These valleys are often separated from each other, in their lower portions, by many leagues of trackless desert, and in their upper portions by impassable mountains. Their inhabitants, therefore, constituted separate communities, independent in government, and with little, if any, intercourse or relationship. In a few instances, however, where several considerable valleys converge and come closely together, as near Truxillo and Lima, large and efficient civil and political organizations were effected, and the united communities took the form and status of a state. But, in general, the inhabitants of the various valleys were isolated and relatively weak, owing their security from the avarice or ambition of their more powerful neighbors to the barriers of mountain and desert which shut them in. We can understand, from these conditions, how it was that the Spaniards encountered no serious opposition when they landed on the coast.

Back of this narrow strip of coast lies the giant bulk of the Cordillera. It is a vast terrestrial billow, bristling with volcanoes and snowy peaks, and supporting a minor net-work of hills and mountains. Although of probably less average elevation than the Eastern Cordillera or the Andes, it is nevertheless the true water-shed of the South American continent. The Andes are pierced by numberless deep valleys, through which most of the waters collected between the two ranges flow, in uncounted streams and rivers, into the Amazon, the Orinoco, and the Plata; but the Cordillera of the Pacific is throughout unbroken.

Its summit often spreads out in broad, undulating plains, or
*punas*, varying from fourteen to eighteen thousand feet above
the sea, frigid, barren, desolate, and where life is only represented by the hardy vicuña and the condor. This inhospitable
region is the great *Despoblado*, or unpeopled region, of Peru.
Here, except on some of the more important trails over the
mountains, where we find the ruins of Inca *tambos*, or huts of
refuge, badly represented by the few and wretched *postas* of
modern times, no trace of human habitation is discovered. The
traveller is happy to obtain the protection of a cave or the shelter of a rock at night, and by day hurries as fast as his starving
and unsteady mule, suffering from the rarefication of the atmosphere, will enable him, across the dreary waste.

The Despoblado, sometimes called the Black Puna, has a general breadth of perhaps a hundred and fifty miles. It narrows
in Northern Peru, and widens as we approach Chili. It varies
also in elevation, but sustains throughout its desolate and repulsive character.

Beyond the Despoblado, we descend into the lower yet lofty
plateau intervening between the Cordillera of the coast and the
glittering Andes. The average elevation of this valley is considerably more than eleven thousand feet above the sea. Though
we cannot characterize it better, by a single word, than *plateau*,
or table-land, yet we must remember that it is an extensive region, with mountains and hills, plains and valleys, lakes and rivers—a microcosm of the earth itself, lifted up into the frosty
air, and held in its place by the mighty buttresses of the Andes
and the Cordilleras.* In some portions of South America these
two great ranges are from one to two hundred miles apart; in

---

* As there will be frequent occasion to speak of these two great chains, and to
distinguish them, I shall use the designations *Andes* and *Cordillera*, as they are used
in the country itself. The great backbone of the South, the Central, and the North
American portions of the continent is, unquestionably, the Eastern Cordillera, bearing in South America the specific name of Andes. Yet the Western Cordillera,
the Pacific, or Volcanic Coast-range, forms, almost throughout, the water-shed of the
entire continent. The streams which gather their supplies between the two chains,
with few exceptions, break through the eastern range, and pour into the Atlantic.

others they approach each other, and at a few points actually come together, forming a "knot," where they become indistinguishable. One of these knots is at the point known as the Pass of La Raya (latitude 14° 30′ south, longitude 70° 50′ west), where, in an inky tarn, is the true source of the Amazon, here represented by the Rio Vilcanota, and whence also flows the Rio Pacura, which falls into the great interior Lake Titicaca. Another point of contact is in Northern Peru, near the important mines of Cerro de Pasco (latitude 10° 15′ south, longitude 76° 10′ west).

To the southward of the pass of La Raya, the Andean plateau is represented by the grand terrestrial basin of lakes Titicaca and Aullagas, to which I have already alluded as having no outlet to the sea, and possessing a fluvial system of its own. In this basin we find ruins of ancient architecture singular in character, and having an antiquity possibly higher than any other of advanced civilization on the continent. It was in the islands of Lake Titicaca that, as tradition affirms, the founders of the Inca Empire had their origin. These circumstances, not less than the remarkable physical characteristics of the basin itself, entitle this portion of the Andean plateau to receive our particular attention. Viewing it from the *cumbre*, or crest, of the Cordillera, we have spread before us a region unlike any we have ever seen, and which seems to be lifted above the rest of the world in spirit as well as in fact, looking down upon it coldly and calmly like the winter stars, sharing none of its sympathies, and disturbed by none of its alarms; the silent, wondering vicuña gazing at us with its large liquid eyes; the gliding llama; and the condor, circling high up in the air, or swooping down towards us as if in menace; the absence of forests; the white clouds surging up from the plains of Brazil, only to be precipitated and dissipated by the snowy barriers which they cannot pass; the clear metallic blue of the sky; the painful silence—all impress the traveller with the feeling that he is no longer in the world that he has known before. There is nothing with which he is familiar, nothing suggestive of other scenes. Not an unfitting region this for the development of an original civilization, like that which carved its memorials in massive stones, and left them on the plain of Tiahuanuco, and of which no tradition remains, except that they are the work of the giants of old, who reared them in a single night.

The American continent affords but three really notable examples of that interesting physical phenomenon to which the basin of Titicaca belongs. The first is the great Utah basin, with its salt lake; the second is the smaller basin of Lake Itza, in Central America; the third is the vaster, more elevated, and, in all respects, more interesting basin under notice. Its greatest length, almost due north and south, is about six hundred miles; its average width may be estimated at not far from one hundred and fifty miles; thus giving a total area of about one hundred thousand square miles. The slope of this basin is gentle towards the south. At or near its northern extremity lies Lake Titicaca, a magnificent body of fresh water, and the recipient of several considerable streams. It discharges its waters through a deep, broad, and swift, but not turbulent stream, El Desaguadero, one hundred and seventy miles long, and having a fall of about five hundred feet, into Lake Aullagas, of which we as yet know next to nothing. The most that seems to be established is, that it has no visible outlet to the sea; that it receives the drainage of Lake Titicaca; that its principal feeder, the Desaguadero, is swollen by some considerable streams, after leaving Lake Titicaca; and that it has itself a number of important feeders. Its size, contour, depth, and the possible disposition of its affluence of waters, are open questions. It must be of vast superficies, indeed, if its excess of water be carried off, as has been suggested, by evaporation. The eastern border of the Titicaca basin is bounded by the loftiest section of the Andes—a vast, unbroken, snow-crowned range, whose loftiest peaks rival Chimborazo in altitude.

The islands and promontories of Lake Titicaca are for the most part barren. The waters hide a variety of strange fishes, which contribute to support a population necessarily scanty in a region where barley will not ripen, except under very favorable circumstances, and where maize, in its most diminutive

size, has its most precarious development; where the potato,
shrunk to its smallest proportions, is bitter; where the only
grain is the quinoa (*Chenopodium Quinoa*); and where the only
indigenous animals fit for food are the biscacha, the llama, and
the vicuña.

In the islands of Lake Titicaca, if tradition be our guide,
were developed the germs of Inca civilization. Thence, it is
said, went the founders of the Inca dynasty, past the high
divide between the waters flowing into the lake and those falling into the Amazon, and skirting the valley of the river Vilcanota for more than two hundred miles, they established their
seat in the *bolson* of Cuzco.

A brief description of these valleys, which nothing can better describe than the Spanish word *bolson*, or "pocket," will
help us to understand the original condition of the various peoples and families which constituted the Inca Empire, and how
the inhabitants of one valley, by uniting with those of another,
through policy or by forcible pressure, grew gradually in power
until they overflowed the Despoblado on one side, and the valleys of the Andes on the other, spreading themselves north and
south past Atacama and up to the equator.

While the narrow valleys of the coast are separated by trackless deserts, the *bolsones* are isolated by ranges of hills or mountains, or by cold, uninhabitable *punas*, and encircled by the
mighty gorges of rivers which, like the Apurimac, are impassable, except by the aid of bridges, swinging dizzily in mid-air.
The *bolsones* are of varying altitudes, and, consequently, of various climates and productions. Some are well drained; others
are marshy, and contain considerable lakes. They discharge
their gathered waters through streams which plunge down
dark and narrow ravines into the gorges of the great rivers.
The passage from one to another is over the intervening elevated ridges and *punas*, frequently among frost and snow, and
always by rocky and wearisome paths, fit only for the vicuña
and the sure-footed llama.

It was in one of these *bolsones*, the centre one of a cluster
lying between the valleys Vilcomaya and Apurimac, that the

Incas built their capital. It is not only central in position, salubrious and productive, but the barriers which separate it from the neighboring valleys are relatively low, with passes which may be traversed with comparative ease; while they are, at the same time, readily defensible. The rule of the first Inca seems not to have extended beyond this valley, and the passes leading into it are strongly fortified, showing the direction whence hostilities were anticipated in the early days of the empire, before the chiefs of Cuzco began their career of conquest and aggregation, reducing the people of the *bolson* of Anta in the north, and that of Urcos in the south.

There remains a comparatively small portion of the Inca Empire to describe. This is what is called the *Montaña*, as distinguished from the *Costa*, the *Despoblado*, and the *Sierra*. The Montaña comprises the eastern declivity of the Andes, or, rather, the valleys of the rivers flowing eastward towards the vast plains of Brazil. The Incas did not extend their empire far in this direction. They pushed down the valleys until they encountered the savage forests, and their still more savage inhabitants. Here their implements were inadequate to the subjugation of nature; and the fierce Antis, creeping through the dense thickets, launched unseen their poisoned arrows against the Children of the Sun, who protected themselves by fortifications from an enemy they could not see, and whom it was vain to pursue. They nevertheless succeeded in securing the upper portions of some of these valleys, with their wealth of tropical products: the cocoa and cotton, the skins of wild beasts, the gorgeous feathers of the birds, and many other articles of use, luxury, or beauty which rigorous nature denied them in their native eyries.

Perpetual war seems to have been waged between the Incas and the savages of the lower valleys. Even in the plenitude of their power, the Incas were unable to carry their conquests far to the eastward, certainly not more than sixty miles from their capital in that direction. The massive and complicated fortresses of Paucartambo, Pisac, and Ollantaytambo define, in part at least, the limit of their sway. They possessed none of the modern auxiliaries to material conquest, and could only

2

look down wistfully and hopelessly on plains where every rood of land might, almost spontaneously, yield a return far greater than their utmost labor could gain from a corresponding portion of their undisputed empire.

The survey of the monuments of Peru brings the conviction that the ancient population was not nearly so numerous as the accounts of the chroniclers would lead us to suppose. From what I have said, it will be clear that but a small portion of the country is inhabitable, or capable of supporting a considerable number of people. The rich and productive valleys and *bolsones* are hardly more than specks on the map; and although there is every evidence that their capacities of production were taxed to the very utmost, still their capacities were limited. The ancient inhabitants built their dwellings among rough rocks, on arid slopes of hills, and walled up their dead in caves and clefts, or buried them among irreclaimable sands, in order to utilize the scanty cultivable soil for agriculture. They excavated great areas in the deserts until they reached moisture enough to support vegetation, and then brought guano from the islands to fertilize these sunken gardens. They terraced up every hill and mountain-side, and gathered the soil from the crevices of the rocks to fill the narrow platforms, until not a foot of surface, on which could grow a single stalk of maize or a single handful of quinoa, was left unimproved. China, perhaps Japan, and some portions of India, may afford a parallel to the extreme utilization of the soil which was effected in Peru at the time of the Inca Empire. No doubt the Indian population lived, as it still lives, on the scantiest fare, on the very minimum of food; but it had not then, as now, the ox, the hog, the goat, and the sheep, nor yet many of the grains and fruits which contribute most to the support of dense populations. The llama was too highly valued to be lightly slain; the huanaco and alpaca were few; and the vicuña, whose soft fleece formed what may be called the ermine and purple of the Inca aristocracy, was protected by royal edict, and no one not of royal blood could use its fleece, under penalty of death. Of other animals available for food there were next to none. These conditions, apart from the scantiness of arable land, must have been a powerful check to the increase of population. This, however, was encouraged by the wise and beneficent social and civil institutions of the Incas, who recognized the right of every human being born into the world, not only to light, water, and air, but to a portion of the earth, and to the direct protection and fostering care of the State.

The present population of the three states which were wholly or in part included in the Inca Empire—namely, Ecuador, Peru, and Bolivia—does not exceed five millions. I think it would be safe to estimate the population under the Inca rule at about double that number, or perhaps somewhere between ten and twelve millions; notwithstanding Las Casas, the good, but not very accurate, Bishop of Chiapa tells us that, "in the Province of Peru alone the Spaniards killed above forty millions of people."

The ancient population of Peru may be divided into the people of the coast and those of the Sierra, the main characteristics of each being determined by the physical conditions of the region in which they dwelt. The people of the Sierra were subdivided into tribes, or families, through physical conditions less strongly marked. The inhabitants of the coast had a comparatively mild climate, although they were sometimes subjected to fervent heat direct from the sun, and augmented by reflection from desert sands and treeless hills. Rain never fell in most parts of the coast, or if at all in any part, it was so rarely and in such small quantities, that to guard against it became a secondary consideration. They had no domestic animals, except, perhaps, the cué, or guinea-pig, and their available lands were too precious to permit the growth of timber and its use in their edifices, except in the smallest quantity. How these conditions would, from necessity, qualify, if not dictate, their architecture, and how they would mould their social and political life, no reflecting mind can fail to perceive.

In the Sierra, on the other hand, where, owing to altitude, the climate is often severe, where rains fall during a great part of the year, where the llama is equally a beast of burden and of

food, and where the stalks of the agave or the forests of the
Amazonian valleys furnish some timber, we can comprehend
that the architecture o' .l'e people would evince a marked difference from that of .i.. .r st, and that very different organizations—civil, social, and religious—must spring up, even though
we were to assume that the people of the coast and Sierra were
originally of one blood and one family.  The great sea, breaking in thunder on the rocky coast, would naturally impress the
dweller on its shores with reverence and awe, lead him to per-
sonify its irresistible power, and induce him to give to Viracocha, the divinity of the ocean, the first place in his rude pantheon.  To the shivering dweller among snowy mountains, or
on frosty table-lands, by an equally natural process, the sun, the
source of light and heat, the visible dispenser of all that supports life, or makes it endurable or even possible, would naturally become the chief object of worship, and would be personified
under some name or symbol.

The general physical characteristics of the land of the Incas,
in relation to the development of the people who inhabited it,
at the period of the Spanish conquest, have now been presented.  To investigate this people in the light of the works
which they constructed, of which the remains, more or less perfect, still exist, was the main design of the travels and explorations the results of which are embodied in this volume.  The
scenes herein described were all visited by me; the ruins were
explored, surveyed, and as far as possible photographed by myself or under my own supervision; and I can vouch for the accuracy of the plans and other illustrations.  To select from the
vast mass of materials gathered by me has been no easy task.
I have performed it as best I could.

## CHAPTER II.

### NEW YORK TO LIMA.

New York to Panama.—The Remains of George R. Gliddon.—The Bay of Panama.
—Embarking for Peru.—The Island of Taboga,—Under Way.—The British Steam-
ship Company.—Dead Man's Island.—The Island of Puna.—The Gulf and City
of Guayaquil.—Balsas.—Pine-apples.—The Rio Guayas.—Las Bodegas.—Along
the Coast.—Paita.—Arrival at Callao.—Disembarking.—The Harbor.—Sea-lions.
—Aspect of the Town.—The Plaza.—Merchandise.—Loungers and Lazy Officials.
—Hotel de la Marina.—The Road to Lima.—First Impressions of the City.—The
Hotel Morin.—New Quarters.

It is not a quarter of a century since the voyage from New York to Lima occupied several months. Under favorable circumstances the journey can now be accomplished in about eighteen days, by steamer from New York to Aspinwall, or "Colon;" thence by rail across the isthmus to Panama; thence by the vessels of the British South Pacific Steamship Company to Callao, the port of Lima. I shall not describe the voyage to Aspinwall, nor the ride across the isthmus; nor even the quaint, dilapidated, picturesque old city of Panama, where we were detained several days awaiting the arrival of the British steamer, which was behind time.

This delay at least gave me time to perform a melancholy duty in caring for the remains of my old friend, George R. Gliddon, known to the world in general as former Consul of the United States in Egypt, and as agent of the Viceroy of Egypt in the United States; known also to the scientific world by having supplied Dr. Samuel G. Morton with most of the material for his "Crania Ægyptica," and as the associate of Dr. J. C. Nott in the production of the "Types of Mankind," and "Indigenous Races." He was also the friend of Humboldt, Jomard, and Lepsius; was a fascinating lyceum lecturer, and contributed largely towards popularizing Egyptian research in America.  Having several years before had important business relations in Honduras, Mr. Gliddon acted as my agent in that country.  On his return to the United States, he was attacked by sudden illness, and died at Panama.

THE RAMPART, PANAMA.

During the flush period of emigration to California, and before the Panama Railroad was built, and while there were no adequate means of speedy communication with California, hundreds and thousands of American emigrants were stricken down with fever at Panama, and died there.  The then prefect of the city assigned a piece of ground in the suburbs as a burying-ground for them.  In this Gliddon was buried ; and, acting in behalf of my associates, I sent to the American consul the materials for erecting an inclosure around his grave, and a marble slab to mark the spot.  It was a sad duty for me now to visit the grave of my old friend.  I early directed my steps to the "American Cemetery." I found it literally a golgotha—"a place of skulls." The shrubbery which had covered it had been cut away, and from numerous little hillocks projected skulls and human bones; many others had been piled up in heaps and burned. A somewhat pretentious building was in course of erection in one corner of the area, and into the walls were built the bricks and head-stones of the few graves which had ever been so marked. The ground had been made over to one of his friends by the very prefect who had originally conceded it for an American cemetery. I sought in vain for the tomb of my friend; all that I could find were two or three half-calcined fragments of the marble slab which I had sent out. I found out a German carpenter, who had acted as undertaker, and with him returned to the cemetery, and with great difficulty we were able to identify the grave, and that only by my recognizing the bricks which I had sent for the foundation of the monument. I caused the remains to be gathered together and sent to Philadelphia, to Mr. Lippincott, his friend and publisher, by whom they were deposited in the Laurel Hill Cemetery, the spot being marked by an appropriate monument.

The Bay of Panama, viewed from the shore, is equally beautiful and picturesque. Its high and brightly tinted islands break what would otherwise be a dull, monotonous horizon, and afford a relief to eyes gazing seawards. But, unhappily, Panama has only a bay. It has, in no just sense of the word, a port. Inshore the bay is shallow and rocky, the black reefs extending out a mile or more beyond the base of the fortifications. The British steamers lie at the island of Taboga, six or eight miles distant, and the American steamers swing at their anchors at points almost as remote. And as the tide rises from eighteen to twenty-two feet, setting in and running out with a strong current, the matter of embarking and disembarking is both difficult and dangerous, and can only be performed with any degree of comfort or safety at what is called "half-tide." Then small steamers, "tenders," and lighters are brought alongside the wharf, where they bound up and down, and lurch "off and on" to the swell of the waves, in a manner startling to delicate nerves. Passengers and baggage are hustled aboard in reckless confusion, and, should it come on to rain, as it is most likely to do, the only refuge is a hot, fetid little cabin, not big enough to hold a fourth of the passengers. If they cannot face the tropical, pouring rain on deck, below they may enjoy the odors of rancid oil from the machinery in the intervals, when not occupied in evading the vagrant trunks and parcels that tumble from side to side with the movements of the vessel.

CITY AND BAY OF PANAMA.

After an hour or more of this discomfort, drenched through and through, the south-bound passenger discerns at last the black sides of the steamer *Bogotá* looming through the blinding rain, like a rampart.

But our troubles had scarcely begun. Getting aboard the tender was bad enough, but getting off her was worse. While the *Bogotá* rocked with a certain gravity to the swell of the sea, our little craft bobbed about like an egg-shell, now banging, in a small way, against the larger vessel, and just as soon as the slippery gang-plank was supposed to be adjusted, falling away to a distance. I know not how many collars were torn from the coats of the men, or how many arms of the women were dislocated by the sailors in dragging — I suppose, in nautical phrase, I should say in "hauling"—us aboard the *Bogotá*. We were more fortunate than some of our fellow-passengers in not having our baggage dropped overboard, and were duly grateful when, saturated with rain from without, and clammy with perspiration from within, we found ourselves in our state-room. It was hot and close; but what with the drifting rain and the splash and spatter of the sea, it was impossible to open the ports, and so we had to sit, sweltering and steaming, until the wretched little tender had gone ashore and brought off a string of lighters, loaded with luggage and freight.

This occupied most of the day, and it was not until near night that we were able to make our appearance on deck, woebegone and bedraggled, to select from a confused heap of dripping luggage our own especial articles. This achieved, and the aforesaid articles, under the persuasive appeal of a half-crown, having been transferred to our cabin, we were able to exchange our saturated habiliments for dry clothes, and to make ourselves relatively comfortable. Our improved temper was further improved when, towards night, the rain ceased, the clouds lifted, and the sun burst in a flood of gold on the island of Taboga, in front of which we lay. The little town looked wonderfully cheerful and picturesque, with its red-tiled and pointed thatched roofs, over which tall palms, with their russet fruit, drooped gracefully, while the broad leaves of the plantain and banana formed a background of translucent green.

Canoes and pit-pans now began to come off the shore, filled with oranges, bananas, pine-apples, cocoa-nuts, aguacates, nisperos, and all the multitudinous tropical fruits that grow on the islands and shores of Panama Bay. We laid in an ample supply of those we liked best, and, moreover, invested in a "monkey." Not one of those gibbering, prehensile creatures that

mock humanity, but a porous earthen jar, in which, if it be sus
pended in front of the open port, water soon becomes delicious-
ly cool.

It was dark when the *Bogotá* lifted anchor and started on her
voyage southward; and when morning came, we found ourselves clear of the Bay of Panama, on the broad Pacific, and out
of sight of land.   The day turned out pleasantly; the deck of
the vessel was clean and dry, and an awning broke the somewhat fervid rays of the sun.   The sea was smooth, and our vessel rose and fell slowly and gracefully to the long, gentle swell
of the mighty Pacific, which contrasts so strongly with the fret-
ful and turbulent Atlantic.   Before night we had forgotten the
trials and disgusts of the preceding day; and as no one was sea-
sick, we began to look upon our voyage in the light of a pleas-
ure-trip.   We were not crowded; the service was good, the officers civil, albeit reticent; the crew prompt and orderly—the
whole in violent contrast with our experiences in that den of
horrors, the steamer from New York to Colon.   It is only just
to say that there is not, under all the adverse circumstances of
the case, a line of steamers better managed than that of the
British South Pacific Company.   It was projected by Mr. Wil-
liam Wheelwright, an American, as an American company, and
he procured the necessary data and concessions for its establishment, all of which he presented to the "merchant-princes" of
New York, from whom he received neither "aid nor comfort,"
and was obliged to take his enterprise to England.   The consequence is that the whole passenger trade of the South Pacific,
and nearly all its commerce, have passed into British hands.
Except a few hulks employed in carrying guano, not an American keel ploughs the Pacific from Panama to Cape Horn!

The morning of our third day out was marked by a yellow
haze through which only the *Isla del Muerto*, "Dead Man's
Island," was dimly visible, looking really like some gigantic
corpse floating on the waters.   This island lies off the Gulf of
Guayaquil, and is an unmistakable landmark for seamen.   Although the main-land was not discernible through the mist,
we could readily detect its odors—a mixture of dampness and

fragrance impossible to describe. Our course was now changed, and we steamed sharply eastward. The fog lifted, and we soon found ourselves in the gulf. On our left was the island of Puna, on which Pizarro bore up so long and persistently against open foes and treacherous friends, and organized that force with which he conquered the richest and most powerful of the ancient empires of America.

The Gulf of Guayaquil is large, and its channel tortuous. At times our steamer ran close to the low, slimy shores, lined with mangrove-trees, among the gnarled roots of which numbers of alligators find congenial repose. The city of Guayaquil stands on the right bank of the river Guayas, sixty miles from the sea. The site is low, and the town itself is utterly without architectural pretension, the houses being mainly of wood, and as flimsy in fact as in appearance. The cathedral is a large edifice of a style that must have been devised by a lunatic architect during an attack of severe indigestion. A broad street extends along the bank of the river, against which is huddled every variety of craft, from the ponderous ocean steamer down to the shallowest canoe.

The voyager can not help being both interested and amused by the incongruity and quaintness of the floating devices that meet his eye, but more especially by the *balsas*, or rafts, constructed of what is known as balsa-wood, as light as cork. These are lineal descendants of the old Peruvian contrivances for navigation, and probably differ little from those which Pizarro saw when he entered the Guayas River. From five to ten of the trunks of the balsa-trees are lashed together with wires and withes; the whole stayed and strengthened by cross-pieces. On a flooring of bamboos or split palms, huts are built, consisting in some cases of several rooms, with a place for cooking, and with hammocks swinging in all convenient positions. Pigs, fowls, parrots and macaws, chattering monkeys, and naked children hardly distinguishable from them, occupy the balsa on terms of easy confidence and familiarity; while bunches of bananas and plantains, and a net-work bag, filled with oranges and pineapples, depend from the rafters.

The *piña blanca*, or pine-apple, of Guayaquil is a proverb of excellence all over South America, on account of its size and flavor.  No traveller fails to secure a dozen or so before leaving port.  When we left, our steamer resembled a first-class fruit-shop.  On deck and between decks, in the purser's cabin and the sailors' forecastle, on every projection from which they could be suspended, swung the fragrant *piña blanca* of Guayaquil; for it is a perquisite of "all hands" to carry along the coast, for sale in the different ports, as many pine-apples as their finances will permit them to buy, or the space at their command enable them to stow away.

Above Guayaquil, although still substantially an estuary, the Rio Guayas narrows and becomes more like a river.  It is navigable for more than sixty miles, and steamers ply to a point or landing-place, called Las Bodegas, whence the traveller for Quito commences his long and weary journey.

The trip to Bodegas takes about six hours, and should not be omitted by the transient voyager to Guayaquil, if his time will permit.  The river-bank is lined with a superb tropical vegetation, relieved at intervals by cane-built and picturesque native huts, in front of which graceful canoes and unwieldy *balsas* are moored, preparatory to being loaded with fruit for the port. The steamer seems utterly out of place in these placid waters and amidst this slumberous scenery, sacred to drooping palms, broad-leaved plants, interlacing vines, gaudy parrots, and dreamy alligators that literally line the shores.  It is well for the traveller, if bound for Peru, to feast his eyes on the verd-ure that surrounds him in such profusion, for he will see little of the grateful green of tree or plant after he leaves Guayaquil. Under favorable circumstances, it is said, the great volcano of Chimborazo, flaunting its banner of smoke over the ranges of high Cordillera, may be seen from the port; but clouds rested on the mountains, and we missed the view.

From Guayaquil southward—which the people persist in say-ing is *up* the coast—there is little to interest the voyager.  The wooded shores of Ecuador soon disappear, and the aspect of the continent becomes entirely changed.  High, bare rocks, frayed

and crumbling, line the shore, and behind them spread out
broad, parched deserts, unrelieved by tree, or shrub, or blade of
grass. From repeated descriptions we have all formed some
faint notion of the deserts of Africa and Arabia, and explorers
have pictured to us the wide wastes of Utah and New Mexico;
but Sahara is a "thing of beauty," and Arizona "a joy forever,"
compared with the coast of Peru.

LAS BODEGAS, GUAYAS RIVER.

The first port in Peru at which the steamer touches is Paita,
the sea-gate of Piura, a considerable city, in the midst of a restricted but rich district, near the base of the mountains, beyond the desert of Sechura. Imagine a series of the mud nests
of the barn-swallow, set close together on a narrow, sandy
beach, at the base of a ledge of pale-gray and disintegrating
rock, with no sign of vegetation far or near, and you will get a
pretty accurate picture of the town of Paita. It is nevertheless a place of some importance commercially, and is a favorite
resort of whalers, who rendezvous here for supplies and repairs.
Its little bay forms a good anchorage, and its blue waters are
relieved by a variety of vessels, European and native; the lat-

ter of a nondescript order, reminding one of the picturesque fishing-boats and coasters of the Mediterranean.

There is here a very good mole and commodious custom-house of iron. Landing is easy, and a visit to the town should n:t be omitted. It consists mainly of a single narrow street, l'ncd by the quaintest shops and dwellings imaginable. The houses are mere wicker-baskets of cane, thinly plastered over with mud, through the walls of which it seems quite feasible to thrust one's fingers Some of them present interiors well completed, and set out with furniture which would not disgrace a Fifth-avenue parlor; but they are few—the residences of expatriated agents of foreign commercial houses, who seem to think that the wealth of Ormus and of Ind might be a compensation for a residence in Paita. We went ashore at Paita, and traversed the narrow, pale-gray streets, between the comical houses of canes and mud; mounted the pale-gray cliffs, and looked out upon the vast plain of pale-gray sand which stretched away twenty leagues to Piura. We were thirsty when we returned from this pale-gray expedition, and were told that the water we drank, to wash out our pale-gray reminiscences, was brought from a distance of thirty miles on the backs of don-keys.

We were not sorry when we left Paita; but were wondering what this portion of burned-out creation was made for, when the captain tells us that we had seen Peru, or at least its coast, fair-ly typified in and around Paita, and that for two thousand miles we would find only this dreary waste of barren rock and sand, treeless and lifeless, traversed only here and there, at long intervals, by ribbon-like valleys of green, marking the course of some small stream or river struggling down from the mountains to the sea.

The route from Paita, passing too far from the shore to en-able us to see the city of Truxillo—around which spread out the vast ruins of Grand Chimu—we find rising before us the isl-and of San Lorenzo, inside of which is the harbor of Callao, with its busy huddle of steamers and forest of masts, standing out in relief against the yellow walls of the Castle of San Felipe, above whose massive battlements the Spanish flag waved for the last time in continental America.

The approach to the harbor of Callao is certainly very fine. As the steamer heads inshore, the high, bare island of San Lorenzo is seen rising boldly on the right, its lofty northern extremity crowned by a light-house, literally a "light-house in the skies," more imposing, it is said, than useful. On the left is a low shore, with trees and a sloping plain, with yellowish verdure, extending back to a series of high brown hills, each receding tier becoming higher, until, above them all, and above a stratum of dim, motionless clouds, we discern the *Nevados*, or Snowy Cordilleras. At the base of these bare brown hills, six miles inland, stands Lima, the renowned "City of the Kings."

In the morning a thin mist almost always rests over the harbor of Callao, the condensation of the moisture of the atmosphere by contact with the cold Antarctic current that sweeps northward along the coast of Peru, and greatly modifies its climate. Through this mist the fleet of steamers, sailing-vessels, store-ships, coke-hulks, lighters, and other craft thronging the harbor loomed up in exaggerated proportions, as did the buildings of the town, and the cheese-shaped turrets of the famous old Castle of San Felipe.

We slowed up among this huddle of vessels to our anchorage, close by the quaint old British store-ship *Naiad*, with high poop-galleries and hanging decks, which had done good service with Nelson at Trafalgar, but is now condemned to swing lazily at her moorings, and eternally rise and dip to the monotonous swell of the sea, her 'tween-decks crammed with musty cordage, rusty chains, and useless lumber of all sorts.

Our anchor was scarcely down before the *marineros*, or boatmen, of Callao came swarming around us like buzzards, in boats of every kind and size; but they were not allowed to come within a certain distance of the steamer until the autocratic captain of the port had made his official visit. This he took his own time to do, and in the interval the captain of the *Bogotá* paced his bridge impatiently, and the purser stood gloomily at the head of the gangway, muttering something probably not complimentary to the captain of the port. Everybody was on deck. The secretary was there, with his long Springfield rifle slung over his shoulder, and arrayed as if about to commence a campaign against the cannibals, while the attorney looked grave and thoughtful, as if already oppressed with the responsibilities of his position. Waiting under such circumstances, with your baggage carefully piled together on deck, after the last scrutiny of your disordered cabin, "to see if you haven't forgotten something," is tedious always, and sometimes provoking.

For a while the chattering of the boatmen — a variegated crowd in color, and polyglot in language—amused us. There were Chinamen and *cholos*, Englishmen and Frenchmen, Swedes and Genoese, among them, vociferating together, in the free jargon of sea-ports all over the world: "Havee boatee?" "Much bueno boatee!" "Ver good embarcation, sare!" "All paints, sweet for lady!" "Tolda boat, mister; keep sun off!" "I take all de Yankee! Good Yankee me!" "Don't mind the yellow beggars, sir! They are only wharf-rats, sir; 'll be sure to wet you, sir!" and so on for half an hour, and yet no sign of the captain of the port.

Meantime the sun's rays dissipated the mist, the ships around us dwarfed in size as they became more distinct, the town contracted and looked shabby, and San Felipe itself ceased to be imposing. Impatience began to run into indignation, and every passenger was fast getting into condition for being disgusted with everything in Peru, its government and officials in particular, when a man-of-war's boat, swept by strong and practiced arms, was seen rapidly approaching, but from quite a different direction from that in which the port official was expected to appear. There was a gratified little flutter, and people began to gather up their bundles, when the boat circled round gracefully under our stern, displaying our own national ensign. She had been sent from the *Fredonia* to land our party; and as we moved cheerfully, if not triumphantly, down the ladder to embark, a perceptible cloud settled over the brows of our fellow-voyagers, and I think their "good-byes" were not altogether so cordial as they would have been had they also been going to land.

On our storm-swept coast the harbor of Callao would scarcely deserve a better name than that of roadstead; but hereabout
the only winds that blow are from the south and south-west,
and from these it is protected by a projecting tongue of land,
marking the site of old Callao, and by the high island of San
Lorenzo. There is, nevertheless, a considerable swell; for the
heave of the great breast of the Pacific is proportioned to its
own vast expanse, and is felt in every nook and corner of the
South American coast, however well sheltered it may be. In
consequence, a kind of mole, or breakwater, has been built out
into the harbor or anchorage, with stairs behind, where all small
boats and lighters receive and land their passengers and car-
g₁es.

As we rowed along, I was startled by the sudden projection
above the water, close by the side of the boat, of a head resembling that of a calf, accompanied with a snort and a spluttering
of the water, like those made by a diver on reaching the surface, after having been a long time under. The captain smiled
as I glanced at him in a bewildered way. " It is only a sea-
lion," he said; "this coast is thronged with every variety of
these great seals, whose diabolical music you will get familiar
with by and by, and who are common enough right here, among
the shipping. They are not at all inclined to be crowded out;
and we who are obliged to live on board ship are often amused
by their gambols, jealousies, and flirtations. There are as ras-
cally Blue-beards and Lotharios among them as you will find on
land, anywhere."

If Callao looked shabby from the deck of the ship at a mile's
distance, how much more rickety and tumble-down and tawdry
did it appear on closer inspection! Built generally of canes,
plastered over with mud and painted a dirty yellow, its flimsy
houses stand askew, with scarcely a perpendicular or horizontal
line among them, and look as if they were trying to straighten
themselves up after a grand debauch, in a vain endeavor to "toe
the line" of the street. There are several modern buildings of
some architectural pretensions in the place. One of these—
the railway-station, close to the mole—is visible from the water.

3

The landing stairs was thronged with a motley assemblage, more variegated even than the crowd of boatmen who had besieged our steamer; a filthy, fetid, hustling crowd, who gaped at the ladies, and obstructed the landing, so that we could with difficulty push our way through their ragged ranks.

We were welcomed warmly by the American consul and other countrymen, and cordially received by some of the officials of the port, arrayed in gorgeous uniforms loaded with gold-lace sufficient to have fitted out a regiment of brigadiers at home. The little plaza at the landing-place presented a strange if not a busy scene. There were gigantic *piscos*, or jars, shaped like Roman amphoræ, and filled with *italia*, a native spirit, ranged in long rows; bales of cinchona-bark from the forests of the distant interior; great heaps of wheat from Chili, waiting to be carried to the mills on the Rimac, and left with impunity in the open air; piles of white and rose-colored blocks of salt, resembling alabaster, from the salt-quarries near Huacho; pyramids of loaves of *chancaca*, or coarse, unrefined sugar, roughly wrapped in dry plantain-leaves, through which the melasses oozed and dripped for the delectation of clouds of flies that hovered around them; and conspicuous among all a stack of massive bars of silver from the mines of Cerro de Pasco, awaiting shipment to England. Mixed confusedly among these products of the country were many commonplace and familiar bales and boxes from Europe and the United States, besides old anchors and iron shafts half buried in the soil, and logs of timber that had evidently lost their owners, and become the prescriptive lounges of idle porters and dozing wharf " bummers."

There were many people with dilapidated hats and greasy ponchos in the plaza, but they seemed to be principally engaged in the easy task of dawdling, or in making up their minds whether they should do any work that day, or creep into the shade between the *piscos*, and go to sleep again. The custom-house officials sat astride their chairs in the corridor of the *aduana*, resting their chins on their arms, with their empty coffee-cups on the stone pavement beside them, lazily puffing their cigars. Everybody looked drowsy and languid, except the dusky

and extremely *décolleté* females who had established their little charcoal braziers in various odd corners, and were engaged
in compounding *picantes*—wonderful aggregations of fish, fresh
and salt meat, potatoes, crabs, the juice of bitter oranges, lard and
salt, but chiefly peppers (the more pungent and fiery the better), ladled out with gleeful alacrity into the earthen dishes or
calabashes of the *cholos* and wharfingers, who have no better
or other fare than this from one year's end to another. Filthy
and incongruous as is the wharf *picante* of Callao, it is certainly fragrant in odor, and we were by no means indisposed for
breakfast when we ascended the stairway of the hotel, to await
the landing of our baggage. I must say, however, that our appetites would have been better, had we not been obliged to
pass the steaming kitchen, with its unwashed and unkempt inmates, and its horrible hangings of mangled flesh, in our way
from our apartment to the dining-room. Still, there was
enough strange and interesting to reconcile or blind us to what
was disagreeable and repulsive, and we were in favorable humor
when we took the train for Lima.

The distance between Callao and Lima, as I have said, is a
little more than six miles; but as Lima is five hundred and
twelve feet above the sea, the ascent is somewhat slow, occupying, with the prevailing wheezy locomotives, the best part of
an hour. The road first takes a sweep along the shore of the
harbor and around the Castillo of San Felipe, now called *Fortaleza de la Independencia*, and then passes through a cane-built
suburb of the town, and strikes off in a right line, past the *aldea*
and cemeteries of Bellavista, to the capital. Throughout it
runs parallel with the old *camino real*, once paved and lined
with trees, but now broken up and deep with loose stones and
sand, through which the big-wheeled carts of the *carreteros* are
dragged with difficulty by struggling mules. The ascent is so
slow that the traveller has ample opportunity to view the country, which is mainly a parched waste, divided up into squares
by ruined mud walls, with here and there a dilapidated, flat-
roofed dwelling, and occasionally a bright green field of *alfalfa*,
or lucern. The whole, however, might be made a garden by

irrigation; and the courses of the *azequias*, or irrigating canals, that do exist are everywhere marked by long lines of willowr, canes, vines, creepers, and flowers. Conspicuous among these were the bright-red, orange, and yellow flowers of the *nasturnum*, which flourishes here with unrivalled luxuriance. Scattered all over the sloping plain are mounds of *mamposterîa* and adobes of greater or less regularity, some of them of immense size. There are the *huacas* of the ancient inhabitants, of which I shall have much to say. They have supplied vast numbers of sun-dried bricks, of excellent composition, for the construction of the towns and villages of the plain.

As we approach the city we come to fruit and vegetable gardens surrounded by high walls, above which rise orange, palta, and plantain trees, with their pleasant contrasts of green and gold. Then we reach the gas-works, and passing through the walls, a section of which is here demolished, enter the city by the Street of San Jacinto, by no means one of its most aristocratic or attractive avenues, and move slowly to the railway-station, which occupies the site of the suppressed monastery of San Juan de Dios.

We found the secretary awaiting us on the platform. He had secured rooms in the Hôtel Morin, and had obtained a cart to transport our baggage; but he had not been able to secure a carriage, and so we were obliged to make our entrance into the capital on foot. The traveller's first impressions of the place are not likely to be pleasing. The houses are squat and irregular, painted fantastically, some of them in squares, like a checker-board; others in stripes, like a barber's pole; and nearly all having Moorish balconies, or *jalousies*, of a size out of all proportion to the buildings themselves, on which they appear to hang by a most uncertain hold, and with which they seldom harmonize in color. The sidewalks are narrow and uneven; but as they are flagged, and less rough than the roadways, they are preferred by the troops of donkeys carrying panniers, filled with offal, lime, sand, bricks, etc., that rush pell-mell along them before the cracking whip of a mounted driver, jostling and crushing against whomsoever may be in their way.

We nevertheless succeeded in reaching our hotel without being bruised or trampled on by the donkeys, and were ushered, under a high archway, into the court of a relatively imposing building, surrounded by three tiers of corridors, on which opened the doors of the various apartments and dormitories of the establishment. One side of the court was occupied by a bar and billiard-saloon, as flashy with mirrors and tinted lithographs as any *biliard* in Paris; another side by a dining-room, through the open door of which we could see a long table, with squadrons of glassware and snowy napkins, which gave us a rather favorable preliminary notion of the resources and cleanliness of the Grand Hôtel Morin. These, however, were not well supported by an inspection of our apartments, which were decidedly dusty and frowzy, and which we only accepted on the assurance of being supplied with better ones on the following day.

Happily, however, we were not obliged to call on the landlord to keep his promise, thanks to the hospitality of our minister, who offered us a suite of rooms in the Legation, a large, new house in the Calle de Coca, in the heart of the city, and not far from the hotel, where we found it more convenient to take our meals than to establish a *ménage* of our own. Here we remained for six months, until my duties as commissioner were concluded; when I started on my explorations. It is to a narrative of these that this book is mainly dedicated, but it would hardly be complete without some account of Lima and its people. Few cities of this continent, historically or in other respects, possess equal interest with the old vice-regal, luxurious, bigoted, and corrupt capital of Peru, the richest and most important of all the kingdoms of Spain in the New World, and which even now has no rival in population, wealth, or importance outside our own country, except perhaps in Rio de Janeiro and Mexico.

## CHAPTER III.

### LIMA—THE CITY OF THE KINGS.

The City of the Kings.—Its Foundation and Aims.—Early Civil and Ecclesiastical Supremacy.—Historical Reminiscences.—Ancient and Modern Sources of Wealth. —Geographical Position.—Climate and Temperature.—Fogs and Mists.—Topographical Situation.—Prevailing Winds.—Health.—Origin of the Name of Lima. —The Walls.—Municipal Divisions.—Population.—The River Rimac.—The Bridge.—Style of Architecture.—Mode of Erection.—Balconies, Courts, and Roofs.—Poultry and Buzzards.—Furniture and Pictures.—The Governor's Palace.—Peruvian Soldiers.—The Cabildo and other Public Buildings.—The Cathedral.—Other Churches.—The Plaza Mayor.—The Arcades.—Fountain, with Statue of Fame.—The Plaza de la Constitucion and Equestrian Statue of Bolivar.—The Paseo of the Barefoot Friars.—The Alameda de Acho.—Monument to Columbus. —Public Institutions.—The General Cemetery.—Flower Gardens.—The Feast of Roses.—Amusements.—Lima under the Viceroys.—Improvements since the Independence.—The Central Market.—Varieties of Fruits.—Fish.—Meats.—The Abattoir.—Poultry.—Cookery.—Puchero.—Chupe.—Picantes of various Kinds.— Other Dishes.—Dulces.—Dietetic Maxims.—A Dinner with a Hidalgo.—A Diplomatic Dinner.

No other city founded by the Spaniards in America possesses so much interest, historical or otherwise, as does Lima. Its site was designated by Pizarro, as the capital of his conquered dominions, on January 6th, 1535, old style, that being the day of the festival of the Epiphany, or the manifestation of our Saviour to the *magi*, called in our English version of the New Testament the "wise men" from the East, and who are by old tradition styled the "Three Kings." Hence Pizarro gave to his projected capital the name of *Ciudad de los Reyes*, the "City of the Kings."* The pompous celebration of the foun-

---

* Many towns of Spanish America derive their names wholly, or in part, from the saints or martyrs upon whose festival days they were captured or founded, or from some doctrine of the Church. Hence there are several towns with such names as "Asuncion," "Santa Fé," "San Pedro," "San Pablo," and "Santa Maria." Each of these had also a special designation; and one or the other is usually dropped in

dation of the city took place twelve days later, on the 18th of January. The arms of the city, granted by the Emperor Charles V., in allusion to the "Three Kings" and the star by which they were guided to "the place where the young child lay," are three golden crowns on an azure field, and a rayed star. The emperor also conceded to it the title of "Most Noble and Most Loyal." The origin of its present name, Lima, will be explained hereafter.

The "City of the Kings" became the seat of the haughtiest, and perhaps the most luxurious and profligate, of the viceregal courts. Its viceroys ruled with almost independent sway, not only over what now constitutes Peru, but also over the vast provinces of Chili, La Plata, and New Granada, including the modern states of Bolivia and Ecuador. Here was the seat of the most important ecclesiastical dependency of the Church of Rome in America. The Inquisition was active and powerful in Lima long after it became inert and decadent in Madrid. Its churches and convents were as magnificent as those of Europe, and were endowed with almost fabulous wealth. The College of San Marcos, the oldest university in America, was founded at Lima in 1551: fifty-six years before the English settlers landed at Jamestown; fifty-eight years before Hudson sailed into the bay of New York; and sixty-nine years before the *Mayflower* touched the shores of New England. Here Pizarro was assassinated by "the men of Chili," the avengers of the stout and generous Almagro; and here his bones repose. Here was born, and here died, Santa Rosa, *La Patrona de todas las Americas*, "the Patroness of all the Americas," the only American woman who has ever attained the honor of canonization. From the turrets of the fortress of San Felipe, in Callao, the port of Lima, the flag of Castile and Leon floated for the last time on the continent of America as the emblem of Spanish sovereignty.

But, apart from these clustering historical recollections, we

popular usage. Thus the full name of Bogotá is *Santa Fé de Bogotá*, and of Tacna, *San Pedro de Tacna*. Children are usually named after the saints on whose day their birth occurred. Hence the frequency of such names as José, Pedro, and Pablo; Maria, Catarina, and Teresa.

know that here centred the products of the mines of Potosi and of Pasco, and the marvellous wealth of Castro-Veireina and Puno. Here, too, in 1681, the viceroy, La Palata, rode through the streets of his capital on a horse whose mane was strung with pearls, and whose shoes were of gold, over a pavement of solid ingots of silver. Here, too, centred the galleons of the East, laden with silks and spices from the Philippines and Cathay; and on the verge of the horizon, off the land, hovered the sea-hawks Rogers, Anson, Hawkins, and Drake, swift to snatch from the heavy "treasure-ships" of Manilla the rich booty which even the Virgin Queen did not disdain to share with the freebooters of the South Sea and the Spanish Main.

Now California quicksilver is carried past the open shafts of the cinnabar mines of Huancavelica; the argentiferous *vetas* of Salcedo are abandoned; the sands of Carabaya are no longer washed for gold; and the infant State of Nevada supplies more silver every year than Pasco and Potosi, and all the mines of Peru put together, ever did. The Indians can no longer be parcelled out to the favorites of power, and the negro no longer pays the tribute of unwilling labor to the rich proprietors of Lima. But the ancient City of the Kings is still rich, still gay, still flourishing, and more luxurious than in her proudest colonial days. If the sources of her ancient wealth have dried up, fortune has opened new and richer fountains, and the rough, rocky, and repulsive guano islands which line the arid Peruvian coast, the terrors of the ancient mariners, and still the haunts of howling seals and screaming sea-birds, pour into her lap a more than Danaëan shower of gold; alas, with all its concomitants of social, civil, and political demoralization!

Lima is situated in latitude 12° 2' 34" south, and longitude 77° 7' 36" west of Greenwich. Its elevation above the sea is 512 feet.* Under these conditions, and being "under the

---

* I follow Paz Soldan because, as I suppose, he must have had, as Superintendent of Public Works, the exact results of the levelling for the Callao and Lima Railway, before him. His figures relate to the height of the Plaza Mayor or Central Square. Humboldt gives the height at 570 English feet; Riveiro at 505; Herndon at 475½; and Gay at 172 Spanish varas, each equal to about 33 inches.

tropics," it might be supposed that its climate would be essentially tropical. Such, however, is not the fact.

During the six months constituting what is called the winter season—that is, from June to November inclusive—it is positively cold, the thermometer ranging from 57° to 61° Fahrenheit, so that thick clothing becomes necessary for comfort within doors, and wrappers almost indispensable without. The mean average of the thermometer during this period, from eight o'clock in the morning to eight o'clock in the evening, for the year 1861, as derived from the observations at the telegraph office, was 56.4° Fahrenheit. During the summer season, from November to May, the average mean is much higher, the mercury sometimes reaching 82° Fahrenheit. This low temperature of Lima may be partially accounted for by the proximity of the snowy Cordillera, and partly from the fact that the great, cold Antarctic current of the Pacific sets from the south-west full on the coast, where it has a temperature of thirteen degrees less than the waters of the open sea a hundred miles from land.* The prevailing winds are also from the south-west, following the direction of the ocean current, and sharing its temperature.

During the winter season (I use the word "winter" in its restricted, local application), it is not the cold which contributes wholly to render life in Lima unpleasant or unbearable, but the fog and the damp. For days and even weeks the sun is invisible, and a drizzle not unlike a Scotch mist makes the sidewalks slippery and pasty, and so permeates the air that the sheets of one's bed are chill and sticky; the walls drip; the hand slips in endeavoring to turn the clammy door-knobs; a feathery and almost ethereal fungus sprouts up in a single night from the depths of one's inkstand, or replaces the varnish on one's boots with a green and yellow mildew. Bone-aches and neuralgies walk the streets, ransack the houses, and outrage

---

* Von Tschudi suggests that the cold waters of the river Rimac, which descends from the glaciers of the interior, may have an influence on the temperature of the city.

their occupants unchallenged, and the noise of the church bell
is stifled in the damp and lifeless atmosphere. We are assured
that "it never rains in Lima;" but the dense permeating mist
not unfrequent'y forms itself into minute drops, when it is called *guara*. These soak through the flat thatched roofs, discolor-
ing the ceilings, trickling upon the floors, and rendering an
umbrella necessary for the pedestrian in the streets.

It is a singular but unexplained fact that while Lima is thus
frequently enveloped in mists, and while its temperature rules
so low, the other towns and villages on the same plain, and not
far distant, generally enjoy a clear sunshine, and are comparatively warm. I have stood on the heights of Morro Solar, overlooking Chorillos, the watering-place of the capital, and only
nine miles distant from it, when the sun was almost blinding,
while a cloud, like that which rests over London in November,
enveloped the city; due, however, not to the smoke of half a
million fires, but to meteorological causes not yet sufficiently
explained. Miraflores is an embowered village, situated on the
same plain as Lima, and about five miles distant. Von Tschudi found that, during ten days in December and January, the
temperature was here ten degrees higher than in the capital.
During the six months for which I have given the mean average in Lima, the mean average in Callao was 67.4°, a difference
of eleven degrees in favor of Callao.

The topographical situation of Lima may help to solve some
of the anomalous meteorological phenomena which I have noticed. It is built at the head of the plain which bears its name,
very nearly at the point where the river Rimac debouches
from the outliers of the Cordillera, which rise close at hand, on
every side except towards the sea. One of these, a buttress of
the range of Amancaes, the Cerro de San Cristobal, a steep, conical peak, surmounted by a cross, and a conspicuous object from
every part of the city, rises, to the north-west of Lima, to the
height of 1275 feet above the Grand Plaza, or 1787 feet above
the sea; while, on the opposite side of the river, and occupying
a position scarcely less dominating, is the Cerro de San Bartolo-
meo, but little inferior in elevation. The cold air, which seems

to pour down the valley of the Rimac with more or less con-
stancy, encounters the sea-winds concentrated at this point by
the funnel-shaped plain, and induces a precipitation of the
moisture of the latter, which, if greater, would descend in rain.
Certain it is that the south-west or prevailing winds are felt
but a little distance up the narrow valley of the Rimac, where
the *guara* is a thing unknown. The precipitation around Lima
is so great as sensibly to affect vegetation, and the arid slopes of
the Cerro de San Cristobal and Amancaes, during the months
of August and September, lose something of their ashy hue under a struggling vegetation, made up chiefly of the plants of
the *amancaes*, a kind of lily with yellow blossoms. This is a
festival period, when all classes of the population resort to the
hills as a *paseo*, or ride, to eat *camarones*, drink *chicha*, and pluck
the flowers, with which every one returns decorated in great
profusion.

But, however they may be accounted for, these meteorological anomalies are not favorable to health; and Lima may be
regarded as the most unhealthy capital in America, Havana not
excepted. Her most ardent eulogists and most enthusiastic
sons have ceased to number salubrity among her merits or attractions. Señor Paz Soldan, while claiming for Lima an ancient good reputation in this respect, admits that she no longer
deserves it, but that, "without doubt, the frequent and rapid
communication with Panama, the immense immigration of Chinese and other foreigners, have produced a notable change in
the atmosphere"—less notable, perhaps, than this apologist im-
agines. It is said that, when the last of the Incas heard where
Pizarro had resolved to found the Spanish city, he was greatly rejoiced, exclaiming that soon none of them would remain
alive. And there is a tradition that, long before the arrival of
the Spaniards, this portion of the valley of the Rimac was set
apart as a kind of *presidio* for criminals — an Inca Cayenne,
in fact—in which conspirators and evil-doers soon ceased from
troubling. Nor can the change have been altogether recent,
since Von Tschudi wrote, more than thirty years ago, when
communication with Panama was rare enough, that it might

"be regarded as certain that two-thirds of the people of Lima are suffering at all times from *tercianas* (intermittent fevers), or from their consequences."

The name Lima is a corruption, or rather modification, of the Quichua word *Rimac*, which was formerly applied to the valley or plain, and is still borne by the river which waters it. The word is the past participle of the verb *rimay*—"to speak" —from a famous oracle that existed here in ancient times, and whose shrine was probably among the extensive ruins near the present little town of La Magdalena.*

The old walls of the city described an irregular oval on the left bank of the Rimac, inclosing an area about three miles long by one and a half broad, within which is the city proper, although there is an extensive suburb—that of San Lazaro—on the right bank of the river. These walls were built by the viceroy, La Palata, in 1683. They were of adobes, from eighteen to twenty-four feet high, and about twenty feet thick, with thirty-four bastions, and were entered by twelve gates. They have been of but little use except to facilitate the collection of local imposts, and affording a *paseo*, or elevated bridle-path, for equestrians. For defensive purposes they were contemptible. They have lately been entirely demolished.

The ground on which the city is built slopes gently towards the river, parallel to which—nearly east and west—the principal streets, eight in number, are laid out. Municipally, the city, including San Lazaro, is divided into 5 quarters, 10 districts, 46 wards, 346 streets, and 33 public squares, exclusive of the principal square. The number of houses in 1864 was stated at 4500, and of doors—a novel item of statistics—at 14,209.

The population of Lima is about 120,000 souls. At the period of the Independence the population was 64,000, showing an increase of upwards of 57,000, or nearly one hundred per cent. since that event. Under the crown, we are informed,

---

* "This name," says an anonymous author, "came from the idol Rimac, and not from the river; for it is only in a poetical and figurative sense that a river can be represented as speaking."

the average annual increase was only 225. Under the republic, it has been 1275. This fact is certainly significant, and is not the only one tending to disprove the common allegation of the decline and deterioration of Spanish America since the Independence.*

The Rimac is an errant stream, variable in volume, flowing through a broad and shallow bed, full of stones and sand-bars, half overgrown with willows and other shrubbery. During the dry season it is separated into a dozen channels, and the water barely dribbles over the stone platform on which the bridge is built. But during the summer season—the season of melting snows and rains among the mountains—it swells into a large, swift, and turbulent stream of yellow water, closely resembling the Upper Rhone. It is tapped at numerous points above Lima, not only for irrigating the valley, but to supply the city and plain of Lima with water. The bridge across it, leading to San Lazaro, is an ancient and ungraceful but massive stone structure of six arches, built in 1610. It has recesses on each side, lined with seats, for foot-passengers and idlers, which are much frequented by the lower orders on summer evenings. The view from the bridge, especially up the valley, is very fine, with the tall willows of the Paseo de Acho on one hand, the bulk of the Church of San Francisco on the other, and in front the Cerro of San Cristobal, with a long succession of brown mountains shutting in the green valleys, altogether forming a grand vista only terminated by the snowy Cordilleras. On the side of the city proper the bridge is reached by a lofty arch, painted in fantastic colors, and supporting a clock.

---

* Navarrete gives the population at different periods as follows: In 1600, 14,262; in 1614, 25,455; in 1700, 37,259; in 1746, 60,000; in 1755, 54,000; in 1781, 60,000; in 1790, 52,627. He, however, suspects that the first census, in 1600, was below the fact, "from the circumstance that the common people refrained from giving correct statements as to their numbers, fearing that the census was only a preliminary to some new tax." This suspicion is borne out by the greatly reported increase at the next census, which shows an augmentation of about eighty per cent. in fourteen years; an increase wholly unwarranted by any thing else in the successive censuses. The decrease in 1746-'55 and 1781-'90 is accounted for by earthquakes and epidemics.

The private buildings of Lima are apparently of a most frail
and unsubstantial character; but the style of architecture is the
result of conditions too imperative to be disregarded. The city
stands in the very centre of a region in which rain never falls,
and in which earthquakes are of frequent occurrence, and may
be looked for at any moment. The most substantial structures
of brick or stone could not resist the severe convulsions to
which the city is exposed, and the buildings are consequently
of the lightest materials—little more than huge cages of canes,
plastered over with mud on the outside, and frescoed in imitation of stone. They are generally of one story, seldom more
than two, in height. The roofs are flat, because the absence of
rain renders a pitched roof unnecessary. They are sometimes
formed of poles, over which is spread cane matting, supporting a layer of sand or ashes to absorb the damp of the *guaras;*
but usually the roofing is of boards, correspondingly protected.
The apparently massive towers and buttresses of the churches
are only great wicker-baskets—deceptive combinations of poles
and canes tied together with hide-thongs, stuccoed over, and
painted. Under a brisk shower, such as we often experience
on a summer afternoon, the whole city would melt away, leaving only a withered cane-brake in a gigantic mud-puddle.

I claim to be versed in the mysteries of house-building in
Lima, for a dwelling went up in the Calle de Joca, during my
stay, right opposite my window. I watched its almost imper-
ceptible growth from day to day, and had a distinct notion of
how little an able-bodied man can contrive to do in a day, if he
really exerts himself in that direction. The site was a little
elevated above the street, which, as regards the matter of drainage, is an advantage. Cellars and basements are things wholly
unknown here. A most unpromising series of poles was set in
the ground, along the front and sides of the proposed building.
Transverse poles were fastened to these by thongs of raw hide,
kept in a proper state of pliancy by immersion in water. This
frame-work, wonderfully like a skeleton, having been finished, split canes were tied to the horizontal ribs, and wattled together, basket-wise. Then came a negro, with two boys, bring-

ing boxes of mud tempered, I should say, with the sweepings
of the nearest stable, which they rolled up in balls and flung
against the wattles, smoothing them down with their hands.
The amount of work accomplished by the man was hardly
worth mentioning. While this was going on, two or three
other men were marking out the interior plan of the building,
dividing it up into *salas*, bedrooms, etc., in the like basket-
making fashion. These partitions were in the same manner
bespattered and jammed with mud by the negro and his juve-
nile assistants, whom he assailed opprobriously and with uncom-
plimentary reflections on their ancestry whenever they bungled
—sitting himself meanwhile on an adobe, smoking his cigar.

At the end of the third month I began to discover indications of a purpose to put up a second story. A ladder appeared, and veritable sawed timber was brought, I suppose
from Maine, to serve as sills for the second floor. These were
tied in place as I have described, while men below, with their
backs braced against the wicker-work, forced it into a perpendicular position. Then came the negro, and his mud, and his
low-born apprentices, and there were more vituperation, and sitting on adobes, and smoking, and at last the second story was
daubed as the first had been before it. Then came the man
who made roofs, and he who tarred them, and he who covered
them with fine gravel; and then the Irish carpenter, who suspended a balcony outside on such frail pretexts of support, that
I never ventured on one thereafter without fear and trembling;
and then a Frenchman came, who stuccoed the mud, and afterwards an Italian with pots of pigments of rainbow hues, who
frescoed the stucco most gorgeously.

I came to look upon this building as in some sort my own;
and when on my return from the Sierra, a couple of years afterwards, although the Italian's work was a trifle faded, I was
more than compensated for the loss of color by glimpses of
dark eyes and ivory shoulders through the tantalizing Venetian
blinds that now formed the front of the balcony.

I should like to know precisely what portion of each day the
beauties of Lima spend in these cages, whence they can look

down on everything that passes in the street below, with the pleasing assurance that no upturned eye can penetrate the mysteries of their retreat, or discover if their toilets have been made. Thrown open on festival days, these balconies are as gay as flower-beds, and as brilliant in color. They are pleasant albeit unsightly contrivances, to which the foreigner takes kindly, happily unconscious of their insecurity.

Most of the houses have courts, with open galleries extending around the four sides. The lower story on the street is usually occupied by shops, and the remaining rooms are devoted to storage, or used as stables and kitchens—the two latter often adjoining and sometimes united. This part of the building is generally damp, and the better class of the people live in the *altos*, or upper stories. These are partly lighted and ventilated by projections above the roof, not unlike the wind funnels which we see on board steamers; but instead of being movable, so as to be turned to catch the breeze, they are fixed with their openings towards the south, the direction from which blows the prevailing wind.

INTERIOR COURT, LIMA.

Some of the older and better class of houses have a *mirador*, or tower, from which some very fine and extended views may be commanded. But from these eminences the views near at hand, although striking, are not usually pleasing, for the shiftless inhabitants and worthless servants heap the flat roofs with every kind of abomination. All the refuse and filth that does not go into the *azequias*, or sewers, and much that ought to go there, is deposited on the roofs. Such rubbish! and occasionally such spectacles! old hats, old shoes, broken crockery, rags, cast-off crinoline, everything worn out and displeasing to the eye, is strewed about or piled up on the roofs of Lima. No wonder the sun refuses to shine for six months of the year. The municipality pass ordinances that are never enforced, bristling with fines and penalties never collected, against the nuisance. The roofs still remain unsightly and offensive, and will do so until the very nature of the population is changed.

Sometimes the *techos*, or roofs, are utilized as grand henneries. The first morning that dawned on us in Lima, at the Hôtel Morin, was ushered in by vehement crowing of cocks, and strenuous gobbling of turkeys, apparently close to my head. I rubbed my eyes, and wondered if I was dreaming, after a surfeiting Thanksgiving dinner, and if the ghosts of slaughtered and undigested *gallinæ* had returned to torment me. I found later, when I ascended to the roof for my first bird's-eye view of the city, that it was a gigantic cage for fowls of every kind; and that when I lay down at nights, only an inch board, two inches of sand, and a crowded chicken-roost intervened between me and the stars and the angels. These roofs are also the roosting-places, and, I suppose, the brooding-places, of the great and noble army of *zopilotes*, or buzzards—those invaluable tropical scavengers. They make deliberate explorations among the garbage and rubbish of the house-tops—stalking about quietly and solemnly, but occasionally quarrelling over the last dead kitten that the lazy servant has thrown there.

Internally, the residences of the better classes of the people of Lima are not only well, but in some instances luxuriously, and even elegantly, fitted up and furnished, too often showily,

4

in a rather exaggerated French fashion, with highly colored carpets and paper-hangings, and furniture, in which veneering and varnish and gilding, satin and brocatel, dispute predominance. Mirrors are abundant, and of the largest dimensions; but pictures are few, chiefly old family portraits of the grimmest kind, or saints and Virgins as grimy as any of those which are sold nightly at auction in cheap shops in the Bowery as the productions of Salvator Rosa and the other masters of lamp-black. But the lithographs are numerous, occasionally somewhat questionable in subject, but always gorgeous in tint.

Excepting the churches, the public buildings are few. The Palace of the Government, which ought to be the best of these, is the meanest—a low, irregular pile, occupying the whole of the right side of the principal square, and entered by a single portal in the centre. A rickety corridor, not a foot of which follows a right line, runs along the front of the second story, beneath which are a great number of low *chucherias, picantrías*, and what may best be described as "junk-shops." Within are several courts, around which are the various Government offices, the official residence of the head of the Government for the time being, and quarters for a detachment of troops.

The Peruvian army is made up almost exclusively of Indians and negroes, or *sambos*. The Indians constitute the infantry, and, being accustomed to travel on foot in the mountainous interior from infancy, they have wonderful rapidity and endurance on the march. The negroes are confined to the plains of the coast, and are accustomed to riding and the management of mules and horses. Hence the peculiar distribution.

The Peruvian soldiers are tractable, and, if well led, as brave as any in the world. The native Indian tenacity and stubbornness are excellent elements in the composition of the soldier. Almost every Peruvian foot-soldier is attended by his *rabona*, who may be, but is not generally, his wife. She marches with him, cooks and mends for him, often carries his knapsack, sometimes his musket, and always the little roll of matting which, when unfolded and supported on a couple of sticks, constitutes his tent. It is of little moment on which side the Indian fights.

PERUVIAN INFANTRY AND CAVALRY.

He knows nothing about the political squabbles of the country, and cares less.

Various improvements have been attempted in the Palace of the Government without the slightest regard to architectural proprieties, but with some success in making a few spacious and comfortable apartments. Altogether, "El Palacio," as described by a native writer, is "a confused, intricate, heterogeneous agglomeration of disproportioned rooms, parlors, and closets of all shapes and eras, forming a veritable labyrinth." It is, however, of some historical interest, having been founded by Pizarro; and from 1535 to 1821, a period of nearly three hundred years, it was occupied by three governors and forty-three viceroys. Since 1821, that is to say, since the Independence, it has been the residence of some fifty or sixty chiefs of state, of various titles, to say nothing of five Councils of Government!

It is only in their churches that the old and new inhabitants

of Lima have undertaken to overcome the physical hostilities
to their position and circumstances.  They have tried to construct imposing temples in spite of the earthquakes, and with a
certain success, making allowance for the semi-Moorish and
somewhat grotesque taste which has ever prevailed throughout
Spain and its former dependencies.  The cathedral, although
the largest, is by no means the most impressive of the religious
structures of Lima.  It was founded by Pizarro, and his bones
are alleged to rest in its vaults.  The original edifice cost
$594,000.  Owing to earthquakes and other retarding causes,
it was ninety years in building.  Nearly destroyed by earthquakes in 1746, the present structure was raised by the viceroy,
Saperanda, and was for a long time surrounded by petty shops,
which obstructed and disfigured the approach from the front.
These were removed many years ago, and a broad platform,
reached by a series of steps, supplies their place.  The lower
part of the building is of stone and brick, but the towers are of
canes and mud.  The whole is stuccoed and painted in a style
which may be designated as the "Eminently Mixed."  The interior is badly cut up, poorly lighted, and without any grand effects.  There are many paintings, but of little merit: among
them, however, is a "Veronica," by Murillo.  The plan and
adornments of the edifice are said to have been closely copied
from those of the great church of Seville, in Spain.  The or-
gan is a fine instrument, and among the bells that clang in its
towers is one of wonderful tone, called the *Cantabaria*, which
weighs thirty thousand pounds.

There are some seventy-six churches, conventual and others,
in Lima, besides the cathedral, but only a few of them are in
any way remarkable.  That of San Francisco is most imposing,
and, with its convent, is said to have cost fifteen million dollars.
That of Santo Domingo is distinguished for its lofty and symmetrical towers, for the spaciousness of its central aisle, and for
having a chapel dedicated to Santa Rosa.  The churches of San
Augustin and La Merced are really remarkable for their elaborate façades, which are wonderful specimens of what may be
called stucco fretwork.  San Pedro has a fine position, a mas-

sive aspect, and is the fashionable church of the city, the favorite worshipping-place of the well-to-do *señoritas*, and consequently of devout young men. Owing to its exceptional popularity, the frayed, flea-infested, rough brick pavement, common to all the churches, was replaced, while I was in Lima, by one of bright encaustic tiles.

The *Plaza Mayor*, or great central square, is spacious, covering nearly nine English acres. Two of its sides are occupied by the Government House and the cathedral. The other two sides are lined by *portales*, or arcades, behind which are shops. The *Portal de Escribanos*, or Arcade of the Scriveners, takes its name from having been the place where this class of persons had their desks, precisely as we see them still under the *portales* of San Carlo in Naples. They have now disappeared, and their place is supplied by the trays and tables of toy-venders. The *Portal de Botoneros*, or Arcade of Trimmers, is still occupied, between the piers, by that class of artisans, who manufacture gold-lace and other similar articles, under a privilege from the municipality. They do not overwork themselves, and are a gossiping set altogether.

As the sidewalks are generally narrow, and not often clean, these arcades are favorite promenades of the ladies of the city and of saunterers of the other sex. They not only afford protection from the sun, but the shops that line them are gay with the fabrics which delight women's eyes, or flash with the jewellery which dazzles them. Although not generally large, these shops, in their fitting-up, and the variety, elegance, and value of their contents, compare favorably with the finest in the great cities of Europe and America. There is scarcely an article of taste or luxury that is not to be found in them, and they are constantly filled by a bright and ever-varying throng of the beauty and wealth of Lima. They are nearly all kept by foreigners, chiefly French and Germans, who spare no money or effort in supplying the extravagance of the capital from every quarter of the globe.

In the centre of the plaza is a bronze fountain, rising from a basin of the same material, supported by lions and griffins, to

the height of forty-two feet, the whole surmounted by a statue
of Fame.  It is very ancient, having been erected in 1578, and
is of the best workmanship of that period.  At the time of my
visit the plaza was an open, unpaved, dusty area, and the fountain was always surrounded by a chattering crowd of water-carriers with their donkeys.  It has since been paved; *pilas* for
the accommodation of the *aguadores* have been placed at the
corners, and the central fountain inclosed within a tasteful garden of tropical plants and flowers.

The only other square worthy of notice is the Plaza de la
Constitucion, formerly called of the Inquisition, from the circumstance that the edifice of that institution fronted on it, as
did also the old college of San Marcos.  Its principal feature
is a spirited bronze equestrian statue of Bolivar, cast at Mu-
nich, from a design by Adam Tadolini.  It is thirteen feet nine
inches high, and closely resembles that of Andrew Jackson at
Washington; but is much superior in design and execution.
The horse is represented as rearing, and is, consequently, supported only by the hind legs and tail; while the *Libertador*, in
the act of salutation, waves his *chapeau* with his right hand, thus
throwing open his cloak and displaying his uniform beneath.
The marble pedestal has let into its side bronze *rilievi* representing the decisive battles of Ayacucho and Junin, which secured Peruvian independence.  Two bronze tablets are sunk in
the ends of the pedestal; that in front bearing the inscription: "A SIMON BOLIVAR, LIBERTADOR; LA NACION PERUANA, AÑO
MDCCCLVIII."  The remaining tablet bears the national arms.

Among the *pascos*, or public walks, that called El Paseo de
los Descalzos, or Nuevo, on the farther side of the suburb of
San Lazaro, is most important.  It is a parallelogram fifteen
hundred feet long, planted regularly with trees, having extending longitudinally through its centre an area surrounded by tall
iron railings, laid out in gravelled walks, with seats, vases, stat-
uary, and a great variety of shrubs and flowers.  It is entered
by a rather elaborate iron gate-way, and at its farther extremity,
a little in front of the Convent of the Barefoot Friars, whence
it takes its name, is a fountain.  In its present form it dates

back only to 1856. In every respect this *paseo* is a tasteful and most creditable public work, worthy of any metropolis.

The Paseo or Alameda de Acho, on the same side of the river, is much more picturesque than that of the Descalzos. A terrace extends along the river for half a mile or more, and here is a paved walk, while the rest of the area is divided by rows of tall willows into long, leafy aisles, terminating in an oval open space, in which is erected an allegorical monument to Columbus. It is a marble group, in which America is represented as a crouching Indian girl, receiving a cross, the symbol of Christianity, from an elaborately draped figure of the great discoverer, while she drops an arrow, the symbol of savage life, at her feet. The whole is supported on a highly ornamented pedestal. The group is from the chisel of Salvatore Revelli, an Italian sculptor of some eminence, and is a work of much merit.

The viceroy Amat projected another paseo on the San Lazaro side of the river—the Paseo de Aguas—but it was never finished. The road leading to Callao was formerly lined with trees and seats, with fountains at intervals, for upwards of a mile, and was called the Alameda del Callao; but it has been suffered to fall into decay and ruin.

The public institutions of Lima of beneficence or charity, if not numerous, are creditable. Principal among them is the Sociedad de Beneficencia, founded in 1825, which has the guardianship and supervision of public charities, and also the direction of the bull-ring, the cock-pit, and the lottery, from the gains of all of which it derives a large part of its resources—much to the scandal of a small minority of the good people of Lima.

The general cemetery, situated outside of the walls, was inaugurated in 1808. The chapel has a pleasant exterior, and the altar in the interior is finely executed. There are pretty gardens, finely kept, and some costly monuments. Vaults are built up, like rows of ovens, tier upon tier, each numbered in order, and in them the coffins are deposited.

One of the favorite resorts of the *élite* of Lima formerly, and

still, to some extent, is Conroy's Garden, on the left bank of the
Rimac. Conroy was an Irishman of cultivated taste and some
wealth, who brought together here, in grounds well laid out, a
great variety of trees and plants, some of them exotics, but
mostly indigenous. Since his death, and in part owing to its
inaccessibility, it has lost most of its prestige, and is becoming
a mere matter-of-fact fruit and flower garden.

There are many fine gardens, private or semi-public, in the
outer squares of the city, especially in that part which is only
partially built up, and known as the Cercado. In all these,
during most of the year, is to be found a vast profusion and

INTERIOR OF THE CHAPEL OF THE CEMETERY, LIMA.

variety of roses, of the most exquisite and marvellous tints.
The pride of the old burgomasters of Amsterdam in their tu-
lips is rivalled by that of the true Limenian in his roses, which
are trained, trimmed, grafted, and attended with the utmost
care, and in a spirit of intense yet friendly rivalry. Perhaps
the fact that Santa Rosa is a native of Lima had something to
do with the growth of this local passion for the queen of the
flowers. Indeed, if a passion for flowers of all kinds can be
taken as evidence of taste and refinement, Lima may claim to
rank among the most refined and cultivated of capitals. High
and low, rich and poor, are more or less adorned or more or less

surrounded by flowers. They bloom in courts and blush on
balconies; they enliven alike the dwellings of the rich and the
humble, and the heavy tresses of the belle as well as the curly
shock of the *zamba*. They tempt you under the Arcade of the
Trimmers, and they have the place of honor in the market-
house. And yet the stranger hears unfeigned lamentations on
the decline of the public taste for flowers! The famed *puchero
de flores*, the matron tells you, has almost disappeared, or is only
to be found, sadly degenerated, at the station of Miraflores, on

VIEW IN THE CEMETERY, LIMA.

the road to Chorillos. It was a grand bouquet of mingled
fruits and flowers, roses and violets and camellias, with cherries
and strawberries and downy peaches, all tastefully arranged, and
(what does the reader suppose?) sprinkled with pungent essences
to give them fragrance! On the whole, it is well enough that
the *puchero de flores* went out with the *saya y manta*, to give
place to a simpler and purer taste.

The public amusements of Lima consist mainly of the thea-
tre, the cock-fight, and the bull-fight, enumerating them inverse-
ly in the order of their popularity. Despite the opposition of

the press, the bull-fight retains its favor, and may be styled the
passion of the Limenians, Sunday being invariably chosen as
the day for the exhibition.  Cock-fighting was formerly practised in the streets and public places.  Many years ago, an attempt was made to suppress it altogether.  This being found
impossible, it was decided to confine the exhibition to a single
building erected for the purpose, and to regulate it by law.
The regulations comprise many chapters, and the official code is
about twice as long as the Constitution of the United States.

One cannot help thinking what a filthy, ill-supplied, uncomfortable city Lima must, after all, have been under the Spanish viceroys, when it was utterly without most of the establishments and appliances which modern civilization regards as indispensable.  There are many of the inhabitants who deplore
the "good old times," when there was no gas, no adequate supply of water, nor a market, nor a slaughter-house, not even a
cemetery worthy of the name, and who fix the date of the Independence as that of the commencement of Peruvian decadence.  Yet four-fifths of all the material ameliorations of the
city have been effected since that event: not precisely as a
consequence of it, perhaps, but with a rapidity that would have
been impossible under the old system.  Although much remains to be done to bring Lima up to the standard of the day,
yet her people deserve great credit for what they have accomplished.  Old customs and habits are hard to be eradicated; and
were it not for the grand institution of death and renovation,
progress would be next to impossible.

The Central Market of Lima is better, in many respects, and
more commodious than any now existing in New York.  It
covers an entire square, being part of the Convent of the Conception, which was, I believe, in 1851, forcibly appropriated by
the Government, at the risk of an outbreak.  It is built around
a great court, with exterior shops and an inner corridor, and is
traversed by pathways, radiating from a fountain in the centre,
forming a series of smaller courts, appropriated to special products.  There are stalls for the principal dealers; but the mass
of venders, who are women, squat on the pavement at the

edges of the galleries or in the open spaces, with their fruits, or fish, or vegetables heaped up in flat baskets, or on mats before them in little piles, called *montones*, each *monton* having a certain price. Like their congeners in all parts of the world, they chatter and "chaff" with each other and their customers, nursing children perhaps, or performing some other less pleasing maternal duty, at the same time. These children, when they have attained the requisite strength, tumble and sprawl about in a very promiscuous way, not at all appetizing to purchasers. People keeping establishments in Lima had better leave their marketing to a confidential major domo possessed of a strong stomach.

The market is certainly very well supplied with products, including those of the tropics and the temperate zone. Most of these are found together in the exceptional climate of Lima and its adjacent valleys, while others are brought down from the mountains, whose elevation and irrigation supply the necessary conditions for nearly every variety of production. Tomatoes, potatoes, the ears of green corn (*choclas*), radishes, and cucumbers are to be found side by side with yucas and plantains; while oranges and peaches, chirimoyas, grapes, granadillas, paltas, and tunas appeal with equal freshness to the eye of the visitor. The people are infatuated with the notion that their paltas, the *aguacate* of Central America, and the alligator-pear of the Antilles, are the best in the world; but they are no more to be compared with the aguacates of Nicaragua and the Isthmus than rancid lard to fresh-churned butter in the clovery month of June!

The waters of Peru abound with fish, which are largely consumed in Lima. The commonest are *bonitos*, a kind of mackerel; *corbinas*, resembling our "weak-fish;" and the *pejerey*, literally, "king-fish," a fine variety of the smelt, which, it is said, for some unknown reason, is fast disappearing from the coast.

Fresh meats—beef, mutton, and pork—are sufficiently abundant in Lima, and of fair quality. One of the best establishments in the city is the *Camal*, the *abattoir*, or slaughter-house, situated just outside of the gate of Monserrat, on the banks of the Rimac, near the so-called Botanic Garden of Conroy.  The Camal was erected in 1855 by the same enterprising person who established the garden, under a contract from the Government.  The place is not easy of access, but it merits a visit, if for no other reason than as showing how much more neatly and efficiently the act of slaughtering the animals is accomplished than with us.  They are fastened to cross-bars extending between stout columns, side by side, in such a manner as to leave an open space between their heads, through which a person may pass. This person is an experienced butcher, who carries in each hand a sharp, thin, broad, triangularly shaped knife.  He pauses before each animal, with his upraised knife firmly clutched, and, cautiously measuring his blow, drives it down in the neck, at the base of the skull, severing the vertebræ at that point.  The animal drops as if struck by lightning, and stiffens out on the instant, while another expert severs the jugular.  According to received theories, sensation' must be suspended the instant the knife falls; but if in no respect more humane than our system of stunning the animal by blows on the head, this certainly appears less brutal to the eye, besides being more rapid and effective.  It is to be regretted that the skill exhibited in slaughtering is not equalled by that of preparing the carcass for market. These are often literally hacked in irregular pieces, such as no American household would permit to appear on its table.  Foreigners stipulate to have their meats cut in a designated manner.

The traveller in Central America who complained that he felt every morning a disposition to perch himself on the first rock and crow, and who examined himself every night to see if his hirsute adornments had resolved themselves into feathers—and all in consequence of his unvarying diet of chickens and turkeys—may visit Peru with safety.  "*Hay gallinas hoy!*" was occasionally the exuberant announcement of Perez, our favorite and especial waiter, as we entered Maury's dining-room.  But when we saw Perez solemn and mysterious, with a deep expression of significance in his eyes, we were pretty sure to be informed in a stage-whisper, "*Pavo hoy!*" (turkey to-day), an announcement too momentous in Lima to be lightly made. And when I tell my readers that turkeys sell at from twelve to twenty dollars each, " in gold," and none of the biggest at that, and that chickens bring from six to eight dollars a pair, and are seldom to be got at that price, they will understand better the impression of rarity and respect they produced on Perez's simple mind.

Lima cookery, like Lima society, is in a transitive state, and is a rather incongruous mixture of foreign and native styles, the latter predominating in private meals, the former in all formal or public repasts. First on the list of national dishes, and that likely to resist longest foreign innovation, and which leads in every true Lima dinner, is the *puchero*. The following recipe for its composition is given by Fuentes, with evident gusto :

" To make a *puchero* according to strict gastronomic rules, put in a kettle a large piece of beef or mutton, some cabbage, sweet-potatoes, salt pork, sausage-meat, pigs' feet, yucas, bananas, quinces, pease, and rice, with annotto and salt [and Chili peppers, of course], for seasoning. Add a sufficient quantity of water, and let the whole stew gently for five or six hours ; then serve in a tureen or deep dish."

*Chupe* is a favorite breakfast dish, having a certain resemblance to *puchero*, but simpler in composition. *Picantes* seem to be going out of fashion with the better classes, although it is said they are pretty freely indulged in by the ladies between meals. On the lower orders, however, they retain their ancient hold, and in some parts of the city almost every second shop is a *picanteria*, around which the water-carriers, porters, and negro and cholo laborers cluster in swarms. There are many varieties of *picantes*, but all have the predominating ingredient of red pepper. The variety called *scoicha* is most pungent, composed of small pieces of fish or crabs, potatoes, and bread-crusts, soaked in the juice of the bitter orange, with an excess of peppers and salt. The other varieties are *carapulca*, composed of meat and potatoes finely pounded; the *lágua*, of Indian-meal and pork; *adoba*, of pork alone; and many others. All are colored more or less red by the peppers and the addition of *achote* (annotto). Formerly it was the custom of the best people after some outdoor *funcion*—a bull-fight, for instance—to resort to the *picanterias* to *picar*. Speaking from long observation and experience, I am confident that there is a certain craving among all dwellers in tropical regions, strangers as well as natives, for stimulating, high-seasoned food, and the free use of the numerous kinds of peppers found there soon becomes a habit, if not a necessity. Salt destroys or neutralizes very sensibly the rank, acrid taste of the peppers, which, after having been treated with it, may be made into a pleasant salad.

Among the numerous other native dishes may be mentioned the *chicharron*, lean pork fried in lard, one of the commonest of the viands cooked by *zamba* women over braziers, on the side-walks and in way-side *tambos*. The *tamal* is a preparation of ground maize, with lard, pistachios, peppers, and slips of pork, grilled, and wrapped in plantain or maize leaves; it is of Central American origin. The *ensalada de frutas* (literally, fruit salad) is a common dish, not generally liked at first, but which improves on acquaintance; as its name implies, it is made up of all sorts of fruits, sweet and sour, mild and pungent, stewed together. *Dulces*, or "sweets," are coincident with Spanish America, and are of infinite variety. *Leche asada* (literally, cooked milk) is a kind of clotted cream. *Maná*, sweetened yolks of eggs, and *empanadas*, gigantic cakes, are among the staples of the dessert. These sweets are taken not for the gratification they may afford to the palate, but in virtue of an ancient dietetic maxim, "*Tomar dulce para beber agua*" (take sweets in order to drink water), for it is orthodox to believe that no dinner can do a man good unless a glass of water follows.

The *Limeños* had formerly many queer conceits and maxims about diet and medicine, which have greatly given way under foreign contact, but which still lurk among the masses. As among the Chinese everything resolves itself into *yin* and *yang*, positive and negative, white and black, male and female, so in Lima all food is held to be *frio ó caliente* (hot or cold), *cosas que se oponen* (things hostile), and which, if introduced into

the stomach at the same time, would be dangerous, if not deadly. It will never do to take chocolate and rice at the same
meal, because *se openen*, "they are opposites;" and a dram of
*italia*, or brandy, on a banana would inevitably produce an *em-
pacho*. Chickens are *frio*, but beef is *caliente*, and *agua de
pollo* (chicken-tea), instead of beef-tea, is the proper thing to
give a patient suffering under acute or inflammatory disease.
You must not take cold water after a fit of anger, nor wash
yourself after a hard ride, or when you have a fever.

We once dined with Señor J——, a thorough representative
of the old school of Limeños, at his house in the Cercado, which
had once been the semi-suburban residence of the viceroys. It
was a spacious, rambling building, repulsive enough on the exterior, presenting more the aspect of a prison than of a palace.
The mountainous line of whitewashed wall on the side of the
street is relieved only by a high *zaguan*, closed by massive
doors, with great bronze knockers, like the heads of Roman
battering-rams, and almost as heavy, and by two or three windows grated like those of the old Bastile. A place roughly
chipped over the entrance showed where the arms of Spain had
been cut away by patriot chisels. Within, however, were wide
and lofty *salas*, wainscoted and draped as in the olden time,
with quaint furniture, and quainter portraits of forgotten digni-
taries arrayed in velvet doublets, and tipped out with plumes,
each with his armorial blazonings and list of titles in opposing
corners of the dark and stained canvas out of which he looked
with stern, unblenching eyes. A few ragged viceregal banners
were draped here and there, and a faded missal or two in parchment rested on marble tables along the walls. The corridor of the building formed one side of a large garden filled
with fruits and rare flowers, divided into terraces, with fountains, pigeon-houses, and graperies, all sufficiently decayed and
out of repair to make the establishment picturesque and the
visitor pensive and poetical. The pigeon-houses had few occupants, and these were old and plethoric; the fountains barely
dribbled; the trees were unpruned and mossy; and the great
brown gnarled trunks of the grape-vines twined themselves in

many a serpentine fold over windrows of stones, which answer
the purpose of trellises, and give out at night the heat they
have absorbed by day, to enrich and ripen the great clusters of
bursting fruit which blushed among the scanty leaves.

We were received by Señor J—— and his daughter with the
lofty ceremonials of other days, but with a cordiality peculiar to
no period.  Our dinner was served in a grand old *comedor*, our
host and hostess occupying the head and foot of the table respectively, but partaking of none of the articles served.  Such
was *haute étiquette* before the Independence, and we were dining
with the representatives of the *ancien régime*.  We had *sopa
teóloga* (priest's soup) and *puchero*, and then came a whole roast
kid; then kid again, in another form; next, mutton in two or
three forms, in one case *almendrado*, stuffed with almonds;
and after that a *picante* (in fact, a *picante* paste was all the time
on the table), pigeons, *tamales*, etc., etc., through twenty courses,
ending with *dulces*, not forgetting a gigantic *empanada*, which
it took an able-bodied man to carry, with fruits and liqueurs, including a glass of ripe and rare *italia*—the supremest stomachic
of their sunny land.

The Second Vice-president, acting in place of the President,
deceased, and the First Vice-president, absent, gave the Mixed
Commission a formal dinner in the rickety old Palacio del Go-
bierno, which was in striking contrast with that which we enjoyed so much in the Cercado.  The diplomatic corps was present, as were the officers of state; but great and grievous had
been the discussions as to where the commissioners should be
placed—those anomalous fellows who were clothed with absolute powers over all questions in dispute between the United
States and Peru, and whose decisions it was impossible to review.  Could they be classed as diplomatists, and sit next the
envoy extraordinary from Ecuador, or with the representative
of the potentate of the Sandwich Islands?  Or were they judicial characters, to be ranked with the Judges of the Supreme
Court?  Or what were they?  How the momentous question
was settled I never knew, but I suspect the matter was com-
promised, as we found ourselves ranged opposite the represent-

atives of Ecuador and Kaméhaméha, with the table between us and their dignity. And then came the dinner, which, like the uniform of the soldiery, was of a Frenchy character. It was a tedious affair, made up of eight courses, with an average of four dishes each, which were all scrupulously served, but with the slight drawback of being exceedingly cold. Patent heaters would be a desirable addition to the culinary apparatus of El Palacio.

A custom of the dinner-table, which was once common, and is not yet entirely in disuse, even in Lima, is the *bocadito*—a demonstration of politeness, or something warmer, consisting in selecting a choice morsel from the dish before you, and handing it on your fork to some lady present, who is privileged to return the attention. In some parts of the country the compliment is intensified, if not rendered a little startling, by the lady's taking the delicate bit between her thumb and forefinger, and placing it in the mouth of the *caballero* who has made the challenge.

5

# CHAPTER IV.

## PACHACAMAC.

DURING my residence in Lima I visited the ruins of Pachacamac, twenty miles south of the capital, on the right bank of the Rio Lurin, close by and overlooking the sea. We started from Chorillos, where we had spent the night, by sunrise, prepared for a stay of several days. Our route lay to the southward, over the dusty Pisco road, and we were soon out of sight of the gardens and cultivated fields of the Rimac Valley, riding over barren and sandy hills, and plains none the less sandy and barren. The sun became scorchingly hot long before we obtained our first view of the green valley of Lurin, and the sparkling waters of the river of the same name, which flow to the southward, and in sight of the celebrated ruins that we had come to visit, and which we found without any difficulty. They cover wholly, or in part, four considerable hills of regularly stratified but somewhat distorted argillaceous slate, the strata varying from two inches to a foot in thickness, breaking readily into rectangular blocks, which were used by the old builders for the foundations of the walls, and to a great extent worked into the structures themselves. The site of the ruins is most forbidding in aspect, and is a waste of sand, which has been drifted into and over a large portion of the buildings within the outer walls, some of which have been completely buried.

The desert extends northward to the valley of the Rimac, and inland to the mountains, that rise, naked and barren, in the distance. In contrast to these are the green and fertile little valley of Lurin on the south, and the blue waters of the Pacific on the west, with its picturesque rocky islands, against which the waves chafe with a ceaseless roar, and over which constantly hovers a cloud of sea-birds. The ruins consist of large adobe bricks, and the ever b already mentioned. Some of the walls are in a fair state of preservation, considering the heavy and frequent shocks of earthquakes to which they are exposed on this coast; but, owing to the absence of rain and frost, they have suffered little from the effects of the weather.

Pachacamac is one of the most notable spots in Peru, for here, as we are told by the old chroniclers, was the sacred city of the natives of the coast, before their conquest by the Incas. Here was the shrine of Pachacamac, their chief divinity, and here also the Incas erected a vast Temple of the Sun, and a house of the Virgins of the Sun, side by side with the temple of Pachacamac, whose worship they were too politic to suppress, but which they rather sought to undermine, and in the end merge in that of their own tutelary divinity. The name Pachacamac signifies " He who animates the universe," " The Creator of the world." The early Spanish priests thought they had discovered in this definition " that it was the Unknown God the people here worshipped, and rendered respect and honor to his name." They also tell us that " it was the same among the Greeks and Latins, with the *Pantocrator* and *Omnipotens,* by which names were invoked the True God, Creator of the Universe, and Verifier of all things. In this way there was established the worship of the Supreme Deity, who from his incomprehensibility was not represented by any figure in this temple, which, although constructed of fragile materials, equalled in wealth of gold and silver those of Cuzco and Titicaca.

" Profuse were the oblations and sacrifices of the Indians in this temple. Of the precious metals the Spaniards took away, among their spoils, twenty-seven *cargas* of gold* and two thou-

---

* A *carga* is two and a half arrobas, or sixty-two and a half pounds.

sand marks (sixteen thousand ounces) of silver, without having discovered the place where were hidden four hundred *cargas* of these two m ls, which is presumed to be somewhere in the desert between Lima and Lurin. Señor Pinelo affirms that a pilot of Pizarro asked for the nails and tacks which had supported the plates of silver, bearing the sacred name on the walls of the temple, as his share of the spoil, which Pizarro granted as a trifling thing, but which amounted to more than four thousand marks (thirty-two thousand ounces). We may judge from this what was the wealth of the temple in its greatness."

After Pizarro had seized on the person of Atahualpa, not satisfied with the immense ransom that he offered, he sent his brother Hernandez from Cajamarca to the coast, to seize on the treasures reported to exist in the Temple of Pachacamac. Hernandez Pizarro had with him one Miguel Estete, by no means an insignificant personage among the *conquistadores*, who wrote a report of the expedition, to which Oviedo had access, and which he seems to have quoted *verbatim*. The expedition appears to have followed the great inner or mountain road from Quito to Cuzco, until it reached a town called Pachacoto, where it left the main road for that of the plains. This was followed for three days to a place called Perpunga, overlooking the sea. Here they took "a very broad road" extending through all the coast towns, and on the fourth day reached Pachacamac, where they were received in a friendly manner and lodged in certain great buildings.

Hernandez then summoned the chiefs, and informed them that he had come for the gold which they were to send for the ransom of Atahualpa. They said it had already been sent; but, nevertheless, they afterwards brought a little, and declared that this was all which remained there. Hernandez pretended to believe them, but said that he wished to see the temple and the idol within it.

"This idol," says Estete, "was in a good house, well painted and finished. In one room, closely shut, very dark and stinking, was the idol made of wood, very dirty, which they call God, who creates and sustains us. At its feet were some offerings of golden ornaments. It is held in such veneration, that none except its priests and servants, whom, it is supposed, he has selected, may enter where it is, or touch the walls. No doubt, the devil resides in this figure, and speaks with his servants things that are spread all over the land. It is held throughout the country as God, and to it they make great sacrifices, and pilgrimages from a distance of three hundred leagues or more, with gold and silver and clothing. These they give to the custodian, who enters and consults the idol, and returns with its answer. Before any of its ministers can enter, they must fast many days, and abstain from all carnal intercourse. In all the streets of this town and its principal gates, and around this house of the idol, are many idols of wood, adorned in imitation of their devil.

"All the people from Tacamez, which is the beginning of the government, pay tribute every year to this temple, having houses in which to place it. They believe all things in the world are in the hands of this idol."

They were greatly scandalized and appalled when Hernandez entered the temple, who, they believed, would be destroyed, and had their faith much weakened when they found this did not occur. Hernandez ordered the vault (boveda) in which the idol was, to be demolished, and broke up the idol itself, and then showed them the cross as an invincible weapon against the devil.

"This town of Pachacamac," continues Estete, "is a great thing; and very near to a part of it, and along-side of the temple, is a house on a hill, well built, with five enclosures or walls, which the Indians say is that of the Sun. There are also in the town many other large houses, with terraces like those of Spain. It must be a very old place, for there are numerous fallen edifices. It has been surrounded by a wall, although now most of it is fallen. It has large gates for entering, and also streets. Its principal chief is called Taurichumbi, and there are many other chiefs."

Many chiefs of Mala, Chincha, and other places, came to see Hernandez, bringing presents, and wondering much at his audacity in confronting the idol. With what they brought and what he got from the temple, he obtained ninety thousand pesos in gold, though the priests had taken away four hundred loads. Such is the account of the first Spanish visit, and the overthrow of the idol of Pachacamac.

During my stay at Pachacamac, I was hospitably entertained at the sugar estate of San Pedro, two and a half miles from the ruins, in the valley of Lurin. By careful irrigation and intelligent industry, this estate has been rendered one of the finest and most productive in the country. I present a view of the residence of a family of laborers on this estate; it is a fair type of the better class of dwellings of the common people along the coast. The large population that once surrounded the great

HUT ON THE ESTATE OF SAN PEDRO.

temple is now reduced to a few families, who live in a little village still called Pachacamac. The houses are built of canes and rushes. And in place of what was once the Mecca of a great empire, we now find only numberless graves, a vast and ancient cemetery among the crumbling ruins, which, however, bear authentic testimony to the ancient greatness of the place.

The South Pacific Ocean off the coast of Chili and Peru is a favorite cruising-ground for whalers, one of which had lately been in these waters, and had left many carcasses to be drifted ashore by the Antarctic current, which here sets full on the land. Two of these were stranded at the foot of the hill on which stands a part of the ruins. A dozen or two condors had appropriated this hill as a resting-place, when gorged with the carrion. Half a dozen would be circling above us at once, sometimes not more than twenty yards above our heads, and again wheeling high up in the air. One day, while I was sketching alone on the top of the ruins, a shadow suddenly fell upon my drawing, and I heard a sharp report like the noise of striking two boards togeth-

er. Looking up, I saw an immense condor, not more than fifteen feet above me, apparently ready to pounce upon me. I sprung to my feet, drew my pistol, and hastily fired. I do not know whether I hit him or not, but he sailed off, "on mighty pens," a few hundred yards, and then turned back and poised himself directly over my head, but at a more respectful distance. I now had a chance for a fair shot at him, and the ball cut out one of the feath-

SHOT AT A CONDOR.

ers of his wing close to the socket. It measured two feet four inches in length. It is hardly necessary to say that I saw no more of my feathered friend for the remainder of the day.

The two principal edifices now traceable (for, as we have seen, some were in ruins at the time of the first Spanish visit) are called "El Castillo," or the Temple, which supported the shrine of Pachacamac, and that reared by the conquering Incas, with the convent of the Virgins, now bearing the name of Mamacuna. The former occupies the summit of a considerable hill, or, rather, headland, projecting from the somewhat ele-

vated level behind, and rising about five hundred feet above the
sea.   It reaches close to the shore, so that the ocean may be said
to break at its feet.

About half-way up the hill commences a series of four vast
terraces built around the natural cone, forming a semilunar
pyramid.   The walls of each terrace are nearly perpendicular,
and are faced with large adobes of uniform size.   They were,
no doubt, at one time painted red, as there are still many spots
of red paint to be seen.   The surface at the top, covering several acres, is reached by a winding passage-way through the
broken-down walls of the terrace.   The rectangular work has

VIEW AT PACHACAMAC.

been greatly injured by excavations, but was originally stuccoed
and painted ; the walls, after all the destructive agencies that
have been employed to effect their ruin, still bearing traces of
the figures of trees and men.   The *terre-plein* is covered with
ruins ; and at the southern corner, behind two rocks that crop
out, stood the shrine.   The most interesting part of these ruins
is a sort of esplanade, at the point commanding the finest view
seaward.   Here, though in an exceedingly ruinous state, can be
made out pilasters and traces of edifices that once adorned
the spot.

The only building among the ruins having the Inca type is

that called Mamacuna, which would seem to imply that it was
a convent rather than a temple.    It is situated about a mile and
a half from the ruins of El Castillo, which we have just described, and stands on low ground near a small lake.    A cluster
of dwarf palms has grown up in what was apparently the court.

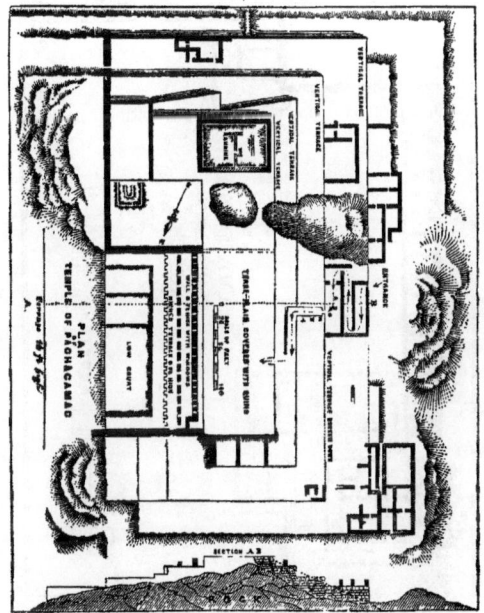

Mamacuna is built of the same material as the other structures,
and in like manner, but differs in style, and is unmistakably
Inca, as the door-ways, niches, and other peculiarities show.    One
of the niches in the inner room, shown in the following plan, is
depicted on page 71.

The principal and remarkable feature is an arch, so rare in American ruins. Indeed, in all my explorations in Central and South America, it is the only proper arch I ever found. It is perfect and well turned, is of adobes, of large size, and surmounts a passage running into the solid bulk of the edi-

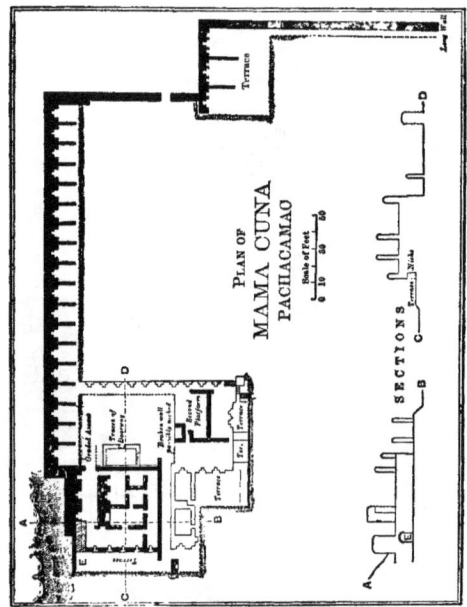

PLAN OF
MAMA CUNA
PACHACAMAO

fice, which may be considered as of two stories. The sides of the passage are the solid walls of the structure. The length of the passage is 14 feet 9 inches, but was, in all probability, much greater. The width is 5 feet 6 inches, its height 8 feet, and the spring of the arch 35 inches. There is no key-stone, but it is filled in with the same material as the adobes.

NICHE IN THE WALL, PACHACAMAC.

This arch is by no means the only example to be found on the coast; for it is said that others also exist among the aboriginal monuments in the vicinity of Tumbez, in Northern Peru. It is certain that a kind of bastard arch, formed by overlapping stones, or flat stones set at a certain pitch against each other, like the rafters of a house, was known among all the relatively civilized nations of the continent; but the true arch is a thing exceptional, and the one to which I have alluded entirely enigmatical, as I can scarcely conceive that the knowledge

ARCH AT PACHACAMAC.

and skill of which it gives evidence could have existed, even among those wonderful architects, the ancient Peruvians, without having a wider or more general application.

In ancient times, Pachacamac was the Mecca of South America; and the worship of the Creator of the World, originally pure, invested the temple with such sanctity that pilgrims resorted to it from the most distant tribes, and were permitted to pass unmolested through the tribes with which they might happen to be at war. Of course, around both the ancient and the modern temple there gradually sprung up a large town, occupied by priests and servitors, and containing *tambos*, or inns, for the pilgrims. But the desert has encroached on the old city, and buried a large part of it, with a portion of its walls, under the drifting sands. Nothing can exceed the bare and desolate aspect of the ruins, which are as still and lifeless as those of Palmyra. No living thing is to be seen, except, perhaps, a solitary condor circling above the crumbling temple; nor sound heard, except the pulsations of the great Pacific breaking at the foot of the eminence on which the temple stood.

It is a place of death, not alone in its silence and sterility, but as the burial-place of tens of thousands of the ancient dead. In Pachacamac, the ground around the temple seems to have been a vast cemetery. Dig almost anywhere in the dry, nitrous sand, and you will come upon what are loosely called *mummies*, but which are the desiccated bodies of the ancient dead. Dig deeper, and you will probably find a second stratum of relics of poor humanity; and deeper still, a third, showing how great was the concourse of people, and how eager the desire to find a resting-place in consecrated ground.

Most of the mummies are found in little vaults, or chambers of adobes, roofed with sticks, or canes, and a layer of rushes, and of a size to contain from one to four and five bodies. These are invariably placed in a sitting posture, with the head resting on the knees, around which the arms are clasped, or with the head resting on the outspread palms, and the elbows on the knees, enveloped in wrappings of various kinds. Sometimes they are enveloped in inner wrappings of fine cotton cloth, and

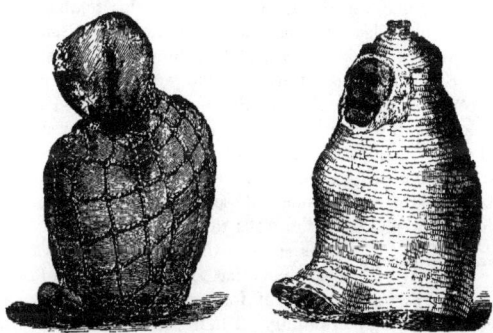

PERUVIAN MUMMIES.

then in blankets of various colors and designs, made from the wool of the vicuña and the alpaca, with ornaments of gold and silver on the corpse, and vases of elegant design by its side. But oftener the cerements are coarse, the ornaments scant and mean, indicating that of old, as now, the mass of mankind was as poor in death as impoverished in life. Fortunately for our knowledge of the people of the past ages, who never attained to a written language, they were accustomed to bury with their dead the things they most regarded in life, and from these we may deduce something of their modes of living, and gain some idea of their religious notions and beliefs. In fact, the interment of articles of any kind with the dead is a clear proof of a belief in the doctrine of a future state, the theory being that the articles thus buried would be useful to their possessor in another world.

To ascertain something more about the ancient inhabitants of Pachacamac than could be inferred from their monuments, I explored a number of their graves, during my ten days' visit there. I shall not try to give the general results of my inquiries, but will record what I found in a single tomb, which will illustrate how a family, not rich, nor yet of the poorest, lived in Pachacamac.

I shall assume that the family occupying this tomb lived in what may be called "an apartment," or one of the tenement-houses in the ancient city, which were, in some respects, better than ours. They were of but one story, and had no narrow, dark, common passages, but all the apartments opened around a spacious central court. Some of these tenements were composed of but a single room. This family probably had three: a large one, about fifteen feet square; a small sleeping-room, with a raised bank of earth at one end; and another smaller room, or kitchen, with niches in the walls to receive utensils, and with

PLAN OF THE TENEMENT.

vases sunk in the earth to contain maize, beans, etc., that seem to have been leading articles of food. The plan is of such a dwelling. The implements, utensils, ornaments, and stores have disappeared; but we find many of them in the family tomb in the neighborhood of the temple.

This particular tomb was one of the second stratum of graves, and was, therefore, neither of the earliest nor latest date. It was walled with adobes, was about four feet square by three feet deep, and contained five bodies: one, of a man of middle age; another, of a full-grown woman; a third, of a girl about fourteen years old; a fourth, of a boy some years younger; and the fifth, of an infant. The little one was placed between father and mother: the boy was by the side of the man; the girl, by the side of the woman. All were enveloped in a braided net-work or sack of rushes, or coarse grass, bound closely around the bodies by cords of the same material.

Under the outer wrapper of braided reeds of the man was another of stout, plain cotton cloth, fastened with a variegated cord of llama wool. Next came an envelope of cotton cloth of finer texture, which, when removed, disclosed the body, shrunken and dried hard, of the color of mahogany, but well preserved. The hair was long, and slightly reddish, perhaps from the effects of the nitre in the soil. Passing around the neck, and carefully folded on the knees, on which the head rested, was a net of the twisted fibre of the agave, a plant not found on the coast. The

threads were as fine as the finest used by our fishermen, and
the meshes were neatly knotted, precisely after the fashion of
to-day. This seems to indicate that he had been a fisherman.
—a conclusion further sustained by finding, wrapped up in
a cloth, between his feet some fishing-lines of various sizes,
some copper hooks, barbed like ours, and some copper sinkers.
Under each armpit was a roll of white alpaca wool, and behind
the calf of each leg a few thick, short
ears of variegated maize. A small, thin
piece of copper had been placed in the
mouth, corresponding, perhaps, with the
*óbolos* which the ancient Greeks put
into the mouths of their dead, as a fee
for Charon. This was all discovered belonging exclusively to the fisherman,
except that, suspended by a thread

PERUVIAN TWEEZERS.

around the neck, was a pair of bronze tweezers, probably for
plucking out the beard.

The wife, beneath the same coarse outer wrapping of braided reeds, was enveloped in a blanket of alpaca wool finely spun,

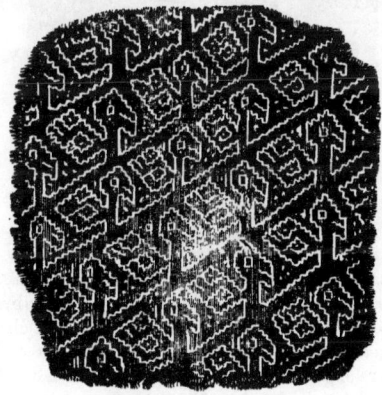

PATTERN OF ALPACA BLANKET.

woven in the style known as "three-ply," in two colors—a soft chestnut-brown and a pure white. The somewhat intricate figure is reproduced on a reduced scale in the engraving.

Below this was a sheet of fine cotton cloth, with sixty-two threads of warp and woof to the inch. It had a diamond-shaped pattern, formed by very elaborate lines of ornament, inside of which, or in the spaces themselves, were representatives of monkeys, which seemed to be following each other as up and down stairs.

PATTERN OF COTTON SHROUD.

Beneath this was a rather coarsely woven, but yet soft and flexible, cotton cloth, twenty yards or more in length, wrapped in many folds around the body of the woman, which was in a similar condition, as regards preservation, to that of her husband. Her long hair was less changed by the salts of the soil than that of her husband, and was black, and in some places

lustrous.  In one hand she held a comb, made by setting what
I took to be the bony parts—the rays—of
fishes' fins in a slip of the hard, woody part
of the dwarf-palm-tree, into which they were
not only tightly cemented, but firmly bound.
In her other hand were the remains of a fan,
with a cane handle, from the upper points of
which radiated the faded
feathers of parrots and
humming-birds.

WALLET, FOLDED.

Around her neck was a
triple necklace of shells,
dim in color, and exfolia-
ting layer after layer when exposed to light
and air.  Resting between her body and
bent-up knees were several small domestic
implements, among them an ancient spindle
for spinning cotton, half covered with spun
thread, which connected with a mass of the
raw cotton.  This simple spinning apparatus

ANCIENT SPINDLE.

consisted of a section of the stalk of the quinoa, half as large
as the little finger,
and eight inches long,
its lower end fitted
through a whirl - bob
of stone, to give it
momentum when set
in motion by a twirl
of the forefinger and
thumb grasping a
point of hard wood
stuck in the upper
end of the spindle.
The contrivance is
precisely the same
as that in universal
use by the Indian

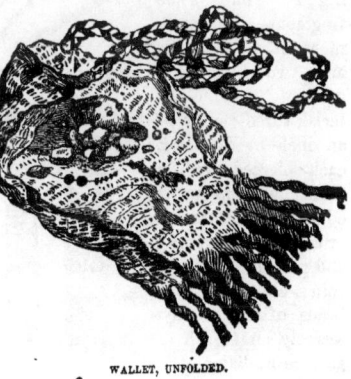

WALLET, UNFOLDED.

6

women of the present day. Only I have seen a small lime, lemon, or potato with a quinoa stalk stuck through it, instead

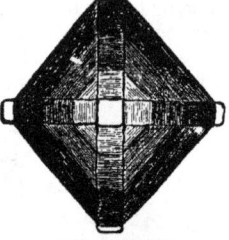

SPOOL OF THREAD.

of the ancient stone or earthen whirl-bob.

One of the most interesting articles found with the woman was a kind of wallet, composed of two pieces of thick cotton cloth of different colors, ten inches long by five broad, the lower end of each terminating in a fringe, and the upper end at each corner in a long braid, the braids of both being again braided together. These cloths, placed together, were carefully folded up and tied by the braids. The packet contained some kernels of the large lupin, sometimes called "Lima beans;" a few pods of cotton, gathered before maturity, the husks being still on; some fragments of an ornament of thin silver; and two little thin disks of the same material, three-tenths of an inch in diameter, each pierced with a small hole near its edge, too minute for ornament apparently, and possibly used as a coin; also some tiny beads of chalcedony, scarcely an eighth of an inch in diameter.

KNITTING UTENSILS.

The body of the girl was peculiar in position, having been seated on a kind of work-box of braided reeds, with a cover hinged on one side, and shutting down and fastening on the other. It was about eighteen inches long, fourteen wide, and eight deep, and contained a greater variety of ar-

SKEIN OF THREAD.

ticles than I ever found together in any grave of the aborigines. There were grouped together things childish, and things showing approach to maturity. There were rude specimens of knitting, with places showing where stitches had been dropped; mites of spindles and implements for weaving, and braids of

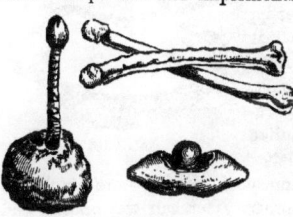

TOILET ARTICLES.

thread of irregular thickness, kept as if for sake of contrast with others larger and nicely wound, with a finer and more even thread. There were skeins and spools of thread; the spools being composed of two splints placed across each other at right angles, and the thread wound "in and out" between them. There were strips of cloth, some wide, some narrow, and some of two and even three colors. There were pouches, plain and variegated, of different sizes, and all woven or knit without a seam. There were needles of bone and of bronze; a

NETTING INSTRUMENT.

comb, a little bronze knife, and some other articles; a fan, smaller than that of the mother, was also stored away in the box.

There were several sections of the hollow bones of some bird, carefully stopped by a wad of cotton, and containing pigments of various colors. I assumed at first that they were intended for dyes of the various cotton textures we had discovered; but I became doubtful when I found a curious contrivance, made of the finest cotton, evidently used as a "dab" for applying the

colors to the face. By the side of these novel cosmetic boxes was a contrivance for rubbing or grinding the pigments to the requisite fineness for use. It was a small oblong stone, with a cup-shaped hollow on the upper side, in which fits a little round stone ball, answering the purpose of a pestle. There was also a substitute for a mirror, composed of a piece of iron pyrites resembling the half of an egg, with the plane side highly polished. Among all these many curious

DRIED PARROT.

things, I dare say, none was prized in life more than a little crushed ornament of gold, evidently intended to represent a butterfly, but so thin and delicate that it came to pieces and lost its form when we attempted to handle it. There was also a netting instrument of hard wood, not unlike those now in use in making nets.

BOY'S SLING.

The envelopes of the mummy of the girl were similar to those that enshrouded her mother. Her hair was braided and

plaited around the forehead, encircling which, also, was a cincture of white cloth, ornamented with little silver spangles; a thin narrow bracelet of the same metal still hung on the shrunken arm, and between her feet was the dried body of a parrot, doubtless her pet in life, brought perhaps from the distant Amazonian valleys.

There was nothing of special interest surrounding the body of the boy; but bound tightly around his forehead was his sling, finely braided from cotton threads.

The body of the infant, a girl, had been

INFANT'S BURIAL-NET.

embedded in the fleece of the alpaca, then

wrapped in fine cotton cloth, and placed in a strangely braided sack of rushes, with handles or loops at each end, as if for carrying it. The only article found with this body was a sea-shell containing pebbles, the orifice closed with a hard pitch-like substance. It was the child's rattle.

Besides the bodies, there were a number of utensils, and other articles in the vault; among them half a dozen earthen jars, pans, and pots of various sizes and ordinary form. One or two were still incrusted with the soot of the fires over which they had been used. Every one contained something. One was filled with ground-

POTTERY FROM PACHACAMAC.

nuts, familiar to us as pea-nuts; another with maize, etc., all except the latter in a carbonized condition.

Besides these articles, there were also some others, illustrating the religious notions of the occupants of the ancient tomb, and affording us scant but, as far as they go, certain ideas of the ancient faith and worship.

.

## CHAPTER V.

### RUINS IN THE VICINITY OF LIMA.

The Valley of Cañete and its Ruins.—The Palace of El Rey Inca.—Ruins of Herval.
—Temple at Magdalena.—Limatambo.—Ruins in the Valley of the Chillon.—
Burial-places of the Ancient Poor.—Relics found in Graves.—Ruins of Cajamarquilla.—Exploring and Surveying.—Meet the Robber, Rossi Arci.—His Subsequent Fate.

In the vicinity of Lima are many ruins, which I visited and
explored. These will form the subject of the present chapter.

In one of the districts of the fertile valley of Cañete, now occupied by rich sugar plantations, stood, at the time of the Spanish
conquest, a grand fortress, which was to a great extent demolished in the seventeenth century by the viceroy, the Conde de
Mendoza, while he was building the Castle of Callao. Of this
fortress a Peruvian author writes: "Where the valley of Guarco
terminates, twelve leagues from Lima, on the south coast, and
near the valley of Cañete, were discovered the remains of a
great fortress overlooking the sea. It was a castle of stone,
situated on an elevation washed by the sea. This edifice had
for its foundations great square bricks (adobes). The doors to
the apartments, and entrances to the various interior rooms,
were of a regular architecture, the whole well arranged, with
spacious courts and antechambers, which gave more dignity to
this invincible fortress. From the highest of these a stairway
descended to the sea. The steps were of great stones, so well
united as to appear of a single piece, nor was any mortar visible between them. Altogether the structure appeared to be of
different construction from the buildings of Cuzco, and at least
exhibiting equal power and magnificence. The Viceroy of Peru,
the Marquis of Cañete, in the year 1595, repaired this fortress,
and appointed an alcalde to guard it, with six soldiers; the for-

mer with a salary of twelve hundred assayed *escudos* annually, and the latter with the pay each of twenty-five *escudos* monthly. But the payment of these sums not having been realized, the guard was withdrawn, and the demolition of the fortress was commenced by the people of the valley, who used the stones for new constructions of their own. The ruin thus made reflects disgracefully on our intelligence, which requires that this work should be restored and preserved."

The ruins known as the Palace of El Rey Inca, in the valley

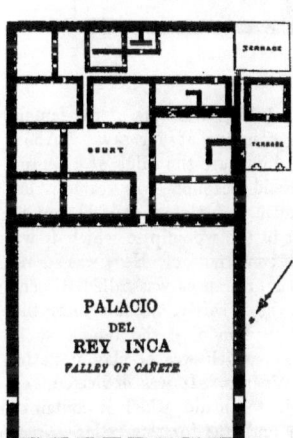

PALACIO
DEL
REY INCA
*VALLEY OF CAÑETE.*

of Cañete, are shown in the plan. On the front, a row of piers gives entrance to an extensive square court, covering as much. ground as the structure beyond, and enclosed by a wall three feet thick. The building itself is divided into rooms, with an open court, and at the side an extension forming one apartment between two terraces. Many of the walls are niched, especially those of the two principal rooms.

The ruins of Hervai, in the valley of Huarcu, one of the branches of the Cañete, show excellent workmanship and materials. As will be seen in the plan, they are remarkable for the numerous flights of well-laid steps, leading from one part to another. The passage-ways through the walls, marked "W," are covered.

Between Lima and the sea, protected by the fortress of San Miguel, is the small village of Magdalena, a place of not more than five hundred inhabitants. A road leads from it to Bellavista, a station on the railroad from Callao to Lima; and as there is a demand for bricks, the ancient adobe structures are fast being destroyed, the material being remade into bricks for the modern towns. The ruins, now in a very dilapidated condition,

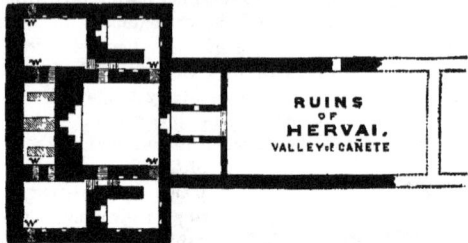

RUINS OF HERVAI, VALLEY of CAÑETE

were once highly important, including a temple of the famous oracle-deity, Rimac. Of this a native author says: "About half a league to the south of Lima are the ruins of a temple which, if we may credit the old accounts, was scarcely less adorned than that of Pachacamac in richness of gold and silver, although differing from it in the worship to which it was dedicated and sumptuousness of construction. Here was adored an idol, which from its oracular utterances was called Rimac,* which word, if you pronounce the *R* softly, means a thing that talks. They pretended that the demon of the temple spoke through the mouth of this idol, which was of clay, imitating the figure and habit of the Moanes. It was dedicated, says Pinelo, speaking of this temple, to an idol which it contained, which responded as an oracle, and was for this called *Rimac*, 'he who speaks.' In this there was nothing more demoniac than astuteness, for the Moanes, to deceive the people, introduced one of themselves beneath the statue, which was hollow, who responded to the consultations according to the character of the offerings made by the people. They painted in this temple, as hieroglyphics, the answers most favoring their ideas. And, to make mysterious these paintings, which are to be seen on the

---

* From this idol, and not from the river on whose banks it stands, the city of Lima takes its name ; the *R* changing into *L*.

walls of this structure, they covered them with other walls,
without allowing the junction of those that served as a curtain
to obliterate the figures they concealed.

"The Padre Calancha adverts to the same things with myself, and with animation says: 'I admired seeing in one of
these palaces or houses two walls, once joined together, which
had been separated by earthquakes, and were painted with
figures of Indians and animals. Asking of some how they
could smooth and paint one wall joining another, they thought
(seeing that the walls are great) that they painted one brick
or section of *tapia*, and quickly joined its ends; then another. But they do not explain how it was that the divisions
between wall and wall remain visible, and the pictures with
lines and breaks show the separation. We are compelled to
believe that the multitude of Indians had a way of making the
wall entire, and, after smoothing and painting it, joining it to
the other; since the number and obedience of the Indians
would make things much more difficult easy.'

"Of the treasures of this temple the authors say nothing
positive; what they write are conjectures, but well founded if
this is the tradition they favor. It says that there are great
riches buried in the ruins. But the area they cover is not great.
With comparatively few workmen the walls may be torn down,
their materials removed, and the centre excavated, in which
case the truth may be ascertained. My doubts do not relate
to the riches which were unquestionably contained in the temple before its ruin, but to those alleged to be buried within its
walls. For such burials there was scarcely time, and if there
had been, it is hardly credible that within the walls of Lima
and around it there can remain until now undiscovered so great
a treasure, there being no difficulty in the way of its discovery,
especially as there are men who love more this kind of work
than any other. I do not deny that there are hereabouts some
burials, sufficient to alleviate the poverty of one or two, but
nothing like the treasures which, without dispute, are hidden
in Chuciuto, Cuzco, Truxillo, Pachacamac, and Cajamarca. If
these were discovered, they would be sufficient to enrich the

world.  It is difficult to find them, from the situation of the
deposits; but it would be easy to discover those of Rimac if
any certain information existed concerning them.  This temple
was called then Rimac-Tam-Pu (house of him who speaks), a
name now corrupted into Limatambo."

When I visited these ruins I found a graded way or inclined
plane leading from one court to another, giving on a small
scale, but in a perfectly satisfactory manner, an explanation and
example of the mode in which ascents were accomplished by
the builders of these works.  The double wall that surrounds
the temple, or *huaca*, and other structures at this place is more
than three miles long, and in some places more than sixteen
feet high.  The gateway, partly closed by a modern wall, has
two inner piers or square columns, standing a few feet from the
wall inside.

DEMOLISHING HUACA, LIMATAMBO.

On the road to Chorillos, nearly on a line with this, is the
modern Limatambo, with extensive remains; but these and similar works at Amacavilca, which overlooks the present fashionable watering-place of Chorillos, need little description.  Those
at Limatambo were also undergoing demolition by the hands of
the brick-makers; but their sacrilege was forgiven in return for
the advantage afforded us of studying more in detail than we

elsewhere enjoyed the mode of construction and system of
building these ancient structures.

In the valley of the river Chillon, ten miles north-west of
Lima, is a fortification similar in design and purpose to the
fortresses of Calaveras and Quisque, in the valleys of the Casma and Nepiña, hereafter to be described. It is situated on the
Hacienda Collique, near the road to Cerro Pasco, over which we
went on our way down to the ruins. The remains are in shape
an irregular oval, the lines being conformed to the outline of
the hill, which is about five hundred feet in height. The area

PORTION OF WALL OF HUACA NEAR LIMATAMBO.

is fifteen hundred feet in its greatest diameter. The two outer walls, with the two supporting ones at the entrance, are of
rough stones without cement; the third and last is of stones
carefully laid in tenacious clay, fourteen feet high, and faced
vertically. There are a number of clusters of ruined buildings
within the walls, and to the left are several small hills, surmounted with adobe buildings in a state of much dilapidation.
After passing the fourth wall, at the entrance we come to an

extensive level area, which I have designated as the Plaza, and
which is partly surrounded by terraces faced with stones; passing which we come to a steep stairway, mainly cut in the solid

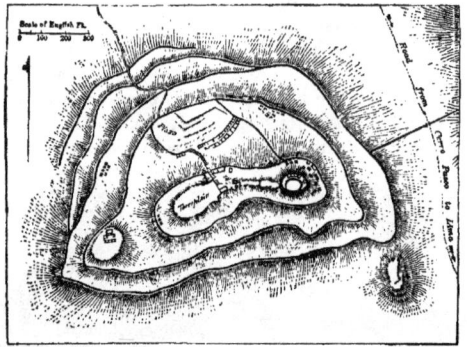

FORTIFIED HILL OF COLLIQUI.

rock, leading to the top of the hill. Here is the *terre-plein*,
nearly level and free from stones, and the round tower or citadel. At the base of the hill, upon the right, is a heavy adobe
wall crossing the valley and the Cerro Pasco road, to another
and somewhat similar fortified hill, on the opposite side of the
valley.

On the Hacienda Arriaga, about three miles north-west of
Lima, on the road to the valley of the river Chillon, there is
an extensive ruin, a plan of a portion of which we give. These
remains are part of a large series, of which they are the best
preserved, and are situated on the flank of a considerable hill
or promontory projecting into the valley which they overlook,
besides commanding a fine view of the harbor of Callao. The
hill is about two hundred and fifty feet high, and the ruins are,
perhaps, one-third of the way up the side. At the place where
the hill is steepest the outer wall is reinforced by two others of
less height. On the opposite side of the hill is a broad sandy
valley running high up the mountain, and covered with re-

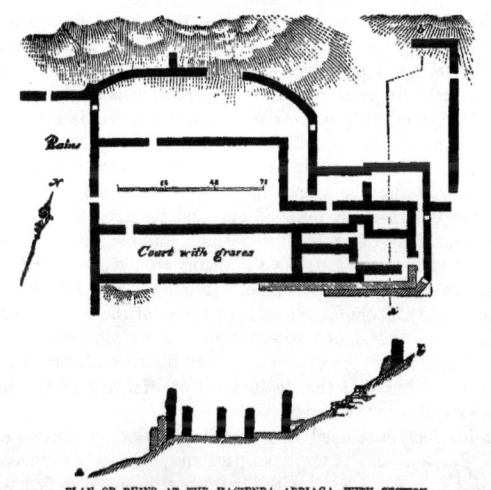

*Ruins*

*x*

*Court with graves*

PLAN OF RUINS AT THE HACIENDA ARRIAGA, WITH SECTION.

mains. It seems formerly to have been in considerable part cultivated by means of an *azequia* tunnelled through the hill a distance of one hundred and fifty yards.

The traces of the tunnel, which is now fallen in or stopped up, are distinct, and are situated about one hundred yards to the left of the works. The remains are distinguished by having several low door-ways through the wall, besides the open ones.

The "lower classes," the "hewers of wood and drawers of water," in Peru, as everywhere else, met in death a treatment corresponding with that meted out to them in life. They were thrust into holes in the nitrous sands of the coast, or into crevices of the rocks among the mountains, with such scant paraphernalia for their wanderings in a future world as their own limited means or those of their humble friends could supply. Few and rude are the relics found with these shrivelled remains: a calabash or gourd; perhaps a carved wooden cup, containing amulets or charms; curious stones, to the natural peculiarities of which the superstitious mind rendered reverence; an implement of toil; and perhaps a rude wooden idol: such were the objects most frequently found with the plebeian dead of the coast, buried in such shallow graves that the winds often exposed them, and the earthquake thrust them up to the day. To utilize the arable land, the ancient inhabitants were accustomed to pile up the stones that encumbered the ground in great heaps. In these, to avoid encroaching upon the areas of cultivation, they often deposited their humble dead. Thousands of such stone-heaps dot the plains around Lima, and the valleys of the Rimac and Chillon. In one of these I found the dried-up body of one of the ancient tillers of the soil. He sat alone among the stones wrapped in rustic cloths, with some pods of beans and ears of maize pressed between his breast and knees, testifying that the distinctions of life, real or adventitious, extended to the grave.

At his feet, enveloped in coarse cotton cloth, were two objects of interest, obviously connected with his superstitions. The first was a kind of idol or mask, cut out of wood, bearing a resemblance to the carved idols brought from distant Pacific islands. It is painted red on the face, and has on top and sides holes through which thin cords, still remaining in place, were passed, as if to attach it in front of some object. A projection beneath the chin, apparently designed to fit into a socket, suggests the possibility that it was carried surmounting a pole or staff. It is seven and a half inches vertically, exclusive of the lower projection, by seven inches broad, and is boldly and freely cut by some sharp instrument. Probably the eye-sockets had been filled by oval pieces of shell, corresponding with what we see in the works of the Polynesian islands, and of the people of the African coast.

CARVED WOODEN IDOL.

There was also a wooden bowl, four and a half inches in diameter, and nearly four inches high, carved with a border of conventional representations of some kind of bird running around its rim. The outer surface is smooth, while the interior shows the marks of sharp tools. It was packed full of layers of variously colored alpaca and vicuña wool, in perfect preservation. Between each layer were deposited pebbles, having some

WOODEN BOWL.

faint likeness to animals, a little strengthened by art. There were fragments of crystallized quartz, and a very good carving

EAR OF MAIZE, IN STONE.

in a variegated talc of an ear of maize, three inches long, and of just proportions. These articles were what are called, according to the Padre Arriaga in his rare book on the " Extirpation of Idolatry in Peru," *canopas*, the household deities, or *lares*, of the ancient inhabitants. We are told that " the most esteemed of these were the bezoar stone (*quicu*) and small quartz crystals (*guispi*). The carvings in stone, in imitation of ears of maize, are specially mentioned under the name of *zaramama*.

Some four or five leagues from Lima, following up the valley of the river Rimac, is a side valley, an amphitheatre among the hills, containing several important haciendas, of which those of Huachipa and La Niverea are the principal. This valley is watered by a large *azequia*, deriving its supply from the river higher up, and which dates from the time of the Incas. The water, however, cannot, or could not, be carried, under the hydraulic system of the ancients, sufficiently high up on the flanks of the hills to irrigate the whole of this subsidiary and remarkably fertile valley. Its upper or higher part, therefore—an extent of several square miles—like all the rest of Peru where not irrigated, is an arid area, without vegetation of any kind; while

the lower or irrigated part is covered with luxuriant grain fields
and meadows.

On this plain, and covering nearly a square league, are the

RUINS OF CAJAMARQUILLA.

remains of an ancient town, now known as the ruins of Cajamarquilla.   These consist of three great groups of buildings
on and around the central masses, with streets passing between them.   It would be impossible to describe this complicated maze of massive adobe walls, most of them still standing,
albeit much shattered by centuries of earthquakes, or to convey

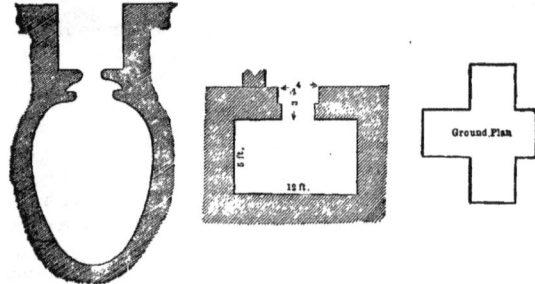

SECTION AND PLAN OF SUBTERRANEAN VAULTS.

an idea of the pyramidal edifices, rising stage on stage, with terraces and broad flights of steps leading to their summits. It is enough to say that many of the buildings of the ruined city, the history of which is lost even to tradition, are complicated

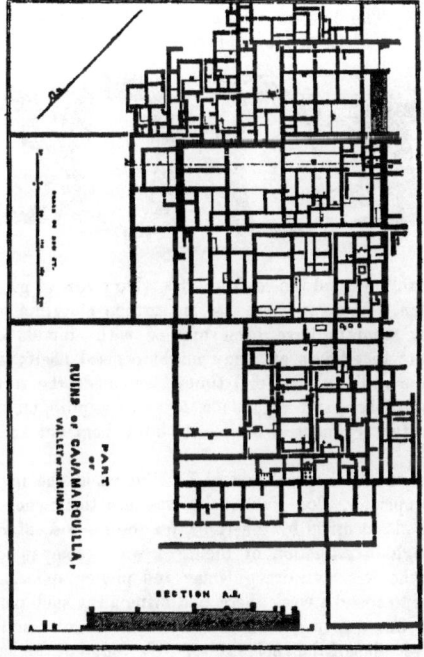

structures, their apartments connecting by blind and narrow passages, and containing many curious subterranean vaults or granaries, which consisted of excavations made in the hard ground, of various shapes and sizes. Some were round, like a vase or jar, and again others were square. They are called

7

*ollas*, or *tinajas* (vases, or jars), and were no doubt intended for the storage of household supplies. The plans on page 92 will afford a better idea of their construction than can be given by words.

The privacy of these rooms was insured by walls in front of the doors. The door-ways are all low, and vary in form, a few of which are given in the engraving. There are no windows

DOOR-WAYS.

in the dwellings, and the roofs are flat. No traces of gables are to be seen. In many there was an earthen elevation or daïs, and they seem to have been supplied with suitable closets. Among these edifices an army might conceal itself; and, in fact, these ruins have several times been made the refuge of bands of robbers and vagabonds, so as to require, on one occasion, a full regiment of soldiers to hunt them out and expel them.

I had gone to the hacienda of La Niverea, at the invitation of its proprietor, Don Pablo, who was also the owner of the waste lands occupied by the ruins, for the purpose of making a thorough investigation of them. I was accompanied by a friend, who was both draughtsman and photographer, and we intended to spend a week there, and bring away such plans and views as would give a clear notion of the singular and undescribed remains of the ancient city. We found at the hacienda a detachment of troops from Lima, a lieutenant and some five-and-twenty men, who seemed to be in no hurry to leave the comfortable foraging afforded by Don Pablo's well-cultivated hacienda, with its acre or two of vineyard, now purple with such grapes as are found nowhere in the world except Peru.

We commenced operations among the ruins the very day of our arrival, assisted by a couple of Chinese laborers, kindly lent us by our host. We went to our work early, and returned late, our interest deepening with every hour's investigation. On the second day, the lieutenant and his squad left, alleging that the *ladrones* had been heard from over the mountains, in the valley of Chillon, whither they went "to persecute them." I suspected that the "persecutors" of the robbers had got some hint of their approach to La Niverea, and, either from fear or through complicity, had determined to give them a clear field.

On our third day among the ruins, my companions succumbed to the heat and glare of the sun reflected from the bare walls, and returned to the hacienda with many symptoms of fever, leaving me with but one assistant, A-tau, a Chinese, who could neither speak nor understand more than half a dozen Spanish words; but who, nevertheless, I had little difficulty in making comprehend all that I required in the way of aiding me in my survey. He carried the measuring-line and stakes, and myself the compass and note-book.

Having long before recognized the utter impossibility of making a complete plan of the whole city, I had determined to run out the most important streets, and make a detailed survey of a section sufficiently large to convey a clear notion of the whole. I ran my lines on the walls, which are in general broad and firm enough to permit one to walk along their tops. We had proceeded on a single, slightly deviating course for nearly half a mile, past the principal pyramidal pile among the ruins, and nearly to their centre, and were silently intent on our work, when, being in advance, I was startled in every nerve by the sudden apparition of three men leaping suddenly to their feet from the earthen floor of one of the smaller rooms, where they had been comfortably reclining on a heap of *piliones* and *ponchos*. They were armed, and their hands were on their weapons in a moment. I gave the universal salutation of the mountaineers, "*Dios y paz*" (God and peace), which was responded to in like manner.

It was Rossi Arci himself, the "Robber of the Ruins," and

his companions, whom I had surprised. I knew that I was in
for it, so I made a bold advance by clambering down the broken
wall, with outstretched hand, which was accepted reluctantly.
I soon found that I was suspected of being a Government agent,
making a plan of the ruins for official use. I knew there was
no time for trifling, and that a fearless manner was my only
guarantee of safety. I offered him my flask, which he declined,
saying, "After you," and for reasons afterwards obvious, I commenced. My excellent friend paid profound respects to the
flask when passed to him; and, as I handed him one of my
cards, and he read the name with the appendage, "*Comisionado
de los Estados Unidos*," he said, "*Bien* [good]; pardon me," and
lifted his sombrero. He followed the explanation of my plans
with apparent interest, but I fear he was not exactly the man to
appreciate archæology. One fellow of the party had encountered me some months previous at the ruins of Amacavilca,
and had seen the great range of my wonderful breech-loading
rifle, and gave a pretty high notion of the efficiency of that
weapon. The robber wished to possess himself of so valuable
an addition to his armory, and immediately made me an offer
of one hundred Bolivian dollars, adding, slowly, "When I get
them; for, señor, we really are not rich." I, however, declined
the generous offer; but I promised to send him a few bottles
of *italia*, such as I had with me. As we parted, he said, "You
may come back to-morrow to your nonsense [*tonterías*] without fear; and I will send a reliable man for the rifle. *Adios,
amigo!*" I sent A-tau to carry the bottles, which he did with
great reluctance. It was after dark when he returned, grossly
intoxicated. It seems that my friend Rossi Arci had insisted
on my drinking first, not from motives of courtesy, but to as-
sure himself that there had been no poisons artfully dissolved
in the tempting *italia;* and when he got hold of A-tau's bottles,
the Celestial wretch was compelled to drink a third of each to
give assurance that a similar "doctoring" had not taken place
at the hacienda. Between fright and an overdose of brandy, I
lost my assistant next day, and Don Pablo a laborer for a week.

Four weeks afterwards, a swollen and disfigured corpse was

exposed in the Grand Plaza of Lima. It was that of Rossi Arci. He had made a bold attack on a Government guard of about a hundred soldiers, who were conveying a remittance of coin, at a place noted in the annals of Peruvian brigandage as Rio Seco, about half-way between Lima and Cerro de Pasco. The fight lasted some hours, and frequently swayed in his favor; and it is not impossible that he would have captured the booty had he not received a severe wound in the groin, which compelled him to retire, and of which he died the next day. His last request was to be buried in the bottom of an *azequia,* so that his body might not fall into the hands of the authorities. His request was complied with; but one of his followers gave himself up, and purchased clemency by revealing the secret of the brigand's grave. A commission was sent to verify the statements of Arci's follower, and the decaying body was identified and brought to Lima amid the rejoicings of the people. The commander of the *remisa* was promoted, and a general feeling of relief pervaded the community.

# CHAPTER VI.

### UP THE COAST TO TRUXILLO.

Starting for Paita.—The Rocky Coast.—Sea-lions.—The Oasis and Port of Huacho.
—The Town.—Rock-salt.—How it is formed.—Supe and Patavilca.—The Rio de
la Barranca.—Ruins of Paramanca.—Traditions.—Ancient Works on La Horca.
—Huarmey or Guarmey.—Casma.—Bays of Simanco and Ferrol.—The Valley of
Chimboto.—Ancient Monuments.—Silver Mine of Micaté.—Port of Santa.—The
Rio Santa.—Ridge crowned with Ruins.—Huaca near Santa.—Ride to Santa.—
The City.—Guano Islands of Guañape.—Eagles, Pelicans, and Vultures.—Port of
Huanchaco.—Singular Craft.—Sardinas.—Getting ashore.—The Prefect of Truxil-
lo.—Departure for Truxillo.—The Grand Chimu.—Beautiful Lizards.—Entrance
to Truxillo.

HAVING completed my official duties as United States Commissioner to Peru, and having explored the ruins at Pachacamac
and those in the immediate vicinity of Lima, I was at liberty to
undertake the far wider researches and explorations which I
had so long meditated. My first expedition was to be northward, up (or as they phrase it here, down) the coast to the ancient ruins of Grand Chimu, near Truxillo. I proposed also, on
my return voyage, to visit the ruins lying in the vicinity of the
coast between the port of Truxillo and Lima. I was accompanied by Mr. P—— as photographer, and Mr. C——, a friend
who was to assist me. After infinite delays, I succeeded, as I
thought, in getting the "dark tent" for use in photographing
completed, just in time to be put aboard the little, low, long
English-built steamer *Inca*, plying coastwise between Callao and
Paita. A more uncomfortable craft could scarcely be found.
The cabin was low and without state-rooms, the compartments
for the sexes being merely shut off by dingy curtains. The
deck was uncovered, with only a narrow seat running part of
the way around it, next the guards. We were too glad to get
off, to be either critical or complaining, especially as we found

that the captain was communicative, pleasant, and even convivial.

It was late in the afternoon, and the two remaining hours of daylight were spent in watching the thousand fantastic forms of the frayed and barren rocks under whose shadows our little steamer glided along. We were so close to them that they shut from sight the higher elevations and *nevados* of the interior, with their rugged escarpments. Early next morning we were awakened by the slowing of the vessel, its occasional stoppages, and the heaving of the lead—indications that we were nearing the land in a fog. Going on deck, we found the atmosphere of the color of milk, thick with moisture that hung in beads from every stay, and stood in pools everywhere. We were cautiously feeling our way into the port of Huacho, more than a hundred miles from Callao. But what noise is that, now loud and apparently close at hand, and then fainter and more distant, a mingled howling and bellowing, rising above the slow splash of our scarcely revolving wheels? A dripping sailor, noticing my amazement, said, with a grim smile,

"They are having a good old time of it this morning."

"Who are?"

"Why, them sea-lions—seals some folks call 'em. They are allers lively in such weather. And a good thing it is too; for you see, sir, the gettin' into this place is full of rocks that these beasts live on, and fight on too; real savage, sir, sometimes, especially when courtin': and if it warn't for them, we should never know where we are in thick weather; for these people would never put up fog-bells."

And so it was; we were really steering by the racket of the seals that swarm on the rocky islets off the coast, and especially in this locality. After a while the man at the lead sung out, "Three fathoms—half!" and the order to anchor was given. A gun was fired, and we awaited the lifting of the fog; waited until breakfast and after breakfast, for four mortal hours, when a light breeze sprung up and the fog began to scatter, unveiling fitfully the shore, which was high and green, with a number of little silvery cataracts from the various *azequias* pouring over the declivity. After a while the whole oasis of Huacho was revealed, a verdant interval extending perhaps a mile along the beach, between two bare, rocky eminences; that to the south projecting into the sea so as to form a partial protection from the prevailing south wind. Near this the Government had constructed at great cost a long iron mole, which was little used; for the boats that put off to our steamer, whether with passengers or freight, all started from the beach through the heavy surf, and landed there, as in the days of old. I was anxious to go ashore for a few hours in Huacho, but found that, in consequence of the delay occasioned by the fog, this would be impracticable.

Huacho is a considerable town, in a high valley watered by the Rio Huaura, containing many rich haciendas and several tolerably large towns. It has about six thousand inhabitants, mainly Indians, engaged in supplying Lima with fowls, pigs, etc., and in working the salt-pits (*salinas*), fifteen miles to the southward. The great blocks of salt which form so conspicuous a feature in the shops of Lima are obtained here. The place where the deposits occur is called *Pampa de las Salinas*, a plain (as its name implies) two miles long by one broad, about three miles from the sea. The centre of this plain is depressed, and here the salt is found in thick layers of different degrees of purity; the upper and poorest being called *sal de barco*, or ship-salt; the intermediate variety, *sal de garza;* and the lowest and best, *sal de corazon.* It is chopped out in blocks of from eighty to one hundred and fifty pounds, varying in price according to quality, from fifteen to forty cents per hundred-weight, at the works.

Whenever the salt is removed, the excavations soon become filled by infiltration with saturated salt-water, and in the course of a year or two they are occupied again by another solid mass of salt. It was long supposed that this infiltration took place from the sea; but the investigations of Professor Raimondi have shown that the supply of water is kept up from the condensation on the surrounding hill-sides, and on the plain itself, of the *guaras*, or fogs, of the winter season. He supposes that

the plain, and the basin of which it is the centre, were once beneath the sea, and raised up suddenly by one of those convulsions of which the whole coast bears so many evidences, thus
forming a great salt lake cut off from the sea, and that by
evaporation thick beds of salt were deposited in the lowest part
of the plain, while the surrounding sands were charged with
it; and that the constant renovation of the pits is due to
the gradual solution of this salt, and its slow accumulation in
depressions formed by the removal of the original deposits.
Hence he rejects the popular notion that these beds are fed
from the ocean, and therefore inexhaustible, and warns the
Government to look to their economical working.

About noon we paddled out of the indentation of the shore
called the bay of Huacho, and passed the low rocky islets.
Many seals were splashing about in the sea, and yet the rocks
were alive with them.

Steaming along and close to the shore, we came in a few
hours to a part of the coast where the high, rocky shore-ridges
broke away, revealing a broad space of sandy beach and rolling
sand-hills, extending back as far as the eye could reach to the
very base of the cloud-capped Cordillera. A cluster of the
rudest possible cane huts near the water, with a few boats and
*caballitos* drawn up in front and a number of horsemen pranc-
ing behind, were the only signs of life within the range of
vision. This is the port of Supe and Patavilca, towns standing
back some distance from the shore, behind the sand-hills, in the
midst of a fertile region watered by three streams; the largest
of them, called Rio de la Barranca, is, during some seasons, a
powerful and impassable stream, bringing down in its course
great rocks, and piling them in confusion on its banks.

In this neighborhood are a number of remarkable monuments
of the ancient inhabitants, the most important of which, situated two leagues from the Rio de la Barranca and one from the
sea, and not far from the pueblo of La Fortaleza, are the ruins
of Paramanca. They are described by Paz Soldan " as occupying the summit of a hill quadrangular in form, consisting of three
lines of mud-walls, the interior ones dominating the exterior.

The greatest exterior length is nine hundred feet, the length of the inner wall six hundred feet. Within the latter are remains of houses separated by narrow streets. Ninety feet from each angle of the exterior wall are bastions [outworks ?] flanking the curtains."

These ruins are described by Proctor as "a large, square mass of mud-work, diminishing towards the summit, and forming large steps. Although," he continues, "undoubtedly of great antiquity, the works do not appear to have suffered materially, as the sides are square, and the edges sharp. They are partly covered by a kind of plaster, on which are seen the uncouth colored representations of birds and beasts."

There is a tradition that this fortress was erected to commemorate the peace between the Inca Capac-Yupanqui and the King of Chimu, who had his capital near Truxillo, far to the northward. But it is more probable that it was a frontier work, defining the limits of the rule of the princes of Chimu as against the chiefs occupying the valleys of Huaura, Pacasmayo, Chillon, Rimac, and Lurin (Pachacamac), to the southward.

A little to the north of the mouth of the Rio de la Barranca, and where the coast begins again to assume its high and rocky aspect, is a considerable hill, presenting a bold, scarped front to the sea, which beats heavily at its base. This is called *La Horca* (the gallows). Its top is crowned by massive ancient works, with wing-walls running down its slope, connecting apparently with other extensive works near the base; the whole being conspicuous from the deck of the passing steamer. Paz Soldan regards these as the prisons of the Chimus, and thinks that the projecting and precipitous headland was a kind of Tarpeian rock, from the crest of which criminals were precipitated into the sea—a suggestion fanciful enough. I passed these fine monuments with the consoling reflection that, in returning, I should be able to investigate them thoroughly, little suspecting on how rich a field of inquiry I was entering, or with what rapidity I should be obliged to return to Lima, if I would not forego my great purpose of a trip to the historic interior.

Our steamer, being a mere coaster, stopped at every little
port and roadstead as she proceeded northward, receiving an
occasional passenger, who seldom indulged in the costly luxury
of the cabin, but took a plank on the forward deck, providing
his own rations.  Going in this direction, little, if any, freight
was brought aboard.  The coast retained its rough, angular outline all the afternoon, and presented a long, ragged perspective,
with a white base-line of spray.

Before bedtime we slowed up in front of a mean collection
of huts, called the port of Huarmey, or Guarmey, which, like all
our other stopping-places, was at the mouth of a river and valley descending from the Cordillera.  The place is of slight importance, distinguished mainly for its *chicha*, which, to my
taste, was only a little less disagreeable than that which I found
elsewhere.

Daylight next morning discovered us anchored close to the
shore in the Bay of Casma, which is a good harbor, under the
protection of a lofty headland that shuts off the south wind.
Here we took in a few passengers, and, hugging the coast, at
noon reached the large and fine bay of Simanco, which, with
that of Ferrol, just to the northward, from which it is separated
only by a sand-spit, constitute the two largest, and perhaps naturally the best, harbors on the whole Pacific coast of South
America.  The river Nepeña falls into the bay of Simanco,
after passing through a rich valley, which, however, is blocked
in by sand-hills and dunes near the coast.

The Bay of Ferrol has behind it the broad valley of Chim-
bote, which has no perennial river, and is consequently now
quite barren and desolate.  It abounds, however, in remains,
temples, dwellings, and other edifices of a large ancient population, who contrived to irrigate it by means of an aqueduct from
the river Santa, sixteen miles distant.  The greater part of this
fine work still exists, and is computed to have a capacity of supplying sixty million cubic feet of water daily.  The somewhat
celebrated silver mines of Micaté are situated twenty-seven
leagues inland from the Bay of Ferrol.

Early in the afternoon we reached the harbor of Santa, be-

hind one of the loftiest and ruggedest of the headlands of this
rocky coast.  The waves and winds have frayed it into a thousand fantastic shapes, and the water has worn a passage through
it, forming a gigantic natural arch.  Myriads of water-fowl soar-
ed and shrieked around its stony pinnacles, or settled in clusters
on its projecting ledges.  We rounded close to this headland—
so close that the spray from the heavy surf almost spattered on
our decks.  A moment later we were out of the swell of the
sea, and gliding along in smooth water towards a cluster of
cane-built and wattled huts that constituted the port of Santa,
behind which we could discern a belt of shrubbery, and still beyond large trees, defining the valley of the river Santa, the longest and largest river on the coast of Peru, and possibly, excepting the Guayaquil, the largest on the Pacific coast of South
America.

The Santa rises far to the south, behind the first range of the
Cordilleras, in a broad and elevated valley, separated from that
of the principal affluents of the Amazon by the true Cordillera,
or dividing ridge of the continent.  Its course is almost due
north for nearly the whole length of the department of Ancachs,
a distance of a hundred and fifty miles, when, receiving a considerable affluent from the north, the Rio Chuquicara, it turns
abruptly to the west, and, after a course of seventy miles, falls
into the Bay of Santa.  The valley of this river is salubrious,
and rich in productions, animal, vegetable, and mineral.  It contains several important towns, and, although reached from various points on the coast through the gorges of the Cordilleras,
its principal commerce is through the town and port of Santa.
Several coasting vessels were loading and unloading in the harbor ; and as we were told that the steamer would not be able to
discharge and receive her cargo until late at night, we determined to go ashore, and visit the town of Santa, situated a
couple of leagues inland.

As we entered the harbor I noticed that the lofty ridge connecting the headland with the main-land was covered with
long lines of walls, terraces, and remains of numerous structures
built of uncut stones.  So, while the agent of the steamer oc-

cupied himself with procuring horses for our trip to Santa, Mr. C——and myself made a reconnoissance of the monuments.

Climbing with difficulty the steep and rocky ridge, we found its summit and flanks for some distance downwards literally covered with vestiges of edifices which had been built among the rocks on terraces laboriously constructed. Some were quite large, especially those upon and near the summit, where a considerable regularity had been observed in their arrangement; but most were small, square or circular, and scattered confusedly wherever a spot could be levelled to support them. There were several large areas, surrounded with ruins of buildings of relatively quite a pretentious character, probably public structures, or the residences of the headmen of the ancient municipality. Flights of stone steps still remained, leading up difficult places, and traces of carefully smoothed streets or roads. These ruins covered an area of half a mile wide by a mile long, terminating towards the sea, on an elevated point of the ridge, in some stone towers eighteen or twenty feet in diameter, and, although much ruined, still of about the same height. These were flanked on and just below the brow of the ridge on both sides by lines of walls, clearly for defence.

As there is little room for cultivation near the harbor of Santa, and as we knew that the valley inland was anciently exceedingly rich and populous, I could not resist the conviction that here was a large fishing town or station, and that its rugged site had been selected in part for its salubrity, and in part for its facilities for defence. The arrangement of the various edifices, so far as the broken nature of the ground would permit, I afterwards found to be substantially the same with that of the cities and towns of ancient Chimu, whose princes held sway over the valley of Santa.

One of the largest and most celebrated *huacas*, or pyramidal structures, of Peru stands not far from the town of Santa. It has been extensively excavated, and many articles of gold and silver, with vast quantities of pottery, have been taken from it; among others an interesting vase or vessel, presented to me by one of the residents of the place, of which an engraving is here

given. It is of well-burned red clay, five inches high, and
represents a squatting human figure supporting a kind of sack

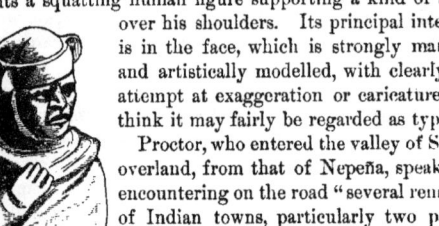

over his shoulders. Its principal interest
is in the face, which is strongly marked
and artistically modelled, with clearly no
attempt at exaggeration or caricature. I
think it may fairly be regarded as typical.

Proctor, who entered the valley of Santa
overland, from that of Nepeña, speaks of
encountering on the road "several remains
of Indian towns, particularly two parallel streets, paved with adobes, with walls
about three feet high on each side, twenty
feet wide, and extending in a direct line
as much as a league."

Returning from our antiquarian ramble, we found Don Federico, the steam-

VASE, FROM SANTA.

er's agent, awaiting us with horses for our trip to Santa. Our
captain, in full uniform, had come ashore, and needed no second invitation to accompany us. We set off at a rapid pace,
over a fair road through swampy ground, covered with bushes, interspersed with pools of water. Seamen are not noted
as equestrians, and for some reason the captain could not
keep up. There was, he said, no "go" in his horse, and he
couldn't get him "to forge ahead." So I changed horses with
him, giving him mine, a spirited animal, which discovered at
once that his new rider was no horseman, and with a wilful
plunge dashed off at full speed. It was now quite dark, the
road was winding, and horse and rider were out of sight in an
instant. We tried in vain to overtake them; but at the end of
half a mile came upon the captain sitting in the road alone, his
coat torn through from top to bottom, and his hair filled with
sand; but he affirmed that he was not hurt in the least. Don
Federico vainly urged him to mount his own horse; but he
had made up his mind, he said, to walk the rest of the way to
Santa, and to return in an ox-cart. Happily the distance was
not great, and we soon entered the town, which looked suffi-

ciently shabby in the evening gloom.  There was one bright
light in a dirty *fonda*, or *pulperia*, where a number of uncouth Indians and half-naked *arrieros* were drinking *chicha*,
and indulging in noisy, incoherent discussion; there was another light in the corridor of Don Federico's house, and a third
streamed from the open mouth of an oven in his court-yard—
for, besides being an apothecary and agent for steamers, Don
Federico was a baker, supplying the town, the port, and the
vessels frequenting it with bread.

Our impression of Santa, derived from a stroll through its
dark and dirty streets, past a tumble-down church, were not
favorable; and we were not sorry, after tasting our host's *italia*,
to return to the steamer, whose captain was fain to forego his
ox-cart and trust himself to a mule, led by one of Don Federico's servants.  The present city of Santa does not occupy
the site of the old town, which was destroyed by the Dutch pi-
rate David in 1685; but it bears the title of "city," given to
it by the crown in recognition of the gallant defence of its inhabitants against the pirates, and particularly for their having
preserved a miraculous image of Christ, the gift of Charles V.

Between Santa and Huanchaco, the port of Truxillo, whither
we were bound, our steamer made no stoppage.  The coast presented throughout its same rugged outlines; but as we now stood
farther off shore, we could see the mighty ranges of the Cordillera, piled rank on rank behind, their summits gleaming with
eternal snow.  We passed to the right of the high guano islands
of Guañape.  Though not of so good a quality as that of the
Chincha, the quantity of guano here is considerable.  Both the
coast of the main-land and these islands are the resorts of
myriads of seals and sea-birds, which find abundant food in the
fishes that swarm in these waters.  All day the sea around the
steamer was alive with the darting, leaping varieties, making
the surface fairly boil with their evolutions.

Mr. Davis, an American engineer, who was engaged in the
survey of these islands, gave me a curious account of the habits
of the birds that frequent them.  Although of a number of varieties, they live together in perfect harmony, and, so far from

quarrelling, some of them, like the sea-eagles, will defend their less powerful neighbors, such as the clumsy and unwarlike pelican. The young of these are regarded by the vultures of the main-land as delicate food, and they will sometimes come off in hundreds, when the wind blows off shore, and make a forray on these plump little lumps of flesh and fat. They select the time of the day when the sea-eagles are accustomed to fish, and when the fish themselves happen to swarm far out at sea. Then they swoop down on the islands, creating the greatest alarm and commotion, except among the stupid pelicans, who will stand stolidly by while their helpless young are disembowelled by their rapacious assailants. But woe betide the latter, when, in response to the alarm carried to them by some fleet messenger, the warriors of the islands return with rapid wing and sharp beaks, and open a fierce attack on the intruders. In vain do the vultures seek safety in flight; the eagles rise high over them, then close their wings and strike down on them with the velocity and force of an arrow from a cross-bow, driving them, wounded and bleeding, into the ocean. The combat is not an equal one; and out of the hundreds of vultures that join in the forray, it will be lucky, indeed, if a tenth part escape. While the fight goes on, the other birds, incapable of coping with the vultures, will nevertheless hang like clouds in the air, and with loud and dissonant cries seem to cheer on and encourage their champions.

The fourth morning after our departure from Callao found us slowing up in the open roadstead, in front of Huanchaco, the place of our destination. The town stands on an unprotected beach which extends for several miles north and south, beneath a high, scarped edge of the sandy plain beyond, relieved by a number of lofty peaks of bare rock, of which the famous Monte Campana — within whose recesses pious ears hear the eternal chime of bells — is most conspicuous. A church on the edge of the plain stands like a sentinel over the mean little town, which is scarcely visible against its amber-colored background, affording a convenient landmark for all vessels bound to this worst of all the so-called ports of Peru.

We fired our gun, and after a while we could discern the great launches or scows, in which landing is effected here, putting off from the shore. But long before they could reach us we were surrounded by a swarm of Indians, mounted astride of probably the most novel craft that the world has ever seen, called *caballitos*, or "little horses." They consist of one or more bundles of reeds or flags, bound together something like sheaves of wheat, only more firmly, from one end to the other, altogether forming a float from eighteen to twenty-five feet long, and of varying width. The taper end is turned up, like the neck of a swan. They are extremely buoyant, and when not in use are taken ashore and placed erect to dry. Generally they consist of two bundles or sheaves of reeds, in which case the *marinero* sits astride, or balanced on his knees in the centre, and propels it by a double-bladed oar, striking the water alternately right and left. Some of the larger ones consist of three sheaves lashed side by side, the largest in the centre, astride of which sits the manager. These will carry several persons, or two or three bales of goods, and are often the only means of communication between vessels and the shore. We declined several urgent offers from the owners of these queer-looking craft to go ashore with them. Among the many quaint earthen vessels which we found in the ancient ruins near Huanchaco, was one rudely representing the *cavallito*, on which is a sitting figure, with two children, engaged in fishing. He is represented as just hauling in a ray.

THE CABALLITO.

The accompanying cut represents a similar and equally interesting one from Chimu.

The lumbering launches were very tardy in reaching the steamer; and it was a long time before the officials who had

8

come off in them were able to get through their duties aboard
—one of which was that of taking a most hearty breakfast, with
the accompaniments.  Finally, after much bumping against the
steamer's sides, we got aboard one of the launches, amidst a confused mass of merchandise and baggage which had been huddled into it without system or order.  The men, at the expense
of much swearing, ultimately got settled at their sweeps, and
began pulling towards the land, two miles distant.  The swell
of the sea was heavy and regular, and we rose and fell with dignified monotony, passing meanwhile through an almost solid
mass of the little fishes, called *sardinas* everywhere on the coast,
which were apparently driven inshore by large and voracious
enemies in the sea, the occasional splash of whose tails told the
story of their insatiable appetites.  The little victims crowded
each other, until their noses, projecting to the surface, made the
ocean look as if covered over with a cloak of Oriental mail.
We could dip them up by handfuls and by thousands.  Vast
numbers had succumbed in the crush, and floated about dead in
the struggling mass.  They filled the sea over a belt more than
a mile broad along the shore, where hundreds of women and
children were scooping them up with their hats, with basins,
baskets, and the fronts of their petticoats, and depositing them
in heaps on the sand.

As we neared the shore, our attention was withdrawn from
the fish and the fishermen by the increased size and more rapid
movement of the rollers, which tossed our heavy launch, now
head, now stern, high up in the air, tumbling boxes and baggage about with little regard to the safety of our legs.  Our
men were very expert in managing the launch so as to evade or
glide over the waves, now pulling vigorously, and next resting
on their oars, until we came to rest just outside the breakers,
holding off and on in a perpetual seesaw.  But now came the
critical part of the business — the landing.  A number of tall,
stalwart *cholos* and *sambos*, naked, except that each had a breech-
cloth, came off through the surf to carry us ashore.  We were
expected to mount, not on their shoulders, with our legs astride
their necks, and clinched under their armpits, but astride their

slippery right shoulders, one leg in front and the other behind. My confidence in this mode of conveyance was not increased by seeing one of our passengers slip from his perch in the thickest of the surf, to be dragged ashore like a half-drowned rat; but I tried it, and got in with a slight wetting. Our baggage was brought off with less difficulty on the heads of the men, who here form a class or guild, with the exclusive right of doing this kind of work.

Huanchaco, unattractive from the sea, was hardly less so when viewed from the shore. *Caballitos* drawn up to dry, with bales of merchandise piled up and covered with hides and old tarpaulins, were scattered along the beach above the reach of the waves, and, with a few high-wheeled and exceedingly rude ox-carts, formed the foreground of the picture that presented itself to us on landing. Back of these, the ground rising rather abruptly, was a kind of shed, formed of a roof of coarse rush-matting and canes, supported on crooked posts, each inclining a different way from any other, beneath which were gathered the leading inhabitants of Huanchaco and its visitors; for this is rather noted as a watering-place, and during "the season" not only attracts many people from Truxillo, but from the towns of the interior. To all of these the arrival of the steamer is an event of importance, to be celebrated by a general gathering under the shed on the shore, where the new arrivals and their mishaps in landing are duly laughed at and criticised.

Happily for us, we were speedily taken in charge by the *contador* of the port, whose acquaintance I had made in Lima, and who occupied a house which was rather stylish for Huanchaco, but which would hardly be dignified by the name of hut in many parts of the world. It was, however, comfortably furnished, and contained a very agreeable family, including a number of young ladies dressed in the height of the ruling fashion at Lima.

During the sitting of the Mixed Commission in Lima, I had been introduced, under very favorable auspices, to Señor K——, the Prefect of Truxillo, who had once been Peruvian minister in Europe, and was reputed to be one of the richest men in

Peru, as well as celebrated for possessing the finest private residence in all South America. He was courtly in manner, speaking English very well, and extended to me a pressing invitation
to visit Truxillo, and investigate the monuments in its vicinity.
His house and influence, personal and official, were put at my
service with a copiousness and warmth of phrase that, from a
man who had lived abroad, and knew something of the value of
words, made me feel not only grateful, but under an obligation
to report myself to him on the instant of my arrival in Truxillo.
It was not, therefore, without satisfaction that I ascertained
from the *contador* that he was then in the port, where he had
also a large and commodious residence. As soon as I could
make myself presentable, I waited on him; but, although the
conversation was sufficiently discursive, and, as I thought, rather
adroitly directed to recalling some of the extravagant proffers
that had been made to me in Lima, I failed to get the remotest
reference to the grand establishment in Truxillo, or to any of
the wonderful facilities I was to have received in prosecuting
my researches. In fact, in reply to the direct inquiry if there
were any thing like hotels in the city, I was told, " None worthy
of the name; nothing except a Chinese *fonda*, Bola de Oro,
and a shabby place, Hotel del Comercio. It was possible I
might find some kind of accommodation there." And, thus enlightened and consoled, I had the honor of wishing the prefect
and ex-minister " Good-morning."

My companions did not receive the report of my interview
with any marked demonstrations of satisfaction. But our good
*contador*, in his modest way, not only gave us a tolerable breakfast, of which the sardines we had seen caught in such vast numbers in the morning formed a principal part, but he also helped
us to get a couple of carts for our apparatus and effects, and
some lean and lazy saddle-horses for ourselves.

Mounting the ridge dominating the town, a broad, barren,
treeless, and somewhat irregular plain spreads out before the
traveller, extending back ten or twelve miles to the base of
the mountains, near which is a belt of verdure, marking the
shallow valley of the river Moche, in which stands the city of

Truxillo. This is properly the plain of Mansiché or Chimu; but the coast is generally level, or interrupted only by isolated mountains, as far north as the valley of Chicama, and as far south as that of Viru, an extent of nearly ninety miles. Practically, these valleys may be considered as one, affording, with their ramifications in the mountains, a rich and ample area for a large and advanced ancient population, the evidences of whose existence are met with almost immediately after leaving Huanchaco. These consist of long lines of massive walls, gigantic chambered pyramids, or *huacas*, remains of palaces, dwellings, aqueducts, reservoirs, granaries, prisons, furnaces, foundries, and tombs, extending for many miles in every direction. These are the ruins of Grand Chimu, the most extensive and populous of all the cities of ancient Peru. The road runs directly through them, and in their centre, solitary and alone, with no sign of life or population around it, stands the little church of La Legua, built here among the deserted and crumbling monuments of the ancient inhabitants, as if to give some sort of Christian sanctity to the relics of *los infieles*.

After a long ride, we emerged from the ruins into cultivated grounds, cut up into fields by thick and high hedges of thorny bushes and climbing plants, under the shelter of which scurried hundreds of lizards, of all sizes and colors, some flashing in metallic green, with heads glowing like rubies, and others splendid in suits of gold. Probably nowhere in the world can be found so many and so beautiful varieties. No wonder the princes of Chimu emblazoned them on their arms, embroidered them in their tissues of cotton and wool, and gave them a prominent place in the insignia of their power.

After passing some crazy reed huts and crumbling adobe houses, the remains of the Indian village of Mauriche, to which the lower orders of the people of Truxillo resort on holidays, we came in full sight of the city, and entered upon a ruined alameda, lined with trees, which had two piers of stone-work, now standing awry, to mark its commencement. One of these bore a half-obliterated inscription, purporting that the alameda was dedicated to the beautiful ladies of Truxillo.

# CHAPTER VII.

A MILE farther on brought us to the walls of the city, at the western, or Mauriche, gate. We entered by a long, ill-paved street, leading directly to the great plaza, which is flanked on one side by the cathedral, and has a fountain in the centre—a large and silent square, with a solitary figure moving here and there in the shadow of the buildings, and a single donkey browsing in the middle. Turning from the plaza to the left, into the Calle del Comercio, the principal street, on which are some pretentious shops, we came to the Hotel del Comercio, a low building, extending around a large court, and entered beneath a heavy archway.

We had difficulty in finding either host or servants, but finally discovered them in certain dark and dirty retreats behind a large room, in which was a dingy bar, and which served the purposes of reception, sitting, and eating room. The proprietor was a lean, sallow man, with black, irregular fangs for teeth, his head bound up in a smouched towel, and his whole person closely enveloped in a rusty blue cloak. His solitary servant, or major-domo, was a fitting counterpart of his master, a saturnine, unkempt *cholo*, who evidently thought guests were nuisances, since they involved some exertion or attention on his part. We finally succeeded in obtaining a large room on one side of the court, which had once served as some kind of a shop, the shelves and counter still remaining, and a room in a low second story, at the front of the house, and looking out on the principal street. Both apartments were full of dust and cobwebs and alive with fleas, on which we persuaded a stray *zambita*, or mixed Indian and negro woman, whom we found strolling in the streets, to make vigorous war. The empty shop answered for a laboratory for preparing our photographic chemicals, and a store-room for our collections.

We retained our quarters in the Hotel del Comercio, but took our meals, when we took them in town at all, at the Chinese *fonda*. This was kept by an association of Chinamen, each taking a special department, and all performing their work harmoniously and well. They had cut off their pigtails; and one of them—the only instance of the kind I heard of in Peru— had married a native *chola*, by whom he had children. The cooking was good, and the food varied and well-served. Altogether, the Chinese *fonda* was second to none of the so-called hotels I found in the country outside of Lima. The enterprise of its managers was shown in establishing relays of mules for bringing down a daily supply of ice from the snowy mountains, four days distant—an enterprise to which we contributed no inconsiderable support during our stay.

Truxillo stands in a little more than eight degrees of south latitude, on a level space, at a slight elevation above the sea, and on ground so flat that the *azequias* by which it is supplied with water have a scarcely perceptible current, and are consequently offensively charged with filth. It was founded in 1535, by Francisco Pizarro, who named it after his native town in Spain, intending it for one of the great capitals of Peru. It is regularly laid out, the streets crossing each other at right angles, leaving here and there small open plazas or squares, on which the various churches usually face. In 1686 it was encircled by a wall of adobes, a regular oval in outline, and, with the excep-

tion of Lima, is the only walled city in Peru. Its present population is about fifteen thousand, made up largely of *hacenda-
dos*, or owners of estates in the surrounding valleys, and *comerciantes*, or traders, with the usual proportions of the lower orders and mixed breeds. It is, on the whole, well built; many
of the houses being of two stories, with spacious and well-furnished interiors, indicative of wealth and a certain amount of
taste. It has still some importance, but insignificant, compared
with what it possessed under the viceroys, when it was the centre of an extensive jurisdiction, with high officers, a royal mint,
and numerous families of high and historic titles among its inhabitants. It was also the seat of a bishop, and had five convents for men and two for women. The former have all been
suppressed; but the latter, largely endowed, are still in existence, covering large areas within the city walls. The richest,
Santa Clara, had, at the time of our visit, only thirteen inmates.
There are thirteen churches within the walls, besides the cathedral. They are generally well built, and some of them, with
their flying buttresses thrown out to support them against
earthquakes, are both quaint and picturesque. The other public buildings are simply mean, neglected, and in decay.

Nearly all the leading inhabitants to whom we had introduc-
tions were absent on their estates at the sea-side; but we were
fortunate in finding the gentleman whom we were most interested in meeting, and to whom I bore special letters from Lima
—Colonel La Rosa, the most experienced, enthusiastic, and persistent treasure-hunter of Truxillo, where rummaging for *tapadas*, or treasures, has been a passion, I had almost said the main
business, of the people since Juan Gutierrez de Toledo commenced the practice nearly three hundred years ago. Years
before, I had seen in London a large collection of articles, both
curious and valuable, obtained by him from the ruins of Chimu,
Moche, and Viru, and which he had confided to a person calling himself "Dr. Ferris" to dispose of, but who claimed to have
discovered them himself, and sold them on his own account.
A part went to the British Museum, and another portion was
bought by the late Mr. George Folsom, and is now deposited

with the Historical Society of New York. I had also seen a considerable collection of the colonel's in Lima, and had purchased some of the more remarkable articles in the precious metals.

The colonel was neither an archæologist nor an antiquary, and had little care for the relics he obtained in his excavations, except in a mercantile sense. He had rather a contempt for pottery, and for implements or utensils in bronze. His interest in Chimu architecture was mainly in the way of finding hidden vaults and chambers; he cared nothing for arabesques or paintings; and his knowledge of the ancient modes of sepulture was limited to ascertaining where the rich and powerful were buried, and where ornaments of gold and silver were most likely to abound. In these directions he had become proverbially expert. Of course, he did not sympathize greatly with my plans of surveying, measuring, and mapping the monuments, and evidently thought my declaration of such a purpose was merely a shallow pretext for diverting attention from my real object—that of finding the *peje grande,* or "great fish," as the yet undiscovered, legendary treasure of the Chimus has been called from immemorial days, and in trying to discover which millions of dollars had been expended. The colonel did not exactly tell me that he was confident I had got hold of some ancient itinerary, map, or guide, drawn up perhaps by the same Indian, Cazique Tello, who had confided to Gutierrez de Toledo the secret of the *peje chica,* or "little fish," and which had been kept hitherto concealed. His manner implied that he was not at all deceived in the matter. He hardly waited for me to suggest that we should take a ride over the ruins next morning, but warmly seconded the proposition. It would be difficult for the possessor of the great secret to wholly retain that composure, when standing over the *peje grande,* which a quick eye and ready wit could not penetrate! Thus, possibly, speculated Colonel La Rosa. But be that as it may, he reported himself early next morning at the hotel; and leaving P—— behind to prepare his photographic chemicals and apparatus, we set out in company with Mr. C—— for a reconnoissance of the ruins of Chimu.

We left the city by the Portada de Miraflores, one of the northern gates, past the Panteon, or Cemetery, through a rich, well-cultivated district, till we reached the hamlet of Miraflores, a league or more from the city, at the foot of the hills that slope down to the plain in that direction. Here we came upon the remains of a great *azequia*, or aqueduct, which had tapped the Rio Moche many miles up towards its source among the mountains for the supply of the ancient city, and which was here carried across the valley on a lofty embankment. This is still more than sixty feet high, built of stones and earth, with a channel on top, originally lined with stones, and of the dimensions of our ordinary canals. We followed this to the point on the slope overlooking the old city, where the water was distributed, through minor *azequias*, over the plain below.

All around us, on the arid slope, were remains of rude stone edifices, suggesting that here, perhaps, had been a suburb of the city, occupied by the poorer class of inhabitants. Below, however, stretching away in a broad sweep from the foot of the declivity to the sea in front, and from the base of the rocky pinnacle of Monte Campana on the north, to Huaman and the Rio Moche on the south, over an area hardly less than from twelve to fifteen miles long by from five to six miles broad, was the plain of Chimu itself, thickly covered over with the ruins of the ancient city. They consist of a wilderness of walls, forming great inclosures, each containing a labyrinth of ruined dwellings and other edifices, relieved here and there by gigantic *huacas*, most conspicuous among which were those of El Obispo, Conchas, and Toledo—great masses, which the visitor finds it difficult to believe to be artificial.

On the side from which we approached the ruins, the city seems to have been protected by a heavy wall, several miles of which are still standing. From this wall, extending inwards at right angles, are other lines of walls of scarcely inferior elevation, inclosing great areas which have never been built upon, and which fall off in low terraces, carefully cleared of stones, each with its *azequia* for irrigation. These were evidently the gardens and pleasure-grounds of the ancient inhabitants.

Descending the slope, we encountered, outside of the great wall, two rectangular inclosures, situated about a quarter of a mile apart, each containing a truncated pyramid, or *huaca*. The first of these inclosures is 252 feet long by 222 feet at the ends. The wall is still 14 feet high by 6 feet thick at the base. The *huaca* is 162 feet square by 50 feet in height, and stands nearer one end of the area inclosed than the other. It is built, as are the walls, of compact rubble; that is to say, of tenacious clay mixed with broken stones, so as to form an indurated mass, almost as hard as mortar. Notwithstanding this, however, it has been much excavated and defaced, revealing that, towards its summit at least, it was made up of sepulchral chambers, from which great quantities of bones have been taken, which now lie strewed about in every direction. These were all slight, and appeared to have been of females, ranging from five to fifteen years old. I had occasion to observe afterwards that a custom of burying the dead of certain ages and sexes together, in certain places, existed among the builders of Chimu.

The other structure referred to corresponds very closely with this. It is 240 feet long by 210 feet wide, the outer walls 20 feet high by 8 thick, and the interior *huaca*, or mound, 172 feet long by 152 wide, and 40 feet high. No human remains were found here, but the summit of the mound showed that it had been divided into sections, or chambers, from five to six feet square, by walls of rubble eighteen inches thick. I could not resist the conviction that this structure, like the other, had been built for sepulchral purposes, but had not been used.

We entered the ruined city through a break in the outer wall, and I was at once struck with the care with which the open areas, which I have called gardens, had been cleared and prepared for culture. The principal *azequias* had been built close along the walls, and carefully lined with stones; while the smaller distributing channels had been carried in zigzags from terrace to terrace, so as to insure an equal and efficient distribution of water. All were dry now, as they had been for centuries, and a nitrous efflorescence covered the once fertile areas that they had made to bloom and blossom in past ages.

Directing our course towards the great *huaca*, Obispo, we passed a number of broad and deep rectangular excavations, their sides terraced and faced with rough but well-laid stones, and with zigzag slopes, or pathways, leading to the bottom. These, Colonel La Rosa insisted, were ancient granaries; but it did not require much intelligence to discern that they had been reservoirs of water. The vast size of the *huaca* became more obvious as we approached it, and the great excavation which had been carried into it from its north side, a century or more ago, made it appear like the crater of some extinct volcano.

The materials—stones, rubble, and adobes—that had been taken out of the excavation were heaped up in a high, irregular mass on the plain, literally covering acres; and close beside it were the ruins of an abandoned village, with a little church, in the plaza of which a cross was still kept up by pious hands. This village was built for the workmen, Indians (*encomendados*) and others, who had been employed, so runs the tradition, for twenty years in penetrating the *huaca*. Presuming that they conducted the work as similar work is still conducted in Peru— in other words, that the materials were loosened by little picks, gathered up by hand, and carried out in baskets on the head, or in improvised sacks made of *ponchos*—I see nothing improbable in the story. But, however accomplished, the undertaking was a gigantic one; yet how insignificant as compared with that of building the structure in the first instance!

I could not learn that treasure, or indeed anything else, was found in the *huaca* to compensate for the great labor and cost of its excavation. And while I could not help regretting the defacement and ruin of this fine monument, yet I was gratified in being able to discover how it was built. Its construction was similar to that of the Castillo at Pachacamac, of nearly equal parts of stones and rough adobes, the whole cast over with a kind of breccia or rubble-work. The excavation had been carried below the level of the surrounding ground; and revealed the natural strata. So the notion of subterranean chambers beneath the mass, evidently once entertained, was not supported by experiment.

We ascended to the top of the *huaca,* from which a distinct view of the whole plain and its monuments is commanded. Turning over an adobe for a seat, I discovered a little scorpion, the first and the only one I saw in Peru. Why he was at the summit of El Obispo, that scorched and arid heap in a scorched and arid plain, I did not stop to inquire, but inveigled him into an empty letter-envelope, and pickled him duly on my return to the city. Whether he belonged to any variety new or rare, I do not know; albeit I sent him, with an earnest solicitation, to a scientific friend, who affects scorpions, but from whom I have never heard a word in reference to the unique and virulent little reprobate.

Subsequently I made a visit to El Obispo, and measured it, with its surroundings, as well as its dilapidation would permit; in doing which, both C—— and myself were overhauled and somewhat roughly questioned by a body of mounted rural police in search of certain *ladrones* who had committed robbery and arson in the neighboring valley of Chicama, and, it was supposed, had taken refuge among the ruins. I shall never forget the blank look of the commander of the squad when he was assured that we were merely making surveys of the monuments. If he did not arrest us, I am sure it was because he doubted if taking charge of idiots and madmen fell within his line of duty.

El Obispo is about one hundred and fifty feet high, and covers an area five hundred and eighty feet square, equal to about eight acres; and as its sides are so abrupt, where unbroken, as to prohibit ascent, its contents may be roughly calculated at about fifty millions of cubic feet. Its summit was probably reached by zigzag inclines or a stairway on its northern face.

From the top of El Obispo, Colonel La Rosa pointed out to me the locality of his latest and most extensive excavations, to which we made our way through an ancient avenue or street, lined on both sides by monuments. The excavations were in what appeared to be a shapeless mound of débris, with very slight external evidence of having been, what it probably was, the palace of the princes of Chimu. The surface was rough and irregular, and we had some difficulty in riding over it.

Suddenly, the colonel, turning abruptly around a huge pile of rubbish, reined up on the edge of a great pit, in which were exposed the lower walls, passages, courts, and apartments of a part of some great structure long ago buried from the day. A single glance satisfied me that, thanks to Colonel La Rosa's passion for *tapadas*, we had before us a revelation of an entirely unique and very beautiful style of aboriginal American architecture. My eye ran with mingled surprise and delight over long walls covered with intricate arabesques in relief, and here and there glowing with brilliant colors, such as I had never seen in all my previous explorations on this continent. The colonel seemed to attach no importance to them, but eagerly directed my attention to the spot where he had found a concealed chamber or closet, piled full of vessels of silver and gold.

As I shall have occasion to speak in detail of these particular remains, I shall pursue the narrative of our reconnoissance. From the palace the colonel led us to another mound, where excavation had revealed what there is good reason to believe were the royal tombs. Hence we took a long sweep past La Legua to an eminence near the sea, on which stands an extensive work with a *huaca* and other monuments inclosed, called, from its position and assumed purpose, El Castillo. The sandy soil in front of its principal entrance, over an area of several acres, is stuffed with skeletons, buried irregularly, as if after a great battle; a supposition supported by the fact that the bones which had been exposed by excavation or laid bare by the winds were all of adult men, and that a large part of the skulls bore marks of violence. Some were cloven as if by the stroke of a battle-axe or sabre; others battered in as if by blows from clubs or the primitive hammer to which the French have given the appropriate name of *cassetête;* and still others were pierced as if by lances or arrows. I picked up a piece of a skull showing a small square hole, precisely such as would be occasioned by the bronze arrow-heads found here and there among the ruins.

I could not resist thinking, in spite of tradition, that perhaps on this very spot had been fought the last decisive battle between the Inca Yupanqui and the Prince of Chimu, and that here were mingled the bones of the slain of both armies: a notion supported by finding mixed together the square, posteriorly compressed skulls of the peoples of the coast, the elongated skulls of the Aymaras, and the regular, normal heads of the Quichuas of the Sierra.

Inside the Castillo we found a terraced cemetery, containing, however, only the skeletons of young women, carefully enveloped in fine cotton cloth. These skeletons were apparently of persons that had died at between fifteen and eighteen years of age.

Returning from the Castillo through a wilderness of excavations and gigantic water-reservoirs, we rode in succession to a series of vast enclosures, themselves containing lesser ones, crowded with buildings, which are strangely called "palaces." One of the most interesting enclosures contained, besides a number of open squares of differing sizes, a great reservoir, and, in one corner, fenced off by massive walls, what we subsequently ascertained to be a prison. We visited also the *huaca* of Toledo, whence Don Garcia Gutierrez de Toledo had extracted his enormous treasures. It has been so worked upon and into, in the course of three centuries, as to have lost all shapeliness; and it now stands, a great uncouth mass, honey-combed, and pierced in every direction by shafts, passages, and adits, some quite recent, that must have cost hundreds of thousands of dollars to excavate.

At four o'clock in the afternoon, with my head in a whirl of surprise and excitement over the wide and unexpected revelations of the day, I was not loath to second the suggestion of my guide to ride along the sea-beach to the little watering-place and projected new port of Truxillo, Huaman. The sand-dunes, at a short distance back from the shore, like almost all vacant and desert spots around Chimu, are vast cemeteries. Skulls and bones projected everywhere above the surface, and were crushed under our horses' hoofs. The whole shore for miles is a veritable Golgotha.

We found at Huaman only a collection of wicker-work huts, built of canes and reeds wattled together, belonging to families living in the city, accustomed to make a *paseo* here occasionally to bathe.   The "masses" disdain these modest refuges, and men and women disport themselves together, *al fresco*, in the waves.   None, however, were bathing this afternoon, for a strong wind was blowing into the shallow bight from the south, in which direction it is open, creating a surf, backed by a mile or more of breakers—a perfect "hell of waters," such as, I think, I never saw before.   The foam from the waves, rolled up like the fleeces of sheep, drifted over the sands inwards, where they were caught on the boughs of the cringing trees and torn into tatters, or tossed high in the air, to fall, pulsating and dissolving, in the open fields.   We were speedily drenched by a penetrating mist, or spray, and rode back to town hurriedly over a level road, which, near the Huaman gate, is glorified into something like an alemada.   In other words, there were willow-trees planted on the edge of the interminably stagnant ditch which flanks it on either side.

Returning to our lodgings, we found P—— in a state approaching frenzy.   In the first place, the dark tent was a failure Wherever the sail-maker's spike of a needle had gone through the oil-cloth, there came in a vicious ray of light, one glance of which on the sensitive plate was utter ruin.   And then the bromide of cadmium, or something of the sort, had been left behind.   I got to know the importance of these things when I was alone in the Sierra ; but just then I was not as tolerant as I should have been of P——'s want of prevision.

Happily, there was a kind of photographer in Truxillo, and from him a few grains of the missing chemical were procured. A *cholo*, who kept black and yellow cotton *manta*, and had a sewing-machine, was also found and engaged to furnish a lining for the dark tent.   As this needful work would occupy a full day, we resolved to utilize our time by visiting the Indian town of Moche and the remains in its vicinity, concerning which we had heard much.

# CHAPTER VIII.

### THE RUINS AT MOCHE.

STARTING early in the morning, we cantered over a level road
through rich green meadows of alfalfa, and fields of cotton,
rice, and the nopal. The cultivation of the latter plant was at
one time quite large, and considerable quantities of cochineal
were produced; but of late years, what with its increased production in Guatemala, and the introduction of aniline and other dyes, this branch of industry has declined. It is stated by
Paz Soldan that the area of arable land around Truxillo was
much larger than now, until the great earthquake of 1687,
which made vast tracts sterile. Stevenson affirms that, after
the severe earthquake of 1729, "some of the valleys near the
coast, which before produced most abundant crops of wheat,
became quite sterile for more than twenty years after."
Some other writers speak of similar effects from earthquakes;
but it is difficult to conceive how the elements of the soil are
affected by earthquakes. If the fact of sterility sometimes following on the convulsions of the earth be established, we may
perhaps find the explanation, at least on the rainless coast of
Peru, in the upheaval of the earth, whereby considerable tracts

.9

of land would be raised above the reach of irrigation. Fertility would follow on any later subsidence of the same areas, whereby irrigation would again be made possible.

About a league from Truxillo, we reached the river Moche, a considerable stream, flowing in a shallow, sandy bed, shut in by alders, acacias, and other trees and bushes. We forded it without difficulty, and, reaching the opposite bank, our ears were saluted by a confused noise of a drum and a *quina*, or Indian fiute, accompanied by shouts and laughter, and in a few moments we came upon an extraordinary scene. A party of Indians and mestizos were excavating an *azequia*, or, rather, clearing out an old and abandoned one, while another party, acting as a relay, all half drunk, sat under the trees near by, around some jars of *chicha* and dishes of *picante*, eating, drinking, drumming, and cheering the men in the trench. Among them were several gaudily dressed women, with dishevelled hair, who formed a fitting adjunct to the bacchanalian scene. They shouted to us to dismount and join them; but as we did not seem inclined to do so, some of them seized our horses by their bridles, and led us into the centre of the throng, where they besieged us with bowls of *chicha* and little gourds of *picante*. We made the best of our situation; that is to say, ate and drank as little as possible. One of the dusky damsels made me the object of her special attentions, calling me familiarly *El Blanquito*. Observing my disposition to shirk the *aji*, she picked out choice bits from her own dish, which she took between her thumb and forefinger, and held them up to my mouth with a ludicrously tender leer, insisting that I should take them "for her own dear sake." I had great difficulty in avoiding the proffered morsels, thereby giving her much offence.

We escaped from our inebriated friends with some difficulty; and a ride of another league, over a flat country and a dusty road, brought us to the Indian pueblo, a considerable town, regularly laid out, of low cane huts, their roofs of reed-matting supported by crooked algarroba posts, and covered with a thin layer of mud to keep them from blowing away. There were a few houses of crude adobes, roofed in like manner, the whole

presenting an aspect of squalid monotony.  We rode directly to
the house of the *gobernador*, a full-blooded Indian.  His dwelling was merely an immense shed, with some compartments
fenced off with adobes or canes, for such of the occupants as
affected privacy.  The bare earthen floor was strewed with the
*aparejo* of mules and rude implements of husbandry, for the
*gobernador* was both muleteer and husbandman.  In front of
the house, and partly in its shade, a sheep-driver from Viru had
halted a flock of sheep, which he was taking to Truxillo.  I noticed among them a very large proportion with three, four, five,
and six horns.

The *gobernador* was not at home; the females were taciturn,
and kept silently and impassibly at their work of spinning cotton, with perhaps the most primitive apparatus ever devised for
the purpose.  It was composed of a thin stem of the quinoa, as
a spindle, stuck through half of a small green lime, for a whirl, or
bob.  Having vainly interrogated these industrious ladies about
*huacas*, we resolved to consult the *cura*, who, we understood,
was an intelligent man.  We rode through the silent streets,
fetlock-deep in dust, to the plaza, one side of which was occupied by the church, a quaint, old, tumble-down edifice, its bell-
tower reached by a flight of stone steps outside the building.
We paused a moment before it, when we were startled by a
stentorian command of "*Quiten sus sombreros!*" ("Take off
your hats!"), proceeding from a stern-visaged, gray-haired man
reclining on a mud-bench under the corridor of a building close
by, which we at once took to be the residence of the *cura*.

We did as we were ordered, and then rode to the house itself,
where we were saluted with a torrent of invective, kept up by
the *cura*, without stopping to take breath, until he was purple
in the face.  "None but Jews and infidels would pass in front
of a church without taking off their hats.  Even the ignorant
Indian brutes of Moche know better; or, if they didn't, I would
teach them!  Holy Mother of God!  I would teach them!"
Here the *cura* shook his stout cane savagely in our very faces.
We endeavored to explain, but he went on.  When he broke
down again, we once more sought to excuse ourselves, but could

get no hearing, for the reason explained by the *cura* himself a little later: "It is of no use talking to me; I have been stone-deaf these ten years; you might fire a battery of artillery in the plaza, and I couldn't hear it. If you have got anything to say, come in here, where there is ink and paper."

He then led the way into his sitting-room, hung around with dusky pictures of saints and martyrs. Helping us with courtesy to seats, he thumped violently on the table with his stick. A meek Indian boy entered on the instant, and received the peremptory order, "Beast! coffee and cigars! Quick! Holy Mother!" One would have supposed the worthy *cura* overcome by rage; but the moment he was seated, his really fine face assumed a benignant expression, and he motioned with a smile to the writing materials, saying, "*Caballeros*, I welcome you to my poor house; it will be my pleasure to serve you. I seldom see white faces, except those of the scoundrel politicians who come down here to corrupt my poor Indians with their lies and their bribes. It was a woful day, gentlemen, when the idiots in Lima gave these simple, innocent people the vote. You should have seen my Moche children forty years ago, when I first came here. They were industrious, sober, devout, and happy. You see what they are now: idlers, liars, drunkards, and thieves! Then, if a stranger or a traveller were to approach the town, the first man in authority would have sent to me a *chasqui* (fleet messenger) to say, 'Our good father, a traveller has come; he is dusty and weary: we will conduct him to you; we will bring alfalfa for his horses; we have eggs and fish, and bread of wheat, which we will bring to you for him. Good father, give us your blessing!' I would have died rather than witness the change that has taken place since. It has all come of the ballot, and the political villains of Truxillo. I have not put my foot within its accursed walls these many years. These poor people are mere children; they must be governed by a father. The Incas were right, after all. This voting is their ruin."

The good *cura* went on for a long time much in this strain, lamenting the part he took in his youth against the viceroys and in behalf of the republic. There was no longer public or private virtue; the duties of hospitality even were neglected, and religion had become a sham and a pretence.

We were not altogether sorry when the *cura's* lamentations were finished, as they were with the entry of the coffee and cigars, and we were enabled to write out a few questions about the *huacas*. The *cura*, I found, regarded them all with aversion: they kept up unholy memories and traditions among the Indians, and he would like to see them levelled to the earth. But they were very strange things, nevertheless, very rich in gold and silver; and that, of course, was the matter in which we were most interested. We had not then entirely ceased to protest against being considered searchers after *tapadas;* but the *cura* would not be convinced that we could have any object except to dig for gold. He advised us to visit Viru, where, he said, the posts and beams of many of the old buildings were still standing, and where there were vast numbers of monuments. The most interesting objects around Moche, he said, were the Temple of the Sun, at the foot of the conical peak called Cerro Blanco, which he pointed out to us from his corridor, and a pyramid *muy disforme* (monstrous), surpassing El Obispo in size. When we inquired for a guide, he volunteered to go with us himself, if we would ride slowly. This he did, mounted on a meek *burro*, his long robe almost trailing on the ground, and carrying over his broad sombrero a bright pink umbrella. One Indian servant led the *burro*, and another the youth whom the *cura* had denominated "a beast" an hour before, trotted by his side, carrying the *cura's* ominous cane and a flask of *chicha*. As we passed through the streets, the Indian women and children hurried to the doors of their houses, and, kneeling with uplifted palms, received the padre's blessing. It was rare, he said, of late years, that he ventured out of the town; it was twenty since he had visited the *huacas*.

We rode for some distance through cultivated fields, striped with lines of verdure following the courses of *azequias*, until we reached the flank of the hills above the reach of irrigation, where the desert commences. Here we fell into a path in the sand skirting the hills, the gray waste relieved here and there by a white human skull bleaching in the bright sunlight—for here, as everywhere amidst Chimu, were scattered mementoes of death.

As we approached the Cerro Blanco, the *cura* pointed out, as the Temple of the Sun, a mass of adobe walls, standing on a bold, rocky projection, or shelf, of the mountain at an elevation of a hundred feet or more. He declined to ascend; so, leaving him below, we clambered up to the structure, which, in position and style, more resembles a fortress than a temple. We entered by an inclined plane, through a massive gate-way, into a broad court, from which passages led off right and left, from one stage or terrace to another, until we reached the last and highest, from which we looked over the whole green valley of the Rio Moche, past the low towers of Truxillo, to the *huacas* of Chimu, El Obispo rising boldly in the distance. The most conspicuous object which met our view was the great pyramid of which the *cura* had spoken, and which, in its magnitude, justified his description. It stands on the edge of the desert slope, at the base of Cerro Blanco, just where irrigation begins—a kind of gigantic landmark between luxuriant verdure and arid sands, between life and death. Viewed from this position, it was the most impressive monument we had yet seen in Peru.

We descended to the *cura*, and rode past the pyramid to a deep *azequia*, which was carried along its base on the side towards the valleys, and was fringed with graceful canes. Crossing it on a shaky bridge of poles, covered with weeds and earth, we entered a grove of fruit-trees, flanking a field of Chili peppers, in one corner of which, and under the shadow of the pyramid, stood a rude Indian cane hut. The occupants welcomed the padre, and treated us to *chicha*. The padre and his attendants soon started back for Moche, while we took a more direct road to the city.

We subsequently returned, and carefully measured and photographed the pyramid, which is sometimes itself called *El Templo del Sol* (the Temple of the Sun). We found it to be a rectangular structure, which the plan alone can make intelligible, having a greatest length of a little more than eight hundred feet, and a greatest width of four hundred and seventy, covering a trifle more than seven acres. Its greatest height,

THE GREAT PYRAMID OF MOCHE.

at the summit of the terraced structure, is upwards of two hundred feet. It is constructed throughout of large adobes, which appear to have been built around a central core, or nucleus, having sides inclining inwards at an angle to the horizon of seventy-seven degrees. The bricks, however, were not laid in a continuous series around this core, but built up in blocks, like

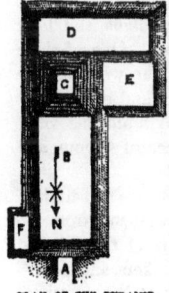

PLAN OF THE PYRAMID.

pilasters, one beside another, unconnected, and supported by common inclination around the centre. The whole seems to have been surrounded by a casing of the thickness of between thirty and forty adobes, interlocking, so that originally its faces were smooth and regular.

To comprehend the structure, we will ascend it from the side on which, if there were any facilities for ascent, they must have existed; namely, from the causeway A. This extends from the base of the pyramid eleven hundred and twenty feet to a

rocky hill, around which are some almost obliterated ruins, and is
about fifty feet wide.  From it there was probably a stairway,
leading up to B, which is a level area, elevated nearly one hundred feet above the plain, and is about four hundred feet long
by three hundred and fifty wide.  It may have been, and prob
ably was, level: possibly it supported buildings; but it is now
covered all over with heaps of rubbish from modern excavations
or from demolished buildings.  At the southern extremity of
this lofty platform, or terrace, rises another, thirty or forty feet
higher, on which stands a terraced pyramid, about two hundred
feet square.  Seven stages are still distinct, but there are traces
of nine.  On its summit, as on most of the more important
monuments of the *infieles*, stands a wooden cross, its elevation
being, by computation, as already said, about two hundred feet.
The platform on which this stands was probably ascended by
steps; but the ascent to the summit of the crowning pyramid
itself seems to have been from the west, and by a graded way.
The long platform D is eighty feet below that on which rests
the terraced pyramid, and E is still lower.

Here I may explain that if my measurements, estimates, and
descriptions are not more specific and exact, it is due to the
devastation which time and the elements — but, above all, the
ruthless hands of men — have wrought in this grand old monument.

Passages and chambers are said to exist in the structure, the
entrances to which are only known to the Indians, and kept
carefully concealed beneath masses of rubbish.  One of these
passages, says common report, descends from the work on the
mountain slope that I have already described, and extends beneath ground to the very sanctuary of the pyramid, the vault
that contains the body of the mightiest prince of Chimu, and
where, perhaps, the *peje grande* lies concealed.

We found neither passages nor chambers, but we did find an
adit, or drift, driven in on a level with the natural soil, from the
eastern side of the great mass, under the centre of the terraced
pyramid C.  This had been dug by treasure-seekers, and the débris from the excavation formed a real hillock at the mouth of

the passage. Having brought candles with us, we followed the passage to its extremity. It was fetid and slippery with the excrement of bats, which whirred past us when disturbed, dashing out our lights, as if they were the sinister guardians of the treasures of the Chimu kings. The survey showed us nothing beyond the constant layers of adobes, with no signs of chambers or passages, nor the slightest variation from the system of construction I have described.

It is hardly possible to assign any other than a religious purpose to this structure, which, with the *huacas* of Obispo, Toledo, etc., in common with the *teócallis* of Mexico and Central America, may have supported buildings sacred to various divinities, or a single *naos* dedicated to the Supreme Essence.

On reaching the Hotel del Comercio, we found a card had been left for us by Señor K——, the prefect; and as a part of the afternoon still remained, we lost no time in returning his visit. We found his residence, in which were also the offices of the prefecture, fronting on the Calle del Comercio, in the very heart of the city, a vast building of two lofty stories, dominating all the other houses of the city. It is of highly ornate modern Italian style, built around a court, with corridors to each story supported by columns. The second story, at the bottom of the court, is omitted, and a colonnade supplies its place. This is for the purpose of better ventilation. Although, from the necessities of the case, built mainly of the ordinary building materials of the country, these have been put together with the utmost care, and stuccoed and frescoed in imitation of marble. Altogether, whether viewed from the exterior or the court, it is an imposing building; and its interior, in arrangement, architectural decoration, and furniture, is in harmony with its palatial exterior, and probably justifies the distinction generally awarded to it, of being the finest private residence in South America. Nothing that money could purchase was spared in its construction and adornment. Workmen and artists were brought from Italy and France, and the furniture was made for it expressly in Paris. Yet, after wandering from room to room, rich in hangings, over floors bright with polish or soft with velvet carpets, it was not without a certain revulsion, when shown into the grand *sala*, we observed the walls hung with meretricious French lithographs of the largest size, representing nude female figures in every voluptuous attitude. But this was not the worst. Bungling attempts at vindicating modesty had been made by sticking strips and patches of green tissue-paper here and there over some of the most indelicate, or, rather, on the glass that covered them. As these patches and slips were attached to the glass by wafers, the reader can imagine the effect! Señor K——'s library was large; that is to say, it was lined with long battalions of the French classics gaudily bound. It was in rather a confused state at the moment, as the shock of a recent earthquake had thrown down some of the book-cases, and shattered the plaster busts of the celebrities, ancient and modern, with which they had been surmounted.

The whole building, not excepting the fine view from the *azotea*, was shown with evident pride by Señor K——; but neither our expressed admiration nor our open appreciation of the señor's munificence and taste, nor yet our natural inquiry as to how he could dispose of so much room, considering that his whole family consisted of himself and a boy seven years old, had the effect of eliciting that conventional, if not warm and cordial, "*Á la disposicion de Vms.*" ("At your service"), so common in Spanish America, and which, after the invitation extended in Lima, we had resolved to accept literally. We returned to our dirty *fonda*, determined to put no more faith in prefects.

# CHAPTER IX.

### EXPLORATIONS AT GRAND CHIMU.

Ride to the Ruins.—Hall of the Arabesques.—The First Corridor.—Figures in Stuc-
co.—The Second Corridor. —Vaults and Store-rooms. —Cotton Mattresses.—An
Upper Edifice. —Walls, Passages, and Chambers. —The Furnace. —Vessels of
Gold and Silver. —Many Relics melted down. —Prospects left for Research.—
Conjectural Features of the Structure. —Exterior Walls probably Decorated.
—The Destruction by Treasure-hunters. —The Necropolis of Chimu. —Niches
with Human Remains. —Fine Cloths of Cotton and Alpaca Wool. —Silver Or-
naments attached to Fabrics.—Decorated Skulls. —A Mysterious Structure. —
Covered Tomb. —Our Way of Life at Chimu. —Plans for the Future. —Ruins
Described by Rivero and Tschudi. —The "First Palace."—Ornamented Court
and Hall.—Forms of Ornamentation.—The Great Reservoir.—El Presidio, or
the Prison.—An Evidence of Former Civilization.—The "Second Palace."—Huaca of Misa.—Barrios, or Wards. —Sub-barrios. —The Cabildo, or Municipal
House.—Dwellings of the People.—Other Squares.—Reservoirs and Gardens.—
Huacas of Las Conchas and Toledo.—Ancient Smelting-works. —Evidences of
Trade Localities.

OUR tent having been finished to P——'s satisfaction, we
hired a cart to convey it, our photographic implements, and a
barrel of water to the ruins of Chimu, whither we directed our
dinner to be sent from the Chinese *fonda*. We then mounted
our horses, and rode direct to the excavation already mentioned, the last made by Colonel La Rosa, in the ruins of what I
shall call the palace. Here, in what we called the Hall of
Arabesques, indicated in the plan by the letter A, we pitched
our tent and commenced operations.

This hall was fifty-two and a half feet wide, but of unknown
length, as on the end by which we approached it the walls are
destroyed. The side walls, however, can be traced for ninety
feet; and it was probably a hundred feet or more in length;
possibly the length was just double the width. The walls on
the right-hand side are much broken down, and covered by

great heaps of débris from the excavation; but the left-hand
wall is very well preserved; and at the height of seven feet
above a low terrace, ten feet wide, running along its base and
thence upwards, is covered with an intricate, unique, and very
effective series of arabesques, or stucco ornaments in relief, on

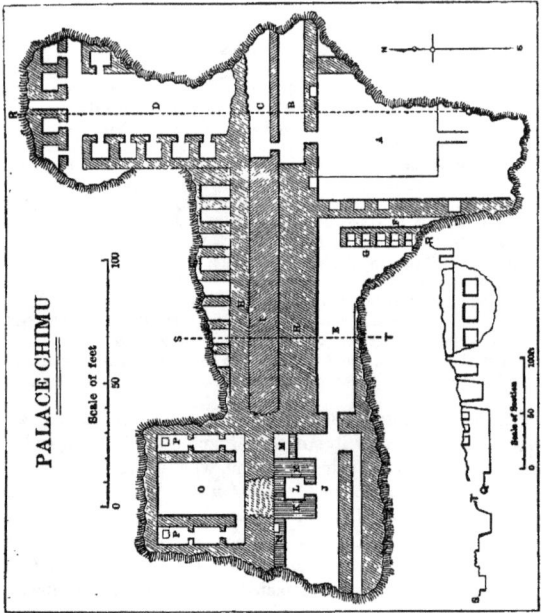

a smoothed surface, made by plastering over the adobes composing the wall. No description can give an idea of the character
of these *relievos*. It will be seen from the illustration that they
consist of a succession of reduplicated figures, raised about an
inch above the surface, and modulating, if I may use the term,
into each other. At an elevation of about twelve feet above

the low terrace alluded to, appears to have been a series of niches five feet wide, and sunk in the wall four feet. Owing to the fact that the upper part of the wall is broken down, their height can not be determined. The arabesque ornamentation, which, however, leaves a kind of smooth frame-work around them, runs up between them, and probably completely surrounded them above.

HALL OF THE ARABESQUES, CHIMU.

Looking directly before you, you will perceive that you are standing on a kind of terrace raised four feet above the general level of the hall, which you may reach, nevertheless, by an inclined plane sunk in the terrace, instead of extending out from it. This lower area is square, fifty-two and a half feet on every side. The end wall in front of you has an elevation of about twenty feet. It is pierced exactly in the middle by a door-way four and a half feet wide; and on each side, near the corners of the hall, is a niche six feet high, five and a half feet wide, and four feet deep. Although this door or passage-way now opens to the very top of the wall, there is reason to believe that it originally reached only to the base of the belt of arabesques, which were continued around from the side. This belt is yet from eight to ten feet wide, but the wall is so much broken down that it is impossible to determine its original breadth.

Entering the door-way through walls tapering slightly upwards, and six feet thick at the base, the investigator finds himself in a corridor twelve feet wide, the floor of which was originally five feet higher than that of the hall or corridor he has just left. How far this corridor originally extended on the right can not be determined, having only been excavated for about forty feet. On the left it has been excavated about ten feet from the door-way, to a barrier of adobes that seems to have been filled in purposely after the corridor was finished, as if to obstruct or close it up. The wall facing the entrance, like that we have just passed through, is covered with arabesques of the same design, but with this difference, that the door-way leading through it and to another corridor beyond is framed in

FIGURES IN STUCCO.

by double pilasters—if I may use this term in default of a better—between which is a line of stucco figures in relief, designed apparently to represent monkeys, each crowned with a kind of ornament, a demi-lune in shape — with which we afterwards became familiar in the pottery and paintings of the Chimus, and which was one of the symbols or insignia of rank and power among them.

Beyond this corridor we enter still another, on a level five feet higher, but only eight feet wide. Its length, for the reasons already assigned, can not be definitely ascertained. The walls are much broken down and defaced; but enough remains to show that they were also covered with arabesques similar to those of the great or entrance hall, apparently differing only in having a border of the monkey-shaped ornaments extending around them.

These apartments and corridors, so far as exposed by the excavations, do not connect with others; but there is little doubt that the corridors led, by ramifications more or less intricate, or by subterranean passages, to vaults and chambers, in the pyramidal structure of which they formed part. We may infer this from the circumstance that, in the adobe mass back of the last corridor, and over which, at a still higher elevation, once stood a large building (D), Colonel La Rosa found several vaults, which he effectually destroyed, completely obliterating the passages leading to them, whether laterally or from above. His recollections of them were very vague. One chamber or vault, however, seems to have been a kind of store-room, containing a great number of cotton mattresses, which had been covered with fine cotton cloth. The cloth had, for the most part, decayed, but the cotton remained perfect, slightly, if at all, discolored. I brought away a portion of one of these mattresses, the cotton of which was, I believe, baled and sent abroad. The fibre is still as strong and good, perhaps, as it ever was.

The edifice D, as will be seen from the plan, had its floor about thirty-five feet above that of the Hall of Arabesques, A. There is no apparent connection between the two, nor yet between the superior structure and the halls or corridors, B and C. This structure seems to have been placed on the summit of the adobe mound, and its interior dimensions, so far as can be ascertained in its present state of mutilation, were seventy-six by twenty-six feet. Its interior has been excavated to the depth of thirty or forty feet, all the way through adobes, without reaching the level of the soil. It was in making this excavation that the vaults to which I have alluded were discovered. The débris from this vast pit is piled all around the structure, burying still deeper the remains of the other structures that once crowned the mound, which must have had on the top an area of two or three acres. The walls of this particular edifice, D, are in places eight feet high. They were built of adobes, stuccoed over smoothly, without ornaments in relief, but with here and there traces of colors. It was entered by passages, skirting the southern wall, flanked on one side by openings, resembling windows, with sills four feet above the floor. These, however. are entrances to little square rooms, seven feet by seven, each floor being on a level with that of the hall itself. These chambers were continued on both sides of the hall, and possibly across the northern end, which has been completely broken down. I found many of these small dependent chambers connected with other buildings, but have been unable to form a clear opinion as to their purpose. They may have been places of deposit or storage, and possibly dormitories. The latter supposition is not unreasonable, when we consider the smallness of some of the sleeping apartments in the dwellings of Pompeii.

Returning now to the Hall of Arabesques, we find its eastern wall broken through near the south-east corner, and are able to pass through the opening into a passage or corridor, E, eighty feet long by fifteen feet wide. Its high walls of adobe have been plastered over and made smooth, as if glazed, but without ornament of any kind. Leading from this to the left is a plain passage, F, only five feet wide, extending until lost in the mass of débris to the north. We next observe an isolated wall, G, eight feet thick, in which, at a height of about six feet above the floor of the passage, are a number of small chambers, precisely like those already described as opening from the superior hall D, only smaller, being but four feet square. The right wall of the passage E is massive; rising first to the height of fifteen feet, when it forms a kind of terrace, H, seventeen feet wide, from which again rises another wall, I, broken down almost to its base, where it is twelve feet thick. Beyond this the terrace, H, is resumed for eight feet, when we come to a succession of oblong, rectangular chambers or vaults, six feet wide and twelve feet long, sunk six feet below the level of the terrace. Some of these are entirely, and the rest partially, covered or filled with rubbish. This description will be made more intelligible by reference to the section.

Advancing along the passage E, we reach a door-way five feet wide, and originally about seven feet high, through a lofty wall eight feet thick, and enter a passage, or rather a chamber, about thirty feet wide, and of unknown length beneath the rubbish in front of us. The walls are plain, the most remarkable feature being a cubical mass, K, K, twenty-four feet long and

eighteen feet wide, and twelve feet high, built up against the
high wall on our right.    In the centre of this is a chamber ten
feet square, open at the top.    Its walls are burned and blistered
like those of a furnace to the depth of twenty inches, and show
every sign of having been exposed to severe and protracted
heat.    By the side of this, and between it and the wall through
which we entered, is a sort of bin, M, with a low wall in front.
This, Colonel La Rosa assured us, was filled with calcined human bones when the hall was excavated; but few traces of
bones, however, were to be found at the time of my visit.    The
colonel considered the hollow mass, K, K, as the place of burning the dead—a practice, however, of which I found no traces
elsewhere, nor do we hear of it among the traditions of the ancient occupants of these regions.    I am more disposed to regard
this mass as a furnace, in some way connected with ancient
metallurgic operations.

Perhaps this hypothesis is better supported than that of Colonel La Rosa, from the discovery by himself of a chamber or
walled-up closet, filled with vessels and utensils of gold and silver, principally of the latter, close to the supposed furnace on
the left, and indicated by the letter N.    This closet, or rather
well, which, according to the colonel's statement, had no entrance, except perhaps from above, was about twenty inches
square, and as many feet deep, and was formed by leaving this
space in a second wall several feet thick, which had been built
up against the original outer wall of the chamber or area.    The
vessels were piled regularly, one layer above another, and, according to the colonel's notion, had been hidden away here at
the time of the struggle between the Chimus and the Incas, to
preserve them from the clutches of the latter.    The vessels
were mostly in the form of drinking-cups or vases, some plain,
and others ornamented, of very thin silver, considerably alloyed
with copper, and oxidized to the extent of making some of
them so brittle as hardly to bear handling.    He had melted
them down, except a few, with very poor return in amount of
exportable silver.

Of the few preserved by him, I have two; one is ten inches
10

in height with a flaring top and bottom, and with a human face, having a marked aquiline nose, and the hair in plaits at the back

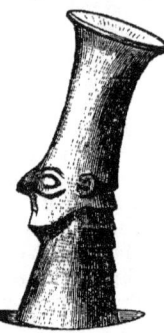

SILVER CUP.

of the head, all struck up from the inside. The thickness of the metal is about that of ordinary tin-plate. There is no sign of soldering in any part, and the whole seems to have been hammered out from a single piece of metal. I can not accept the suggestion that it was cast, of which there is not the slightest indication. The other is a similar but less ornate vessel, somewhat smaller in size. Colonel La Rosa affirmed that he had found some gold vessels here, which he had sold by weight, for exportation as bullion. It will probably be always a source of regret to antiquarians that these

articles, infinitely more valuable in an artistic and scientific view than in any other, should not have fallen into more enlightened hands.

The outline of the treasure-well is distinctly marked on the opposite wall, twelve feet thick, and twenty-eight feet high, which has been excavated through, affording admission to the oblong rectangular chamber, or hall, O. Flanking this are two passages, P, P, eight-feet wide, divided by projections into two rooms, and entered by narrow passages. Near the farther extremity of each inner apartment, sunk in the floor, was found a vault, three feet by two, and four feet deep, which, when discovered, I was assured, was full of silver utensils similar to those to which I have just alluded.

I have here, as clearly as I am able, described the excavated portion of the mound which I have ventured to designate the "Palace," and which, as I have said, covers several acres. What valuables are still hidden under the present shapeless mass, what secrets of architecture and art, of ancient skill and industry, are here concealed, remain to be disclosed. The glimpses we have got are due to the blind greed of treasure-hunters, who spent

many thousands of dollars over and above the spoils they obtained in their operations, and who have fortunately been discouraged from extending the ruin they have already wrought.
There remains, consequently, a rich mine for the antiquarian
student to explore: but he must have command of ample
means; as, area for area, the amount of material to be removed here is twice that required to be taken away to reach
the streets and dwellings of Pompeii, while fewer facilities for
excavation and the removal of the débris here exist.

I would not undertake to reconstruct the Palace from hints
afforded by the comparatively small portion of it uncovered;
but I have no doubt it was a broad, and rather low, artificial
mound, built of adobes throughout, containing many small subterranean chambers, or vaults, and rising from the plain by a
succession of three or more terraces, each covered with buildings of various designs and purposes; some of them connected
by passages, others detached; some ornamented by reliefs or
colors, but all arranged in a harmonious whole—at least, in exterior aspect. If it was the residence of the Prince of Chimu,
it contained, perhaps, as did some feudal castles of the Old
World, store-houses and armories, rooms and shops for attendants and servants, and perhaps, like the Vatican, a place for cun-
ning workmen in metal and in clay, spinners, weavers, and dyers.

Nowhere in the excavations here could we find out if the exterior walls of the structure had been in any way decorated;
but we may infer that they were, from the fact that the outer
walls of some of the buildings surrounding and standing apart
from the mound were elaborately ornamented with a kind of
crochet-work of small squares, surrounded by a border of vo-
lutes, the former in *intaglio*, the latter in bass-relief. The interior walls of some of these outstanding buildings had been
painted with vivid colors, among them a delicate purple. The
areas of some of them had been excavated to the depth of fifty
or sixty feet, all the way in the gravelly, semi-stratified drift
of sand, gravel, and pebbles that makes up the plain of Mansiché. Evidently, the excavators had but slight acquaintance
with geological conditions!

About a hundred yards to the westward of the great mound in which the excavations just described were made, is another low, broad mound, in which treasure-seekers had also been at work, exposing some interesting features, indicating that here was a cemetery, probably the necropolis of the princes of Chi-

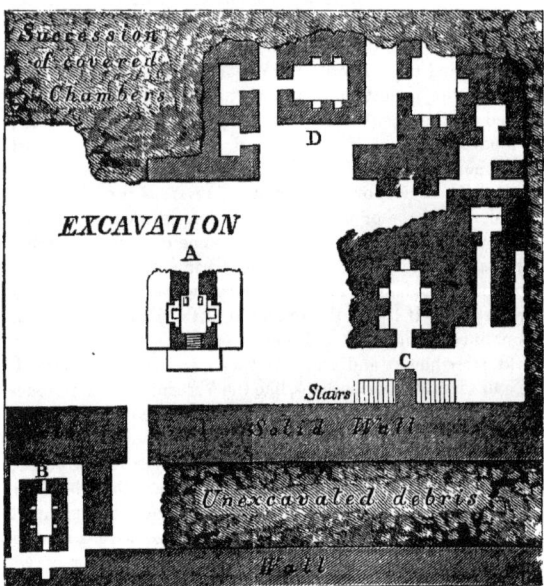

EXCAVATION OF THE NECROPOLIS, CHIMU.

mu. The excavation is about 100 feet long by 60 feet wide, and 14 feet deep. It reveals a portion of two sides of a square, defined by thick, solid rubble walls. The extent of these walls, and consequently of the area they enclose, is unknown. From the northern wall projects a platform, C, with a flight of steps descending on either side into the area. This area seems to have been mainly occupied by masses or blocks of rubble-work, separated by streets or passages, and covering chambers or vaults of varying sizes, but of the uniform height of about nine feet. Nearly all have niches at the sides or opposite the entrances. Two or three have two rows of niches, one above the other. Occupying the niches in all these chambers or vaults were found skeletons and desiccated bodies, elaborately clothed and plumed, and accompanied by ornaments of gold and silver and various insignia of rank.

These interesting relics were all taken away or destroyed. I nevertheless found fragments of the cloths and garments in which the bodies had been wrapped, some of cotton, others of the wool of the vicuña, called *chumbi*. The cotton cloth was

SPECIMEN OF CLOTH, CHIMU.

remarkably fine and even, with sixty-two threads of warp and
woof to the inch.  I have a piece of what is regarded as a very
fine specimen of Egyptian mummy-cloth, from the wrappings
of a priest unrolled in the Egyptian department of the Paris
Universal Exposition, which has but forty-four threads to the
inch.  The finest was plain, or without color, except a yellowish tinge, probably from age.  Specimens from graves newly
opened were perfectly white.  Some specimens (of which the
cut affords an example, greatly reduced from the original) were
woven in ornamental figures, and those of animals.  In this instance the border is made up of a narrow strip of white, followed by dark brown, relieved by little squares of white.  Succeeding this is a broad stripe of bright red, relieved by yellow,
leaf-shaped figures.  Next a stripe of white, then of black,
shading off into dark brown, which seems to have been the prevailing tint of the article of which the fragment formed part.

Woven in this ground are a succession of figures of yellow lizards, with
eyes in red, alternating with birds with
red eyes and feet, and yellow legs and
bills.  They appear to be striking the
heads of the lizards with their bills,
which are represented longer than
their legs.  This device has been observed in several fragments.  One of
these was a little square rug, with a
brick-colored ground, on which are
sewed plates of silver, ornamented in
relief, the whole having a double
border of feathers, blue and yellow,
with feather tassels held in silver
knobs.  This specimen, with many
others, larger and smaller, was obtained from the tombs of Chancay, to

SILVER ORNAMENT FROM CHIMU.    the north of Chimu.

This instance of the ornamentation of cloth by fastening on
it plates of the precious metals, instead of embroidery with

threads of the same, is by no means an exceptional one. Among the cloaks or wrappers taken from the Chimu tombs by Colonel La Rosa, and now preserved in the museum of the Historical Society of New York, is one spangled over with silver plates cut in the form of fishes, of which a representation is here given. The original is nine and a half inches in greatest length, and five and a quarter in greatest breadth, and is in the form of the fish known as the "skate." It was sewed upon the cloth through small holes punched in it. Thin plates of silver, also cut in the forms of fishes, with their eyes, fins, gills, and other features "struck up" as if from dies, had been found elsewhere, notably in the guano islands of Chincha. The other cuts give

FISH ORNAMENTS FROM THE CHINCHA ISLANDS.

FISH ORNAMENTS FROM THE CHINCHA ISLANDS.

examples, natural size, of a number in my own possession, taken by Captain John Pardo, an Italian, from the guano at a depth of about thirty-two feet below the surface. At the same time, and in connection with these, was found the body of a female, lacking the head, which, however, was discovered at some distance from the skeleton. The breasts and the ribs were covered with thin sheets of gold, and the whole would have been a valuable relic, had it been preserved as found. But the workmen divided the gold, part of which was sold to captains of ships loading guano, and the body thrown into the sea.

FISH ORNAMENTS FROM THE CHINCHA ISLANDS.

It is not improbable that the silver fishes had been attached to some envelope or article of clothing which had decayed in the lapse of time.

Many fragments of human skulls and other bones were scattered about this excavation, some of the former showing signs of having been painted red, and affording some ground for crediting Colonel La Rosa's statement that among the skulls discovered here were several that had been gilt, or were encircled by ornamented bands of gold or of brightly colored braids of thread, in which, and rising above the forehead, were stuck feather-shaped ornaments of thin gold, which vibrated with every movement, giving motion to little disks of the same metal, suspended in corresponding openings in the plate. I

subsequently found a number of these in Lima, of which the
cut is an example. They were all of very
pure gold.

Certainly the strangest, if not the most interesting, object disclosed in excavating these
tombs was the regular and somewhat elaborate
mass of adobes and rubble-work indicated by
the letter A, and of which the cut on the following page, from a photograph, will give a
better idea than the plan. The end towards
the spectator is partly broken down; but, presuming it to have corresponded with the other, the structure was sixteen feet square, and
twelve feet high, entered at each end by a
door-way or passage three feet wide, leading
into a kind of area, ten feet long by five wide.
The sides of this area or court were furnished
with a series of platforms and demi-niches impossible to describe, and only to be comprehended by reference to the engraving. They
were all plastered smooth, as were also the upper surfaces of the walls themselves, and here
and there exhibited traces of having been
painted. I am utterly at a loss to suggest
even the purposes of this strange monument,
unless indeed it was connected with unknown
burial rites, in the course of which different
grades of functionaries occupied the various
graduations or seats of the interior. It obviously had never been covered so as to form
a vault, and seems to have stood wholly isolated from the other
masses containing hidden chambers.

GOLD FEATHER ORNA-
MENT.

In an open space outside of the excavated area, reached by a
passage through the northern wall, is an isolated, covered tomb,
twelve feet long by six wide, nine feet high exteriorly, and six
and a half feet inside. It has entrances at both ends, one twice
the width of the other, the narrowest showing evidences of

A STRANGE STRUCTURE.

having been once closed with adobes. There are eight niches, four on each side, in two rows of two each, one above the other.

TOMB B, NECROPOLIS, CHIMU.

Small openings lead from the tops of the upper ones into the open air. The walls are smooth-cast, and were once painted in red and yellow. The whole is a compact mass of rubble; and, as the ceiling supports itself, was probably built over a solid core or model, which was removed when the mass had become hard and firm. When this was first discovered, the excitement of the discov-

erers was intense: they felt sure that this was the traditional
"big fish;" and they sent to Truxillo for a force to protect
their anticipated wealth from the workmen, who were eager
to break down the adobe barrier between them and the countless millions the vault was supposed to contain. But, alas for
their golden visions! it proved to be only a tomb, containing
some of the most striking relics disclosed by the excavations,
including the alleged gilt skulls. A number of vaults besides
those shown in the plan had been excavated, but were covered
up again by the débris of those finally left exposed.

In studying, planning, sketching, and photographing the remains of the palace and the necropolis we spent a week, coming
early and leaving late. Our practice was to rise at daylight, get
a cup of coffee at the Bola de Oro, mount our horses, and gallop
to the ruins. At eleven o'clock our Chinese purveyors would
send out a boy with edibles, wine, and ice for our breakfast.

The remains we had investigated were those exposed last;
but there was a vast number of others, uncovered years and
even centuries ago, which claimed our attention. I was at a
loss what to do. To make a good plan of the ruins would occupy a large corps of engineers for months, and I did not like
to undertake to do less. I calculated my time, and came to the
conclusion that, by swift movements, passing over some points
of interest on the coast, I might get back to Lima early enough
to enter on my expedition to the Sierra, and yet have two weeks
more in Chimu, besides a week in each of the valleys of Nepeña and Casma. I took my measures accordingly.

I have said that among the ruins of Chimu are many great
blocks, or rectangular areas, enclosed by massive walls, and containing within themselves courts, streets, dwellings, reservoirs
for water, etc., etc. Of two of these, Rivero and Tschudi have
published plans and brief descriptions, calling them, strangely
enough, "First Palace" and "Second Palace." These plans I
determined to verify before proceeding farther; for if they
were accurate, there was so much gained.

The so-called "palaces" stand not very widely apart, about a
mile south of the remains which I have described. Both are

rectangular.  The first is sixteen hundred feet long by eleven
hundred feet wide at its widest part.  The outer wall varies
from twenty-five to thirty feet or more in height, by ten feet
thick at the base, the sides inclining towards each other; so
that on top the wall is probably not quite half that thickness;

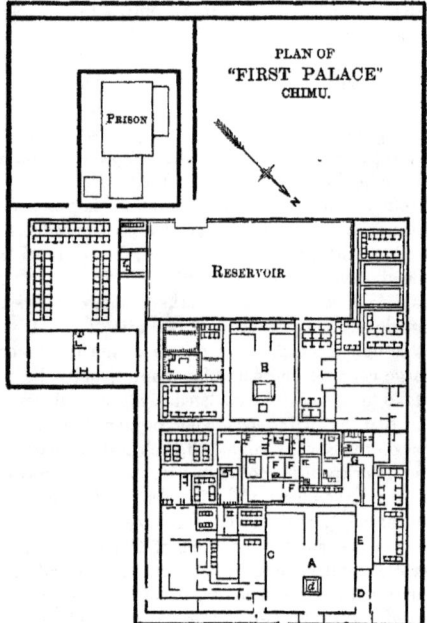

PLAN OF
"FIRST PALACE"
CHIMU.

PRISON

RESERVOIR

for from five to seven feet from the ground it is built of rough
stones, laid in tenacious clay, which may have some intermixture
to give it greater cohesion over that.  At intervals of a few feet
may be seen, projecting above the wall, the tops of tall stems
of the *caña brava*, or bamboo, which may have been planted in

the ground to give greater firmness to the wall. It is possible they were laced together horizontally by other stems, thus giving

greater strength and cohesion to the mass. Inside this wall, which appears to have had but a single entrance, from the north (although there are now two others, apparently broken through forcibly), we find five lesser rectangular enclosures, three of them

SECTIONAL VIEW OF WALLS, CHIMU.

filled with minor squares, dwellings, and reservoirs, one vacant, and the fifth containing a strongly walled interior square, in turn enclosing a strange structure, called *El Presidio* (the Prison). The relations of these squares and the plans of the buildings they enclose can only be understood by reference to the general plan of the grand enclosure itself, corrected on the spot, from that published by Rivero and Tschudi. This plan is on so small a scale that many of the minor features of the work are necessarily lost, or but imperfectly indicated.

FIGURE ON WALL, CHIMU.

Entering the grand enclosure from the north, and turning to the right, we find ourselves in a kind of antechamber, evidently never roofed, from which a gate-way opens into a large, open *plaza*, or square, A. In front of the entrance is a raised plat-

form, *d*, forty feet square, and three feet high.   Beyond this is
a graded way, leading to a narrow *terre-plein*, or platform, from
which there is a narrow street, or passage, to the left.   The left-
hand wall of this court is composed of adobes, stuccoed over, and
covered with ornaments in relief, in which the figures shown in
the cut are constantly reproduced.   A single line of these occupies the face of the wall, which is twelve feet high.   The opposite, or right-hand, wall may also have been ornamented, but
of this there are now no traces.   To the right of this court, but
not entered directly from it, are two long and relatively narrow
halls or passages, E, F, the walls of which are also highly ornamented in figures of which the following cut affords an example.   The design is in relief, as are also what may be called the borders, above and below.   The wall is of adobes, and
the *relievos* were formed by their projections when built in the
wall.   The ground on which they appear is of stucco, scratched,
or roughened, horizontally with numerous undulating lines, producing the effect of what we call "rustic work" in architecture.   In this way, the *relievos*, having their faces smooth, are
made conspicuous.   Here, as elsewhere, there are traces of color.

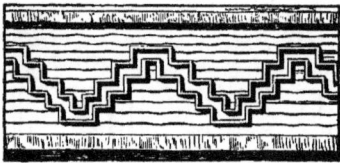

FIGURE ON THE WALL, CHIMU.

From these ornamented halls we pass into another *sala*, or
hall, G, which has a *terre-plein*, or platform, running around two
sides, with a graded way leading up to it on the third.   The
walls of this, although much broken down, are remarkable.   On
the face of a solid backing is a wall of adobes, so arranged as to
form regular, lozenge-shaped figures, as shown in the cut.   Several other rooms or courts are ornamented in like manner.   In
a few instances, the lozenge-shaped opening is carried quite

RUINED WALLS, CHIMU.

through the wall, giving the effect of a trellis. Another kind of ornamentation is to be observed in several places, formed of square adobes, in which every alternate block is in relief, as shown in the cut. Occasionally these blocks are so arranged that every alternate space is an opening entirely through the wall, which is as thick as the adobe is long—about three feet. The honey-combed effect of these walls, when looking over the ruins from an eminence, is very striking.

Passing now to the rectangular court, B, we find nearly a similar arrangement with that marked A — the raised square, the inclined plane, and the *terre-plein*. A little beyond this to the south, past a row of houses, we come to a wall five feet high standing on the *berme*, or near the edge of a deep excavation, presumably a reservoir for water. I give a plan, and a section of this structure, of which the description must stand for that of a hundred others, of greater or less size, among these ruins. It is 450 feet long by 195 broad,

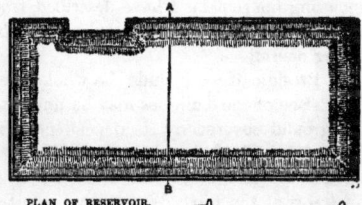

PLAN OF RESERVOIR.                SECTION.

and 60 deep. The sides fall off by two steps, or gradients, and were, from top to bottom, faced with unwrought stones, carefully fitted in place. On the southern and near the left end is a projection like a wharf, from which there is reason to believe stairways led to the bottom of the excavation. This is 78 feet long, and projects 15 feet. The wall on the southern *berme* of the excavation is double the height of that on the northern side, and has only one or two gates; while through that on the north, or populated side, there are several, as also at the ends.

The bottom of this area sunk so far below the general level is comparatively moist, sufficiently so to nourish a number of fine fig-trees (probably planted by some enterprising citizen of Truxillo), from which we obtained a by no means ungrateful

11

supply of fruit. Rivero and Tschudi mention certain aqueducts, or *azequias*, leading from the Rio Moche into this reservoir as "still visible." I did not discover such, but it is probable that they existed anciently.

I shall not stop to describe the groups of structures at the
extremities of the great reservoir, of the purposes of which, except in so far as they may have been used as dwellings, I can
form no better judgment than my reader. I therefore come at
once to what I regard as the most remarkable and interesting
feature in the group I am describing, namely, *El Presidio*,
which fills the north-west corner of a large square, defined by
high and massive adobe walls, entered, as is the great rectangle
enclosing the remains I have described, from the north. Other
openings exist, but they are modern breaches to facilitate excavating operations.

El Presidio (if we include the whole area under that name, as
the Palace of the Tuileries may be understood to give name to
the ground covered by its dependent squares and gardens) is
320 feet long by 240 wide. The wall surrounding it is 5¼ feet
thick at the base, 25 feet high, narrowing to about two feet in
thickness at the top. Within the area thus enclosed we find
the most conspicuous object to be a rectangular mound of
*mamposteria*, measuring at the base 175 by 135 feet, and 17
feet high, the sides inclining inwards. It is level on the top,
which is reached, as shown in the plan, through a rectangular
enclosure, passing several apartments or guard-houses by a
graded way or inclined plane. A low wall of adobes is carried
around the edge of the mound at its summit, where we find, at
the north-east corner, an enclosure 55 feet long by 30 wide. A
trench has been excavated nearly through the mound longitudinally, which, while it has greatly disfigured it, has revealed its
construction. The foundation seems to have been of large,
rough stones, placed on the ground, on which the body of the
work, of most compact *mamposteria*, was raised. This, however, was not solid throughout, for no fewer than forty-five cells
or chambers, arranged in five rows of nine each, were left in
the mass, as shown in the longitudinal section.

The roofs of these cells are six feet below the level of the summit of the mound, and the cells themselves are 13 feet long, 7 wide, and 6½ high, entered from above by gradients like steps. The dimensions of the orifices by which they were entered, owing to the general ruin, cannot now be exactly ascertained, but they were probably only sufficiently large to admit the body of a man—a supposition supported by the circumstance that a

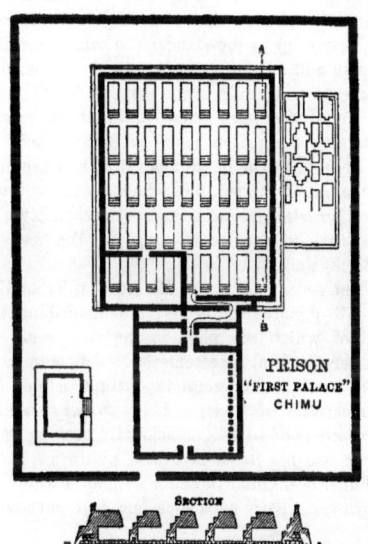

PRISON
"FIRST PALACE"
CHIMU

SECTION

number of heavy quadrangular stones are scattered about, the only intelligible purpose of which was that of covering over the entrances to the vaults or cells below. The hypothesis that the structure was really a prison derives favor from the fact that not only the foundation is composed of heavy stones, through which a convict could not dig, but that such stones are

also built firmly in the *mamposteria* between the cells, as if to
prevent excavation horizontally.   The manner in which the
approach to the mound is guarded ; the platform to the left,
with a parapet running around its upper edge, and which commands the only entrance to the great enclosure—all go to indicate the character of the work, which was first suggested to me
by its popular name, *El Presidio.*

If I am not mistaken in the matter, this monument is evidence of an advanced condition of society and government in
Chimu very nearly up to the standard of what we call civilization.   The plan and size of the cells would suggest that "solitary confinement" was a rule in the penal code of Chimu, probably supplemented with hard labor—of which the vast block of
edifices containing the prison shows so many proofs.   To the
right of the mound, and built up against it, is a supplementary
and lower one, much ruined, but which seems to have had a
number of rather elaborate apartments or chambers; whether
intended as penal cells or as dwellings for the keepers of the
prison, I will not undertake to say.

This detailed account of what Rivero and Tschudi call the
"First Palace" obviates the necessity of describing the "Second Palace," of which the plan, on the same scale with the
first, gives a very faithful representation.   In common with the
other, it is a great parallelogram in outline, defined by heavy
double walls capable of resisting field-artillery; some are of
*mamposteria,* others of adobes, occasionally backing one against
the other.   It also has its open courts, platforms, and squares
of houses; but it is singular in being without a water reservoir.
There is, however, a very capacious one just outside its walls
to the right.

Near its south-east corner is an enclosure, not unlike El Presidio in the "First Palace," also containing a mound known as
the Huaca of Misa.   It is, however, very different from that in
El Presidio; originally it was perhaps fifty or sixty feet high;
but now, excavated in every direction, it is a shapeless mass.
Passages and interior chambers, some of considerable size, are
nevertheless still traceable.   Rivero reports these to have been

lined with cut stones, of which, however, I found no sufficient
evidence.  He also states that many relics were discovered here:
mummies, mantles of cloth ornamented and interwoven with gold
and bright feathers, figures of men and animals, in metal, implements of various kinds, an idol of wood, and many fragments of pearl shells.

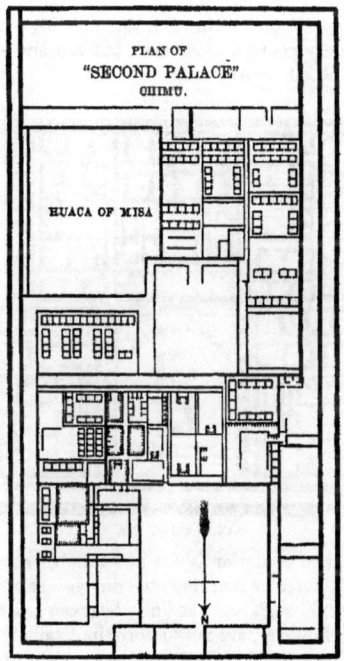

I made surveys of several other grand enclosures similar to
those noticed, which might, with equal propriety, be called
"palaces."  They may better be described as sections, *barrios*,

or wards, each with its special population separated and kept
apart for municipal purposes or social reasons.   True, it would
seem that this kind of isolation could be equally well effected without constructing such high and massive walls as define
these *barrios,* and which are quite as strong and imposing as
those which seem to have enclosed the city on its land side.
Yet each division or square may have been designed to be in itself a fortress or citadel.   However that may be, some of these
squares not only contain lesser ones, but are also subdivided,
as shown in the subjoined plan.

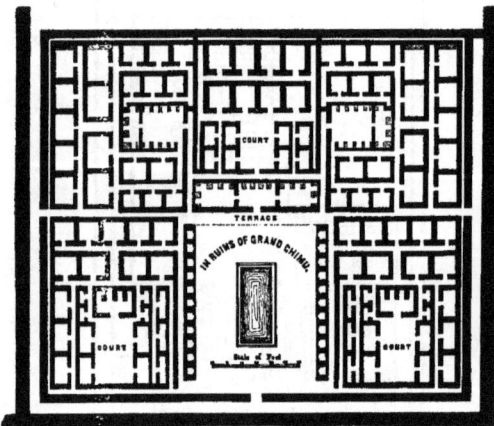

PLAN OF SUB-SQUARE.

This sub-square or section is one of a number contained in a
great enclosure three or four times the dimensions of that called
by Rivero the " First Palace," and may be taken as a type of the
others, which, however, are not uniform in details.   The heavy
outer walls shown in the plan are by no means those of the
grand enclosure, but of a series traversing its area at right angles.   Within these walls is an open space, ten feet wide, after
which comes another lesser wall, with openings or entrances on

three sides.  The main entrance, or that from the north, leads
into an open plaza, in the middle of which is a reservoir for water, about sixty feet long by thirty broad, and twelve feet deep,
the sides falling off by steps, and are faced with stones.  On
the right and left are rows of what originally appear to have
been shops or market-stands, only a few feet square, opening
on the plaza.  A low and comparatively thin wall crosses each
door-way, like a threshold, and separates the interior from the
area outside.  A terrace three feet high extends across the end
of the plaza, opposite the entrance, in front of the largest building in the group.  This contained three apartments, along the
walls of which are projections like pilasters, too high for seats,
forming what may be called niches between them.  Even our
Chinese attendant recognized the probable purpose of this
building, when, in pointing to it, he ejaculated, "*Cabildo!*"
Three streets, two crossing the square north and south, and one
east and west, intersect each other on this terrace of the *cabildo*,
dividing the whole area of the *barrio* into six subordinate
squares or blocks, exclusive of that which I have called the
plaza.  Each of these in turn has its minor court or plaza, and
four of them have their own small *cabildos*, or municipal houses.

Around each plaza the dwellings of the ancient inhabitants
are grouped with the utmost regularity, but in a manner baffling
description, and which can only be made intelligible by reference to the plan, which also shows many curious and enigmatical features which it would be tedious to enumerate.  Some of
the houses or apartments are small, as if for watchmen or people on guard; others are relatively spacious, reaching the dimensions of twenty-five by fifteen feet inside the walls.  These
walls are usually about three feet thick, and about twelve feet
high.  The roofs were not flat, but, as shown by the gables of
the various buildings, sharply pitched; so that, although rain
may not have been frequent, it was, nevertheless, necessary to
provide for its occurrence.  Each apartment was completely
separated from the next by partitions reaching to the very peak
of the general roof.  There are no traces of windows, and light
and air were admitted into the apartments only by the door.

It will be observed that, except on the plazas, the doors of none of the buildings open opposite each other. How far this feature may be due to regard for individual or family privacy, in a community organized with an order and system that a socialistic philanstery might despair of rivalling, I do not undertake to say, but we must believe that it was not without a clear design. Altogether there seems to have existed in this sub-barrio thirty-nine separate buildings, with from two to five apartments each, or one hundred and eleven in all, without counting the twenty-two little *tiendas*, or shops, facing upon the central square.

The long, narrow, open spaces, or corridors, running around the several squares and along the walls of the principal square itself, are enigmatical, especially as we find them interrupted, on one side at least, by cross-walls. We might otherwise imagine them to be the places where refuse and filth of various kinds were cast temporarily.

The sole entrance to this particular square, it will be observed, is from the south-east corner, and through another but open square, which seems to have been a garden, the indurated ground still showing traces of cultivation. The square to the north of this under notice corresponds very nearly with it in size, and contains a large but ruined truncated mound, surrounded by buildings. Some open squares succeed, followed by others filled with edifices in perplexing variety, a few standing on the natural surface of the earth, others on terraces; some in absolute ruin, others relatively perfect; and altogether so numerous as to forbid a survey except by a corps of engineers, limited in their work neither by time nor considerations of cost.

Outside of these walled enclosures, and scattered with more or less regularity over the intervening spaces, are the foundations and other remains of a vast number of small buildings, apparently of ruder construction than those within the enclosures. Some of the spaces, however, are clear, or marked only by small piles of stones scattered over them here and there. We were told that these covered graves; but I removed several, and excavated the earth beneath them, without finding any remains.

I have alluded to reservoirs for water; these are more numerous outside than inside the enclosures, and exist in considerable numbers. They are popularly supposed to be granaries, but I think their purposes are obvious, especially as there are traces of *azequias* leading to several of them. They could not have been roofed over; and the intelligent people who built Chimu would certainly not have left their grain exposed in a region where, although rarely, rain sometimes falls in torrents. Three or four instances have been known in the historical period when great damage was done, and indelible traces left on the plain and its monuments.

Besides these reservoirs, there are a number of large excavated areas in the sands towards the sea, in the direction of Huaman, obviously for gardens, in conformity with a practice, anciently wide-spread on the coast, and not yet extinct, of removing the sand in desert places until a stratum of earth was reached sufficiently moist to support vegetation.

In speaking of the *huaca* of El Obispo, I alluded to two others, those of Toledo and Las Conchas. The latter, like all the others, has been excavated from above and from the sides. Tunnels have been driven into it at various elevations; and outside a shaft has been sunk, and a drift carried beneath it, in search of subterranean deposits. This last experiment was made only a few years ago, by a company of treasure-seekers of Truxillo, but without much success. They found some passages and chambers, one of the latter ornamented with shells inserted in the *mamposteria* of the walls. They found the roofs of the passages supported in places by hewn cross-beams of algarroba wood, of which I brought away one, perfectly preserved. It is five feet long, nine inches wide, and five thick, hewn flat on the lower surface and the sides. One end is cut squarely, the other roughly to a point. The marks of the tool are large, bold, and sharp, as if from an instrument quite as effective as the iron axe now in use in Peru. The drifts and passages are dark, noisome with bats, and quite unsafe, so that

I did not undertake to penetrate far into Las Conchas. The same reasons deterred me from venturing into the labyrinthine excavations of the *huaca* of Toledo farther than to ascertain its construction. Its core, or central mass, seems to have been of very hard concrete, in thick layers, inclining to the centre, and the whole faced over, both on the sides and top, with adobes to the depth of ten or twelve feet, perhaps more. I can only repeat that the ruin here, as in the case of most of the *huacas*, is so absolute that close measurements are impossible.

I have omitted reference, up to this point, to a remarkable sub-barrio, or enclosure, in one of the larger squares, notice of which now will naturally lead to a fuller consideration of what may be called the minor works of art of the ancient Chimus. This enclosure is very nearly of the dimensions of that last described, but with a different arrangement. It has a double row of buildings on its northern side, but along its southern wall is a succession of what were perhaps ancient furnaces or smelting-places, so much ruined as to prevent any clear understanding of their construction. Their thick walls were burned deep, and fragments of slag still clung to them, while in a large open space near by was heaped a great quantity of slag, or scoriæ, which is proved by analysis to be mainly of copper and silver ores. We have here proofs of a certain proficiency of the Chimus in metallurgy, in addition to those furnished by their ornaments and other relics in gold, silver, and bronze. Here, too, we have further evidence of the hypothesis that the various great enclosures were occupied by artisans or mechanics of cognate pursuits, and the smaller divisions, by those who followed out the details of each pursuit—by those who reduced the metals from the ores, and those who wrought them into articles of use or ornament; by those who produced and cleansed the cotton from its seed, and those who spun, wove, and dyed it.

# CHAPTER X.

## LEGENDARY HISTORY OF THE CHIMUS.

Accounts by Feijoo and Garcilasso de la Vega: Extent of their Territory.—Their Chief, Chimu-Canchu.—The Invasion by the Inca Yupanqui.—Stubborn Resistance.—Final Submission of Chimu-Canchu.—Beneficent Measures of the Inca.—Relation by Montesinos: The Inca Empire threatened by the Chimus.—Wars between the Chimus and Incas, from the Eleventh to the Twenty-fifth.—The Chimus conquered by Topa-Yupanqui, the Ninety-seventh Inca.—Relation by Balboa: War between the Inca Capac-Yupanqui and Chimu-Capac.—The Chimus subjugated by Topa-Inca.—The Account by De Leon.—Different Customs and Dialects among the Chimus.—Some Legends of their own Origin.—The Idol Llampallec at Chot.—Its Removal, and the Consequences.—Accession of Chimu-Capac, who was conquered by the Incas.—The Ancient Language of the Chimus still spoken at Eteng.—Different from the Quichua and that of the Incas.

THE history of Chimu and its princes, beyond what can be deduced from its monuments, is exceedingly vague and scanty. The relation of Feijoo, although dedicated exclusively to the city and province of Truxillo, contains little more on the subject than was presented by Garcilasso de la Vega in his "Comentarios Reales." According to this authority, the coast of Peru from the valley of Parmunca (now Barranca), province of Chancay, northward to Truxillo, was under the dominion of Chimu, a powerful chief who was greatly feared by all his neighbors, north, east, and south. Feijoo states that the authority of Chimu extended northward of Truxillo to Tumbez, which would have given his dominions an extent of six hundred miles along the coast. Of the origin of the people of Chimu, Garcilasso says nothing, and Feijoo only observes that it was very remote, and he is not sure that it did not antedate that of the Incas.

During the reign of Pachacutec, ninth Inca, the Chimu territory was ruled by a chief whose name was Chimu-Canchu.

At this time Yupanqui, the warlike son of Pachacutec, was engaged in extending Inca authority and influence along the coast; and having, partly by force and partly by diplomacy, secured the adhesion and qualified submission of the chiefs of the valleys of Pachacamac and Rimac, he continued his march northward to the Chimu frontier, reaching the valley of the Barranca with thirty thousand men.   Hence he despatched messengers to demand of the Chimu chief that he should become a vassal of the Inca, accept the worship of the Sun, and abandon the adoration of fishes and animals.   Anticipating a refusal from Chimu-Canchu, and knowing the strength of the latter, he sent hurriedly to Cuzco for a reënforcement of twenty thousand men.   The refusal of Chimu-Canchu was absolute and defiant, and a bloody war commenced, in which the Inca was successful, forcing his way northward to the valley of Santa.   Here he met with a stubborn resistance, such as the Inca arms had never before encountered, and was held in check until the arrival of the reënforcements from Cuzco.   The Chimu chief, finding further resistance hopeless, reluctantly accepted the terms of the Inca, and accompanied him through all the valleys of his dominions, in which the conqueror directed the construction of various royal edifices, new and more extensive *azequias* for irrigating the soil, wells, and other things, as the beneficent Incas always did.   He also, in commemoration of his hardly contested struggle with the chief of Chimu, directed the construction at the Barranca, where the war commenced, of a great fortress, strong, and very beautiful with paintings and other royal adornments.   He then left Chimu-Canchu in great favor.

To this relation of Garcilasso the early chroniclers add but little in the way of confirmation or otherwise.   Montesinos, in his apocryphal history, speaks of a body of strangers, called Chimus, who had introduced themselves on the coast, bringing new idolatries, and, by superior valor, reducing the scattered tribes between the mountains and the sea.   They were represented to have come by water, in canoes, and to be giants, and warlike.   The tidings of their arrival caused alarm in Cuzco,

and Ayatarco-Cupo (the eleventh Inca, according to Montesinos) raised a large army to stop their advance southward, and
prevent their entrance into the mountains.  He does not appear to have encountered them; but his son, Huascar-Titu, continued the preparations against them, having meantime heard
that they had reached as high up the valley of Pisco as Guitera, and even to Caxamarca, and threatened Cuzco.  Huascar-
Titu died without checking their advance, as did his son, Quis-
pi-Tutu, when the kingdom fell to Titu-Yupanqui, also called
Pachacuti, the fourteenth Inca.  He moved against the Chimus, but was refused passage by the cacique of Vilcas, against
whom he consequently threatened war, but died without striking a blow.  Nor did his successors, until Marasco-Pachacuti,
twenty-fifth Inca, who marched along the coast against the
Chimus, but was unable to make head against them; so he directed his course along the flanks of the mountains, inflicting
great loss on them, and checked their advance inland.

We hear no more of the Chimus in Montesinos relatively
until the reign of the ninety-seventh Inca, Topa-Yupanqui,
who, marching from Quito along the coast, found the Chimus
in full revolt (Montesinos nowhere mentions their reduction).
He attacked and defeated them, the survivors taking refuge
among the mountains.  They subsequently descended on the
Inca garrisons, and destroyed them; whereupon Yupanqui, instead of attacking them directly, sent a large force to divert the
streams watering their territories, by which means they were
forced to submit, and became afterwards loyal vassals of the
Inca.

Balboa, whose relation is more in accord with that of Montesinos than that of Garcilasso, states that when the Inca Capac-
Yupanqui had finished a campaign against the Changas, he turned against their allies, the Conchucos, who had their capital in
Caxamarca.  Their chief made an alliance with Chimu-Capac,
a monarch ruling in the plains from Guarmey to Tumbez; but
he was slain, and his capital captured.  The garrison left by
the Inca in Caxamarca was repeatedly attacked by the Yungas
of the hot plains, of whom Chimu-Capac was king, and the

most redoubtable enemy of the Incas; being not less powerful in the plains than they were among the mountains.

Topa-Inca, the son of Yupanqui, made a war on the Chimus, of which Balboa confesses himself unable to give any details, since the Indians have lost nearly all their traditions, and the Spaniards preserved none; but, after many terrible combats, the Incas conquered the whole country, ravaging all the region watered by the river Pacasmayo. Later, after subduing the Chimus and other nations, and building a great fortress at Tumbez, he sent his uncles, with a large force, to traverse the plains "occupied by warlike nations, who bore impatiently the yoke of Chimu-Capac, instructing them to raise fortresses and leave efficient garrisons to maintain his authority." These generals traversed the plains with little resistance, finding considerable riches in gold, silver, and precious stones in the valley of Chimu, the chief of which had gone to pay his duty to the Inca at Caxamarca.

Cieza de Leon, corresponding generally with Garcilasso in his list of Inca emperors, makes the reduction of Chimu by Topa-Yupanqui take place from the north, on his return from Quito. He represents the struggle in the valley of Chimu as very severe, and at one time doubtful, and that Yupanqui built the fortress of Parunquilla on leaving the Chimu territory.

If we accept the statement that the Chimu authority extended as far north as Tumbez, we must do it with the qualification that there were considerable differences in language, if not in origin, between the intervening families, some of which are traceable to this day. Balboa affirms that Tumbez was peopled by natives from the mountains, as were the banks of the Rio Chira, the valleys of Catacaos, Piura, etc. The people of Olmos, a town still existing two days' journey to the north of Lambayeque, he says, "in language and customs differ entirely from their neighbors," although claiming also to have come from the mountains.

The people of the valleys farther south give different accounts of their origin. Those of Lambayeque declare that they came, at a very remote period, from the North, on an immense raft, under a chief of great talent and bravery, named Naymlap, having with him many followers and concubines. They landed at the mouth of a river, called Faquisllanga, near which they constructed a temple, at a place called Chot, placing in it Llampallec, an idol of green stone, representing their chief, which they had brought with them. Here the new-comers greatly multiplied. But, after a long succession of chiefs, in an evil hour they ventured to remove the idol in the temple at Chot to another place. This enraged the deity, and it commenced at once to rain, a thing unknown before, and continued for thirty days. The destruction thus occasioned was followed by a year of drought and famine. The chief under whose direction this sacrilege was committed was tied, hand and foot, and thrown into the sea. Lambayeque took its name from the idol Llampallec. After the death of the last chief, as recounted above, the district was governed for a long time as a republic, when it fell under the dominion of the powerful Chimu-Capac, who appointed governors over it until the conquest by the Incas, who appointed the chiefs until the arrival of the Spaniards.

The inhabitants of the Indian village of Moche still speak, in confidential intercourse, the ancient language of the Chimus, which, from all I can learn, is identical with that spoken in the village of Eten, or Eteng, about one hundred miles to the north, on the coast. Of this language I have a brief vocabulary. The statement that the Chinese coolies can converse freely with these villagers is only a version of that which has been told of every Indian tribe or family from Behring Strait to the Horn. The most that can be said of the language of Eteng is that it has no relationship with the Quichua, or with that of the Incas; and if it were that spoken by the people and princes of Chimu, it goes far to show that the latter were a distinct family.

# CHAPTER XI.

## THE ART, CUSTOMS, AND RELIGION OF THE CHIMUS.

Skill of the Chimu Artificers.—Their Productions easily Recognized.—Their Conventional Symbols.—Animals, Birds, and Reptiles.—The Lance as an Emblem of Royalty.—Vases and other Works in Gold and Silver.—Groups of Figures.—Some Remarkable Examples.—Implements and Weapons.—Their Chief Excellence in Pottery.—Various Forms of Vases and other Vessels.—Ornamentation of these.—Pictures on Pottery.—Musical Instruments and Performers.—Representations of the Human Head.—Of Animals and Fruit.—Sacred Character of their Ceramic Art.—The Best Source of our Knowledge of their Religion.—Symbolical Character of their Religion.—The Symbols of the Four Elements.—A Debasing Fetichism coincident with their Purer Religion.—Padre Arriaga's Book on the Extirpation of the Idolatry of Peru.—His Account of their Various Superstitions.—Their Village, Household, and Personal Idols.—Worship of Ancestors.—Results of Arriaga's Efforts to extirpate Idolatry. — The Purer Religion of the Chimus.—Worship of the Original, Pure, Incorporeal Being.

In reporting the conquest of Chimu by the Inca Yupanqui, Cieza de Leon relates that the victor took with him to Cuzco many of the artisans of the country, "because they were very expert in the working of metals and the fashioning of jewels and vases in silver and gold." We may infer from this that the Inca regarded the workmen and smiths of Chimu as not inferior to those of his own capital. I have already given some examples of their skill in working silver. Objects of gold are of course rare, after three centuries of ransacking their ancient depositories by men who sought gold for itself alone, and sent to the smelting-pot the finest productions of ancient art, without bestowing thought on their artistic or antiquarian value. Yet some specimens have been preserved in private and public collections, where they are generally loosely classed as "Peruvian." The student, however, will seldom fail to distinguish the Chimu relics by their style and ornamentation. They are marked and peculiar, distinguished by certain figures and designs of constant recurrence; sometimes woven into fabrics of cotton, painted or embossed on pottery, or engraved or "struck up" in relief on vases and other objects of metal.

Among these figures I have already mentioned the lizard as conspicuous. The fish, the serpent, and a long-legged bird, like the flamingo, are frequent. The monkey is not uncommon. But the most characteristic is the lance, which nearly all the representations of the sovereigns and divinities of the Chimus carry in their right hands, and which has been perpetuated as a symbol in Truxillo, where a huge lance, like a flag-staff, occupies the centre of every public square. Crowning the heads of the representatives of sovereigns and divinities are a number of conventional figures, evidently symbolical and significant. One of these, in shape like an inverted leather-cutter's knife, is shown crowning the heads of the stuccoed monkeys in the palace of Chimu. It is constantly found on pottery and in works of metal.

GOLDEN VASE, CHIMU.          SILVER VASE, CHIMU.

The golden vase represented in the accompanying cut exists in the museum of Lima, and may be taken as a very fair example of the better kind of articles in metal. The material is very thin, and the ornaments are struck up from the inside. The silver vase is also in the Lima Museum, and bears some resem-

12

blance to one in my possession, already described.  The three
succeeding cuts represent a plate of gold, bearing a rude figure

of a bird in relief, en-
closed in a border also
in relief ; a silver disk
or medal, with engraved
figures; and some small
thin pieces of gold, sil-
ver, and copper, round
and square, each pierced
with a small hole as if
intended to be strung
like the coin of the
Chinese.

Besides works in met-
al, like those described
above, a large, essen-
tially different, and very interesting class has been found in
Chimu, consisting of representations of men, animals, and reptiles cast, sometimes hollow, sometimes solid, with scales, feathers, and other minor features indicated by engraving on the surface.  The lizard, fish, and the serpent represented on the following page may be taken as examples.

GOLDEN PLATE, CHIMU.   ONE-FOURTH SIZE.

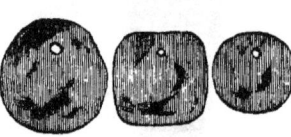

SILVER MEDAL, CHIMU.
ONE-FOURTH SIZE.

GOLD AND SILVER COINS, CHIMU.   FULL SIZE.

Another and more interesting class of relics in silver are
groups of figures, of men, animals, trees, etc., of such complex-
ity, and exhibiting such striking evidences of proficiency in
modelling and casting, that I was for a long time skeptical as

to their genuineness. I possess one of these representing **three**
figures, one of a man and two of women, in a forest. It rises
from a circular base about six inches in diameter, and weighs
forty-eight and a half ounces. It is solid throughout, **or rather**
is cast in a single piece, and rings, when struck, like a bell. **The**
trees, whose twisted trunks resemble those of the algarroba, with

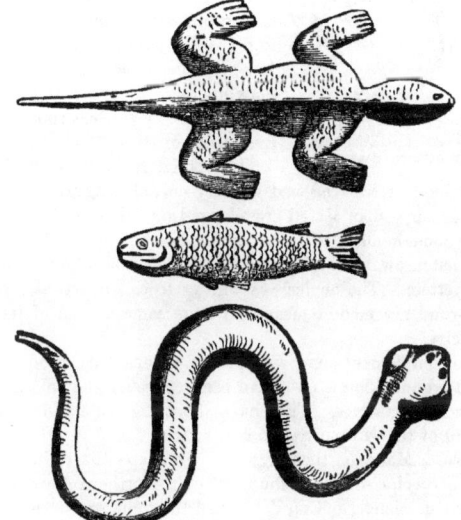

SILVER LIZARD, FISH, AND SERPENT, CHIMU. REDUCED.

their branches spreading in every direction, are well **represent-**
ed. The human figures are well proportioned and full of **action.**
Unfortunately the scene is not of a kind to bear being **engraved.**
How the mould for this complicated piece of work was **made, is**
a difficult question to answer. The most plausible **suggestion**
is, that the device now in use, of making a model of wax, **which**
is melted out when the material composing the mould is **suffi-**

ciently hardened, was known to the ancient founders of Chimu. But we have no evidence that wax was known anywhere in

BIRD CAST IN ALLOYED GOLD.
FROM CAÑETE.  HALF SIZE.

Peru. It is possible, however, that the model was made of some plastic gum or other material removable by heat or soluble in water.

Another group, of like workmanship, represents a hammock containing a child swinging between two trees, up one of which a serpent is crawling as if to attack the infant, while close by a kettle is represented over a fire of sticks.

Colonel La Rosa introduced me to a friend of his who had a badly corroded figure in silver, representing a man seated cross-legged on a kind of daïs, holding in one hand a plate or tablet, bearing some characters, much eaten away, which an active imagination might conceive to be letters. The owner was willing to sell it, but at a price far beyond my modest means. I have some doubts of its authenticity.

Many implements and weapons of bronze have been found in and around Chimu, and have been collected and sold by the ton, in former times. They have about the same alloy of copper and of tin with corresponding articles found in other parts of Peru. Many of them resemble in shape the ruder forms of bronze celts found so abundantly in Northern Europe and the British islands, and no doubt had the same use. They may be described as a kind of chisel, of varying size and weight, rather broader at the edge than at the shank, which has a socket to receive a handle. This socket has a slit on one side, so that the staff or handle might be tightened in its place when the instrument was used. We notice the same device in some of our present agricultural implements. The European celts, having closed sockets, were often attached to their handles by cords passing through a little loop on one side. The first of the accompanying cuts is a very good type of this class of imple-

ments. It is nine and a half inches long. Precisely similar
tools are still in common use among the agricultural laborers of
Nicaragua, only iron is substituted for bronze. They are used
for loosening and mellowing the soil, somewhat as we do with
a spade.

AGRICULTURAL IMPLEMENTS OF BRONZE.

But the Peruvian agriculturist had other implements coming
nearer our spade in shape, two of which, one engraved with
figures, are here given. The plain one is 11 inches long and
4 broad, forming a very efficient implement in experienced
hands. That with ornamental engravings is 14 inches long by
4½ broad at its widest part. Another agricultural implement,
with a curved blade not unlike some tools now in use, is also
engraved. It measures 10 inches in total length, and shows
that the ancient inhabitants of Peru knew perfectly how to
adapt the forms of their implements to the objects they had in
view.

Vast numbers of a kind of implement, of which an example
is here given, are found not alone in Chimu, but along the whole
Peruvian coast. Although varying in dimensions from a few
inches to nearly two feet in length, they are unvarying in shape.
They are cut, apparently, from thin but stiff plates of bronze,

and the curved lower edge is invariably sharp, as is the upper one occasionally.  We know that the knives of the Peruvians

generally were almost identical with those used by saddlers, having an upright and often ornamented handle.  Of one of these, the handle terminating in the figure of some animal supporting a smaller one on its back, I give a representation below.  Other specimens look more like chopping-knives, the blade being five inches wide, and weighing nearly two pounds.  Neither of these last, however, seems to have the same design with the preceding one.

TROWEL.

This, since the ancient inhabitants of the coast worked so largely in clay, in their architecture as well as in their pottery, I have come to regard as a kind of trowel.

KNIVES, CHIMU.

The most common of the weapons found in Chimu are bronze javelins or lances, some long, thin, and light, others comparatively short and heavy.  They are hammered four-sided from the shank, which is round, to the point.  The handle of the spear fitted into a socket, and not the shank of the spear into the handle.  The finest lance in my collection is twenty-two inches long, and only six-tenths of an inch in diameter at the shank.  It contrasts with a spear-point, which is but thirteen inches long, with a diameter at the shank of one inch and two-tenths. The sockets of all of these are slit on one side, as in other bronze implements already described. The shank of the spear last mentioned still bears the marks, for an inch from its base, of the cord by which the slit was partly closed, and the weapon fastened firmly to its handle. The arrow-heads of the ancient inhabitants were made in like manner with the lances, varying in length from three to five inches. If arrow-heads of flint, or weapons of stone, were ever found here, I

WAR-CLUB.

failed to learn the fact. I heard of bronze swords, but saw none, although some of the skulls, found near the enclosure called "The Fortress," appeared to have been cleft by swords rather than by hatchets. Several varieties of bronze war-clubs, or what the French aptly call *cassetêtes* (head - breakers), are

PERUVIAN POTTERY.

found here as elsewhere, of which a specimen is given. Among the fractured skulls found near "The Fortress," the larger part seem to have been broken by blows from some such weapons. Not a few show the clean, square hole produced by the bronze arrows. In fact, I found a portion of one skull with the arrow still wedged fast in it.

Remarkable as were the works of the Chimus in metal, their chief excellence was in pottery. In this the coast tribes to the south of them also excelled; and it is safe to say that three-fourths of the pottery found in the museums of Europe and America, and called

PERUVIAN POTTERY.

Peruvian, came from the coast or near it, and of this probably much the largest portion from the region ruled by the princes of Chimu. In variety of forms and freedom of execution, as also in fineness of material, the pottery found around Truxillo is superior to that of any other portion of Peru, Cuzco not excepted. There is a broad distinction also between the coast pottery and that of the interior in shape, style, and ornamentation; and, although in places the styles may have run into each other, and examples from the two regions been interchanged, the difference is absolute.

A distinguishing feature of the coast pottery, or of that class which is most prized by collectors, is the occurrence of a double spout, or, rather, a bifurcate one, like an inverted Y, with two orifices opening into it from the vessel. The simplest form is shown in the cut, in which the spout serves also as a handle. I have one of this shape, covered with a most elaborate picture of figures, etc., which is more fully described further on. The next advanced form is where the spout rises from one side of the vessel, and a handle is curved inwards from it to a corresponding projection, terminating in the head of a bird or animal on the other, the last, perhaps, with openings for nostrils, or with open mouth, so that, in pouring water out of the vessel, air is not only admitted to supply the vacuum, but in passing in or out often causes a sound imitating the note or cry of the bird or animal represented. Occasionally there are two spouts. Very many of these vessels are double. One of these, given on the opposite page, represents a stag and doe, having an interior connection at the point of contact; others are treble and quadruple. There are other forms, more in the shape of modern vases, of which the cut, ornamented with a line of fishes, is an example.

It would be impossible to enumerate the countless varieties of forms and combinations of the coast pottery of Peru. There are hardly two specimens alike. Not only do we find almost every combination of regular, or geometrical, figures, but earth, sea, and air are laid under contribution to supply shapes for the potter. Men, birds, animals, fishes, shells, fruits, and vegetables all find their reproductions in clay. Even the physical features of the ancient inhabitants—their architecture, arts, customs, and religious notions — find illustration and record in these most fragile, and yet almost imperishable, remains.

The architecture we find represented is not unlike that of the Indians of Moche at this day, except in that the roof is pitched instead of being flat. It is shown in the extract (if I may so call it) from a very elaborate painting on a Chimu vase in my possession, and represents a building raised on a mound of four stages, ascended by steps (omitted in the engraving), and constructed of *mamposteria* or of adobes, with a corridor in front, and the roof of thatch, supported by crooked poles. Seated apparently on a dais in the interior is the figure of some important personage, with an elaborate plumed helmet or headdress, and holding in his hands a kind of goblet, suggesting that *chicha* was known in ancient as well as modern Chimu.  He is approached by a helmeted figure of a warrior who holds his sword, or some equivalent weapon, as if in attitude of salute.

PICTORIAL DESIGN FROM A VASE, CHIMU.

Behind him, in the original painting, is represented a long procession of men and women, some borne in palanquins, and some on foot, all hurrying forwards, with every expression of eagerness, to the dwelling of the supposed chieftain.  What the painting as a whole signifies, I will not undertake to say; but it is not very difficult to suppose that it is a rude pictorial story of a general returning with an array of prisoners from a successful forray into an enemy's country.

Forming an integral part of another vase is a representation of the houses of that large part of the population of Chimu which we may call "the lower classes," which justifies the notions of the character of their edifices that we might deduce from the ruins. The building is of a single story, with a pitched roof, a single door-way, and a circular window or ventilator in the gable.

Abundant proof of a musical taste, vocal and instrumental, is discoverable in the Chimu relics in clay, not only in the form of musical instruments themselves, but in representations of musicians in the act of performance. Who can doubt the existence of a musical taste when he sees the illustration below, a reduced copy of a painted vase, representing a person singing and accompanying himself on some kind of tambourine?

MODEL OF AN ANCIENT HOUSE, FROM A VASE. CHIMU.

The instruments oftenest represented are the tambourine, a kind of drum, the syrinx, or Pan's-pipe (of which an example in stone is shown on the following page), a kind of flute, and the trumpet. All these are common to this day.

TAMBOURINE-PLAYER.

The pottery representing the human head has a special interest, not only as probably presenting to us the characteristic features of the ancient people of the coast, the Yungas and Chinchas, but as also illustrating their styles of wearing their hair and the kinds of head-dress and ornamentation common among them. I have reproduced a few examples, all accurate copies of photographic originals, which will afford a ready means of comparison. How nearly these concur in type with the existing remnants of the Indian population may be seen from the cut on page 184, giving the profile of a servant-boy of mine, having a slight infusion of Spanish blood, as compared with the profiles of two of the *huacas*.   Many of these relics are painted in the prevailing color of the Indians of the day, thus making the resemblance more nearly complete.

SYRINX, OR PAN'S-PIPE.

How well the different varieties of animals, fruits, etc., were represented will appear from the accompanying cuts, which are reductions from a large number of originals and photographs in my collection.

I have said that these works in pottery not only illustrate the

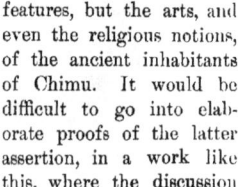

features, but the arts, and even the religious notions, of the ancient inhabitants of Chimu.   It would be difficult to go into elaborate proofs of the latter assertion, in a work like this, where the discussion

TRUMPET, BAKED CLAY.

would occupy far too much space.   I shall here confine myself to a *résumé* of the results I have thus far reached, always reserving the right to alter, modify, or abandon my present conclusions.

The most we learn directly from the ancient chronicles concerning the religion of the Chimus is, that when they were reduced by the Inca Yupanqui, they worshipped animals and fishes; a worship which they agreed to abandon, and adopt that of the sun. This was one of the conditions imposed by the Incas.

If research into primitive religions has proved anything, it is that what is called animal-worship is purely symbolical. The animal, for reasons usually obvious, is in some way the type or hieroglyphic of a power, or a conception of the mind, and is, or was originally, venerated only in that sense.

PERUVIAN VASE.

But before going further I must premise that the class of vessels in pottery of which I have just given so many examples were not devoted to secular, but to religious uses. They were *huaca*, "sacred," dedicated to religious and mortuary services. To them, in default of other

PERUVIAN VASES.

probable or possible means of recording a religious symbolism, we must look for all the scanty illustrations we are ever likely to obtain of the religious ideas and conceptions of their makers. And on them we do find representations, which from their clearly mythological character, close identity, and frequent recurrence, indicate that they originated in prevailing notions, and are exponents of a common system. These representations

MODERN PERUVIAN HEAD.

are in reliefs or paintings, and from them I make the following deductions: The Chimus adored, as almost every primitive people has done, the powers of nature, in their various manifestations. The visible dominions of these powers, or elements, are Earth, Air, and Water. In these all life is centred; from them it proceeds, and in them it disappears.

In the absence of written language men employ signs and symbols to indicate their ideas and conceptions; and these symbols are usually obvious and easily intelligible. Among the Chimus the symbols of Water were the fish, the turtle, or the crab; of Earth, the serpent and the lizard; and of the Air, the "thunder-bolt," represented by a lance or spear, the typical symbol of the lightning in many parts of the world. The divinities

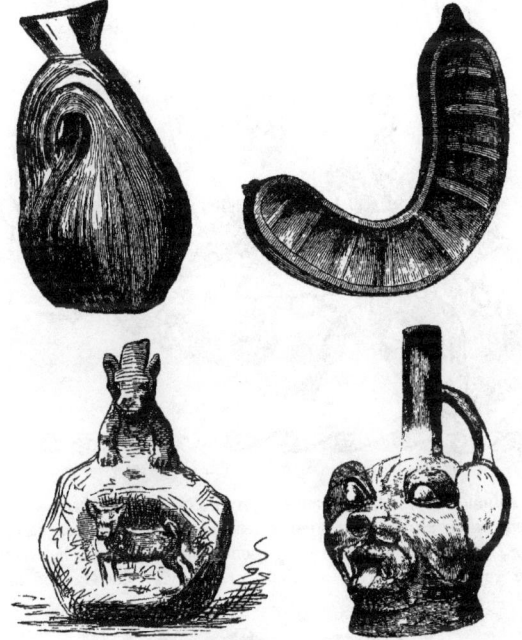

PERUVIAN VASES.

presiding over "the three elements" are not only to be identified by their bearing these symbols, but by peculiar head-dresses or crowns, best illustrated by the following engravings from some interesting vases from Chimu, in which the hypothetical divinities of Air, Earth, and Water appear with their distinctive crowns, bearing their characteristic symbols—symbols or insignia constantly repeated in an important class of remains from Chimu and its dependencies.

COMBAT BETWEEN THE MAN OF THE EARTH AND THE MAN OF THE SEA.

Among the symbolic scenes or mythological illustrations that have fallen under my notice, whether in the reliefs or paintings, the most common are representations of contests between the gods of the Earth and those of the Sea: the Man of the

THE SERPENT SYMBOL.

Earth crowned with a serpent or lizard, and the Man of the Sea in an armor of the shell of the crab, the lobster, or the turtle.

The first, in all cases, seems to be aggressor and victor. I give
a single illustration of this point from a painting on a vase
now in Lima. In many of its accessories, such as the plumed
helmet, the predominant figure recalls the style of the ancient
Mexican and Central American paintings. The serpent, represented in the same conventional style, occurs among many of
the paintings, as shown upon a vase covered with phallic scenes
and representations. We also find a gigantic horned or plumed
snail on some of the vases.

As a rule, the Chimu representations of their divinities do
not assume the extravagant
shapes, the strange and often
repulsive symbolic accessories, of those of the Mexican
gods; yet there are some

SNAIL FROM CHIMU VASE.

which remind us strongly of the representations of Tlaloc, the
Mexican god of water, as shown in the terra-cottas and in paintings.

I do not intend here to follow out this abstruse subject; I
shall only add, from the work of Mr. Bollaert, an engraving of
a mythological figure, shown in the following page, copied from
a vase now in the British Museum, found at Viru (or Berue), the
valley next south of that of Chimu. It will be seen that the figure is volant, and bears the lance, symbol of the God of the Air.

But while it seems very evident that the Chimus had more
advanced religious notions, a loftier religious system, and wor-
thier objects of worship than their Inca conquerors chose to
accord to them, there is no doubt there existed a popular form
of worship little removed from fetichism, and marked by all the
extravagances of a degraded superstition, such as has always existed among all peoples contemporaneously with religions relatively exalted and pure.

On this point our evidence is neither scanty nor uncertain.
It exists abundantly to-day; but I prefer to take it from an
earlier date, when both the State and the Church, scandalized
by the superstitions and idolatries of the Indians, especially
those of the coast northward of Lima, sent commission after

commission, secular and clerical, "to extirpate the idolatries, superstitions, rites, fables, and antiquities of the native infidels." The reports of many of these commissions are embodied in a very rare and important work entitled "Extirpacion de la Idolatría del Perú," by the Padre Pablo Joseph de Arriaga, of the Company of Jesus, and published in Lima in 1621. The Padre Arriaga was himself one of the commissioners, and wrote with authority.

GOD OF THE AIR.

He tells us that in many parts, particularly among the mountains, the natives, perhaps following the teachings of their Inca conquerors, worshipped the Sun under his proper name of *Inti;* and also *Punchao*, or the Day; *Quilla*, the Moon; certain stars, especially *Oncoy*, the Pleiades; *Libac*, the Lightning; *Mamacocha*, the Sea; *Mamapacha*, the Earth; *Puquias*, Springs; and *Razu*, the Snowy Mountains. To these their adorations were least imposing, consisting of the act of bowing, raising the hands in reverence, pulling out hairs from their eyebrows and blowing them aloft, and taking water in their palms and throwing it into the air.

As the Hindoo races worship, besides their celestial gods and their representatives, three classes of divinities — the *Grâma devetâ*, or village god; the *Kula devetâ*, or household god; and the *Ishta devetâ*, or personal or patron god—so, too, the Chimus, and the whole Yunga and Chincha family, had their village or communal deities, their household *huacas* (their *lares* and *penates*), and their patron or personal *huacas ;* and it was to these that their most conspicuous idolatry was paid.  The communal *huaca* was carefully preserved by a class of priests and their assistants ; the family *huaca*, or *canopa*, was kept in the family dwelling, and descended from father to son ;* while the personal *huaca*, generally a very insignificant object, was buried with its possessor.

"Ordinarily," says Padre Arriaga, speaking of the communal *huaca*, "they are of stone, without any figure ; but others are in the form of men and women.  Some are in the form of animals, and all have special names by which they are invoked ; and there is not a child who does not know the name of the *huaca* of his *ayllo* (tribe or clan), and how to invoke it, often taking its name for his own.  Some of these *huacas* are regarded as guardians or protectors of certain towns, and are called *marca-aparac*.

"All have their special priests, who make the sacrifices to them ; and although every body knows where they are kept, few ever see them, as the priests do not care to have the people see what kind of objects they so much fear and worship. The very places where these *huacas* are deposited are held sacred ; and so far does this reverence extend, that those that

---

* "The *canopas*, called *chancas* in the mountains, are probably their *lares* and *penates*, and are also called *huacicamayoc, mayordomo,* or master or owner of the house.  They are of various substances, of extraordinary figure, and stones peculiar, whether in shape or color.  An Indian finding any singular object at once repairs to his sorcerer and asks him what it is.  If the latter says *canopa*, he at once cherishes and reveres it.  The *canopa* descends from the father to the eldest son, who always has charge of the clothing (regalia) used in the festivals.  Some *canopas* are of bezoar stone, called *qvieu ;* some are little crystals, called *lacas*.  There are special *canopas* of maize, called *zarap-canopa ;* others of potatoes ; others called *caullama*, for the increase of herds, sometimes in the shape of llamas.  All *canopas* have the same kind of worship with the *huacas*, except that the latter is public, and the former in its own house, not at fixed intervals, but on occasions of sickness, at seed-time, etc."—ARRIAGA.

have been destroyed by the visitors are still invoked by their names.

"Wherefore," continues the padre, "in throwing the *huacas* into the seas or rivers, or otherwise destroying or disposing of them, care must be taken not to allow any Indian to witness the act, not even the most faithful; for there is nothing these people will not do to recover their idols, even to tearing down the bridge of Lima."

After the village *huacas* of stone, the padre assures us, the objects most venerated were "the *malquis*, called in the plains *munaos*, which were the bones, or rather entire bodies, of ancestors, sons of the Huancas. These were preserved in the fields in places quite apart, in ancient sepulchres, called *machays*. They were wrapped in *cumbi* (cloth of vicuña wool), and sometimes adorned with feathers. These had also a class of priests who conducted the sacrifices made to them, the same as to the *huacas*. With the *malquis* were deposited the implements and arms used in life, and passages or tubes were left in the sepulchres, through which food and drink could be conveyed to the dead, in vases of clay or wood, but sometimes of silver, etc."

It was one of the complaints made in Arriaga's time against these Indians, that "in many parts, and in all where possible, they had taken the bodies of their dead from the churches, and carried them to their *machays*, giving as a reason *cuyaspa*, the love they bore the departed."

As regards the rites and ceremonies attending the worship of the *huacas*, etc., "it is necessary," continues the padre, "to witness, some day, the Indians coming together, and bringing all the instruments of their idolatry! The various *ayllos*, or families, come, carrying the entire dried bodies of their ancestors, together with those taken from the churches, as if the living and the dead were coming to judgment! Also the higher and the lower priests, dressed in their robes and plumes, with the offerings for the *huacas*, the pots, jars, and vases for holding the *chicha*, with copper and silver trumpets, and large sea-shells, on which they blow to convene the people, who come with tambourines, well made, hardly a woman being without one, bringing also great numbers of *cunas*,* well carved horns of deer, skins of foxes and lions of the mountains, and many other things, which it is necessary to see in order to credit."

It would occupy too much space even to epitomize Padre Arriaga's long and minute account of the idolatries, superstitions, rites, and ceremonies of the Indians visited by him and other commissioners, notwithstanding whose zeal and labors " it was pitiful to think how little was or could be done towards the extirpation of idolatry among the nations," who, the moment the visitors turned their backs, renewed their ancient practices. It was difficult to find their *huacas, canopas, malquis*, and other objects, as they sedulously hid them away, even in the churches, so that "when it was supposed they were devoutly worshipping God, they were secretly adoring the abominations concealed beneath the altars!"

Notwithstanding his discouraging account of his labors, the padre did good work; for in his first visit to the Northern provinces in 1618, he tells us he "confessed 6794 persons; detected 679 ministers of idolatry, and made them do penance; destroyed 603 principal *huacas*, 3418 *canopas*, 45 *mamazaras*, 189 *huancas* (large stones raised in gardens), 357 *cunas*, and burned 617 *malquis*, and 477 bodies taken from the churches, to say nothing of many *chacpas* and *chuchas*,† besides chastising 73 witches: and all this in only thirty-two towns, many of them very small."

All of the superstitions of the Yungas do not appear to have been as gross as those above described by the Padre Arriaga, for he himself tells us that they believed in invisible spirits: spirits of the air, of the snowy mountains, of springs and

---

* *Cuna*, "cradle," formed like a litter, the wooden side-pieces or bearers being carved, each end terminating in the representation of the head of some animal, by which it became *huaca*.

† " *Chacpas* are the bodies of children born feet foremost, which are dried and preserved in jars in the houses of their parents. If they live to grow up, they bear the name of *chacpa*, in addition to their own. Their sons are called *Masco*, their daughters, *Chachi*. *Chuchas* are the bodies of twins dying young. They are believed to be children of the lightning."—ARRIAGA.

streams; also in elves or spirits of the groves; as in the town of Tauca, where, under the name of *huaraclla*, they appeared among certain clumps of alders near the town, and made responses to the love-lorn maidens who sung songs to them, and offered them libations.

But, above all and beyond all, above and beyond the worship of ancestors and *huacas*, spirits of sea and land, and the powers of nature, they probably adored the original, pure, incorporeal essence, the uncreated Pachacamac—not with noisy and fantastic rites and sacrifices, but "in their hearts," in silence, and in awe. We cannot deny the prevalence of this spiritual worship among all, or nearly all, the nations of the coast, without discrediting the authorities that have reached us bearing on the subject.

# CHAPTER XII.

## EXPLORATIONS NEAR THE COAST.

THE day for leaving Chimu came round too soon. I had not only become attached to the dry and dusty ruins, but every hour their purposes, so enigmatical at the outset, became more obvious. Constantly the evidences of harmonious design, intelligence, industry, skill, and well-directed authority in their construction became more apparent; and, having half unravelled the tangled skein of their purposes, I was loath to leave my work unfinished. But neither my time nor my resources, if I were to carry out my original programme of exploration, would permit me to remain here any longer. So I reluctantly packed my effects, the trophies of our explorations, settled my bill at the Bola de Oro without disputing any of the items, since the whole was in Chinese characters; and, disdaining to pay the landlord of the Hotel de Comercio the poor compliment of an *adios*, rode out early from his filthy and flea-bitten *fonda*, through the now familiar ruins, marked out boldly in light and shade by the morning sun, to the port of Huanchaco.

From the high natural terrace behind the town we saw with pleasure the smoke of the steamer *Peruano*, on her way back from Lambayique to Callao. With pleasure, because every hour's delay, in view of my limited time, was at the cost of work I was eager to perform, and of results I was anxious to achieve. Our good friend the *contador* urged us to join him at breakfast, but I knew I could breakfast on board, and my impatience banished appetite. We were off in the first launch, and were the first to clamber over the churning guards of the steamer. I say guards, because the *Peruano* was an American-built vessel, brought into these waters, and put in competition with the coasters of the British Pacific Steamship Company by a shrewd American captain, her principal (if not sole) owner, who well knew that her superior accommodations would soon force the company to purchase her at double her real value, besides retaining him as her commander at double the salary he could command elsewhere—all of which the company did. The enterprising and excellent captain was not on board, but his purser, another American, was, and by him we were received with the utmost cordiality.

Unlike the little *Inca*, the *Peruano* was broad in beam, with a hurricane deck, over which in fair weather—and in these waters it is always fair—an awning could be stretched. The dining-saloon was on deck, as also a double row of well-ventilated state-rooms, all in violent contrast with the dingy, cramped, unventilated cabin of the *Inca*.

No wonder the *Peruano* ran full of passengers when the other vessels of the line, of English build, were empty. The meanest *cholo*, escorting his sacks of algarroba beans or coop of chickens to Callao, waited for the *Peruano;* so that its popularity became its greatest drawback. Outside of the Levant steamers, perhaps no more extraordinary spectacle could be witnessed than its decks afforded. Few of the coastwise passengers in Peru cared for berths or state-rooms. It is enough for them to find a place on the bare deck, which, on the whole, is a great improvement upon their usual dormitories. The better classes had their mattresses, and the lower orders their sheep-skins, all with utensils seldom exhibited in other countries, a dish of *picante* and a gourd of *chicha*, and took possession of the first vacant plank they could find, from which they never moved. Comely *cholas*, bejewelled and in silks or gay alpacas, as well as ragged *sambos*, sprawl promiscuously over the deck, the only difference in rank being between a plank in front or one abaft the engine—the latter part of the vessel being most aristocratic here, as all over the world, although the bad odors naturally drift to that quarter, and the motion there is greatest.

I spent the day on a settee in the purser's cabin, well away from our none too savory passengers, from which I could look out on the ever-changing yet monotonous shore—a diversified waste of rock and sand, frayed headlands and shelving beaches, fringed by a lace-work of surf, contrasting strongly with the deep blue of the sea. Beyond a long, dark belt of brown, bare ridges, and a stratum of motionless clouds, rose the pale, sepulchral crest of the snowy Cordillera.

Late in the afternoon, we anchored a second time in the Bay of Santa. Don Federico insisted on our stopping over another steamer with him, and investigating the monuments of the valley; but the old longing for the interior forbade, and we went on to the port of Samanco, where we found ourselves anchored next morning. A schooner from Callao, laden with lumber, supplies, and workmen for Mr. Swayne's estate of San Jacinto, had arrived the previous night. Before leaving Lima, Mr. Swayne had given me letters to Señor B——, his *mayordomo*, which I had despatched to him on my upward trip, with a request that he would send down horses for us from San Jacinto, eleven leagues inland, at the date of our return. The letter had miscarried; and on landing, we found no animals had arrived, but we learned that they might be expected next morning.

Reconciling ourselves to the inevitable delay, we took a survey of the place—a squalid collection of cane and wattled reed huts, with but a single building, worthy of the name of a human habitation, going up for Mr. Swayne's use as a warehouse and stopping-place, but as yet only half finished. It nevertheless was a shelter, and into it our effects were removed.  The beach here has a gentle declivity, and is of the purest sand, the whole port so well protected that the heavy surf outside comes in softly, with a purr like that of a well-pleased kitten.  A little to the north of the town, behind a tall mass of disintegrating rock, through which there is a picturesque natural archway, the river Nepeña enters the bay.  Although the waves of the bay are not heavy, they are strong enough to sustain an unending conflict with the somewhat sluggish current of the stream, so as sometimes, in bad weather, to form a bar across the mouth, through which, a little later, the dammed-up water breaks, sweeping away the sandy barrier, and renewing the labor of the ocean.

Back of the port, for some miles, the country is a mere desert of sand-dunes, unrelieved except by the skulls and skeletons of men and animals, the former in such numbers as to justify the belief that the ancient occupants of the valley had a considerable fishing-station at the port.

We had been so busy during our stay at Truxillo that our forced inaction at Samanco was unbearable.  So we photographed the beach, the one squalid street of the town, and the picturesque natural archway in the rock.

As the afternoon wore away we became conscious that we had nothing to eat.  The coarse provisions on board the schooner, owing to her protracted passage from Callao, supplied only half-rations to the men, and there were no signs of food visible in any of the wretched huts of Samanco.  The *rancho* of the captain of the port was rather more pretentious than the rest, and had one or two close apartments, which our imaginations filled with edibles, and hence we made ourselves very agreeable to the captain; but he was reserved and distant, and evinced not the slightest curiosity to know whether we had dined or not.  It was finally arranged that C—— should intimate to the captain that while, for his own part, he could share rations with his men, or even fast altogether, it would be a great shame if the Commissioner of the United States should go hungry in Samanco.  He did not think it worth while to say that I was then ex-commissioner. The little ruse succeeded, and by dark the captain had prepared what, under the circumstances, seemed a sumptuous repast, which he served with his own hands. All the recompense he desired was that "His Excellency the Commissioner" should say a good word for him to the officials in Lima, which that functionary certainly agreed to do.

We slept on the bare floor of the unfinished house, but our rest was not so sweet and refreshing as to make us regret the coming of the dawn. We had coffee with the captain, and soon after the animals began to come in. They were all cargo-mules. And then began the task of mounting the workmen, two and two, on the backs of the obstinate and wayward brutes. Some were thrown off at once, others held on while their animals bolted through the village, only to be deposited head-foremost in the sands beyond. It was an amusing sight, but annoying enough to Mr. De C——, who was anxious to get his men at the hacienda without delay. After a single trial, most of them preferred to go on afoot, but some of the more persistent determined to ride.

It was ten o'clock before the last straggler was started on his way, and then came our trouble. Three rather sorry horses had come down for the use of the muleteers, who, however, gave them up to us for a consideration, and finally we also got off. We soon overtook the rear-guard of the men, struggling through the deep sand of the desert, and at about two leagues from the port struck the river, here considerably larger than at its mouth. A rude bridge of loose poles spanned it, over which our horses stumbled, in imminent danger of breaking their legs. Our path now lay along the base of the rocky hills which bound the valley on the north, the valley itself here spreading out several miles in width, and overgrown with scrubby trees. Two leagues farther brought us to a rough building, half farm-house, half tambo, where we got some cheese and *chicha*, and a little *charqui*, which we broiled for breakfast on the end of a stick.

Overlooking the establishment is a rocky, conical hill, on the slopes of which were evidences of ancient buildings, but so ruined that we could not make out their plan. From the summit, however, we descried two objects of interest: one, a single huge rock, standing on the very top of a high, bare hill, a conspicuous object from a great part of the valley; the other, a mass of ruins, covering a considerable area, in a dry, transverse valley entering that of the Nepeña from the north. Leaving our companions to pursue their journey, Mr. De C—— and myself rode first to this strange rock, so much resembling those scattered over the hill-tops of the British islands and Scandinavia. The people of the tambo told us that it was still regarded as *huaca*, and that there was a cavity at its summit, in which offerings were yet made to Huari, the god of strength.

By leading our horses part of the way, we managed to reach it. We found it to be an isolated mass, about sixteen feet in height and eight feet in diameter at its base, somewhat flaring towards the top, and standing upon some deeply embedded rocks of the same material with itself, that is, of the prevailing rock of the region. By leading one of the horses close up against it, Mr. De C—— managed to clamber to its top, but found no concavity or traces of recent sacrifice. From its position and peculiarity, it was, no doubt, once regarded as very sacred, and it is not improbable that the extensive building half a mile distant to which I have alluded, and from which this singular stone is in plain view, was in some way connected, as a temple or convent of priests, or both, with the worship paid to it by the ancient inhabitants.

This edifice which bears the name of Huacatambo, and of which the plan only can give an idea, has a greatest length of about four hundred and fifty by two hundred and fifty feet in greatest breadth, and consists of several open courts of various sizes, with platforms at their ends and sides, the former ascended by graded ways. The outer walls, which are of adobes, are in places twenty feet high; the interior ones are from eight to twelve and from three to six feet thick. All the courts marked *N* have niches, square or slightly oblong, in their walls. They do not resemble those in Inca edifices, which are narrower at the top than the bottom, and are taller. These niches are three feet above the floors, preserving the same elevation above the

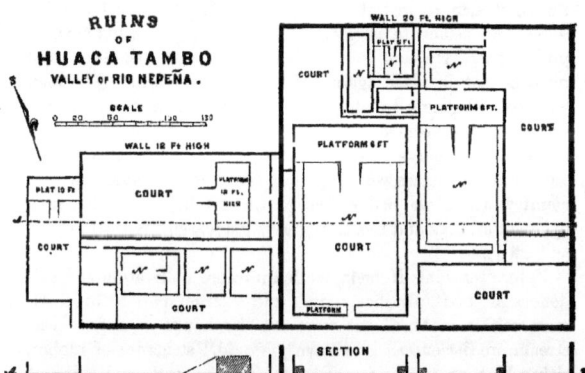

platforms also; they are twenty inches deep, twenty-four wide,
and twenty-eight high; their tops are covered by a kind of lintel of cane. Obviously no part of the structure was adapted for
residence except, perhaps, the small and somewhat intricate portion represented in the upper part of the plan. Unless cane
or other huts were built in the courts, of which there is no evidence, we must conclude that this was a temple, probably connected in some way, as already suggested, with the reverence
or worship of the extraordinary and conspicuous megalithic
monument on the hill in front.

Regaining the main road, which now led nearly through the
centre of the valley, over low and, in places, marshy ground, we
resumed our course. We had not gone far, when we met one
of the mules, with its pack-saddle turned under its belly, rushing down the road. We stopped it with difficulty, and, fastening its bridle to my crupper, went on, with apprehensions of
trouble ahead, which were soon realized; for, at a distance of
a mile or so, we came up to a very dilapidated group by the
roadside. One man, with his head bound up and covered with
blood, sat leaning against a tree; while another, lying on the
grass, and partly held down by his companions, was having

his right arm tugged at vigorously by Mr. P——, who added some pretensions to surgical knowledge to his other accomplishments. He said the man's shoulder was dislocated, and must be got in place again before swelling set in. The man writhed and groaned under the operation, which, however, was successfully performed. We sent the damaged men back to the tambo under charge of their friends, and hurried on as fast as our wretched horses would permit us, over the same low, flat country which we had struck at the tambo, but which now opened out, here and there, in grassy glades, covered with sheep and cattle.

Before reaching Nepeña, we found more cultivation and evidences of thrift, a richer region and a larger population. Almost within sight of the town, on the banks of a fine clear stream, we discovered a massive pyramidal structure of adobes, rising high above the forests, with lines of walls and ruins of buildings surrounding it. This we were told was called the Fortaleza de Tierra Firme.

Leaving it behind, for future examination, we rode on into the town of Nepeña, a rather large, straggling, tumble-down place, in which the principal traffic seemed to be *pisco*, a kind of brandy made from grapes of exquisite quality, which are found in great profusion in the neighboring vineyards. Riding into one of these vineyards, where we saw an old woman gathering the luscious clusters, she literally loaded us down with them for the small sum of a *medio* (six cents), and would have given us more, if we could have carried them away.

Proceeding through a cultivated country, rich in grapes, cotton, and sugar-cane, our course was again deflected to the desert belt of sand skirting the bare hills in that direction—deflected, not because that was a better way or a more direct one, but because the owner of the great hacienda of San Juan, lying in front, chose to build his fences across the highway, and block up.

Just before leaving the proper highway, we passed a rocky mass, covered and surrounded with ancient remains, called *Huaca de la Culebra*, or "Huaca of the Serpent," from a gigan-

PYRAMID OF TIERRA FIRME.

tic representation of that reptile cut in one of the faces of the eminence, and which commenced and terminated in a reservoir. It also bears a name equivalent to sun-serpent. I shall not enter into a discussion of the symbolical problem, or of the connection between sun-worship and serpent-worship, but shall confine myself to the single statement, that among the sun-worshippers *par excellence* of this continent the most frequent, almost the only, sculptured object we find is the serpent.

Warned by the approach of night, we pushed ahead over the stony desert which the owner of San Juan had compelled us to traverse: it seemed to have no end. Our horses stopped every few paces, thoroughly tired out, and we were at last compelled to dismount and lead them, often losing the trail in the darkness, and becoming involved among rocks and crags, until at last we determined to stop and wait for morning. Just then we caught glimpses of a light, which seemed to be approaching us over a gloomy spur of the mountains in front, and which

was borne by men sent from the San Jacinto estate to hunt us
up and bring us in.   They led three fine horses, well saddled,
on which we soon galloped to the hacienda, where Mr. De
C—— and the *mayordomo* had made the culinary and other arrangements proper for hungry and exhausted travellers, and
where we were warmly welcomed.

The hacienda, or estate, of San Jacinto was anciently one of
the largest and finest in the valley of Nepeña; but when purchased by Mr. Swayne, a few years before our visit, it had very
much run down.   It was deserted by the negro slaves soon after their emancipation; the dwellings had fallen out of repair;
the roof of the church connected with it had tumbled in; the
walls of the cemetery behind it were crumbling down; the *azequias* had broken their banks, and were dry or only half filled;
while chapparal and scrub, broom and acacias, had invaded the
irrigated grounds, and the desert had encroached on them as
the supply of water on the higher levels had diminished.   Its
extent will appear when I say it was nine miles long by not
less than three in average width, covering the entire valley
from one mountain range to the other.   Sugar had been the
principal product of the estate, but Mr. Swayne had supplanted
it in great part with cotton, and was bending every effort to increase its production.   Ginning-mills and cotton-presses had
been erected, and we found at the hacienda quite a colony of
English, German, and American engineers, mechanics, and over-
seers.   The long, narrow, half-ruined dwelling-house, large
enough to shelter a regiment, was in course of renovation; the
church was undergoing repairs; and quarters for the Chinese
and other workmen were going up, arranged and finished with
proper regard to health and comfort.   Men were mending
broken walls, restoring *azequias*, making bricks, and planting
the garden.   On every side was seen the movement and heard
the inspiriting sound of industry.   The household service was
prompt and efficient, and performed entirely by Chinese.

The buildings of the hacienda stand on the very northern
edge of the valley, so that their rear rests on the desert slope of
the mountain, while the *azequia*, which passes in front, waters

and fertilizes the grounds in that direction. The position is high, dry, and commanding. Around all is a heavy wall, almost like that of a mediæval fortress, entered by a lofty archway.

The arid, sandy, rocky slope behind is thickly covered with the ruins of ancient stone buildings, comparatively rude, it is true, with their little plazas and terraces, some perched on projecting shelves of rock, others half buried between great fallen masses, and all showing the shifts and straits of a redundant population, with whom life was little more than a prolonged struggle for bare existence. Still behind these poor and almost pitiful remains of the past, high up on the bleak mountainsides, may be seen parallel walls of stone, bending in and out with every curve of the declivities, and at first suggestive of lines of fortification. But a little reflection dispels this idea, and the notion that they were designed to check or prevent the fall of stones and rocks during earthquakes becomes the natural solution of their purposes. They are to be found almost everywhere, and especially in places where ancient populations existed at the foot of the mountains. I have observed as many as five or six concentric and approximately parallel lines on a single declivity. These walls are not high, seldom more than four or five feet, but stout and well suited to check whatever may be tumbled from above.

Our first day in San Jacinto was spent in looking over the estate, and in finding out what were the monuments for which the valley was most distinguished, and in arranging for a week's excursion among them. We found that they were numerous and interesting; indeed, from the corridor of our apartment we could discern a number of gigantic *huacas* rising above the shrubbery of the valley, and standing out boldly on the mountain slope beyond, while along the brow of a headland to our left we could trace the line of a great *azequia*, which, in the olden time, conducted to a vast water reservoir in a lateral valley among the hills, whence the water was distributed through the valley, during seasons of drought in the Sierra, and when the river ran low.

In a region like the coast of Peru, where possible rains and storms are eliminated from the calculations for irrigation, it seems to me agriculture, and especially the production of cotton and sugar, should be carried to the highest and most successful points ; for where the supply of water is constant and sufficient, and judiciously distributed at proper times, ample crops become certain. But, generally, the *hacendero* exercises little judgment or foresight in the matter, and leaves the direction of his estate to his *mayordomo*, whose notions of cultivation of the soil are purely traditional or empirical. A few, however, like Mr. Swayne, make irrigation a study, and with remarkable results. Not only was his yield of cotton large and uniform, and the quality of the staple good, but the irrigation was so well directed that each field was ripened in succession, at short intervals of time, thus enabling a large crop to be picked with a minimum number of hands, and distributing over weeks the work that is with us crowded into days. Yet the scarcity of labor, and especially skilled labor, is so great, and the area of cultivable land so small, that, except for manufacture on the spot, I doubt if cotton can be produced profitably in Peru.

My first day's excursion from the hacienda was up the valley to the town of Mora, situated near the foot of a spur of the Cordillera, which, starting from the great divide near Cajatambo, in latitude 10° 30' south, runs north and nearly parallel to it for two hundred miles, forming the rich and populous valley of Huaraz, drained by the Rio Santa. Passing the ginning-mill and cotton-press of the establishment, over a good cart-road lined with trees and shrubbery, and alive with doves of several varieties, we found ourselves, at the end of a league, obstructed by the rapid river, fretting and foaming over a rocky bed, forcing us to fall into a narrow and treacherous path that skirted the flank of the mountain. This soon led us up into the dry bed of an ancient *azequia*, partly excavated in the steep slope, and partly built up against it, which constituted the only roadway. This *azequia*, at the height of several hundred feet above the river, was that which had fed the reservoir I have already referred to.  Abandoned water - conduits throughout the country are often utilized in this way; sometimes, indeed, where there is not room or foothold enough for both road and existing *azequia*, the traveller has to ride for miles through the latter in water up to his saddle-girths.  I had not yet travelled among the Andes, and must confess to a certain nervousness in riding along the almost vertical face of the mountain, with the angry river beneath; and when we had scrambled down again into the valley, at a point where several copious springs gushed out from among the rocks in a stream sufficiently large to work a mill, I must confess that I experienced sensible relief.

Our way now led over a low plain, much cut up by errant channels of the river, and by beds of sand and stones, which the stream, after the melting snows of the interior swell its sources, spreads far and wide, leaving only room for occasional clumps of dwarfed and distorted trees.  Fording the river, here flowing through a broad and stony channel, our horses stumbling dangerously over the loose, water-worn stones, we finally reached higher ground, consisting of several distinct terraces, and covered with fruit - gardens and vineyards.  The latter were numerous and luxuriant, chiefly of the large white or Malaga grape, and the air, swarming with bees and other insects, was fragrant with their rich odor.  The gnarled trunks of the algarroba-trees supporting the vines were weighed down with great golden clusters, in a profusion amazing even to one who had seen the grape-gardens of France, Italy, and Spain in their glory.

One of the finest of these vineyards, El Padrejon, gives its name to an ancient stone work, El Palacio del Padrejon, on a terrace overlooking it, and of which I present a plan.  As will be seen, it consists of a series of enclosures, reached by a stone stairway, C, from the terrace below.  Partly within, and, to a certain extent, forming part of one of these enclosures (to the right in the plan), is another enclosure, surrounded by walls of cut stone, topped with adobes.  The ground within is raised about twelve feet, reached by a winding stairway of stone, through a gate-way, A.  A parapet wall of adobes runs around this platform, which supports three rectangular, truncated pyr-

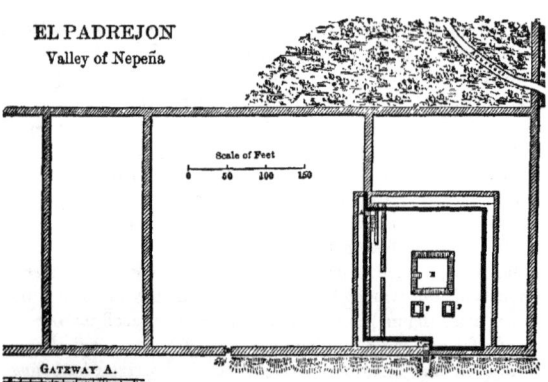

EL PADREJON
Valley of Nepeña

Scale of Feet

GATEWAY A.

amids or elevations of adobes, E and F; F, the first, reached by a stairway from the east. No part of the structure seems to have been roofed. The gate-way, or entrance, B, had been covered by a lintel of wrought stone, eleven feet long by two and a half wide, and two feet thick.

Two miles beyond this monument, still riding through vineyards, gardens, and cultivated fields, the mountains rising gloomily over our heads, we reached the flourishing little town of Mora, where we were hospitably received by the first *alcalde*, and plentifully regaled with fruits and grapes of several varieties. Here we heard of another great stone work, two and a half miles to north-east of the village, on a partially detached headland, dominating the pass of Pamparomas, leading to the valley of Huaraz. Like that just described, it consists of a series of vast open areas and terraces, surrounded by heavy walls of stone, with entrances which had been covered by massive lintels, from nine to twelve feet long, now fallen in the lapse of time or under the destroying hands of man. In many places, and especially at the point marked *b b*, the walls had been un-

dermined in search of concealed treasure, and the ground had
been deeply excavated here and there within the courts with
the same object.   The walls, in places yet twenty feet high, are
turned at their angles, and the entrances faced with large cut
stones.   The fallen lintel, *a a,* has the figure of a condor cut on

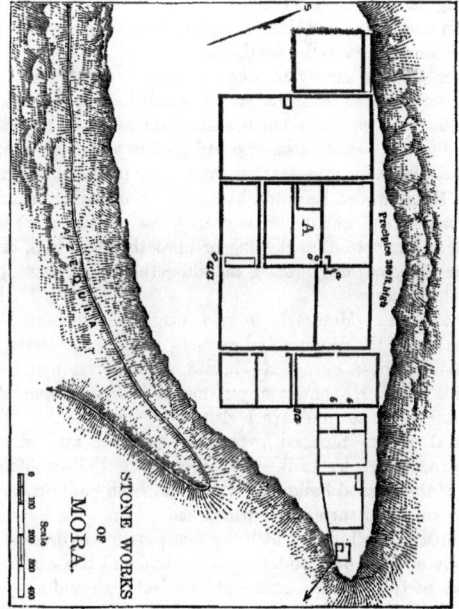

one of the surfaces in outline, but there were no other sculptures discovered.
    Two minor enclosures, contained in that marked **A,** are full
of fallen stones, and the whole surface of the eminence **around**
the grand structure itself is covered with the stone **foundations**

of buildings, indicating the former existence here of a considerable town.  The purposes of the work, which has a total length
of about sixteen hundred and fifty feet, are not obvious; but
from its commanding position, difficulty of access, and massiveness, it may be regarded as having been a kind of temple-for-
tress — a conclusion favored by the existence of a heavy wall
running off from the work and across the neck of land, connecting the eminence on which it is built with the steep and inaccessible mountains to the south-east.

After a rapid survey of this monument, which I shall call
the "Stone Works of Mora," we descended again into the valley, and struck off to the north-west, to the estate of Motocáche,
belonging to a Señor Salas, who had invited us to visit him, and
on whose lands we were assured were many interesting remains.
Señor Salas, whose hacienda had long been distinguished for
the quantity and quality of its grapes, was putting every available acre into cotton, neglecting or uprooting his vines, diverting *azequias*, building presses, and altogether displaying a great
amount of energy.

We arrived at Motocáche at an inauspicious moment.  That
very morning the ginning and pressing mills of the estate, just
finished, had been burned down, and our host was half frantic
over his loss.  He, however, put me in charge of one of his
men, under whose guidance I visited the monuments.  These
consisted of four terraced, pyramidal structures situated on as
many conical, rocky eminences, overlooking the smouldering
ruins of the burned buildings, which had been built, in part, of
the cut stones of the edifices which had crowned the pyramidal
structures.  The hill on which the first pyramid in order stands
is about one hundred and fifty feet high, and the work itself
consists of two terraces, each eighteen feet high and sixty feet
wide, reached by stairways at their south-east corners.  There
are traces of rectangular buildings on the upper platform.

On a lower natural eminence, to the north-east, is a square
work of three stages, supporting the walls of a single building,
much ruined.  In the masonry of the lowest southern platform
are embedded six great vases of pottery, eight feet deep by five

wide at their widest part (interior measurement), of the shape
here given, and in some respects
resembling those found at Cajamarquilla.    The material, well
burned and firm, is an inch thick.
Each vase has an opening large
enough to admit the body of
a man.    I cannot divine their
purposes, except as reservoirs of
grain or for water.    The remaining structures are similar

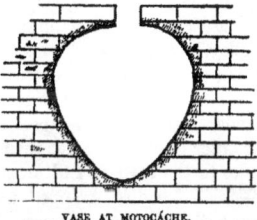

VASE AT MOTOCÁCHE.

to the two just described, but neither had the feature of the
vases.

The buildings of the hacienda were as spacious as those of
San Jacinto, but rather more out of repair.  Its church was
also dilapidated, and the area enclosing it had been converted
into a corral for cattle, which had tumbled down the cross that
once stood in its centre, and in various ways defiled the church
itself.

It was nearly dark when we left Motocáche, but by a different road than that by which we had reached there.  It led
through a rocky pass in the rocky ridge behind the estate into
a dry, desert valley nearly parallel to that of the river, and
which enters the latter not far from San Jacinto.  As we urged
our horses through the heavy sands, I saw rising on every hand,
through the exaggerating twilight, the spectral walls of extensive ruined structures, similar, so far as I could discern, to those
occupying a relative position at Huacatambo.  The señor informed me that there were traces of ancient *azequias* in this
now utterly arid valley, and evidences that it had once been
highly cultivated.  But I saw none, owing to the darkness, and
found no opportunity of investigating the point afterwards.

It was late when we reached the hacienda, and by the time
we had finished our well-relished supper, all except our immediate attendants were " wrapped in slumber."  I thought this
a good opportunity for committing a burglarious, not to say a
sacrilegious, act in the interest of science.  I have mentioned

the little cemetery of the estate behind the ruined church. Its walls were dilapidated and its gate prostrate; but it continued to be the burial-place of the poorer classes of this part of the valley, as it had been for a long period and in its palmy days the graveyard of the negroes, *cholos*, and other laborers of San Jacinto. These had crowded its narrow area, and the later intruders were forced to expose the bones of the former occupants in order to find room for their own. These were heaped up in piles in the corners, and attempts had been made to burn the desiccated bodies, wrapped in their poor ragged habiliments, but with only partial success. From among the skulls scattered about, I had already put aside a typical series, which I was anxious to transfer to the recesses of my trunk, without scandalizing the superstitious people of the estate, who, while themselves quite capable of digging up their dead friends, and irreverently tossing their remains aside in a corner, were yet jealous of having them meddled with by strangers. So C—— and myself, putting out our light, quietly stole away in the darkness, stepping lightly over the prostrate forms of the sleeping workmen in the corridor, and reached the cemetery without creating alarm. Returning with a skull under each arm, we had almost got to our rooms again, when a restless Hibernian, who had lighted his pipe in the interval of our absence, not only perceived us, but, by its fitful glow, our ghastly plunder also. "Holy Mother!" followed by a score of ejaculations, roused all the sleepers in real alarm. Before the story of the terrible apparition, with astonishing exaggerations, could be told, we had thrust our spoils under our sheets, and were closely covered up in our beds. We, of course, explained the incident to the *mayordomo* and Mr. De C——; but they were obliged to find another dormitory next night for the men, whose conviction that San Jacinto is haunted no doubt remains unshaken to this hour.

Returning from San Jacinto to Samanco, we resumed our voyage to Lima, stopping by the way to visit many of the ruins near the coast, some of which I shall briefly describe. Everywhere are the remains of towns, temples, pyramids, fortifications, and *azequias*, indicating the former existence of a dense and industrious population.  They fringe the hills and line the valleys.  Large stones are almost entirely wanting in their construction, their place being supplied by rubble - work, adobes, and compacted clay.

Among the most notable of these ruins are those of Calaveras, or Chancayillo, near the head of the valley of Casma.  They

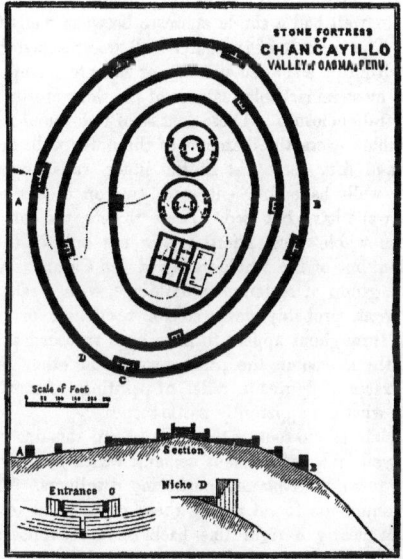

form an irregular oval, three-quarters of a mile in circuit, occupying the summit of a steep rocky hill.  The exterior line consists of three walls, the outer one twenty-four feet thick and twenty-six feet high, and is really five separate walls, built against and supporting each other.  The inner walls are somewhat less in height and thickness, but constructed on the same general plan.  The slope between these walls, and that be-

tween the outer one and the brow of the hill, was filled up to
a level. The outer wall had five gate-ways, or entrances, the
second four, the third and inner, only one. The gate-ways were
differently constructed. Those in the outer wall had two stairways, meeting and leading upwards, the lintels being of the
hard and durable algarroba wood. Those of the second wall
had a single stairway, and a protecting outwork. The entrance
of the inner wall had a single staircase between walls flanking
inwards. The summit of the outer wall was reached from the
corridor within by a sunken stairway of seventeen steps.

But the most remarkable features of the work are those within the central enclosure. These consist of two round towers, or
rather double towers, the diameter of the outer walls being one
hundred and fifty feet, that of the inner walls seventy feet.
The outer walls have four entrances, two on each side, while
the inner walls have but two. These towers, the loftiest portion of the whole work, afford a view not only of the entire
fortification, but of the whole valley of the Casma. Near the
towers is a group of rectangular buildings, with a raised esplanade in front, probably designed for residences or barracks.
The walls throughout appear to have been stuccoed and painted. On the stucco in the passage-ways and other protected
parts are traces of figures in relief, of paintings of men and animals, and what are apparently battle-scenes.

In the plain at the foot of this fortress are remains of works
of stone, well laid, but without cement, which seem to be the
ruins of a town, with plazas, courts, and dwellings. The most
curious monuments found among these ruins stand on a ridge
running in nearly a right line back of the supposed town.
They consist of thirteen solid structures, thirty-six feet by
twenty-five, and from ten to fourteen feet high. They are all
ascended by insunk stairs. These structures could not have
been designed for defensive purposes, but were probably used
as stands from which long processions could be observed filing
between them; or perhaps sacrifices may have been offered
upon them. The entire plain is now covered with sand, which
has in the course of time overspread it.

Another fortification near the coast is situated in the valley of the Nepeña—or, rather, overlooking it, at an elevation of twelve hundred feet—on the side of the mountains which encircle it. This, which is known as the Fortress of Quisque, differs from that at Calaveras in having the stones at the angles and entrances finely cut. The walls may be called cyclopean, in the same sense that some of those in South-eastern Europe

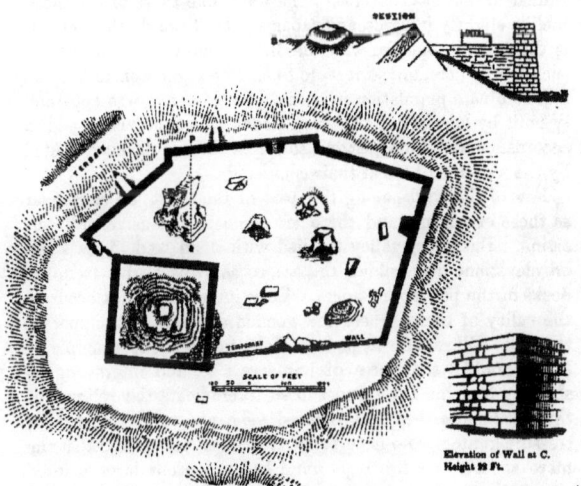

PLAN OF THE FORTRESS OF QUISQUE.

and Central America are thus designated. The horizontal blocks of large stones alternate with layers of thin stones adjusted to the irregular forms of the larger ones. The entrances are by interior walls and stairways, as at Calaveras. There are also salients. Some of the stones are very large, measuring nine feet in length, six feet six inches in breadth, and three feet in thickness. The work was evidently never finished. The levelling made by cutting away and filling up, elsewhere universal, is here only partial. Some of the walls surrounding square or irregularly shaped rocks, which were evidently held sacred, are only partly finished, as if the labor had been interrupted; and there are walls, evidently temporary, to be removed when the whole structure was finished.

The work appears to be of a composite character; partly Inca, as is shown by the cut stones, and partly of workmanship similar to that at Calaveras. The walls, like those of the Incas, incline slightly inwards, and taper a little towards the top. It is difficult to conceive why the Incas should have undertaken such works here, unless it were to shelter a garrison to keep an insubordinate population in check. The fortress was apparently built by laborers of the coast, under Inca supervision, and in accordance with Inca designs, so far as they could be executed by the workmen here at their command.

Few of the works along this part of the coast are as regular as those of Chimu, and there are none so extensive or interesting. But every valley is filled with them, and many stand on elevations overlooking the sea, so as to be visible from the decks of the passing steamers. Very interesting ones occur in the valley of Santa, where the wooden columns that supported the roofs still remain in place. Here, too, is a fine example of the pyramidal structures of immense size, and interesting, as showing how the Incas endeavored to eradicate the religion of the inhabitants they had reduced. Thanks to the energy of treasure-hunters, who have penetrated its sides, we find that the more ancient or original pyramid had numerous large painted chambers, was built in successive diminishing stages, ascended by zigzag stairways, and was stuccoed over and painted in bright colors. The conquerors filled up these chambers, and recast the edifice with a thick layer of adobes, made a straight ascent, and built on the top a stone temple dedicated to the sun.

Many, if not most, of the pyramids, or *huacas*, however, were originally solid, built up of successive vertical layers of bricks or compacted clay, around a central mass or core. The probable method by which the clay or earth was compacted is shown even at this day. The traces of the boxes or moulds, and of

the devices resorted to to keep the successive layers in position
till they had become sufficiently hardened to stand, can be easily detected by an observer.  The firmness and durability of
these walls, after standing for centuries, is the best proof of
the skill of the builders.

Not far from the ruins of Quisque is a series of terraces on
the north - west, and facing it are the remains of an ancient
stone-work and *huaca*, known as the ruins of Alpacote.  It is

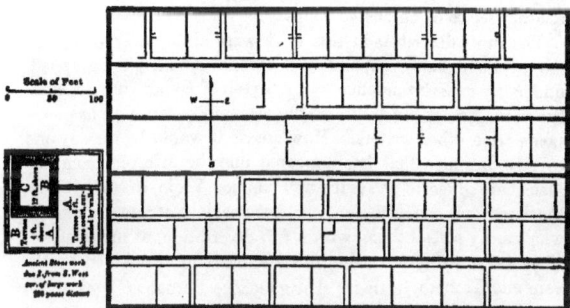

PLAN OF THE RUINS OF ALPACOTE.

a vast structure, of quadrangular form, 510 feet front by 313 in
depth.  The walls are built of ordinary rounded stones, from 4
to 10 inches in diameter, laid up with care in a cement or mortar of kneaded clay.  The outer walls are still from 4 to 10 feet
in height.  The interior is divided into six rows of apartments,
30 to 40 and 50 feet wide, fronting on corridors running the
length of the building, with occasional cross corridors opening
on these.  Some of the rooms in the centre of the building
were apparently of twice the usual size.  The inner walls are
nearly of the same height as the exterior, and are 4 or 5 feet
thick at the base.  The walls between the apartments are not
so thick or high as those running along the corridors.  About
500 yards westward of this quadrangular ruin rises a *huaca* of
adobes to the height of 100 feet.  Directly south of the south-

west corner of the large work, and 200 paces from it, is another ancient stone work, 110 feet square, enclosing within its walls two terraces separated by a wall, 3 feet above the plain, occupying one-half the square; the other containing two terraces, the smaller 4 feet above the first, and the larger, with its well-defined slope, rising 12 feet above this last.  On the hills called Cerro de Palenque, beyond the river, is a fortification, with a triple line of walls.  Near it is an ancient reservoir, with an *azequia* winding around the hill, and between it and the river another series of defensive walls.

The ruins described in this work were all actually visited by me, explored, surveyed, and, to a certain extent, photographed, under my superintendence or by myself.  Experience in similar work enables me to attest the accuracy.  Nothing has been taken from other writers.  How unsafe it would be for any one to rely on much that has appeared may be inferred from the plans here given of the ruins of Huánuco Viejo, as surveyed by the laborious and conscientious antiquary Antonio Raimondi, who kindly placed them, with a full description, at my disposal.  They vary utterly from the plan and elevation presented by Rivero and Tschudi, in their "Antigüedades Peruanas," and in the translation of their work by Dr. Hawkes:

"These ruins occur in the province of Huamalies, eighteen leagues west of the present town of Huánuco, and north-west of the great silver-mines of Cerro de Pasco.  They are 12,156 feet above the sea, and are of great extent, covering more than half a mile in length.  These remains consist of two distinct portions.  The smaller is a quadrangular *terre-plein*, A, with a parapet, generally called El Castillo; the other a much larger structure, somewhat irregular in outline, but filled with curious buildings of rectangular form, some of them entirely without doorways or entrance of any kind.  History is entirely silent as to the origin of these great monuments, which seem to have contained a palace, and show work of the same character as those at Cuzco.  A part of the works are of limestone, cut accurately, and laid without cement, but with the utmost nicety.  The remaining structures and the outer wall are of rough stones, ce-

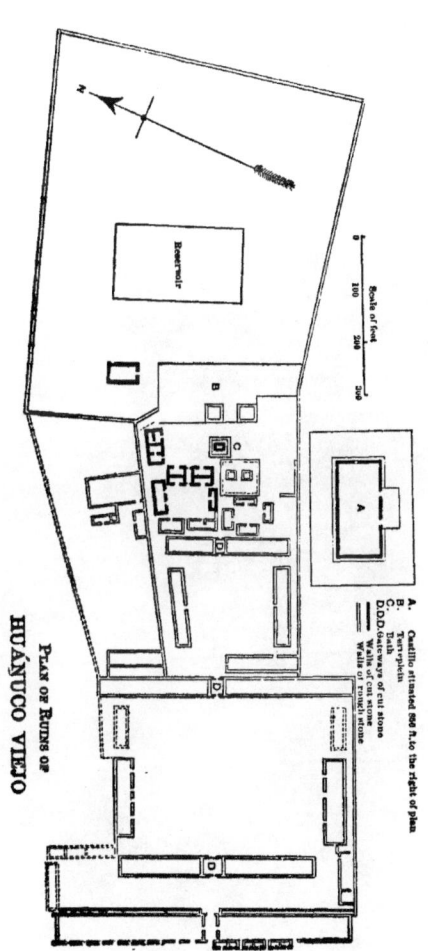

PLAN OF RUINS OF
HUÁNUCO VIEJO

A. Castillo situated 950 ft. to the right of plan
B. Terraplein
C. Baths
D.D.D. Gateways of cut stone
===== Walls of cut stone
===== Walls of rough stone

Scale of feet
0    100    200    300

Reservoir

A

B

N

mented. This wall has been broken down in most places; but where it is still standing it is 16 or 18 feet high, and 3 or 4 feet thick. Entering from the road leading from Huánuco, you come upon an open space, in the centre of which is an excavation known as the *estanque*, or reservoir, 250 feet long by 130 wide. The Indian tradition is, that in the time of the Incas wild animals were kept here; but as an *azequia* runs near it, the idea of a reservoir naturally suggests itself as the most plausible explanation. The only other work in this portion is a house of cut stone, still well preserved. Beyond this portion is a *terre-plein*, B, 20 feet high, on which are a number of houses, of cut and of rough stone, most of them divided into

THE CASTILLO OF HUÁNUCO VIEJO.

several apartments. Here is also a bath, C, of cut stone, the stone aqueduct still remaining to remove all doubt, in this case, as to its use.

"Leading from this portion of the works is a double doorway of cut stone, with a long, doorless, rectangular room on either side. Opposite, at a distance of 240 feet, is a similar structure, and still farther on is the outer door-way of the works. The perspective through this series of portals is the finest to be found in the ancient works of Peru. The doorways are narrower at the top than at the bottom, and each is crossed above by a slab 13 feet long. The stones forming the side are rectangular, slightly convex on the face, and very well cut, the joints being perfect. The first one is overgrown with

15

the luxuriant *Ephedra Andina.* Above the second portal and
at the sides are rudely cut animal figures, with a square niche
near each. The doorless rooms show no sign of steps for entrance, and no subterranean avenues to them have been discovered. At right angles to the lines of these structures were others, now greatly ruined. Beyond the second portal, and seventy
feet from it, is another structure, with its double portal, not,
however, of cut stone. Between these portals, on either side,
are door-ways leading into the rectangular rooms, which have
also various openings, from without, and six small chambers.
The Castillo is about 275 yards from the larger structure. It is
180 feet long by 80 wide, and has a fine cut-stone wall 13 feet
high. An inclined plane leads up to the *terre-plein,* which is entered by two portals, with animals rudely sculptured at the top.
The wall has a cornice of projecting stones, and forms a parapet
3½ or 4 feet high. A canal to drain this work is still discernible."

The system of irrigation of the ancient Peruvians is well
worthy of attention. Even in those parts where the rain falls
during six months in the year, they constructed immense irrigating canals. They not only economized every rood of ground
by building their towns and habitations in places unfit for cultivation, and buried their dead where they would not encumber
the arable soil, but they terraced the hill-sides and mountains
to heights of hundreds and thousands of feet, and led the waters of mountain springs and torrents downwards, until they
were lost in the valleys below. These *azequias,* as they are
now called, were often of considerable size and great length,
extending in some instances for hundreds of miles. I have
followed them for days together, and have seen them winding amidst the projections of hills, curving in and out as topography required; here sustained by high walls of masonry,
there cut into the living rock, and in some cases conducted in
tunnels through sharp spurs of the obstructing mountain. Occasionally they were carried over narrow valleys or depressions
in the ground, on embankments fifty or sixty feet high; but
generally they were deflected around opposing obstacles on an
easy and uniform descending grade.

It is on the desert Pacific coast of Peru, however, where no vegetation could otherwise exist, except on the immediate banks of the streams descending from the Cordillera, that we find the most extensive irrigating works of the ancient inhabitants.  They not only constructed dams at different elevations in the stream, with side weirs to deflect the water over the higher slopes of the valleys, but built enormous reservoirs high up among the mountains, as well as down nearer the sea, to retain the surplus water of the season when the snows melted, and the rains fell in the interior.  One of these reservoirs in the valley of the Nepeña is three-fourths of a mile long by more than half a mile broad, and consists of a massive dam of stone eighty feet thick at the base, carried across a gorge between two lofty, rocky hills.  It was supplied by two canals at different elevations; one starting fourteen miles up the valley of the Nepeña, and the other from living springs five miles distant.

The system was universal, for without irrigation nearly the whole country would be a desert, although not from any absolute defect of the soil; for the vast ash-heap, as it appears to be, has every element of fertility.  Only give it water, and it will produce luxuriant crops.  Occasional meteorological phenomena show that even in the most arid soils are the germs of plants, fruits, and flowers, which in some remote cycle, and under entirely different conditions of the globe, blushed and ripened there.  Several years ago, there fell on the desert intervening between Piura and Paita a series of heavy rains, a thing never before known within the memory of man.  Within a few days after the rains were over, the desert, forty miles broad and of indefinite length, was thickly covered with sprouting plants and grass, and shortly after was brilliant with flowers of kinds both known and unknown.  Gourds and water-melons sprung up in profusion and ripened, furnishing abundant food for the cattle of the neighboring valleys.

During the American civil war, when cotton commanded its highest price, the people of Peru rushed into its cultivation as if the price of the staple would never fall.  Cochineal and sugar plantations were ploughed up and put into cotton.

Lands augmented in value; and in the vicinity of Arica the people, unable to obtain lands capable of irrigation from the few running streams, sunk wells near the sea, where fresh water from the mountains, having leached through the sands to the sea-level, was found in abundance. It was raised by pumps, and distributed over what appeared to be an irreclaimable desert, on which were raised some of the finest cotton crops in the world. The Incas achieved a similar object in a very different way. They removed the sand from vast areas until they reached the requisite moisture, then put in guano from the islands, and thus formed sunken gardens of extraordinary richness. A large part of the vineyards around the city of Iça are planted in these old Indian excavations, which are only visible when one stands on their very edges.

## CHAPTER XIII.

### FROM LIMA TO TACNA.

Start for Explorations Southward.—Voyage along the Coast.—Islay the Port of
Arequipa.—Arequipa and the Earthquake of 1868.—Author's Experiences of
Earthquakes in Peru.—Arica the Port of Tacna.—The Earthquake at Arica.—
A Peruvian Railway.—Tacna.—Its Architecture and Trade.—The Alameda.—
The Bola de Oro.—Preparations for a Journey among the Andes.—Berrios, our
Muleteer.—On the Way.—About Mules.

I HAD already explored and surveyed the ancient remains existing in the vicinity of Lima, visited Grand Chimu, and those
ruins lying near the coast northward of the capital.  But the
great objects of investigation lay far to the south, and high up
among the Andes and Cordilleras.  The expedition to Chimu
had enlarged my ideas of the preparations necessary to be made;
but I had been informed that I should find at Tacna, where the
journey was properly to begin, everything needful.  In this, as
will be seen, I was sadly disappointed, and my outfit at last was
far less than it should have been.

For a hundred miles up the coast to the port of Pisco, the
shore preserves its aspect of a desert, with the single interruption of the small but productive valley of Cañete.  At Pisco
the stream of the same name comes down to the sea, through
a valley literally purple with the grape.  Off this valley lie the
high, rocky guano islands of the Chinchas.  Beyond Pisco the
bare, treeless, silent mountains come down close to the sea.  I
call them mountains, and so they appear to us; but they are
only the broken edges of a high desert plateau, undermined by
the ocean and corroded by the ceaseless south wind.  One or
two streams succeed in penetrating this high desert; but their
beds are mere cañons, or narrow gorges, with no intervals of
land, and affording no soil for cultivation.  The towns stand

back at the foot of the Cordillera, sixty or a hundred miles
from the coast, where the streams emerge from the snowy
mountains in a full and perennial volume before they are drunk
up by the thirsty sands. We touch at but one harbor, as we
sail along under the shadow of this desolate table-land—that of
Islay, the port of Arequipa, the second city of Peru until it
was partly destroyed by the earthquake of August 13th, 1868.

I did not have the time to visit Arequipa, and shall briefly
speak of it as it appeared just before and just after the earthquake. It stands ninety miles inland, on a plain or oasis, ele-

MEDANOS.

vated 7560 feet above the sea, watered by the river Chile, at
the foot of the symmetrical volcanic cone of Misti, 18,538 feet
above the sea. It was, until recently, only to be reached from
Islay by a ride over a sandy desert, in which there is not a drop
of water nor a single blade of grass to be seen.* The surface

* There is a railroad at present, built for the Peruvian Government by Henry
Meiggs, running from Mollendo, a short distance south of Islay, across the desert to
Arequipa, thence up the Andes to Puno; and it is proposed to continue the line to
Cuzco, a part of which is now graded. The reader will be able to judge somewhat
of the importance and value of such a road when he is informed that the natives prefer to walk from Puno to Arequipa, a distance of 218 miles, to riding in the train,
although the Government carries them free.

is broken only by crescent-shaped shifting sand-hills (*medanos*), and the skeletons of men, horses, and mules that had perished on the way. The Incas had here established a station for facilitating communication between Cuzco and the coast, and called it *Ari-quepai* ("Yes, rest here"), from which comes the name of the modern city, founded by Pizarro in 1540. Through it most of the commerce with the vast interior departments of Cuzco and Puno is carried on. Probably no other town in the

GRAND PLAZA AND MARKET-PLACE OF AREQUIPA.

interior of South America was so well built as this before the earthquake; the houses, massive in structure, with vaulted roofs, although seldom more than one story high, were constructed of hard volcanic stone, a style of architecture adopted after the earthquake of 1821, which laid most of the city in ruins, as a security against similar catastrophes. The cathedral, now greatly damaged, was a vast and imposing structure, of a *bizarre* style of architecture: the inhabitants fancied it one of the finest in the world. It contained a great bell, cast in the city itself, said to be larger than that of St. Paul's in London.  Its population is about fifty thousand, many of whom are Indians.  In point of science and art it is the foremost city of Peru.  Most of the men distinguished in modern Peruvian history, whether in literature, art, commerce, war, or politics, belong to Arequipa.  It has suffered much during the various political struggles of the country, and in December, 1867, was bombarded for three days by President Prado.

Notwithstanding its inland situation, Arequipa has been visited by earthquakes nearly as often as Lima itself.  Among the most notable on record are those of January 2d, 1582; February 18th, 1600; November 23d, 1604; December 6th, 1609; one in 1613; May 20th, 1666; April 23d, 1668; October 21st, 1687; August 22d, 1715; May 13th, 1784; one in 1812; July 10th, 1821; June 3d, 1825; October 9th, 1831; and that of August 13th, 1868.  The most destructive of these were those of 1582, 1821, and 1868.  An eye-witness, writing three days after this last earthquake, thus describes it:

"At about four minutes past 5 P.M. of Thursday, the 13th, a slight movement of the earth was noticeable by persons who chanced to be seated; there was no rumbling.  In about eight to ten seconds more the movement became strong enough for persons not seated to notice.  This movement gradually increased in strength until, after about thirty seconds, pieces of timber began to fall from the houses.  In about a minute all were satisfied that a great earthquake was at hand.  Then began a terrible rumbling, similar to the noise of an avalanche.  Every one ran to the open spaces.  The earth shook, and every structure swayed to and fro from north to south.  In about three minutes it was almost impossible to keep one's feet.  The strongest buildings began to cast off stones, bricks, pieces of wood, etc., and the weakest began to fall, almost all of them level with the ground.  In about five minutes from the first movement the whole city was enveloped in clouds of dust and darkness, and resounded with the crash of falling buildings.  There is not one house left standing in Arequipa.  The only church tower left is that of Santa Catalina; but it, like the cathe-

AREQUIPA AND THE VOLCANO OF MISTI.

dral, will have to be pulled down.  Santo Domingo Church is levelled to the ground.  The Portal de Flores is in ruins, as well as all the surrounding blocks.

"We are now living in a tent on the river-bank.  No one dares go to town, as the shocks still continue to bring down what little is left standing.  They occur at intervals of half an hour each.  This evening some of the shocks have been very violent.  So far there have been about seventy-six shocks. Everything is confusion, and the cries and lamentations are heart-rending.  Thus the work of the Arequipeños for three hundred years has been destroyed in a few minutes; it will take an age to do the same work over.  The débris of the Jesuits' church was hurled to a distance of one hundred yards.

"The picture presented by our desolate city is sad indeed. Mount Misti is vomiting lava, clouds of smoke, and quantities of mud, and darkness hides its side from our view.  We hear the constant noise of falling rocks and earth, and the river is impassable, owing to its black color and sulphurous odor."

As already said, Arequipa stands at the foot of the great volcano Misti,* which had not been in eruption during the historical period, but which now burst into activity.  At the time of the eruption, those who were outside the city saw huge pieces of rock split off from it, and, together with heavy avalanches of snow and ice, tumble down to the bottom, making a fearful noise.  The river, fed by the snows of the mountain, increased at least one-third inside of six hours.  Indeed, the rise in the water was so great and rapid as to inundate several of the towns in the valley of Arequipa, sweeping away the ruins the earthquake had made, together with the dead and wounded.

The prefect of the city reported officially: "All the edifices have been thrown to the ground, and the few walls that remain are so racked that they must be demolished."  Another report

---

* The Misti was ascended for the first time in September, 1873, by Dr. Isaac T. Coates, of Chester, Pennsylvania, who from measurement found its height to be 18,538 feet.  He saw no signs of recent eruption.  His account of the ascension is printel in No. VIII. Bulletin of the American Geographical Society, 1874.

states that between four and five thousand buildings, among them the cathedral and twenty-one other churches, were destroyed. The prisoners in the jails, and the patients in the hospital, unable to escape, were crushed among the ruins. Besides these, about three hundred persons were killed outright, and more than one thousand severely injured. Thanks to the warning given by the premonitory shocks, the strength of the buildings, and their small height, the ruins did not cover the whole width of the streets when the walls fell; otherwise the casualties must have been far more numerous.*

Islay is merely a collection of huts perched on a corroded cliff, full of dark caverns, in which are to be discerned only the flash of the ocean spray, or the gleam of the white wings of the sea-birds, which, with multitudes of howling seals, give all there is of life to the shores and islands of Peru.

The great table-land, along which we sail so closely that its

---

* I myself have had three several experiences of considerable earthquakes on the coast of Peru, not including numerous slight tremors of the ground, hardly to be distinguished from the vibrations occasioned by passing carriages. The first of these was preceded by a slight rumbling sound, which continued during the movement. This shock was felt along the whole coast from Arica northward, doing little damage, however, except at the city of Truxillo. The second occurred while I was making a survey of the ruins of Amacavilca, nine miles south of Lima. I had just exposed a plate in my photographic camera, and was timing the exposure, when I heard a noise from the southward, something like that of a wave striking the shore. I recognized the sound as that of an earthquake, and noted the interval between its first reaching my ear and the commencement of the tremor of the earth where I stood. It was just five seconds, a fact of some scientific value, as indicating the velocity with which earthquake shocks are propagated. The movement was sufficiently great to ruin my photographic negative, which, however, I preserved, as probably the first one ever produced during an earthquake. My third experience was when I was descending to the coast from the lofty table-lands of Huancavelica. We were entering upon the desert extending from the mountains to the sea, when the ominous sound was heard coming from the south. My mule pricked up her ears, and stopped suddenly in extreme terror. I dismounted, and took out my watch. Not counting the time taken for this, it was ten seconds before the movement was felt under our feet. In looking southward, I could distinctly see the vibrations of the mountains in that direction for four seconds before those nearest us began to tremble. Assuming that the trembling of the mountains could be detected by the naked eye at a distance of two miles, we have a means of determining approximately the velocity of the movement of this shock as about thirty miles a minute.

PORT OF ISLAY.

rugged edges hide from view the monarch mountains beyond, extends all the way to Arica, the last port but one in Peru, and the chief one in its southern department of Moquegua, whence we shall start inland on our rough mountain journey.

TAMBO OF LA JOYA, PAMPA OF ISLAY.

It is gray morning when our steamer slacks up before the port, and moves slowly to her buoy in the open roadstead. To the right, projecting boldly through the thin mist, half made up of spray from the surf that beats on the rocky shore, and which exaggerates its proportions, we discern the great *Morro*, or headland, of Arica. Its face is frayed, seamed, and corroded, and is full of caves, and dark, inaccessible grottos which our glasses show us to be the roosts and refuges of countless water-fowl. To the left of the headland there is a low line of verdure, a cluster of modern-built houses, a gayly painted church, and a mole—the latter giving us comforting assurance that here

CHART OF THE HARBOR OF ARICA.

we are not to be obliged to perform the difficult feat of landing on the shoulders of a stalwart *cholo*, staggering over rolling stones through a thundering surf. This is San Marcos de Arica, the port of Tacna, forty miles distant inland, in the direction of the snowy Cordillera that lies, in a long line, crowned with frosted silver, high up beyond a great and ominous range of umber-colored and treeless mountains. A railway connects Arica with Tacna.

We look with unspeakable interest towards the great mountain billows before us, each succeeding one higher and more mysterious, and wonder what marvels of rock and stream and what remains of ancient human greatness they conceal, and what will be our own sensations when, after days of travel and toil, and nights of cold and exposure, we shall be swallowed up

THE PORT AND MORRO OF ARICA.

in their unknown recesses.  In one who had read and written of Peru and its wise and powerful Inca rulers, and with whom a journey to the centres of its ancient civilization had been a dream of life, this standing at the portal of the land, and this realization of a wish which had before scarcely assumed more than the outlines of a hope, inspired a feeling of awe and responsibility rather than of eagerness or romance.

Sweeping back from the Morro and behind the town, forming a kind of amphitheatre, is a great windrow of yellow sand, unrelieved by shrub or blade of grass.  This ridge is a huge cemetery of the ancient inhabitants, and is crowded with the dried-up bodies of those who patiently and skilfully cultivated the narrow valley on the borders of which they are buried, or fished from balsas in front of the Morro.

Here, as the workmen were digging away the sands to fill up the little pier and to open a track for the railway, they found, not alone the poor fisherman wrapped in his own net, and the humble laborer enveloped in braided rushes and stained fabric of cotton, but the more pretentious personage of his day, now equally grim and ghastly, wrapped in a shroud of beaten gold, which rough hands rudely tore away from his dry and crumbling bones, and left them to dissolve in the keen sea air.

At Arica, also, the earthquake of 1868 was severely felt.  The United States war-steamer *Wateree* was in the port, and was stranded high on the beach.  I abridge the account given by an officer of this vessel of the earthquake at Arica:

"At about twenty minutes past five o'clock, immense clouds of dust were seen at a distance of some ten miles south of Arica.  The volume of clouded dust came nearer and nearer, and it was observed from the deck of the vessel that the peaks of mountains in the chain of the Cordilleras began to wave to and fro like reeds in a storm.  A few minutes after, it was observed that from mountains nearer to Arica whole piles of rock rent themselves loose, and large mounds of earth and stone rolled down the sides.  Very soon it was noticed that the whole earth was shaking, and that an earthquake was in progress.  When the convulsion reached the Morro, it also began to move.

16

Pieces of from ten to twenty-five tons in weight began to move from their base and fall, altering the whole front view of that part of the coast. At the same moment the town commenced to crumble into ruins. The noise, the rumbling like the echoes of thunder, the explosive sounds, like that of firing a heavy battery, were terrific and deafening; and the whole soil of the country, as far as it could be seen, was moving, first like a wave, in the direction from south to north; then it trembled, and at last it shook heavily, throwing into a heap of ruins two-thirds of all the houses of Arica. Shock after shock followed. In several places openings were becoming visible in the ground, and sulphurous vapor issued from them. At this juncture a crowd of people flocked to the mole, seeking boats to take refuge on the vessels in the harbor. As yet the shipping in the harbor felt not the least commotion from the disturbances on land. After the first shock there was a rest. The *Wateree* and the *Fredonia* sent their surgeons ashore to assist the wounded. Between fifty and sixty of the people of the town had reached the mole by this time to take to the boats. But the surgeons had hardly landed, and but few of the others had entered the boats, when the sea quietly receded from the shore, leaving the boats high and dry on the beach. The water had not receded farther than the distance of extremely low tide, when all at once, on the whole levee of the harbor, it commenced to rise. It appeared at first as if the ground of the shore was sinking; but the mole being carried away, the people on the mole were seen floating. The water rose till it reached a height of thirty-four feet above high-water-mark, and overflowed the town, and rushed through the streets, and threw down what the earthquake had left. And all this rise and overflow of the waters took only about five minutes. The water rushed back into the ocean more suddenly than it had advanced upon the land. This awful spectacle of destruction by the receding flood had hardly been realized when the sea rose again, and now the vessels in port began dragging. The water rose to the same height as before, and on rushing back it brought not only the débris of a ruined city with it, but even a locomotive and tender and a train of four cars were seen carried away by the fearful force of the waves. During this advance of the sea inland, another terrific shock, lasting about eight minutes, was felt. At this time all around the city the dust formed into clouds, and, obscuring the sky, made things on land quite invisible. It was then that the thundering approach of a heavy sea-wave was noticed, and a minute afterwards a seawall of perpendicular height to the extent of from forty-two to forty-five feet, capped with a fringe of bright, glistening foam, swept over the land, stranding far inshore the United States steamer *Wateree*, the *America*, a Peruvian frigate, and the *Chañarcillo*, an English merchant-vessel."

Tacna—properly San Pedro de Tacna—stands about 2000 feet higher than Arica; and as the ascent is accomplished in forty miles, the grade of the railway is in places very heavy, so that the locomotive which carries one up travels slowly and painfully. It took us four hours to accomplish the ascent—four hours over a waste of sand, loose or indurated, without a semblance of life or verdure, except at the half-way house or station, El Hospicio, where there is a subterranean flow of water, and where a few scrubby bushes attest its existence deep in the sands.

The entrance into the valley of Tacna is marked by one of those sudden transitions from desert waste to luxuriance of vegetation which so greatly impress the traveller in Peru. The *azequias* are always carried as high up on the borders of the valleys as possible, and the water is distributed below, so that they constitute an abrupt and strongly marked boundary between the barren sands and cultivated fields, which are as sharply defined as if clipped out with a shears from a sheet of green paper.

We alighted from the train in a very respectable depot, with thrifty piles of merchandise on all sides, just delivered or awaiting transportation, and I handed over the "checks" for my baggage to a man with a cart, who undertook to deliver it at the Bola de Oro, the hostelry whither I had been directed. There was quite a gathering around the depot and in the adjacent streets, inasmuch as the day had been set apart for patriotic purposes—that is to say, for listening to denunciations of the Spaniards, and for the glorification of Bolivar. A squad of soldiers were at the depot, quite drunk with enthusiasm and *cañaso*, and looked as though they would be a useful riddance to Tacna, and could depart amidst ardent aspirations from the entire community that they might all realize the soldier's loftiest ambition, and "die in the arms of victory!"

Tacna has little of the prevailing Oriental aspect of Spanish-American towns. Stone and adobe scarcely enter into the construction of its buildings, which are mostly of wood brought from Chili, from California, or around the Horn, and are run up after the fashion prevalent in our mushroom Western cities. Generally of but one story, the houses of Tacna recall the description of Albany by the excellent old geographer Jedediah Morse: "A city of one thousand houses and ten thousand inhabitants, all standing with their gable-ends to the street." The population of Tacna, however, is about 15,000. The long, low, monotonous lines of gables, with no attempt at architectural relief, are poor substitutes for the heavy arched door-ways, Moorish balconies, and jalousies of the older cities, and which, however neglected and tumble-down, convey an impression of strength and respectability. Nor is Tacna exceptional in its architecture alone. It has two theatres, and but one church.

The public buildings are as mean as are the private houses. The theatres were closed during my visit, and I had no opportunity of judging of their accommodation or effect, which is reported to be very creditable. Outside they are simply hideous, barn-like structures, resembling rusty wooden breweries or tan-houses. A rather pretentious stone church, the Parroquia, was commenced in the principal plaza of the town many years ago, but before it could be finished it was so racked by earthquakes that all work on it was abandoned. The stone is a light-colored trachyte, found in the neighborhood, and well adapted for building purposes.

The market-place is a hollow square, surrounded by a colonnade, and entered by archways from parallel streets. The oc-

cupants squat on the stones, and display their wares before
them in shallow baskets, or on cloths long innocent of washing.
Considering the size of the town, the stock in trade is small,
and painfully suggestive of short rations.    Tacna is, however,
a considerable mart.

The principal evidence of public spirit is the Alameda, lying
quite to one side of the town—a long and rather narrow area,
planted with willows, with a broad *azequia* paved with stones in
the middle, and crossed at intervals by stone bridges, modeled
after those pictured in Chinese paintings, each surmounted by
a coarse marble allegorical statue.    There are also stone seats
here and there for visitors; but, in common with all the alame-
das, or public walks, of the cities of Peru, that of Tacna is the
one place above all others deserted.    A very fine view is commanded from here of the brown, bare mountains of Pachia, with

THE ALAMEDA OF TACNA.

the snowy peaks of Tacora and Chipicani rising brightly beyond.

My hotel, the Bola de Oro, was one of the quaintest of caravansaries. The entrance was through the shop of the proprietor, surrounded by shelves gay with bottles of fanciful fashion and labelling, some containing wines and liqueurs, and others comfits and preserves. Every vacant space of wall was covered with chromo-lithographs of the latest French victories. The hot sunset colors of Solferino and gorgeous tints of Magenta were sufficient to start a perspiration on the coldest day. And then the little round tables sacred to *eau sucré*, coffee, and dominos! Everything had a French look, not omitting the comfortable-looking *Madame la Propriétaire*, who sat at her sewing behind the counter, and dispensed smiles, bonbons, bon-mots, absinthe, and cigars with equal alacrity and grace. Beyond the shop was, of course, the inevitable *billard*, opening on a court set round closely with little wooden buildings, resembling on a slightly exaggerated scale those sold in the toy-shops, and all presenting their gables to the court. Each gable was penetrated by a door, and over the door was a window hung on a pivot, opened and shut by a cord inside, which afforded light and air to the interior—a single room, with a cot, a small table, a smaller wash-stand, a single chair, and a tall candle. From the farther end of the court rises a perpetual fragrance of onions; and there is a gentle and constant sizzling of frying meats, appetizing enough, but suffering some detraction from the circumstance that the way to the closets is through the kitchen, dirty as French kitchens always are, and which are clean only by comparison with the Spanish.

It might be supposed that ample facilities would exist in Tacna for the journey inland, and that no difficulty would be encountered in obtaining the supplies and equipments necessary for it. I was assured in Lima that "everything" could be had in Tacna; but, fortunately, I was too old a traveller to neglect making some provision for the trip. Fortunately, I say, for it was with the greatest difficulty I could obtain the cooking utensils, pans, kettles, coffee-pots, and other requisites for travel in an uninhabited region, or among a people ignorant of the appliances of civilization.

After long search I found a broken *cafetera*, in which alcohol could be used for boiling coffee. This I repaired with my own hands, after the job had been given up by the clumsy native tinman as impossible; and it proved to be my best friend on many an occasion when neither wood nor other material for lighting a fire or heating water was to be found, sometimes for days together. The hammock—that supremest device for human rest, repose, and enjoyment, afternoon siesta or midnight slumber, the solace and reliance of the traveller in Central America and Mexico, in which he may suspend himself in happy security above the filth of his dormitory, and out of the reach of its vermin — is useless among the sierras of Peru. There are no trees between which to swing it in the uninhabited regions, and the mud and stone huts of the Indians and *lomeros*, besides being generally too low, afford no projections to which it may be fastened. Unless, therefore, the traveller has made up his mind to rough it in roughest fashion, wrapped only in his blanket at night, or to take the risk of finding now and then a filthy sheep-skin for his couch, he must literally carry his bed with him — a necessity imposed also by the severe cold of the interior. So I had a mattress made in Tacna, light and easily handled, covered with leather on the under side to prevent the absorption of damp from the ground, and as a protection, when rolled up and on the mule's back, against the rain, which saved me, no doubt, from indefinite rheumatism, not to say something worse. It took five days to get my mattress made. I had to buy the wool in one place, the ticking in another, the leather elsewhere, and, when I had collected all these, the dusky individual who condescended to put them together demanded, in a tone equally reproachful and imperious, "But where are the needles and the thread?" I acknowledged my oversight, apologized in fact, and proceeded to obtain them. I only wonder now that the mattress-maker of Tacna allowed me to keep on my hat in his august presence.

There is but one mode of reaching the interior from Tacna,

and that is on mule-back.   But to obtain mules is both difficult
and expensive.   I had been recommended to an arriero named
Berrios, who had had the honor of conducting the American
minister to Bolivia over the Cordillera, and who had also accompanied Mr. Forbes in his geological explorations, and in his
ineffectual attempt to reach the as yet untrodden summit of
Tacora.   But Berrios looked yellow and ill, and complained
that two nights among the snows of Tacora had nearly finished
him.   Besides, his mules had not had time to recover from the
fatigues of their last trip over the mountains two months before.   Furthermore, they were at pasture in the valley of Lluta,
fourteen leagues distant, beyond the desert.   Finally, however,
after much diplomatizing and a great concentration of mercantile influence, to say nothing of the offer of about double the
usual rate of hire, Berrios undertook to supply me with mules,
and to accompany me himself, aided by two *mozos*, all the way
to Puno.

After the day had been fixed two or three times, and I had
as often been disappointed, the echoes of the *patio* of the Bola
de Oro were startled one afternoon by the clatter of hoofs, the
jingling of spurs, and a general rush of a dozen mules, which
hustled in before the cracking whips of Berrios and his *mozos*.
We were to have started at daylight, and slept at Palca, the last
*aldea*, or village, on the road inland, before finally plunging
among the mountains and entering on the Despoblado.   But
now we could get no farther than Pachia, three leagues distant.
Having been waiting, booted and spurred, since dawn, I was
not in the best of humor; and my ruffled temper was by no
means soothed on discovering two mules already loaded with
baggage not my own, and learning that it belonged to a party of three Bolivians, who had arranged with Berrios for the
mountain trip subsequently to his engagement with me.   It
was to suit their convenience that I had been detained in Tacna; and they had, moreover, already gone on to Pachia, where
they would, no doubt, monopolize the limited accommodations
of the little tambo at that place.

I confess to a decided liking for mules—not less for their patience, sure-footedness, and faithful service, than for their little wicked ways. The cargo-mule thinks that every moment his load can be evaded is an hour of happiness gained; and although, when it is once on his back, he will walk off resigned, if not contented, he will resort to every expedient his thick head is capable of devising to avoid receiving it. It was amusing to see Berrios and his *mozos* chase around the *patio* after a mule that would dodge in and out among its fellows until cornered, and then lay back its ears, put its nose to the ground, and kick out with vicious vehemence, until the lasso was once around its neck, when it would surrender itself tamely, and receive its load with an expression of face as gentle and demure as if it rejoiced in its lot, and had years before repented of all mulishness. There was one, however, the largest and most powerful of the lot, who held out to the last; and nothing could be done with him until a poncho was thrown over his head and tied under his throat, leaving only his nose uncovered. But the spite and malice that quivered in the withdrawn upper-lip, and glanced from his broad, yellow teeth, and nestled in every wrinkle, when the girths were tightened by two men surging on each side, with one foot braced against his ribs, were past description. He became quiet enough, however, long before we got to Puno, and as humble as the rest.

## CHAPTER XIV.

### OVER THE CORDILLERA TO TIAHUANACO.

A TRAVELLER accoutred for a journey among the Andes is a picturesque, if not an imposing, personage.   Heavily clothed and booted; a felt hat with a broad brim, capable of being bound down over his ears, for the double purpose of warmth and security against being blown away by the currents of wind that suck through narrow gorges or sweep over unsheltered heights with hurricane force; his neck wound round with a gayly colored *bufanda;* a thick, native-made poncho of vicuña or llama wool over his shoulders, and falling to his knees; a serviceable knife stuck in his boot-leg; spurs that look like cart-wheels minus their perimeters, and not much smaller, which jangle as he treads and tinkle as he rides; a rifle hanging at the bow of his saddle; and a well-filled *alforja* fastened behind him—these go to make up the equipment of the advent-

urer among the mountains; that is to say, if he have what the
Spaniards call *sabiduria*, and we call "gumption." It only requires the addition of a large pair of green goggles, to protect
the eyes from the glare of sun and snow, to make one's best
friend irrecognizable.

EQUIPPED FOR THE CORDILLERA.

The road from Tacna to Pachia lies straight across the sandy
desert, into which the traveller enters soon after leaving the
town, while the narrow, cultivable valley deflects in a curve to
the right. The distance is ten miles, and the rise 1630 feet,
but scarcely perceptible to the eye, probably from being regular
and constant. It was dark when we reached the tambo, a collection of mere huts, but for default of a better place a resort
of the *jeunesse* of Tacna, who gallop out here to eat *dulces*,
drink *chicha*, fight cocks, and in other modes gratify the universal Spanish passion for play.

As I had anticipated, the intruding Bolivians were already on the spot, and had taken possession of the mud-banks that ran around the solitary apartment of the tambo, and which, throughout the interior, are the sole substitutes for bedsteads. Some young foreigners, however, out for a holiday, who had a kind of club-house or club-hut close by the tambo, invited me to share it and their supper with them, which I was glad to do ; and I was especially pleased to observe my Bolivians still hungry after their meal of sloppy *chupe*, sneaking around the door of our hut, and glancing with longing eyes at our table, on which were heaped the edibles of three continents.

And as *chupe* is the eternal and almost always the sole dish obtainable in the interior of Peru and in Bolivia, I may as well dispose of it at once. It may be described as a kind of watery stew, which on the coast and in the principal towns is made up of vegetables and fragments of different kinds of meat and fish, boiled together and seasoned with salt and *aji*, or peppers, and is sometimes rather savory, or at least eatable. As we go into the interior, it decreases in richness as the materials for making it become fewer and tougher, until it consists of only a few square pieces of lean mutton and some small, hard, bitter, water-soaked potatoes, floating about in a basin of tepid water, which at most has simmered a little over a smouldering fire of the dung of the llama or cow, from the smoke of which it has absorbed its predominant flavor. A little brown salt from the native salt-quarries, in which it is mixed with a variety of other and astringent ingredients, constitutes the only seasoning. One wonders how life can be kept up in these frigid regions on such thin and unsubstantial fare. Unhappy is the traveller here who has not made provision for the frequent occasions when nothing but the most diluted *chupe* can be obtained, and for the not infrequent occasions when not even this poor substitute for food can be procured. Detesting it in its best form, I literally loathed it in its degeneracy, and only ate it with inexpressible stomachic protests.

We left Pachia at three o'clock in the morning. The air was chill, and we already experienced the usefulness of our thick ponchos. Our cavalcade was strung out in a long line, and as we followed each other silently over the echoless sand, we might have been mistaken for a ghostly procession. When day dawned, we found ourselves already hemmed in by the steep slopes of the Quebrada de la Angostura, through which descends, with a rapid current and many a leap and bound, one of the brawling affluents of the stream that fructifies the oasis of Tacna. A few dwarf molle trees, which somewhat resemble our willows, but which bear a berry in taste much like that of our red cedar, found scant foothold here and there along the stream, far below our narrow path, which was little more than a shelf worn in the abrupt hill-side by the tread of countless mules and llamas. The ascent was steep, and the gorge narrow and barren for two leagues, when we came to a point where the *quebrada* widens out into something like a valley. Just before entering this valley, at the right of the mule-path, we came upon a rock or boulder covered with figures, which Berrios pointed out to me as a rare relic of antiquity. Roughly pecked in the rock, barely penetrating its ferruginous crust, I observed a great number of circles and semicircles, some angular figures, and rude representations of llamas, mules, and horses. The latter appeared no fresher or later than the former, and all looked as if they might have been worked in the stone yesterday by the same idle and unskilful hand.

In the narrow valley which now takes the name of the Quebrada de Palca, there were many desperate attempts at cultivation, particularly of lucern, always in great demand as fodder for the mules entering the Despoblado, and Berrios bought here a little and there a little — there was not much in all — which was packed on the sumpter-horse and the lightly laden mules, and behind the *albardas* of the *mozos*. It was a wise prevision of Berrios, as we found out afterwards.

At 11 o'clock A.M. we came in sight of Palca, a poor but picturesque little *caserio*, or village, with a small white church gleaming out against the dull brown of the bare mountain side. The village is five leagues from Pachia, and 9700 feet above the sea. There were some scant fields of maize and lucern around it, and the lower slopes of the mountains were thinly sprinkled with stems of the columnar cactus. Here and there in the valley, standing on little natural knolls or artificial eminences, we saw a number of ancient burial towers, which afterwards became familiar to us under the name of chulpas. They are rectangular in plan, from 6 to 10 feet square at the base, and from 10 to 15 feet high.

Beyond Palca the *quebrada* narrows again, and the path was at one time high up on the slopes of the mountains, at a dizzy elevation above the fretting torrent below, and next in the very bed of the rapid, stony stream, not unfrequently between rocks almost closing above our heads, giving to the atmosphere a chill, sepulchral feeling that made us shiver beneath our heavy ponchos. Here we began to meet *atajos*, or trains of mules. descending from the resting-place of La Portada, laden with bags of barilla (powdered copper or tin ore). which are brought by llamas. These *atajos* are always led by an educated horse, with a sonorous bell attached to his neck, to warn approaching travellers to stop at some spot where the road is wide enough to prevent their being run down outright, or toppled over the precipices, by the heavily laden train that plunges down behind the equine leader. The fear of being thus run down is what most disturbs the traveller in the Sierra, where there are many long and dangerous passes, with paths so narrow as not to admit of two animals passing each other. It is customary to shout or to blow a shrill blast on a pandean pipe, which every arriero carries for this purpose, before entering on these dangerous sections of road, which is responded to by whoever happens to be struggling along it. If not answered, the road is supposed to be clear.

We passed several great stacks of bags of barilla as we went on, and one or two store-houses of corrugated and galvanized iron for receiving ores, and, still ascending, came to a little open space, where, on the shelves of the steeps around us, we observed a number of burial-towers similar to those which we had noticed, two leagues below, at Palca. I dismounted to examine them, and, in my eagerness to reach them, ran a thorn or spine of the cactus into my foot through the thick leather of my boot, which it took half an hour to extract.

Primarily these chulpas consisted of a cist, or excavation, in the ground, about four feet deep and three feet in diameter, walled up with rough stones. A rude arch of converging and overlapping stones, filled in or cemented together with clay, was raised over this cist, with an opening barely large enough to admit the body of a man, on a level with the surface of the ground, towards the east. Over this hollow cone was raised a solid mass of clay and stones, which, in the particular chulpa I am now describing as a type of the whole, was 16 feet high, rectangular in plan, 7½ feet face

CHULPA, OR BURIAL-TOWER.

by 6 feet on the sides. The surface had been roughcast with clay, and over this was a layer of finer and more tenacious clay or stucco, presenting a smooth and even surface. At the height of fourteen feet was a cornice or projection of four inches, and of about six inches in vertical thickness, formed by a layer of compacted ichu, or coarse mountain grass, placed horizontally, and cut off evenly as by a shears. Above this the body of the chulpa reappeared, a little frayed by time and weather, to the height of about eighteen inches. The whole structure rested on a square or rather rectangular platform of roughly hewn stones, extending about four feet around it on every side.

The stuccoed surface of the chulpa had been painted in white and red, as shown in the engraving, where the shaded parts represent the red, and the light parts the white, of the original. The opening was towards the east, on a level with the platform, and was about eighteen inches wide and high. But every other face of the chulpa had a painted opening, which led me to think that the real one had once been closed and also painted over, so that the fronts corresponded in appearance. However that may be, I wedged myself through the opening into the cist or vault, the bottom of which was covered a foot deep with human bones and fragments of pottery. There were no entire skulls, but many fragments of skulls, in the cist; a circumstance by no means surprising, as these remains are close by a principal road or trail from the coast to the interior, which has been more or

AYMARÁ SKULL

less traversed by curious and Vandalic people for three hundred years. Although I did not obtain a skull from these chulpas, I secured one from another point, a few leagues distant. It is a fine specimen of the Aymará skull, artificially distorted and lengthened.

At the chulpas our mules had begun to pant and stagger under the *soroche*, or rarefaction of the air, but which Berrios insisted was from the *veta*, or influence due to mineral substances (*vetas*, or veins of metal) in the earth. And, in reality, at a little distance farther on, although meanwhile our ascent had been constant, they seemed to have sensibly recovered, but still showed signs of the *soroche*.

At three o'clock we turned abruptly from the gorge of the torrent, which we had been following, now reduced to a trickling rivulet, and began to climb the steep mountain-side on our right, zigzagging towards the *cumbre*, or crest. Two hours were occupied in this slow and painful ascent, the mules suffering much, and frequently stopping to recover breath. From

the summit of the ridge—which was the divide between two of
the sources of the Rio de Tacna—although bleak mountains
still rose above us, cutting off from view the still higher nevados, or snowy mountains, beyond them, we could, nevertheless, look down with scarce an interruption on the great sandy
plateau of the coast, in which the valley of Tacna appeared only
as a speck.  A thin white, but confusing, haze cut off our view
of the ocean; but the intervening desert, dull and monotonous,
was clearly defined.

On what may be termed the saddle of the crest are the remains of tambos, or stone edifices, which the provident Incas
had erected as hospices, or refuges, for the travellers between
the coast and the interior.  So-called Spanish civilization has
supplied nothing of this kind.

Descending from this ridge, we found ourselves in another
gorge or valley somewhat wider than that by which we ascended, and watered by a larger stream.  Following up this, it being now late in the afternoon, we began to experience the cold
consequent on our great altitude, and became aware of an unnatural distention of our lips and swelling of our hands, due to
diminished atmospheric pressure.  Icicles depended from the
dripping rocks in shaded places, and the pools of the stream
were bridged over with ice.  Suddenly we came to a point
where the rocks closed so nearly as to permit but one loaded
animal to pass at a time, stumbling through the stream among
loose stones and the skeletons of mules—a dark, cold, shudder-
ing place!  Fortunately the pass, which is that of *La Portada*,
"The Portal," is not long, and we soon emerged from it, in
sight of the great corral and depository of barilla, of the same
name, standing upon a kind of shelf on the mountain-side, with
the stream chafing close to it on the left.

The merchants of Tacna have built here a rude enclosure for
the droves of llamas that come from the interior with products
for the coast, and here also is a little cluster of buildings for
persons connected with the trade, homely and poor, but a welcome refuge for the tired traveller.  As we rode up, a troop of
more than a thousand llamas, with proudly curved necks, erect

17.

THE LLAMA.

heads, great, inquiring, timid eyes, and suspicious ears thrust forward as if to catch the faintest sound of danger, each with its hundred pounds of ore secured in sacks on its back, led, not driven, by quaintly costumed Indians, filed past us into the enclosure of the establishment.

We obtained hospitality in one of the buildings of La Portada. But let not my readers mistake the meaning of the word hospitality. In Peru it consists generally in permitting you, with more or less of condescension, to spread your own bed on the mud floor of an unswept room, alive with vermin, with a single rickety table for its chief and often its only article of furniture. It consists in permitting you to cook your own food, with fuel for which you will not be obliged to pay your host, or his servant acting under his direction, much more than four times its value, and who expects that you will permit him to take the lion's share of your preserved meats, and no inconsiderable portion of your last bottle of the stimulant you most affect, which cannot be replaced, and which is here often vitally necessary.

I have crossed the Alps by the routes of the Simplon, the Grand St. Bernard, and St. Gothard, but at no point on any of them have I witnessed a scene so wild and utterly desolate as that which spreads out around La Portada. There is neither tree nor shrub; the frosty soil cherishes no grass, and the very lichens find scant hold on the bare rocks. In altitude La Portada is 12,600 feet above the sea, or about 1000 feet higher than the hospice of the Grand St. Bernard, and but little lower than the untrodden summit of the Eiger. The night was bitterly cold. The *aguardiente*, or native rum, which I had purchased for making coffee in my *cafetera*, refused to burn, and extinguished the lighted match thrust into it as if it were water. I was obliged to abstract some refined alcohol from my photographic stores to supply its place, with which my Bolivian companions made themselves free, besides taking the best places for their beds, and leaving only the table and a narrow bench for H—— and myself.

Before going to bed I went out to the corral. The llamas had been fed each with a handful of maize, and were crouching on their bellies, with their legs mysteriously folded beneath their fleeces, and invisible, but with their heads erect, and ears thrust forward, chewing their cuds with an expression of distant contemplation such as we often observe in confirmed smokers. If I were to paint a picture of Rest, it would not be of a child in slumber, of a Hercules leaning on his club, nor yet

THE NEVADOS OF TACORA AND CHIPICANI, FROM THE PASS OF GUAYLILLAS.

mits yet untouched by human foot, is a broad but shallow valley covered with hardy puna grass, now sere and withered, but affording food for a flock of graceful vicuñas, which lift high their heads and stare straight at us as I fire my rifle, the report of which sounds wonderfully hollow and weak in the thin atmosphere.

While we sat gazing on this grand but bleak and wintry scene, the distended nostrils and heaving sides of our animals telling painfully how great was their difficulty in breathing, we were startled by the sudden fall from his saddle of one of our Bolivian companions under the effects of the *soroche*. On lifting him from the ground, we found him nearly senseless, with blood trickling from his mouth, ears, nostrils, and the corners of his eyes. Copious vomiting followed, and we administered the usual restoratives with good effect. In doing this I drew off my gloves, and was surprised to find my hands swollen and covered with blood which appeared as if it had oozed from a thousand minute punctures. Excepting this, a tumefaction of the lips, and occasionally a slight giddiness, I did not suffer from the rarefaction of the air or from the *veta* while in the interior of Peru, although for six months I was seldom less than thirteen thousand and often as high as eighteen thousand feet above the sea.

We wound down by an easy path into the valley that intervened between us and the base of Tacora, at the bottom of which we came to the Rio de Azufre. Its banks, as its name implies, are yellow and orange, with sulphurous deposits, and lined with the skeletons of horses, mules, and llamas that had ventured to drink its poisonous waters. I tasted the water, and found it abominably acrid and bitter. Indeed, all the water of the Despoblado, even that which to the taste does not betray any evidence of foreign or mineral substances in solution, is more or less purgative, and often productive of very injurious effects. In many parts of the country the thirsty traveller discovers springs as limpid and bright as those of our New England hills; yet when he dismounts to drink, his muleteer will rush forward in affright with the warning cry, "Beware; *es agua de verruga!"* The verruga water is said to produce a terrible disease, called by the same name, which manifests itself outwardly in both men and animals in great bleeding boils or carbuncles, which occasion great distress, and often result in death.

From the Rio de Azufre our path wound round the base of Tacora, which is of volcanic origin, and 22,687 feet in elevation,

THE VICUÑA.

and gradually ascended to a broad plain, sloping gently to the right, covered with stones, sere ichu grass, and clumps of a low resinous shrub called tola. Groups of vicuñas were scattered over the plain, and at a low, marshy spot, near where a patch of ground, white with the efflorescence of some kind of salts, showed the existence of a shallow pool in the season of rains, we observed a belt of light green grass, on which a troop of llamas were feeding.  They were interspersed with vicuñas, which grazed by their side as if members of the same community.

I need not say that we were eager to get a shot at the vicuñas, but they were shy, and kept well out of reach.  I dismounted, and endeavored to steal from one clump of bushes, and from one rock to another, until within reasonable range; but always at the critical moment the male of the family—they always run in groups of ten or a dozen, females and young ones, under the lead of a single patriarch—would stamp his foot and utter a strange sound, half neigh, half whistle, and away they would dart with the speed of the wind, only, however, to stop at a safe distance and stare at us intently, not to say derisively.  After several attempts and failures, I ventured a random shot at a group fully half a mile distant.  They bounded away, all but one, which after going a few yards stopped short.  *"Es herido! es herido!"* ("He is wounded! he is wounded!") shouted my companions, who threw off their ponchos and *alforjas*, and, calling to me to follow their example, started on a chase after the wounded animal.  And such a chase I venture to say was never before seen at the foot of solemn old Tacora!  The shot had broken one of the forelegs of the vicuña just below the knee, but we soon found that with his three sound legs he was more than a match for us, on a stern chase.  After half an hour's hard riding we stopped to arrange a little piece of strategy, and the vicuña stopped also, as if to say, "Take your time, gentlemen!  I am a little sore, but in no kind of a hurry!"  Our plan was soon fixed, and we separated, making long detours so as to surround our victim, whom we were to despatch with our revolvers as he attempted to break through our line.  He regarded the whole proceeding with complacency, and never moved, except to contemplate us one after another as we closed slowly and cautiously around him.  Nearer and nearer, and still he never moved.  We were almost within pistol-range, and our fingers were already on our triggers, when with a bound he dashed between me and Berrios, who had joined in the chase, with the velocity of an arrow. I fired twice rapidly, and Berrios discharged his rusty horse-pis-

tol, loaded with a half-pint of slugs, without effect, when our
excited Bolivians, closing in, commenced an irregular fusillade,
sending their bullets singing around us in most unwelcome
proximity.  I suspect I came much nearer being shot than the
vicuña, and, not choosing to take more risks, gave up the chase.
But the Bolivians kept on, while Berrios, H——, and myself
toiled back to the mule-path and onwards to the tambo of Tacora.

This tambo, which is a favorable type of what in Switzerland
would be called "refuges," consists of four low buildings of
stones and mud, thatched with ichu, and surrounding a small
court, in which the travellers' animals are gathered at night.
Sometimes, and for the accommodation of the troops of llamas,
there is a large supplementary corral, or enclosure, constructed
of loose stones, or stones laid in mud.  Often these tambos are

NEVADO AND TAMBO OF TACORA.

without keepers, occupants, or furniture of any kind; but that
of Tacora had a resident, who occupied the principal building,
in which he had a scant store of wilted alfalfa, and a few articles of food, principally the flesh of the vicuña. Another building served as a kitchen; a third for the storage of cargo and as
a dormitory for the arrieros; while the fourth was reserved for
travellers. It had no entrance or opening except the door-way,
elevated two feet above the ground, and barely large enough
to permit a full-grown person to squeeze through. This was
closed with a flap of raw hide. The interior was dark and dirty
beyond description. I doubt if it had been swept, or if any attempt had been made to cleanse it, for many months. This den
had no furniture whatever, only there was the usual mud-bank
on every side, whereon the traveller might spread his bed.

The keeper of the tambo, wearing a slouched felt hat, and
wrapped in a blue cloak with a fur collar and a gilt clasp at
the neck as big as one's hand, complied loftily and somewhat
haughtily with our request for some cebada, or barley, for our
mules, and motioned to one of his Indian women to cook some
chupe for our *mozos*. We preferred to open a can of stewed
beef and a box of sardines for our dinner. I observed that
the proceeding arrested the attention of our distant host, with
whom we had signally failed to open conversation, but who
now seemed to have been suddenly called down from his con-
templations to a cognizance of what was going on around him.
I think I never saw a more fixed and eager gaze than that he
fastened on our edibles and on our bottle of brandy. His eyes
followed every morsel from the plate to our mouths with an expression of indescribable longing. There was no evading the
conclusion that the man was ravenously hungry; but if there
had been any doubt, the alacrity with which he responded to
my invitation to join us, and the unctuous "*Como no?*" ("Why
not?") of his reply would have dispelled it. He certainly did
justice to his meal, if not to us, for he made no pause until the
last morsel had disappeared, which it did just as our Bolivians
came in, panting and exhausted, from their fruitless chase after
the wounded vicuña.

Under the circumstances, I could not resist encroaching a little on my stores in their behalf, and gave them also a can of beef and a box of sardines. Our host did not wait to be invited to join them, and when I left the tambo for a ramble in its neighborhood I observed that the larger part of this feast also was disappearing behind the wonderful gilt clasp. But all this did not prevent him from demanding a price for his cebada and chupe which made Berrios speechless with astonishment.

Beyond the tambo the ground becomes a little undulating and broken, but soon subsides into a broad plain, white with efflorescence of some kind, at the lower part of which appeared La Laguna Blanca, a considerable but apparently shallow sheet of water, along the edges of which we discerned vast numbers of water-fowl. Several mountain streams, fed from the snows, descending from the slopes on our left, had taken the mule-track for their channel, and we splashed along for a mile or more through the icy water. The plain now became less stony, and more thickly overgrown with tola. Vicuñas, too, were more numerous and less shy, and towards evening we were able to approach so near them that I might have shot a dozen, if I liked, with my revolver. We contented ourselves with one, taking with us only the saddle, and leaving the rest to the condors.

The ground over which we rode during the afternoon, and after leaving La Laguna Blanca behind us, rose gently in a broad swell or billow, which here, although nearly a thousand feet lower than the ridge of Guaylillos, is the real divide, separating the waters flowing into the Pacific from those discharging into the lakes of the great terrestrial basin of Titicaca. From its summit a fine view is obtained, stretching southwards to an immense distance, with the smoking cones of the undescribed volcanoes of Pomarope and Sahama on the horizon. At the foot of this dividing ridge we come to the considerable, clear, and rapid stream of Uchusuma, flowing into the Rio Maure, which in turn falls into the Desaguadero, or outlet of Lake Titicaca, itself pouring its flood into the mysterious lake of Aullagas.

Night began to close around us soon after passing the river, and we turned abruptly to our right, across the *tolares*, or tola-fields, into a shallow valley near the stream, where Berrios said there was some grass for the animals, and some *casitas* for ourselves. We soon reached a little group of low stone huts, hardly bigger than the houses the beaver builds, and quite as rude. They had been erected by a couple of Indian families, who undertook to pasture a drove of llamas on the banks of the Uchusuma, but who had all died of small-pox about two years

THE CASITAS OF UCHUSUMA.

before our visit. The *casitas* had fallen rapidly into ruin. The wind had torn great holes through the thatch of the roofs, and the frost had made breaches in the rough walls. Our Bolivians, who always contrived to get in ahead of us, took hasty possession of the best-preserved and largest of the huts, and we were fain to take the next best, which had been the chapel. It was not an imposing structure, the interior being barely seven feet long by five feet wide, and so low as to prevent a man of ordinary height from standing erect. At the farther end was a little altar of mud, and a little wooden cross hung undisturbed

OUR DORMITORY AT CCHUSENA

against the rough stone-wall. There was barely room to stow
away our saddles and *alforjas*, and spread our two beds. We
closed the orifice which answered for a door with a blanket, and
then set about cooking our saddle of vicuña. All hands turned
out to gather the dry stems and roots of the tola, which burn
fiercely and rapidly, and we soon had a bright fire blazing in
one of the half-unroofed huts which we had improvised as a
kitchen. Our baggage was arranged in a square, and a tarpau-
lin spread over all, forming a sort of tent, which here and subsequently was the sole protection of Berrios and the *mozos*, and
which we were often too glad to share with them.

I cannot say much for vicuña flesh on first trial and when
freshly killed, and should prefer good mutton to it at any time.
We nevertheless had chupe of vicuña, and vicuña steaks, and
might have had a joint of vicuña, if we could have had a fire
constant enough to roast it by. On the whole, I do not think I
had a good appetite that night, and fell back early on coffee,

the traveller's best reliance under all circumstances and in every clime.

We had burned out the last stem of our supply of tola before we stole to our couches in the chapel. The sky was dark as a pall, and the stars burned out on the still, bitter air with unnatural lustre. I watched them through the openings in the roof of our rude dormitory until midnight, and then fell asleep and dreamed that they were golden-tipped spears, darting down from the sky. Berrios did not rouse us early next morning, nor until the sun was up, for every one was cold and stiff, and needed thawing out. My beard was matted with ice, and the blanket around my head was spangled over with the frost.

We were now fairly entered on the cold, arid region known as the Despoblado — that drear, desolate, silent region which forms the broad summit of the Cordillera. It has the aspect of an irregular plain, and is diversified with mountain ridges and snowy and volcanic peaks, imposing in their proportions, notwithstanding that they rise from a level fourteen thousand feet above the sea. In all directions spread out vast tola fields, with here and there patches of ichu grass, which grows in clumps, and at this season is dry and gray, stiff and needle-like. Towards noon we came to many broad dry run-ways, or channels, between disrupted beds of trachytes, indicating that, during the rainy season, heavy volumes of water descend from the Ancomarca and Quenuta mountains and ranges to the north. Just at noon we reached the Rio Caño, a rather broad and shallow stream, flowing in a sandy bed, and which is here the boundary between Peru and Bolivia. On its opposite bank rises a cliff of porphyry, fissured and broken into a thousand shapes, which deflected our path to the southward until we reached a point of practicable ascent for animals.

Among the rocks we saw for the first time the biscacha, almost the only quadruped, except those of the llama family, that is found in the Altos of Peru. It is of the chinchilla family, about the size and shape of a rabbit, gray on the back, reddish-brown on the belly, but with a long tail, like that of the squirrel, which it curves up over its back in sitting erect, as is its custom, like the latter animal. It has some of the quaint and amusing habits of the prairie-dog of our own country, and delights to perch itself on some point of rock, whence it will contemplate the traveller silently and without motion, only, however, to plunge down suddenly into some covert with the quickness of light; but as often without as with apparent reason. After a few moments' absence it will very likely appear again, first projecting its head above the rocks, then the shoulders, and, should the reconnoissance prove satisfactory, it will resume an erect position, perhaps, however, to repeat the previous gymnastic feat a second after. The biscacha is esteemed good food, provided the tail is cut off immediately after it is killed. If this is not done, the natives maintain the animal is *corrompido.* For myself, I class the flesh of the biscacha with that of the vicuña as a possible alternative against starvation.

An hour later, some very regular elevations, or table-rocks, appearing on our right in the distance, we came to the Rio Maure, a large stream flowing in a deep channel between high cliffs of purple porphyry-conglomerate, which is here fissured and weather-worn into a thousand castellated and fantastic shapes. The descent to the water is by a steep, breakneck path, partly worn and partly worked among the rocks, and down which it seems incredible that a loaded animal can pass. In the dry season the stream is fordable, the water reaching only to the saddle-girths; but in the rainy season it is often impassable. The water is remarkably clear and pure, and I observed a few small fishes in the pools.

The Maure falls into the Desaguadero about midway between lakes Titicaca and Aullagas. Its left bank is less precipitous than the right, though abrupt, and we toiled slowly up its acclivity to the broken plain, in which the bed of the river is only a fissure or rent, invisible at the distance of a few hundred yards. At three o'clock the ground became more broken, and we became involved among a series of hills, our path ascending and descending, and crossing at intervals narrow, swampy valleys, where patches of green and tremulous sod alternated with dark, deep pools of water, affording a scant pasturage for some droves of alpacas, which find a congenial home in these localities. At various points we observed rough stone enclosures in which the alpacas are herded for clipping and other purposes, and which, perhaps, date beyond the Conquest. But nowhere could we discern a trace of human habitation. In some sheltered spots we noticed a few dwarf quinoa or wild olive trees, with trunks rarely over an inch in diameter, and which are carefully protected by the arrieros, to whom they afford a desirable substitute as fuel for the dung of the vicuña and llama. The latter, as I have said, is about the only kind of fuel to be had in the Altos of Peru; and even this would be scant and difficult to get if it were not the unvarying habit of all the members of the llama family to make their droppings in certain fixed spots, where they form accumulations or mounds often from ten to twelve feet broad, and from two to five feet high. These black heaps are characteristic features in the *puna* landscapes.

Towards night we began to climb the high ridge known as the Pass of Chuluncayani. The summit of the ridge, according to Pentland, is 15,160 feet above the sea, and from it we caught our first view, over lofty and rugged intervening ridges, of the Nevados of the Andes—that magnificent snowy range that dwarfs the Alps, and stretches in a glittering line along the horizon for three hundred miles. The descent of the ridge was almost as difficult and dangerous as that into the gorge of the Rio Maure, but much longer and wearisome. Both H——and myself broke the cruppers of our saddles under the sudden plunges of the mules, and in many places, in common with our arrieros, we were obliged to dismount and proceed on foot. At the base of the ridge we came to a small wet pampa, sloping somewhat rapidly to the right, and traversed by half a dozen bright and brawling rivulets, falling from a high ridge on the north. On the farther edge of the plain, which, from its abundance of water and favorable exposure to the sun, was relatively fresh and green, we saw the buildings of the tambo of Chuluncayani—a welcome sight through the cold mist that had already begun to settle over the damp surface of the pampa.

The keeper of the tambo, which is much larger and better-appointed than that of Tacora, is by far the most enterprising and active man whom I met with in Bolivia. He had several flocks of alpacas scattered in the surrounding valleys, kept a store of barley-straw for the mules of travellers, and was able to furnish the traveller himself with a chicken, if he chose to pay therefor the sum of three dollars. His chupe was less thin than we found to be the average quality of that kind of delicacy; and, in bottles, bearing labels gorgeous in crimson and gold, he had brandy of the kind that Berrios called *muy endemoniado* (much bedevilled), and in which red pepper seemed to be the predominant ingredient. And, although the floor of the room set apart for travellers was the bare earth, innocent of brush or broom, yet were not its walls gay with paper only less dazzling than the labels of his brandy-bottles? We had a chupe and two chickens, returned one of the two bottles of brandy, and had barley-straw for our mules, for which our enterprising host charged me sixty-four dollars! There was no charge for bedding and lights, for these we supplied ourselves. From this statement, the adventurer in Southern Peru and Bolivia may form some estimate of the expense of travel in those interesting regions. Sixteen cents a pound, or at the rate of three hundred and twenty dollars a ton, is the current charge in Chuluncayani for green barley-straw, and the market is always "firm." I left my Bolivian friends disputing with the landlord because he had charged *them* four dollars each.

Beyond Chuluncayani the road winds through a hilly country, constantly descending, until, in a beautiful little savanna, or pampa, completely hemmed in by hills, it crosses the Rio Santiago, a stream flowing nearly due east, between parallel ranges of hills artificially terraced, and where we discovered the first signs of cultivation since our departure from Palca. These *andenes*, or terraces, became familiar enough before we left the Sierra, but here they were welcome indications of the proximity of human beings. The crops were all gathered, but we learned that barley, quinoa, and potatoes were cultivated on these sunny hill-sides. Barley does not ripen, and is grown

only for fodder.  Following down the Rio Santiago, we finally
came to some isolated buildings, in one of which was a cretin
afflicted with concomitant goitre, who, except in color, might
be mistaken for one of the miserable wretches so common in
Switzerland and the Tyrol.

The valley now began to widen, and soon spread out into a
broad plain, on a slight eminence in which we discerned the
village of Santiago de Machaca.  The stream or river here deflects to the left, and not to the right, as laid down in the maps,
and pursues a north-eastern course.  Numberless water-fowls,
including geese, ducks of various kinds, several varieties of wa-

STREET VIEW IN SANTIAGO DE MACHACA.

ter-hens and ibises, disported themselves in its icy waters, or
flew away, screaming, on our approach.

At noon we reached the village, which has a population of
between five and six hundred souls, chiefly occupied in raising
llamas, for which the broad plain is favorable.  The plaza in
the centre of the town is large, and the streets entering it at
each corner are covered with arches and flanked by little open
chapels of adobes, in each of which is a mud altar surmounted
by a wooden cross covered with tinsel, and weighed down with
withered mountain flowers.  A low, rambling church, with a
dilapidated bell-tower standing apart, occupies one side of the

plaza, facing the *cabildo*, with a prison on one hand confining
two or three dirty and emaciated wretches, and a school-room
on the other, in which a dozen children were learning a prayer,
*vivá voce*, but in which they stopped short as we rode past, and
seemed to relish the opportunity to exclaim, "*Buenos dias, caballeros!*" We had been recommended to the *cura*, who was
rather noted in the Sierra for his intelligence and hospitality,
but found that he had died a few weeks previously, and that his
house was shut up. There was, however, a kind of *pulperia*,
or shop, fronting on the plaza, where *bayeta*, or baize, was sold,
and some rough woollen cloth of native manufacture, besides
cheese, *charqui* (sun-dried beef), and eggs. We purchased the
entire stock of the latter, and took our dinner on the sunny
side of the building.

The houses are built of adobes, and, without exception, are
thatched with ichu grass.
They seldom consist of
more than a single apart-
ment, entered by a low
and narrow door, closed
by a dried hide inside, the
sill of which is raised so
as to prevent the water
from flowing in from the
street. The walls of all of
them incline inwards after
the style characteristic of
all the Inca edifices that
we afterwards had occa
sion to examine; and the
doors were also narrower
at the top than at the bottom, precisely as in the ancient structures. There
are no "party-walls" or
single walls answering for
contiguous houses, but each

AYMARÁ FEMALE HEAD-DRESS.

building has its distinct gables. Here we saw, for the first time, the extraordinary *montero*, or hat, universally worn by the women of the Aymará race or family. It may be compared to a coffin, with a kind of black valance suspended around a stiff body of pasteboard, covered with red cloth and tinsel. Nearly all the Indian women had children—silent, uncomplaining little creatures—slung in a thick shawl over their shoulders.

Striking across the plain of Santiago, which extends to the north-east almost to the outlet of Lake Titicaca, where it is relieved by a number of mammiform hills, or buttes, and which is dotted all over with heaps of llama dung, and sprinkled with the llamas themselves, we came to a little isolated church, with no building near, and with scarcely a hut in sight. I suppose some sort of pilgrimage or procession to it takes place on occasion; but as the church of Santiago was disproportionally large for the town, this edifice seemed entirely supererogatory. Just beyond it, in a little hollow, was the dead body of a mule, from which a group of condors were tearing the flesh in great strips, while a dozen or more of king-vultures, gorgeous in color, were ranged in a circle around, respectfully waiting until their masters were gorged, when it would be their turn to take part in the unsavory feast. I fired at the group from the back of my mule; but owing to the wonderful trajectory of my rifle, with whose vagaries I had not yet become familiar, I missed my aim. After a series of ungraceful leaps, flapping their wings the while for a hundred yards along the ground, the great birds succeeded in rising in the air, and commenced to circle in defiant and threatening evolutions above our heads. I dismounted for surer work, and with my second shot brought down one of the largest with a broken wing. But, like the wounded vicuña on the stony plain of Tacora, he was more than a match, on his legs, for our worn and battered mules; and after a chase of half a mile I gave up pursuit, consoling myself with the reflection, "What could I have done with the gigantic scavenger had I caught him?"

Our halting-place for the night was fixed at the village of

San Andres de Machaca, and we pushed forwards over some low ranges of hills with all our energy, to reach it before dark. We passed some terraced slopes, subdivided by stone-walls, resembling fortifications, which were the *huertas*, or gardens, of San Andres; crossed some streams flowing northward in shifting channels through an alluvial valley, and at five o'clock reached the irregular and rambling village for which we were bound. Our Bolivians, whose feet were literally "on their native heath," had taken great airs on themselves at Santiago, but they now became imperious. They rode to the house of the *gobernador* as if he were a born vassal; but that official had discovered our approach and hidden himself — a common expedient with alcaldes not addicted to hospitality—or else he was really absent from home. At any rate, his poor habitation was shut up and tenantless. Our next recourse was to the *cura*, who lived in a relatively grand house behind the church; but he, too, was absent. His *suplente*, or substitute, a pleasant young man, was in charge of the establishment, and gracefully accepted the situation, giving us a vacant room, and treating us to chupe and eggs.

The church of San Andres was the first one we had seen of that series of fine temples reared by the Jesuits in their days of prosperity and power in all parts of the Titicaca basin. Almost every squalid village has its church—always of good architectural design, and often of grand proportions and wonderful solidity. That of San Andres had never been finished, but was nevertheless imposing. Its façade is relieved by a lofty archway with a bold sweep, and its towers rise with a strength showing that the designer of the building was no feeble or timid architect. In front is an elaborate cross of beautiful white *berenguela*, or alabaster, taken from extensive quarries of that material not far distant. Slabs or plates of this supply the place of glass in the windows of many of the churches of the Sierra, and give to the transmitted light a soft and mellow tinge like that let through the painted windows of old cathedrals.

We left San Andres before daylight, and resumed our course towards Nasacara, or, as the point is sometimes called, the Bal-

sas oi Nasacara, on the Rio Desaguadero. The morning was
bitterly cold, and we suffered much until the sun rose and
thawed the icicles from our beards. The country retains its aspect of a high plain, without cultivation, and covered with tola.
At nine o'clock, having travelled five leagues, we came to the
edge of the table-land, and obtained our first view of the valley
of the Desaguadero, covered with sward, broken here and there
by small patches of cultivated ground, and traversed up and
down, as far as the eye can reach, by the broad and placid river.

BALSA BRIDGE OVER THE RIO DESAGUADERO.

At our feet, built partly on the hither, but mainly on the farther bank of the stream, is the village of Nasacara, distinguished
chiefly for its bridge of balsas, or floats of totora, and as being
the point where the Bolivian custom-house is established, where
passports are scrutinized and baggage examined.

The bridge of Nasacara is a type of a considerable number
of bridges in South America, and merits more than a passing
notice. It is a floating bridge, not unlike that across the Rhine
at Cologne, except that, owing to the entire absence of timber

in the country, the floats are of dried reeds, bound together in huge bundles, pointed at the ends like canoes. These are fastened together side by side by thick cables of braided reeds, anchored to firm stone towers on both banks. The roadway is also of reeds resting on the floats, about four feet wide, and raised above the floats about the same height — a rather yielding and unsteady path, over which only one or two mules are allowed to pass at a time. The causeways leading to both extremities of the bridge are barred by gates at which toll is collected. When the river is swollen and the current very strong, it is usual to cut the cables at one extremity or the other, and let the bridge swing down the stream so as to prevent it being swept away.

At the point where the bridge crosses the Desaguadero the river is one hundred and fifty feet wide and thirty deep, flowing with a strong but even current. This point is about forty miles below where the river debouches from Lake Titicaca, and one hundred and thirty feet, according to Mr. Pentland's observations, below the level of the lake; thus giving to the river a fall to Nasacara of three and a half feet to the mile. I nowhere saw rapids in the stream, nor did I hear of falls, and was told that it was easy to ascend the river in canoes to the lake itself. However that may be, nothing can be more absurd than the story which once found place in some educational publications, that the waters of Lake Titicaca sometimes flow into Lake Aullagas, and *vice versâ*, varying with the amount of rainfall, etc., in the northern and southern parts of this great terrestrial basin. Mr. Pentland fixes the level of Lake Aullagas at five hundred and seventy feet lower than that of Lake Titicaca, and the distance between the two at about one hundred and seventy miles, which would give an average fall throughout corresponding with that between Lake Titicaca and Nasacara. I have no doubt the river is everywhere practicable for small boats, and that no serious interruption by rapids exists at any point.

We experienced no detention from the custom officers of Nasacara, although they exhibited unnecessary curiosity regarding my breech-loading rifle, which I really believe they would have confiscated if they could have satisfied themselves how to use it, and how to replace the fixed ammunition without which it would have been useless. They gave us chupe, and sold us cheese and a little Puno butter, which comes packed in small bladders, like snuff.

Here our Bolivians separated from us to pursue their road to La Paz, and Berrios coolly proposed to do the same thing, and leave us in charge of a dark and sinister-looking *mestizo* whom he had met, and who was in some way a dependent of his, but who had never been over the road we were to follow, and could not speak a word of Aymará or Quichua, now the universal languages of the country. My remonstrances were equally forcible and effective; and as they were made in the open street and in a sonorous tone, they must have been edifying to the good people of Nasacara.

At noon we struck off from the town at right angles to the La Paz road, following up the valley of the river, over an undulating but uninhabited plain, to Jesus de Machaca, situated in marshy ground, near the base of the high ridge that separates the valley of the Desaguadero from that of Tiahuanuco. Its inhabitants are all Indians of the Aymará family, who eke out a scanty subsistence as shepherds and cultivators of the bitter variety of potato to which I have alluded, and which grows on the sunny hill-sides. Like San Andres, it has a great church in good repair, and containing some large pictures, of the excellence of which we were unable to judge under the "dim religious light" that stole through the alabaster windows. Having no place of refuge, we rode direct to the house of the *cura*. He was an intelligent, meek, earnest man, who did for us all that we were unable to do for ourselves, and made no apologies for deficiencies which were obviously inseparable from his position. We passed the evening pleasantly in his society. He showed us through his church, in which five times the population of his village might easily assemble, and pointed out the beauties of its architecture with a faint flush of pride. His hectic cheek and rasping cough told us then that he verged on the close of his earthly career; and we were not surprised, although we were grieved, to hear a few months later, and before we left the Sierra, that Manuel Valdivia, the good *cura* of Jesus de Machaca, was dead.

The ridge behind Jesus de Machaca reaches close up to Lake Titicaca, and extends southward for a hundred miles, nearly parallel with the Desaguadero. The path over it is little frequented, rough, and in some places dangerous. We were from six o'clock in the morning until noon in reaching its summit, marked by the inevitable cairn of stones, standing at an elevation of three thousand six hundred feet above the valley of the Desaguadero, and over sixteen thousand feet above the sea.

From this point we obtained our first view of Lake Titicaca, or rather of the lower and lesser lake of Tiquina, with its high islands and promontories, and shores belted with reeds. Here, too, the great snowy chain of the Andes, of which we had only caught glimpses before, burst on our sight in all its majesty. Dominating the lake is the massive bulk of Illampu, or Sorata, the crown of the continent, the highest mountain of America, rivalling, if not equalling in height, the monarchs of the Himalayas. Observers vary in their estimates and calculations of its altitude from twenty-five thousand to twenty-seven thousand feet; my own estimates place it at not far from twenty-six thousand. Extending southward from this is an uninterrupted chain of nevados, nowhere less than twenty thousand feet in height, which terminates in the great mountain of Illimani, twenty-four thousand five hundred feet in altitude. Between the eminence on which we stand and these gigantic mountains are, first, the deep valley and plain of Tiahuanuco, with a high table-land succeeding, and a range of mountains beyond, which look small only from contrast with their snow-crowned neighbors.

Looking back, the view, if not equally imposing, is nevertheless as interesting. We can trace the windings of the Desaguadero through its shallow valley until lost in the distance in the direction of Lake Aullagas. There, too, is the broad plain of Santiago over which we have toiled, its inequalities scarce-

ILLAMPU (THE CROWN OF THE ANDES) AND LAKE TITICACA.

ly discernible from our elevation.  Beyond it, distinct, white, grand, and solemn, are the volcanic peaks of Sahama, Poma-rape, and Tacora, the pinnacles of the Cordilleras, themselves reflecting their silver crests in the Pacific.

Nowhere else in the world, perhaps, can a panorama so di-versified and grand be obtained from a single point of view. The whole great table-land of Peru and Bolivia, at its widest part, with its own system of waters, its own rivers and lakes, its own plains and mountains, all framed in by the ranges of the Cordillera and the Andes, is presented like a map before the adventurous visitor who climbs to the *apacheta* of Tiahuanaco.

The descent into the valley or plain of Tiahuanaco is more abrupt than in the direction of the Desaguadero, and the most reckless travellers find it requisite to dismount and proceed on foot.  It was dark when we struck the edge of the plain, and ascertained that we had yet nearly four leagues to go before reaching the village of Tiahuanaco.  This border of the plain receives the wash of the adjacent ridge, and is covered thickly with rocky débris, and seamed with shallow torrent beds.  To get at the soil and protect the ground when once reclaimed, the stones in many places have been heaped together in mounds, or long, heavy ridges, capable of resisting or diverting the rush of the waters descending from the hills.  This work seems to have been in great part, if not wholly, performed by the ancient in-habitants; showing that here, as everywhere else, they were avaricious of arable soil, and spared neither time nor labor to rescue the scantiest portion of it to cultivation.

At a distance of two leagues from the western border of the plain we came to a considerable swell of land, free from stones, and of which patches were broken up for crops; and a league and a half farther, after fording a shallow stream of clear run-ning water, we reached the village of Tiahuanaco itself, situated upon another slight elevation, in a well-chosen position.  The narrow unlighted streets, lined by low huts of rough stones laid in clay, covered with thatch, destitute of windows, and en-tered only by low and narrow door-ways (closed, for the most part, with raw hides), were silent and deserted ; the wretched inhabitants have hardly fuel wherewith to cook their scanty food, and are fain to slink away into their dark and squalid habitations, as soon as the sun withdraws his genial rays. The traveller who emerges in the morning, blue and benumbed, from his bed on the ground in an unventilated, gloomy hut of the Sierra, where pigs are his least unpleasant companions, to thaw himself into life on the sunny side of the wretched *choza* that has sheltered him, will readily comprehend how the people of Peru became worshippers of the sun.

We were not long in finding the plaza of Tiahuanaco, where a faint light shining out from a single *portada* in front of the church gave us the first evidence that the town possessed inhabitants. The house proved to be the *posta*, and the most we could learn from the saturnine Indians in charge was that the master of the post was absent. They neither invited us to come in, nor made any movement to assist us when we dismounted, but disappeared one by one into dark dormitories, leaving us standing alone, hungry and cold, in the open court. However, the arrival of our arrieros, some of whom spoke Aymará, changed the aspect of affairs. They pushed open the door of the principal or travellers' apartment, and, piling the barley in stalk which it contained at one end, cleared a space for a broken table, the single piece of furniture in the room, and with imperative words and acts as emphatic, finally secured for us a dish of diluted chupe.

While this was going on we received a visit from the *cura*, on his return probably from some nocturnal adventure. His face was red and bloated, deeply scarred by small-pox, but retaining traces of original manly beauty. He was quite drunk and not very coherent, and when we began to question him about the celebrated ancient ruins of the neighborhood he became suddenly silent, and drew me into a dark corner of the court-yard, where, in a mysterious whisper, he told me that he knew all about the hidden treasures, and that we could count on his guidance in obtaining them, for an equitable division of the spoils. It was in vain I protested that we were not money-diggers. He could not conceive how any stranger should

evince an interest in the " vestiges of the Gentiles" not founded
on the hope of discovering treasure among them.

And here I may mention that throughout all of our explorations, in all parts of Peru, whether in the city or in the field,
we were supposed to be searching for *tapadas*, and were constantly watched and followed by people who hoped to get
some clew to the whereabouts of the treasures through our indications. Often, when engaged in surveys of fortifications or
buildings, we found the marks left by us at night, to guide us
in resuming our work in the morning, not only removed, but
the earth deeply excavated below them. The ancient monuments of the country have suffered vastly more from the hands
of treasure-seekers than from fanatic violence, time, and the
elements combined. The work of destruction from this cause
has been going on for three hundred years, and still actively
continues.

# CHAPTER XV.

### TIAHUANACO, THE BAALBEC OF THE NEW WORLD.

Tiahuanaco a Centre of Ancient Civilization.—Difficulties.—The Chuño Festival.—
Death of my Photographer.—Studying the Art.—My Assistants.—The Edifices of
Ancient Tiahuanuco.—The Ruins a Quarry for Modern Builders.—Their Extent.
—The Temple.—The Fortress.—The Palace.—The Hall of Justice.—Precision of
the Stone-cutting.—Elaborate Sculptures.—Monolithic Gate-ways.—The Modern
Cemetery.—The Sanctuary.—Symbolical Slab.—The great Monolithic Gate-way.
—Its Elaborate Sculptures.—Monuments described by Cieza de Leon and D'Or-
bigny.—Material of the Stone-work.—How the Stone was cut.—General Résumé.
—Tiahuanaco probably a Sanctuary, not a Seat of Dominion.

TIAHUANACO lies almost in the very centre of the great terrestrial basin of lakes Titicaca and Aullagas, and in the heart
of a region which may be properly characterized as the Thibet
of the New World.  Here, at an elevation of twelve thousand
nine hundred feet above the sea, in a broad, open, unprotected,
arid plain, cold in the wet and frigid in the dry season, we find
the evidences of an ancient civilization, regarded by many as
the oldest and the most advanced of both American continents.

It was to explore and investigate the monumental remains
that have made this spot celebrated that I had come to Tiahuanuco, and I lost no time in commencing my task.  This was
not an easy one, for even with the aid of the drunken *cura*
we were unable to procure laborers to assist us, for not only
had we reached the village on the eve of the Chuño, or potato
festival, a remnant of ancient observances, but before we had
finished our work the Feast of Corpus Christi had commenced.
*Chicha* flowed like water, and the few inhabitants that the
Chuño festival had left sober deliberately gave themselves up
to beastly intoxication.

This was not my only difficulty.  While we were toiling our

way upwards through the mountain road, my photographer, on whose skill I had depended, became dangerously ill. One bitter night, under an ebon sky, with no one to assist us save some kindly Indians, we tried in vain to relieve his sufferings and compose his mental hallucinations. The disease baffled all our efforts, and before sunrise death brought him relief and release. He murmured something in the Gaelic tongue, in which only the endearing word "mamma"—sacred in all languages—was intelligible, and died with that word lingering on his thin, blue lips.

I had provided myself with a complete and costly set of photographic apparatus, which I regarded as indispensable to success in depicting the ancient monuments; but I had little knowledge of the art, and must now become my own photographer, or lose many of the results of my labor. With no instruction except such as I could gain from Hardwick's "Manual of Photographic Chemistry," I went to work, and, after numerous failures, became tolerably expert. I had but a single assistant, Mr. H——, an amateur draughtsman, and only such other aid as I could get from my muleteer and his men, who were eager to conclude their engagement, and simply astounded that we should waste an hour, much more that we should spend days, on the remains of the heathens. Still, the investigation was undertaken with equal energy and enthusiasm, and, I am confident, with as good results as could be reached without an expenditure of time and money which would hardly have been rewarded by any probable additional discoveries. We spent a week in Tiahuanaco among the ruins, and, I believe, obtained a plan of every structure that is traceable, and of every monument of importance that is extant.

The first thing that strikes the visitor in the village of Tiahuanaco is the great number of beautifully cut stones, built into the rudest edifices, and paving the squalidest courts. They are used as lintels, jambs, seats, tables, and as receptacles for water. The church is mainly built of them; the cross in front of it stands on a stone pedestal which shames the symbol it supports in excellence of workmanship. On all sides are vestiges

19

of antiquity from the neighboring ruins, which have been a real quarry, whence have been taken the cut stones, not only for Tiahuanaco and all the villages and churches of its valley, but for erecting the cathedral of La Paz, the capital of Bolivia, situated in the deep valley of one of the streams falling into the river Beni, twenty leagues distant. And what is true here is also true of most parts of the Sierra. The monuments of the past have furnished most of the materials for the public edifices, the bridges, and highways of the present day.

The ruins of Tiahuanaco have been regarded by all students of American antiquities as in many respects the most interesting and important, and at the same time most enigmatical, of any on the continent. They have excited the admiration and wonder alike of the earliest and latest travellers, most of whom, vanquished in their attempts to penetrate the mystery of their origin, have been content to assign them an antiquity beyond that of the other monuments of America, and to regard them as the solitary remains of a civilization that disappeared before that of the Incas began, and contemporaneous with that of Egypt and the East. Unique, yet perfect in type and harmonious in style, they appear to be the work of a people who were thorough masters of an architecture which had no infancy, passed through no period of growth, and of which we find no other examples. Tradition, which mumbles more or less intelligibly of the origin of many other American monuments, is dumb concerning these. The wondering Indians told the first Spaniards that "they existed before the sun shone in the heavens," that they were raised by giants, or that they were the remains of an impious people whom an angry Deity had converted into stone because they had refused hospitality to his vicegerent and messenger.

I shall give only a rapid account of these remains, correcting some of the errors and avoiding some of the extravagances of my predecessors in the same field of inquiry. I must confess I did not find many things that they have described; but that fact, in view of the destructiveness of treasure-hunters and the rapacity of ignorant collectors of antiquities, does not necessarily discredit their statements; for Tiahuanaco is a rifled ruin, with comparatively few yet sufficient evidences of former greatness.

The ruins are about half a mile to the southward of the village, separated from it by a small brook and a shallow valley. The high-road to La Paz passes close to them—in fact, between them and some mounds of earth which were probably parts of the general system. They are on a broad and very level part of the plain, where the soil is an arenaceous loam, firm and dry. Rows of erect stones, some of them rough or but rudely shaped by art; others accurately cut and fitted in walls of admirable workmanship; long sections of foundations, with piers and portions of stairways; blocks of stone, with mouldings, cornices, and niches cut with geometrical precision; vast masses of sandstone, trachyte, and basalt but partially hewn; and great monolithic door-ways, bearing symbolical ornaments in relief, besides innumerable smaller, rectangular, and symmetrically shaped stones, rise on every hand, or lie scattered in confusion over the plain. It is only after the intelligent traveller has gone over the whole area and carefully studied the ground, that the various fragments fall into something like their just relations, and the design of the whole becomes comprehensible.

Leaving aside, for the present, the lesser mounds of earth of which I have spoken, we find the central and most conspicuous portion of the ruins, which cover not far from a square mile, to consist of a great, rectangular mound of earth, originally terraced, each terrace supported by a massive wall of cut stones, and the whole surmounted by structures of stone, parts of the foundations of which are still distinct. This structure is popularly called the "Fortress," and, as tradition affirms, suggested the plan of the great fortress of Sacsahuaman, dominating the city of Cuzco. The sides of this structure, as also of all the others in Tiahuanaco, coincide within ten degrees with the cardinal points of the compass. Close to the left of the Fortress (I adopt this name, and the others I may use, solely to facilitate description) is an area called the "Temple," slightly raised, defined by lines of erect stones, but ruder than those

which surround the Fortress. A row of massive pilasters
stands somewhat in advance of the eastern front of this area,
and still in advance of this are the deeply embedded piers of
a smaller edifice of squared stones, with traces of an exterior
corridor, which has sometimes been called the "Palace." At
other points, both to the south and northward, are some remains to which I shall have occasion to refer.

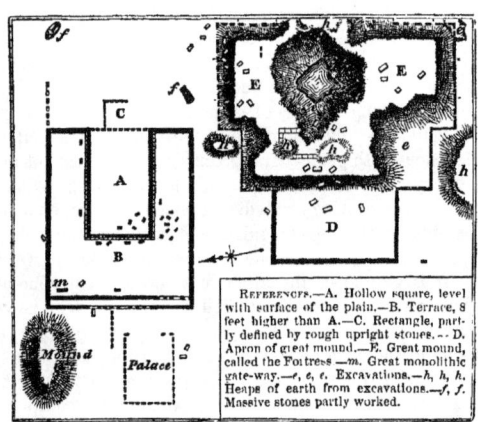

REFERENCES.—A. Hollow square, level
with surface of the plain.—B. Terrace, 8
feet higher than A.—C. Rectangle, partly defined by rough upright stones.— D.
Apron of great mound.—E. Great mound,
called the Fortress —m. Great monolithic
gate-way.—r, e, e. Excavations.—h, h, h.
Heaps of earth from excavations.—f, f.
Massive stones partly worked.

PLAN OF A PART OF THE RUINS OF TIAHUANACO.

The structure called the Temple will claim our first attention;
primarily because it seems to be the oldest of the group, the
type, perhaps, of the others, and because it is here we find the
great monolithic sculptured gate-way of Tiahuanaco, which is
absolutely unique, so far as our knowledge goes, on this continent.

The body of the Temple forms a rectangle of 388 by 445
feet, defined, as I said before, by lines of erect stones, partly
shaped by art. They are mostly of red sandstone, and of irregular size and height; those at the corners being more carefully
squared and tallest. For the most part, they are between 8 and

10 feet high, from 2 to 4 feet broad, and from 20 to 30 inches
in thickness.   The portions entering the ground, like those of
our granite gate-posts, are largest, and left so for the obvious
purpose of giving the stones greater firmness in their position.

These stones, some of which have fallen and others disappeared, seem to have been placed, inclining slightly inwards, at
approximately 15 feet apart, measuring from centre to centre,
and they appear to have had a wall of rough stones built up
between them, supporting a *terre-plein* of earth, about 8 feet
above the general level of the plain.   On its eastern side this
*torro-plein* had an apron or lower terrace 18 feet broad, along

THE AMERICAN STONEHENGE, TIAHUANACO.

the edge of the central part of which were raised ten great stone
pilasters, placed 15½ feet apart, all of which, perfectly aligned,
are still standing, with a single exception.  They are of varying
heights, and no two agree in width or thickness.   The one that
is fallen, which was second in the line, measures 13 feet 8 inches
in length by 5 feet 3 inches in breadth.   It is partly buried in
the earth, but shows 32 inches of thickness above-ground.
Among those still erect the tallest is 14 feet by 4 feet 2 inches,
and 2 feet 8 inches; the shortest 9 feet by 2 feet 9 inches, and
2 feet 5 inches.   These are less in dimension than the stones
composing the inner cell or sanctum of Stonehenge, which

range from 16 feet 3 inches to 21 feet 6 inches in height; but they are nearly, if not quite, equal with those composing the outer circle of that structure. They are much more accurately cut than those of Stonehenge, the fronts being perfectly true, and the backs alone left rough or only partially worked. The tops of the taller ones have shoulders cut into them as if to receive architraves; and as this feature does not appear in the shorter ones, it may be inferred that their tops have been broken off, and that originally they were all of one length. And here I may call attention to another singular feature of this colonnade —namely, that the sides or edges of each erect stone are slightly cut away to within six inches of its face, so as to leave a projection of about an inch and a half, as if to retain in place any slab fitted between the stones, and prevent it from falling outwards. The same feature is found in the stones surrounding the great mound or Fortress, where its purpose becomes obvious, as we shall soon see.

Such is the general character of the exterior propylon, if I may so call it, of the structure called the Temple. But within the line of stones surrounding it there are other features which claim our attention. I have said that the interior is a mound of earth raised about eight feet above the general level. But in the centre and towards the western side is an area sunk to the general level, 280 feet long by 190 feet broad. It was originally defined on three sides by walls of rough stones which rose above the surface of the mound itself, but which are now in ruins. If this sunken area communicated in any way with the more elevated interior parts of the structure, the means of communication, by steps or otherwise, have disappeared. Across the end of the area not shut in by the mound, the line of stones which surrounds the Temple is continued without interruption; but outside and connected with it is part of a small square of lesser stones, also erect, standing in the open plain.

Regarding the eastern side of the Temple, marked by the line of pilasters which I have described, as the front, we find here, at the distance of 57 feet, the traces of a rectangular structure, to which I have alluded as the "Palace," which was

composed of blocks of trachyte admirably cut, 8 to 10 feet long
by 5 feet broad, with remains of what appears to have been a
corridor 30 feet broad extending around it.  The piers which
supported the Palace still remain, sunk deep in the ground,
apparently resting on an even pavement of cut stones.  Remove the superstructures of the best-built edifices of our cities,
and few, if any, would expose foundations laid with equal care,
and none of them stones cut with such accuracy, or so admirably fitted together.  And I may say, once for all, carefully
weighing my words, that in no part of the world have I seen
stones cut with such mathematical precision and admirable skill
as in Peru, and in no part of Peru are there any to surpass
those which are scattered over the plain of Tiahuanaco.  The
so-called Palace does not seem to have been placed in any symmetrical relation towards the Temple, although seemingly dependent on it; nor, in fact, do any of the ancient structures here
appear to have been erected on any geometric plan respecting
each other, such as is apparent in the arrangement of most of
the remains of aboriginal public edifices in Peru.

The Fortress stands to the south-west of the Temple, the
sides of the two coinciding in their bearings, and is 64 feet distant from it.  As I have already said, it is a great mound of
earth, originally rectangular in shape, 620 feet in length and
450 in width, and about 50 feet high.  It is much disfigured
by the operations of treasure-seekers, who have dug into its
sides and made great excavations from the summit, so that it
now resembles rather a huge, natural, shapeless heap of earth
than a work of human hands.  The few of the many stones
that environed it, and which the destroyers have spared, nevertheless enable us to make out its original shape and proportions.
There are distinct evidences that the body of the mound was
terraced, for there are still standing stones at different elevations, distant horizontally nine, eighteen, and thirty feet from
the base.  There may have been more terraces than these lines
of stones would indicate, but it is certain that there were at
least three before reaching the summit.  This coincides with
what Garcilasso tells us of the mound when first visited by

the Spaniards. He says, speaking of the ruins under notice: "Among them there is a mountain or hill raised by hand, which, on this account, is most admirable. In order that the piled-up earth should not be washed away and the hill levelled, it was supported by great walls of stone. No one knows for what purpose this edifice was raised." Cieza de Leon, who himself visited Tiahuanaco soon after the Conquest, gives substantially the same description of the so-called Fortress.

OUTER TERRACE WALLS OF FORTRESS, AND SCATTERED BLOCKS OF STONE.

On the summit of this structure are sections of the foundations of rectangular buildings, partly undermined, and partly covered up by the earth from the great modern excavation in the centre, which is upwards of 300 feet in diameter, and more than 60 feet deep. A pool of water stands at its bottom. This latest piece of barbarism was, however, only in continuation of some similar previous undertaking. All over the Fortress and on its slopes lie large and regular blocks of stone, sculptured with portions of elaborate designs, which would only appear when the blocks were fitted together.

Some portions of the outer or lower wall are fortunately nearly intact, so that we are able to discover how it was constructed, and the plan and devices that were probably observed in all the other walls, as well as in some parts of the Temple. In the first place, large, upright stones were planted in the ground, apparently resting on stone foundations. They are about ten feet above the surface, accurately faced, perfectly aligned, and inclining slightly inwards towards the mound. They are placed seventeen feet apart from centre to centre, and are very nearly uniform in size, generally about three feet broad and two feet in thickness. Their edges are cut to present the kind of shoulders to which I alluded in describing the pilasters in front of the Temple, and of which the purpose now becomes apparent. The space between the upright stones is filled in with a wall of carefully worked stones. Those next the pilasters are cut with a shoulder to fit that of the pilaster they adjoin; and they are each, moreover, cut with alternate grooves and projections, like mortise and tenon, so as to fit immovably into each other horizontally. Vertically they are held in position by round holes drilled into the bottom and top of each stone at exact corresponding distances, in which, there is reason to believe, were placed pins of bronze. We here see the intelligent devices of a people unacquainted with the uses of cement to give strength and permanence to their structures. Nearly all the blocks of stone scattered over the plain show the cuts made to receive what is called the T clamp, and the round holes to receive the metal pins that were to retain the blocks in their places, vertically.

The Fortress has on its eastern side an apron, or dependent platform, 320 by 180 feet, of considerably less than half the elevation of the principal mound. Like the rest of the structure, its outline was defined by upright stones, most of which, however, have disappeared. The entrance seems to have been at its south-east corner, probably by steps, and to have been complicated by turnings from one terrace to another, something like those in some of the Inca fortresses.

The tradition runs that there are large vaults filled with

treasure beneath the great mound, and that here commences a subterranean passage which leads to Cuzco, more than four hundred miles distant. The excavations certainly reveal some curious subterranean features. The excavation at its south-west corner has exposed a series of superimposed cut stones, apparently resting on a pavement of similar character, twelve feet below the surface. It is said that Von Tschudi, when he visited the ruins, found some "caverns" beneath them (but whether under the Fortress or not does not appear), into which he endeavored to penetrate, but "was glad to be pulled out, as he soon became suffocated." I found no such subterranean vaults or passages in any part of Tiahuanaco; but I do not deny their existence.

To the south-east of the Fortress, and about two hundred and fifty paces distant, is a long line of wall in ruins, apparently a single wall, not connected with any other so as to form an enclosure. But beyond it are the remains of edifices of which it is now impossible to form more than approximate plans. One was measurably perfect when visited by D'Orbigny in 1833, who fortunately has left a plan of it, more carefully made than others he has given us of ruins here or elsewhere. Since 1833, however, the iconoclasts have been at work with new vigor. Unable to remove the massive stones composing the base of what was called the Hall of Justice, they mined them, and blew them up with gunpowder, removing many of the elaborately cut fragments to pave the cathedral of La Paz. Enough remains to prove the accuracy of D'Orbigny's plan, and to verify what Cieza de Leon wrote concerning these particular remains three hundred years ago.

The structure called the Hall of Justice occupied one end of a court something like that discoverable in the Temple. In the first place, we must imagine a rectangle, 420 feet long by 370 broad, defined by a wall of cut stones, supporting on three sides an interior platform of earth 130 feet broad, itself enclosing a sunken area, or court, also defined by a wall of cut stones. This court, which is of the general level of the plain, is 240 feet long and 160 broad. At its eastern end is, or rather was, the massive edifice distinguished as the Hall of Justice, of which D'Orbigny says:

"It is a kind of platform of well-cut blocks of stone, held together by copper clamps, of which only the traces remain. It presents a level surface elevated six feet above the ground, 131 feet long and 23 broad, formed of enormous stones, eight making the length and two the breadth. Some of these stones are 25½ feet long by 14 feet broad, and 6½ feet thick. These are probably the ones measured by Cieza de Leon, who describes them as 30 feet long. 15 in width, and 6 in thickness. Some are rectangular in shape, others of irregular form. On the

LESSER MONOLITHIC DOOR-WAY.

eastern side of the platform, and cut in the stones of which they form part, are three groups of alcoves, or seats. One group occupies the central part of the monument, covering an extent of fifty-three feet, and is divided into seven compartments. A group of three compartments occupies each extremity of the monument. Between the central and side groups were reared monolithic door-ways,* similar in some respects to the large one, only more simple, the one to the west alone hav-

---

* One of these, not, however, standing in its original position, is shown in the view of the "Gate-way at Cemetery."

ing a sculptured frieze similar to that of the great gate-way. In front of this structure, to the west, and about twenty feet distant, is a wall remarkable for the fine cutting of its stones, which are of a blackish basalt and very hard.  The stones are all of equal dimensions, having a groove running around them, and each has a niche cut in it with absolute precision.  Every thing goes to show that the variety of the forms of the niches

GATE-WAY AT CEMETERY—FRONT VIEW.

was one of the great ornaments of the walls, for on all sides we find stones variously cut, and evidently intended to fit together so as to form architectural ornaments."

So much for the description of D'Orbigny.  I measured one of the blocks with a double niche, which is shown in the engraving of the terrace walls of the Fortress.  It is 6 feet 2 inches in length, 3 feet 7 inches broad, and 2 feet 6 inches thick.  The niches are sunk to the depth of 3 inches.

One of the monolithic door-ways originally belonging to this structure is unquestionably that forming the entrance to the cemetery of Tiahuanaco.   This cemetery is an ancient rectangular mound, about a hundred paces long, sixty broad, and twenty feet high, situated midway between the village and the Fortress.   Its summit is enclosed by an adobe wall, and, as I have said, the entrance is through an ancient monolithic gate-

GATE-WAY AT CEMETERY—REAR VIEW.

way, of which I give a front and rear view.  It is 7 feet 5 inches in extreme height, 5 feet 10½ inches in extreme width, and 16½ inches thick.  The door-way, or opening, is 6 feet 2 inches in height, and 2 feet 10 inches wide.  The frieze has a repetition of the ornaments composing the lower line of sculptures of the great monolith, but it has suffered much from time and violence.  The ornamentation of the back differs from that of the front, and seems to have been made to conform to the style adopted in the interior of the structure.

In making our measurement in the cemetery we disturbed a pack of lean, hungry, savage dogs of the Sierra—an indigenous species—which had dug up the body of a newly-buried child from its shallow, frozen grave, and were ravenously devouring it. They snarled at us with bristling backs and bloodshot eyes as we endeavored to drive them away from their horrible feast —by no means the first, as the numerous rough holes they had dug, the torn wrappings of the dead, and the skulls and fragments of human bodies scattered around too plainly attested. I subsequently represented the matter to the *cura*, but he only shrugged his shoulders, ejaculating, "What does it matter? They have been baptized, and all Indians are brutes at the best."

Returning to the Hall of Justice, we find, to the eastward of it, a raised area 175 feet square, and from 8 to 10 feet high, the outlines defined by walls of cut stone. This seems to have escaped the notice of travellers; at least, it is not mentioned by them. In the centre of this area there seems to have been a building about fifty feet square, constructed of very large blocks of stone, which I have denominated the "Sanctuary." Within this, where it was evidently supported on piers, is the distinctive and most remarkable feature of the structure. It is a great slab of stone 13 feet 4 inches square, and 20 inches in thickness. It is impossible to describe it intelligibly, and I must refer to the engraving for a notion of its character. It will be observed that there is an oblong area cut in the upper face of the stone, 7 feet 3 inches long, 5 feet broad, and 6 inches deep. A sort of sunken "portico" 20 inches wide, 3 feet 9 inches long, is cut at one side, out of which opens what may be called the entrance, 22 inches wide, extending to the edge of the stone.

At each end of the "portico" is a flight of three miniature steps leading up to the general surface of the stone, and sunk in it, while at the side of the excavated area are three other flights of similar steps, but in relief. They lead to the broadest part of the stone, where there are six mortises, 8 inches square, sunk

SYMBOLICAL SLAB.

in the stone 6 inches, and forming two sides of a square, of 3 feet 7 inches on each side, and apparently intended to receive an equal number of square columns. The external corners of the stone are sharp, but within six inches of the surface they are cut round on a radius of twelve inches.

I cannot resist the impression that this stone was intended as a miniature representation or model of a sacred edifice, or of some kind of edifice reared by the builders of the monuments of Tiahuanaco. The entrance to the sunken area in the stone, the steps leading to the elevation surrounding it, and the *naos* opposite the entrance, defined perhaps by columns of bronze or stone set in the mortises and supporting some kind of roof, constituting the shrine within which stood the idol or symbol of worship—all these features would seem to indicate a symbolic design in this monument. The building in which it stood, on massive piers that still remain, was constructed of blocks of stone, some of them nearly fourteen feet in length and of corresponding size and thickness, and was not so large as to pro-

hibit the probability that it was covered in.  Looking at the
plan of the Temple, and of the enclosure to the area, one side
of which was occupied by the building called the Hall of Justice, we cannot fail to observe features suggestive of the plan
cut in the great stone which I have called symbolical.

The most remarkable monument in Tiahuanaco, as already
intimated, is the great monolithic gate-way.  Its position is indicated by the letter *m* in the plan.  It now stands erect, and
is described as being in that position by every traveller except

FRONT OF GREAT MONOLITHIC GATE-WAY.

D'Orbigny, who visited the ruins in 1833, and who says it had
then fallen down.  I give two views of this unique monument,
both from photographs, of some interest to me, as the first it
was ever my fortune to be called on to take.  It will be seen
that it has been broken—the natives say by lightning—the fracture extending from the upper right-hand angle of the opening,
so that the two parts lap by each other slightly, making the
sides of the door-way incline towards each other; whereas they
are, or were, perfectly vertical and parallel —a distinguishing

feature in all of the door-ways and sculptures of Tiahuanaco.
This monolith has attracted so much attention, and the drawings that have been given of it have been so exceedingly erroneous, that I have sought to reproduce its features with the
greatest care, using the line, the pencil, the photograph, and the
cartridge-paper mould.

We must imagine first a block of stone, somewhat broken
and defaced on its edges, but originally cut with precision, 13

BACK OF GREAT MONOLITHIC GATE-WAY.

feet 5 inches long, 7 feet 2 inches high above-ground, and 18
inches thick. Through its centre is cut a door-way, 4 feet 6
inches high, and 2 feet 9 inches wide. Above this door-way,
and as it now stands on its south-east side or front, are four
lines of sculpture in low-relief, like the Egyptian plain sculptures, and a central figure, immediately over the door-way,
sculptured in high-relief. On the reverse we find the door-
way surrounded by friezes or cornices, and above it on each

20

side two small niches, below which, also on either side, is a single larger niche. The stone itself is a dark and exceedingly hard trachyte. It is faced with a precision that no skill can excel; its lines are perfectly drawn, and its right angles turned with an accuracy that the most careful geometer could not surpass. Barring some injuries and defacements, and some slight damages by weather, I do not believe there exists a better piece of stone-cutting, the material considered, on this or the other continent. The front, especially the part covered by sculpture, has a fine finish, as near a true polish as trachyte can be made to bear.

The lower line of sculpture is 7½ inches broad, and is unbroken; the three above it are 8 inches high, cut up in *cartouches*, or squares, of equal width, but interrupted in the centre, immediately over the door-way, by the figure in high-relief to which I have alluded. This figure, with its ornaments, covers a space of 32 by 21½ inches. There are consequently three ranges or tiers of squares on each side of this figure, eight in each range, or forty-eight in all. The figures represented in these squares have human bodies, feet, and hands; each holds a sceptre; they are winged; but the upper and lower series have human heads wearing crowns, represented in profile, while the heads of the sixteen figures in the line between them have the heads of condors.

The central and principal figure is angularly but boldly cut, in a style palpably conventional. The head is surrounded by a series of what may be called rays, each terminating in a circle, the head of the condor, or that of a tiger, all conventionally but forcibly treated. In each hand he grasps two staves or sceptres of equal length with his body, the lower end of the right-hand sceptre terminating in the head of the condor, and the upper in that of the tiger, while the lower end of the left-hand sceptre terminates in the head of the tiger, and the upper is bifurcate, and has two heads of the condor. The staves or sceptres are not straight and stiff, but curved as if to represent serpents, and elaborately ornamented as if to represent the sinuous action of the serpent in motion. The radiations from the

CENTRE FIGURE ON GREAT MONOLITH.

head—which I have called rays, for want of a better term—
seem to have the same action. An ornamented girdle surrounds the waist of this principal figure, from which depends
a double fringe. It stands upon a kind of base or series of figures approaching nearest in character to the architectural ornament called *grecques*, each extremity of which, however, terminates in the crowned head of the tiger or the condor. The
face has been somewhat mutilated, but shows some peculiar fig-

ures extending from the eyes diagonally across the cheeks, terminating also in the heads of the animals just named.

The winged human-headed and condor-headed figures in the three lines of squares are represented kneeling on one knee, with their faces turned to the great central figure, as if in adoration, and each one holds before him a staff or sceptre. The sceptres of the figures in the two upper rows are bifurcate, and

SCULPTURED FIGURE ON GREAT MONOLITH.

correspond exactly with the sceptre in the left hand of the central figure, while the sceptres of the lower tier correspond with that represented in his right hand. The relief of all these figures is scarcely more than two-tenths of an inch; the minor features are indicated by very delicate lines, slightly incised, which form subordinate figures, representing the heads of condors, tigers, and serpents. Most of us have seen pictures and portraits of men and animals, which under close attention resolve themselves into representatives of a hundred other things, but which are so artfully arranged as to produce a single broad effect. So with these winged figures. Every part, the limbs, the garb, all separate themselves into miniatures of the symbols that run all through the sculptures on this singular monument.

The fourth or lower row of sculpture differs entirely from the rows above it. It consists of repetitions—seventeen in all —smaller and in low-relief, of the head of the great central figure, surrounded by corresponding rays, terminating in like manner with the heads of animals. These are arranged alternately at the top and bottom of the line of sculpture, within the zigzags or *grecques*, and every angle terminates in the head of a condor.

The three outer columns of winged figures, and the corresponding parts of the lower line of sculpture, are only blocked out, and have none of the elaborate, incised ornamentation discoverable in the central parts of the monument. A very distinct line separates these unfinished sculptures from those portions that are finished, which is most marked in the lower tier. On each side of this line, standing on the rayed heads to which I have alluded, placed back to back, and looking in opposite directions, are two small but interesting figures of men, crowned with something like a plumed cap, and holding to their mouths what appear to be trumpets. Although only three inches high, these little figures are ornamented in the same manner as the larger ones, with the heads of tigers, condors, etc.

These are the only sculptures on the face of the great monolith of Tiahuanaco. I shall not attempt to explain their significance. D'Orbigny finds in the winged figures with human heads symbols or representations of conquered chiefs coming to pay their homage to the ruler who had his capital in Tiahuanuco, and who, as the founder of sun-worship and the head of the Church as of the State, was invested with divine attributes as well as with the insignia of power. The figures with condors' heads, the same fanciful philosopher supposes, may represent the chiefs of tribes who had not yet fully accepted civilization, and were therefore represented without the human profile, as an indication of their unhappy and undeveloped state.  By parity of interpretation, we may take it that the eighteen un-finished figures were those of as many chieftains as the ruler of Tiahuanuco had it in his mind to reduce, and of which, happily, just two-thirds had claims to be regarded as civilized, and, when absorbed, to be perpetuated with human heads, and not with those of condors.  Another French writer, M. Angrand, finds a coincidence between these sculptures and those of Central America and Mexico, having a corresponding mythological and symbolical significance, thus establishing identity of origin and intimate relationship between the builders of Tiahuanaco and those of Palenque, Ocosingo, and Xochicalco.

Leibnitz tells us that nothing exists without a cause; and it is not to be supposed that the sculptures under notice were made without a motive.  They are probably symbolical; but with no knowledge of the religious ideas and conceptions of the ancient people whose remains they are, it is idle to attempt to interpret them.  Nowhere else in Peru, or within the whole extent of the Inca empire, do we find any similar sculptures.  They are, as regards Inca art, quite as unique in Peru as they would be on Boston Common or in the New York Central Park.

The reverse of the great monolith shows a series of friezes over the door-way, five in number, of which the engraving will give a better idea than any description.  Above the entrance on either hand are two niches, twelve by nine inches in the ex-cavation.  It will be observed that those on the right have a sort of sculptured cornice above them which those on the left have not.  The second one on the left, it will also be observed, is not complete, but evidently intended to be finished out on another block, which was to form a continuation of the wall of which the gate-way itself was designed to be a part.  Indeed, as I have said, nearly all the blocks of stone scattered over the plain are cut with parts of niches and other architectural feat-ures, showing that they were mere fragments of a general de-sign, which could only be clearly apparent when they were properly fitted together.

The lower niches, now on a level with the ground, show that

the monolith is sunk deeply in the soil. They exhibit some peculiar features. At each inner corner above and below are vertical sockets, apparently to receive the pivots of a door, extending upwards and downwards seven inches in the stone. D'Orbigny avers that he discovered the stains of bronze in these orifices; and I have no doubt that these niches had doors, possibly of bronze, hinged in these sockets, and so firmly that it was necessary to use chisels (the marks of which are plain) to cut into the stone and disengage them. These large niches are 28.2 inches by 18.2 inches wide. On the face of the monolith, on each side of the door-way, but near the edges of the stone, are two mortises 10 inches by 9, and 6 inches deep, and 12 inches by 6, and 3½ inches deep respectively, which are not shown in the drawings published by D'Orbigny and some others.

I very much question if this remarkable stone occupies its original position. How far it has sunk in the ground it was impossible for me to determine, for the earth was frozen hard, and we had no means of digging down to ascertain. D'Orbigny, as I have already said, states it was fallen when he visited it. Who has since raised it, and for what purpose, it is impossible to say. No one that we could find either knew or cared to know anything about it. It seems to me not unlikely that it had a position in the hollow square of the structure called the Temple, in some building corresponding with that called the Hall of Justice. Or, perhaps, it had a place in the structure enclosing the stone I have ventured to call symbolical. It is neither so large nor so heavy that it may not be moved by fifty men with ropes, levers, and rollers: and although we do not know of any reason why it should have been removed from its original position, we know that many of the heaviest stones have been thus moved, including the monolithic door-way at the entrance of the cemetery.

In addition to the various features of Tiahuanaco already enumerated, I must not neglect to notice the vast blocks of unhewn and partially hewn stones, that evidently have never entered into any structure, which lie scattered among the ruins. The positions of two or three are indicated in the plan. The one to the north-east of the Temple is 26 by 17, and 3½ feet above-ground. It is of red sandstone, with deep grooves crossing each other at right angles in the centre, twenty inches deep, as if an attempt had been made to cut the stone into four equal parts. Another of nearly equal dimensions, partly hewn, lies between the Temple and the Fortress. Another, boat-shaped and curiously grooved, lies to the north-west of the great mound. It measures upwards of forty feet in length, and bears the marks of transportation from a considerable distance.

There were formerly a number of specimens of sculpture in Tiahuanaco besides the two monolithic gate-ways I have de-

HEAD OF STATUE NEAR TIAHUANACO.

scribed. Says Cieza de Leon: "Beyond this hill [referring to the Fortress] are two stone idols, of human shape, and so curiously carved that they seem to be the work of very able masters. They are as big as giants, with long garments differing from those the natives wear, and seem to have some ornament on their heads." These, according to D'Orbigny, were broken into pieces by blasts of powder inserted between the shoulders, and not even the fragments remain on the plain of Tiahuanaco. The head of one lies by the side of the road, four leagues distant, on the way to La Paz, whither an attempt was made to carry it. I did not see it, but I reproduce the sketch of it given by D'Orbigny, merely remarking that I have no doubt the details are quite as erroneous as those of the figures portrayed by the same author on the great monolith. The head is 3 feet 6 inches high and 2 feet 7 inches in diameter; so that if the other proportions of the figure were corresponding, the total height of the statue would be about eighteen feet.

D'Orbigny found several other sculptured figures among the

ruins; one with a human head and wings rudely represented;
another of an animal resembling a tiger, etc.  Castelnau mentions "an immense lizard cut in stone," and other sculptured
figures.  M. Angrand, whose notes have been very judiciously
used by M. Desjardains, speaks of eight such figures in the village of Tiahuanaco, besides two in La Paz, and one, broken, on
the road thither.  I found but two; rough sculptures of the

COLUMNS AND FIGURES IN STONE IN TIAHUANACO.

human head and bust, in coarse red sandstone, one of a man
and the other of a woman, standing by the side of the gate-way
of the church of Tiahuanaco.  They are between four and five
feet high, roughly cut, much defaced, and more like the idols
which I found in Nicaragua, and have represented in my work
on that country, than any others I have seen elsewhere.

Among the stones taken from the ruins, and worked into

buildings in the town of Tiahuanaco, are a number of cylindrical columns cut from a single block, with capitals resembling the Doric. One of these stands on each side of the entrance to the court of the church, 6 feet high and 14 inches in diameter. There are also many caps of square columns or pilasters, besides numbers of stones cut with deep single or double grooves, as if to serve for water-conduits when fitted together—a purpose the probability of which is sanctioned by finding some stones with channels leading off at right angles, like the elbows in our own water-pipes.

The stones composing the structures of Tiahuanaco, as already said, are mainly red sandstone, slate-colored trachyte, and a dark, hard basalt. None of these rocks are found *in situ* on the plain, but there has been much needless speculation as to whence they were obtained. There are great cliffs of red sandstone about five leagues to the north of the ruins, on the road to the Desaguadero; and, on the isthmus of Yunguyo, connecting the peninsula of Copacabana with the main-land, are found both basaltic and trachytic rocks, identical with the stones in the ruins. Many blocks, hewn or partially hewn, are scattered over the isthmus. It is true this point is forty miles distant from Tiahuanaco in a right line, and that, if obtained here, the stones must have been carried twenty-five miles by water and fifteen by land. That some of them were brought from this direction is indicated by scattered blocks all the way from the ruins to the lake; but it is difficult to conceive how they were transported from one shore to the other. There is no timber in the region of which to construct rafts or boats; and the only contrivances for navigation are floats, made of reeds, closely bound into cylinders, tapering at the ends, which are turned up so as to give them something of the outline of boats. Before they become water-soaked these floats are exceedingly light and buoyant.

As to how the stones of Tiahuanaco were cut, and with what kind of instruments, are questions which I do not propose to discuss. I may, nevertheless, observe that I have no reason to believe that the builders of Tiahuanaco had instruments differing essentially in form or material from those used by the Peruvians generally, which, it is certain, were of *champi*, a kind of bronze.

I have thus rapidly presented an outline of the remains of Tiahuanaco—remains most interesting, but in such an absolute condition of ruin as almost to defy inquiry or generalization. Regarding them as in some respects the most important of any in Peru, I have gone more into details concerning them than I shall do in describing the better-preserved and more intelligible monuments with which we shall have hereafter to deal.

We find on a review that, apart from five considerable mounds of earth now shapeless, with one exception, there are distinct and impressive traces of five structures, built of stones or defined by them—the Fortress, the Temple, the Palace, the Hall of Justice, and the Sanctuary—terms used more to distinguish than truly characterize them. The structure called the Fortress may indeed have been used for the purpose implied in the name. Terraced, and each terrace faced with stones, it may have been, as many of the terraced pyramids of Mexico were, equally temple and fortress, where the special protection of the divinity to whom it was reared was expected to be interposed against an enemy. But the absence of water and the circumscribed area of the structure seem to weigh against the supposition of a defensive origin or purpose. But, whatever its object, the Fortress dominated the plain; and when the edifices that crowned its summit were perfect, it must have been by far the most imposing structure in Tiahuanaco.

The Temple seems to me to be the most ancient of all the distinctive monuments of Tiahuanaco. It is the American Stonehenge. The stones defining it are rough and frayed by time. The walls between its rude pilasters were of uncut stones; and although it contains the most elaborate single monument among the ruins, and notwithstanding the erect stones constituting its portal are the most striking of their kind, it nevertheless has palpable signs of age, and an air of antiquity which we discover in none of its kindred monuments. Of course, its broad area was never roofed in, whatever may have

been the case with smaller, interior buildings no longer traceable.   We must rank it, therefore, with those vast open temples
(for of its sacred purpose we can scarcely have a doubt), of
which Stonehenge and Avebury, in England, are examples, and
which we find in Brittany, in Denmark, in Assyria, and on the
steppes of Tartary, as well as in the Mississippi Valley.   It
seems to me to have been the nucleus around which the remaining monuments of Tiahuanaco sprung up, and the model upon
which some of them were fashioned.   How far, in shape or arrangement, it may have been symbolical, I shall not undertake
to say ; but I think that students of antiquity are generally prepared to concede a symbolical significance to the primitive
pagan temples as well as to the cruciform edifices of Christian
times.

We can hardly conceive of remains so extensive as those of
Tiahuanaco, except as indications of a large population, and as
evidences of the previous existence on or near the spot of a considerable city.   But we find nowhere in the vicinity any decided
traces of ancient habitations, such as abound elsewhere in Peru,
in connection with most public edifices.   Again, the region
around is cold, and for the most part arid and barren.   Elevated
nearly thirteen thousand feet above the sea, no cereals grow
except barley, which often fails to mature, and seldom, if ever,
so perfects itself as to be available for seed.   The maize is
dwarf and scant, and uncertain in yield ; and the bitter potato
and quinoa constitute almost the sole articles of food for the
pinched and impoverished inhabitants.   This is not, *primâ
facie*, a region for nurturing or sustaining a large population,
and certainly not one wherein we should expect to find a capital.
Tiahuanaco may have been a sacred spot or shrine, the position
of which was determined by an accident, an augury, or a dream,
but I can hardly believe that it was a seat of dominion.

Some vague traditions point to Tiahuanaco as the spot
whence Manco Capac, the founder of the Inca dynasty, took
his origin, and whence he started northwards to teach the rude
tribes of the Sierra religion and government; and some late
writers, D'Orbigny and Castelnau among them, find reasons for

believing that the whole Inca civilization originated here, or was only a reflex of that which found here a development, never afterwards equalled, long before the golden staff of the first Inca sunk into the earth where Cuzco was founded, thus fixing through superhuman design the site of the imperial city. But the weight of tradition points to the rocky islands of Lake Titicaca as the cradle of the Incas, whence Manco Capac and Mama Oello, his wife and sister, under the behest of their father, the Sun, started forth on their beneficent mission. Certain it is that this lake and its islands were esteemed sacred, and that on the latter were reared structures, if not so imposing as many other and perhaps later ones, yet of peculiar sanctity.

But before starting on our visit to that lake and its sacred islands, I must relate some of the incidents of our stay in Tiahuanaco.

# CHAPTER XVI.

### AT TIAHUANACO, AND TO THE SACRED ISLANDS.

I HAVE no doubt the *cura* of Tiahuanaco believes to this day that our visit to the ruins was for the purpose of digging for treasures, and that we had some *itinerario*, or guide, obtained from the archives of Old Spain to direct our search.

What the Indians themselves thought, they did not tell us. But on our very first day among the monuments, and within an hour after we had pitched our photographic tent and got out our instruments, we became aware of the presence of a very old man, withered, wrinkled, and bent with the weight of years. His hair was scant and gray, his eyes rheumy, and his face disfigured by a great quid of coca that he carried in one cheek. He wore tattered pantaloons of coarse native cloth, made from the fleece of the llama, kept together by thongs; his poncho was old and ragged; and the long woollen cap, that was pulled low over his forehead, was greasy from use and stiff with dirt. He had an earthen vessel containing water suspended from his waist, besides a pouch of skin containing coca, and a little gourd of unslacked lime. In his hand he carried a small double-edged stone-cutter's pick or hammer. He paid us no perceptible attention, but wandered about deliberately among the blocks of cut stone that strew the ground, and finally selected one of a

kind of white tufa, which he rolled slowly and with many a
pause up to the very foot of the great monolith, then seated
himself on the ground, placed it between his legs, and after preparing a new quid of coca, began to work on the stone, apparently with the purpose of cutting it in halves.  He worked at
it all day with small effect, and during the whole time neither
noticed us nor responded to our questions.  Just before returning to the village, in the edge of the chill night, I prevailed on
one of our arrieros, who could speak Aymará, to ask him what
was his occupation.  He got the curt answer from the old man,
that he was "cutting out a cross."  Every morning he was at
the ruins before us, and he never left until after we did at
night.  All day he pecked away at the stone between his knees,
apparently absorbed in his work and oblivious of our presence.
After a time we came to look upon him as an integral part of
the monuments, and should have missed him as much as the
great monolith itself.

One evening I mentioned the old man to the *cura*, who again
put on mystery, took me out for a turn in the plaza, and explained in whispers, heavy with fumes of cañaso, that the old
man was nothing more nor less than a spy on our doings, and
that we made no movement in any direction that he did not
carefully observe.  "He is," said the padre, "one of the guardians of the *tapadas*.  He is more than a hundred years old.
He was with Tupac Amaru when he undertook to overturn the
Spanish power, and he led the Aymarás when they sacked the
town of Huancane, and slew every white man, woman, and child
that fell into their hands.  He is a heathen still, and throws
coca on the *apachetas*.  Ah! if I only knew what that old man
knows of the *tapadas*, señor," exclaimed the *cura*, with fervor,
" I should not waste my life among these barbarians!  You can
pity me!  And for the love of God, señor, if you do come across
the treasures, share them with me!  I can't live much longer
here!"  And the padre burst into a maudlin paroxysm of tears.

Von Tschudi, when he was at Tiahuanaco, found or obtained
some ancient relics—small stone idols, if I remember rightly—
but had not proceeded many miles on his way to La Paz before

he was surrounded by a party of Indians from the town, and compelled to surrender them. We suffered no molestation, although there is no doubt we were closely watched, and that the deaf and apparently almost sightless old stone-cutter was a spy on our actions.

I have already said that our visit to Tiahuanaco was coincident in time with the Chuño and Corpus Christi. The population of the place, as indeed of the whole region, is Indian, the white priests, officials, and landed proprietors being so few as hardly to deserve enumeration. These Indians are of the Aymará as distinguished from the Quichua family, and are a swarthier, more sullen, and more cruel race. Their celebration of the Chuño feast, a ceremony dating back of the Conquest, and of the feast of the Church, were equally remarkable, and, as throwing some light on their earlier practices and present condition, probably not unworthy a brief notice.

I have mentioned an acrid variety of the potato as among the principal articles of food in the Sierra. It is rendered more palatable than when used in its natural state, and better capable of being preserved, by being spread out on the ground, and exposed for some weeks to the frosts at night and the sun by day, until it becomes chuño, when it is stored away for consumption. The chuño had just been housed when we reached Tiahuanaco ; and on the second night after our arrival the preparations for celebrating the event were commenced by large indulgences in chicha and cañaso, with corresponding uproars in different parts of the village, strangely compounded of cheers, howls, whoops, and shrieks, not favorable to sleep, and not altogether assuring to travellers among a people notoriously morose, jealous, and vindictive. On the morning of our third day, as we started out for the ruins, we noticed that the sides of the plaza were lined with venders of chicha, chupe, coarse cakes, and *charqui*, or jerked meat, and that several posts had been erected in various parts of the square. During the day the bells of the church clanged incessantly ; there was an irregular fusillade of *cohetes* (diminutive rockets) and an unceasing drumming, relieved, or at any rate varied, by the shrill notes of the syrinx, or Pan's-pipe, and the wild, savage shouts of the revellers.

I shall never forget the extraordinary scene that startled us on our return to the village in the evening. The streets were deserted, and the entire population of the place was gathered in the plaza, grouped along its sides, where glowed fires fed by stalks of quinoa, while the central part of the square was oc-

cupied by four groups of male and female dancers, dressed in ordinary costume, except that the men in each group had handkerchiefs, or squares of cotton cloth of different colors, fastened, as a distinguishing badge, over their right shoulders, and falling down their backs. They wore head-dresses of various-colored feathers or plumes, lengthened out by slips of cane, and rising to the height of from five to six feet, like an inverted umbrella, from a head-band tightly fitting around the forehead. Under the left arm each man held a rude drum, large in circumfer-

HEAD-DRESS OF INDIAN FEMALE DANCER.

ence, but shallow, which he beat with a stick grasped in his right hand, while in his left he held to his mouth a Pan's-pipe, differing in size and tone from that of his neighbor. With each group were a number of females, all dressed in blue, but, like the men, wearing scarfs of differently colored cloth over their left shoulders crossing their breasts. They, too, wore hats or head-dresses of stiff paper, the rim perfectly flat and round, plaited and cut so as to represent the conventional figure of the

21.

sun with its rays.  The crown was composed of three semi-
circular pieces, placed triangularly, with the rays, in different
colors, radiating from little square mirrors set in their centre.

Each group danced vigorously to its united music, which
made up in volume what it lacked in melody—wild and pierc-
ing, yet lugubrious; the shrill pipe and the dull drum, with
frequent blasts on cow's horns by amateurs among the spectators, filled the ear with discordant sounds.  Every man seemed
anxious to excel his neighbor in the energy of his movements,
which were often extravagant; but the motions of the women
were slow and stately.  The music had its cadences, and its
emphatic parts were marked by corresponding emphatic movements in the dance.  The "devilish music" that Cortez heard
after his first repulse before Mexico, lasting the livelong night,
and which curdled his blood with horror, while his captured

INDIANS CELEBRATING THE CHUÑO, OR POTATO FESTIVAL, TIAHUANACO.

companions were sacrificed to Huitzlipochtli, the Aztec war-god, could not be stranger or more fascinating, more weird or savage, than that which rung in our ears during the rest of our stay in Tiahuanaco.   All night and all day, still the festival went on, growing wilder and noisier, and only culminating when the feast of the Church commenced.   It was an extraordinary spectacle, that of the symbols of Christianity and the figures of our Saviour and the saints carried by a reeling priest and staggering Indians through the streets of Tiahuanaco, while the Chuño revellers danced and drummed around them.   The chants of the Church were mingled with the sharp tones of the syrinx while the bells pealed, and the foul smoke of wretched candles, combined with the odor of damp powder, obscured and poisoned the atmosphere.   In the church, before the dim altar, when the Host was raised in the unsteady hands of the sot who affronted Heaven and debased religion, the saturnalia reached their height, and we left the scene with a clear conviction that the savage rites of the Aymarás had changed in name only, and that the festival we had witnessed was a substantial rehearsal of ceremonies and observances antedating the Discovery.

The road northward from Tiahuanaco is raised above the general level in consequence of the flooding of the plain during the rainy season, and marked every league by adobe columns.   Passing some large buildings, situated at the base of the western hills, which had belonged to the Jesuits, who obtained, and at one time held, almost absolute control of this entire region, and reared in every village temples emulating in massiveness those of the Incas, we reached, at a distance of four leagues, the village of Guaque, distinguished not alone for its vast church, but for containing in its plaza half a dozen quenua, or wild olive-trees, with trunks at least five inches in diameter —isolated and, in this part of the Sierra, mammoth products of the vegetable world.   Here, too, the Indians were celebrating Corpus Christi, but instead of the syrinx they played on a kind of flute of cane; their drums were smaller, and their head-dresses different from those of their neighbors of Tiahuanaco, but quite as gaudy. They wore similar insignia over their shoulders, but were not so utterly gone in intoxication.

A little beyond Guaque the road strikes the shore of the Lake of Titicaca, or rather the lesser body of water connected with it, and sometimes called Tiquini or Chucuito. For a considerable distance from the shore the water is shallow, and is full of a kind of lake-weed which grows to the surface, where it forms an evergreen mat. This weed is freely eaten by the oxen and cows of the Sierra, and is their principal food when

CATTLE FEEDING ON LAKE-WEED, LAKE TITICACA.

drought and frost destroy the pasturage. They wade into the water until their backs are scarcely visible, in order to obtain it, advancing farther and farther from shore as the lake-level falls, so that there is always a clear space of water near the land, and an emerald belt of verdure beyond. All along, overhanging the road and the lake shore, is a cliff of red sandstone, great blocks of which have fallen down and obstruct the path. This stone is precisely the same with many of the blocks in the ruins of Tiahuanaco, and the latter were no doubt obtained from some portion of the great ledge under the shadow of which we travelled.

Five leagues from Guaque and nine from Tiahuanaco we reached the Desaguadero a second time.  It forms here the boundary between Bolivia and Peru, and each state has a customs establishment and a dozen soldiers on its own bank.  One of these peremptorily ordered us up to the tumble-down building which bears the name of Aduana; but the officer in command, who had heard of our approach, permitted us to pass on without dismounting.

TOTORA BRIDGE OVER THE OUTLET OF LAKE TITICACA.

We crossed the river at the point where it debouches from the lake, on another floating bridge of totora.  A few balsas of the same material were moored just above the bridge, as was also a rough wooden barge, sloop-rigged, built at great expense by Mr. Forbes, for transporting hither copper ores from the opposite shore of the lake.  The river flows out through a low and marshy plain, bounded by high disrupted cliffs of lime and sandstone, with a strong, majestic current.  After a course of a few miles it spreads out in a series of shallow lakes or marshes (*totorales*), full of reeds, fish, and water-fowls, in which the remnants of a wild Indian tribe, the Uros, have their abodes.  They live on floats or rafts of totora, and, it is alleged, subsist on fish and game, cultivating only a few bitter potatoes and ocas in the recesses of the Sierra of Tiahuanaco. *

The village called El Desaguadero is built on the Peruvian bank of the river, under the shadow of a high, rocky eminence, on which stand the gray ruins of an old *calvario*, or church. The village is mean, with a dilapidated, half-roofed church, in the plaza in which the *cura* and principal inhabitants were enjoying the *fiesta*. Across the entrance of the plaza, stretched between two crooked poles, was a rope, from which depended what were meant to be decorations. These consisted chiefly of silver valuables belonging to the people — cups, goblets, plates, platters, soup-tureens, spoons, strings of Spanish dollars, and one or two articles of domestic use which will hardly bear to be designated, and which certainly, whether of silver or other material, are seldom conspicuous in well-conducted households. In the corners of the plaza were improvised altars adorned with mirrors, paintings from the church, highly colored lithographs, and gay hangings, such as bedspreads, scarlet table-cloths, variegated sashes and handkerchiefs and other flaming finery. To the left of the plaza was a kind of open tent or awning spread over a space carpeted with a mat of reeds, within which were seats, and here were the *élite* of the place, of both sexes, engaged in celebrating the *fiesta*, while some Indians, fantastically dressed, were dancing to discordant music in front of the little church.

The scene was equally droll and barbaric, and we involuntarily checked our horses as we passed beneath the extraordinary string of treasures that garnished the entrance to the

---

* These Indians and their modes of life are mentioned by Herrera in his "History." "They were so savage," he affirms, "that when asked who they were, they answered they were not men, but *Uros*, as if they had been a different species of animals. *In the lake there were found whole towns of them living on floats of totora, made fast to rocks, and when they thought fit the whole town removed to another place.*" This illustration of the modes of life of a rude, primitive people has interest in connection with the discovery of the remains of what are called "lacustrine" dwellings in the Swiss lakes.

plaza. We had hardly time to take in the view before we were approached by the *cura* himself, holding in one hand a bottle, and in the other a small silver cup. His face was red and glistening, his eyes watery and blinking, his step decidedly unsteady, and his accents thick. He insisted on our taking a *trago* (drop), and then on our dismounting, and being introduced to the party beneath the awning, where, in answer to our inquiries, he said we would find the comandante, to whom we had let-

ENTRY INTO THE PUEBLO OF EL DESAGUADERO.

ters, and on whose hospitality we proposed to trespass. So we complied, and were formally introduced to each and all of the caballeros and señoritas, for it is the custom to designate all the women of Peru, young and old, married and single, by this diminutive designation. And with each and all we had to take a *traguito* (little drop), happily in cups not much bigger than a thimble. The señoritas were certainly affable, and the gentlemen almost affectionate—it was late in the afternoon, and this

was the third day of the *fiesta* — so that we had some difficulty in getting away with the comandante to his house, which,
like all the others, was small and poor.  The comandante was
an old man, and yet only a colonel, in a country where every
third man is a general, and every tenth one a grand marshal.
He, nevertheless, claimed a historic name, and relationship with
the last of the viceroys.

I shot some ducks in the half-frozen pools behind the comandante's house, and what with these, some articles from my
stores, and a mess of a very good fish called *suches*, from the
lake (the sole contribution of the comandante), we did not sup
altogether badly in El Desaguadero.  My bed was spread on a
settle of rough poles on one side of the room, under which the
dishes from our table were hustled away by the solitary Indian
*pongo*, or servant; for such a thing as cleansing the cups and
plates for the next meal until the time for it comes round is
unknown in Peru.  H—— contrived to dispose himself on
some bags of barley in a corner, and the comandante, under
the hallucination consequent on three days of festivities, mis-
took my wax-candles for his fetid dips, and disappeared with
them, two boxes of sardines, and a can of biscuits, in another
apartment.  I fear he was not an early riser, for he had not
made his appearance when we left next morning.

Climbing the abrupt ridge behind the town of El Desaguadero, we descended again to the shore of the lake, along which
the road runs to the town of Zepita, a rambling, shabby place,
hanging on the skirts of a long and steep ridge just above a low,
marshy plain.  We found here a kind of tambo, in which were
gathered a great number of drunken natives, returning from
the fair of Vilque, near Puno, and were obliged to breakfast on
the tough flesh of a veteran llama which had been killed that
morning, eked out with a few eggs.  Mule meat, especially
from an animal that has been killed because he is too much reduced to travel, is not highly esteemed by epicures; but I can
testify that it is preferable to that of the llama in its best estate,
and even llama meat is better than none at all.

At Zepita we turned off from the direct road to Puno to the

right, over the marshy plain of which I have spoken, for the
purpose of visiting the peninsula of Copacabana, and the island
adjacent.  The path runs on a causeway of earth and stones
which keeps it above the pools and creeks of the low plain, over
which were scattered great flocks of water-fowls of almost every
kind, including vast numbers of gulls, white and mottled, fla-
mingoes, ibises, geese, ducks, water-hens, and divers.  These
would whirl up in clouds, with a noise like that of a high wind
in a forest, on our approach, and circle, screaming, in the air,
and then settle down again on some new spot, literally hiding
the ground from sight.  The bridges across the water runways
are curious constructions of turf, each layer projecting over
that beneath until the upper ones touch and brace against each
other, forming a rude kind of arch, which is curious, but not
calculated to inspire any strong sense of security.  The absence
of wood and timber has led the people of the Sierra to adopt a
great many novel and striking devices to remedy the deficiency,
in architecture and navigation as well as in road-making.

At the distance of a league the ground becomes higher and
firm, sloping gently to the south, and dotted over with houses
and flocks.  Nowhere in the interior of Peru does the traveller
find more evidences of industry and thrift than here.  The
wealth of the people consists almost entirely in herds and flocks.
They supply La Paz and Arequipa with cattle, and produce
a valuable annual crop of wool.  Owing to some advantage
in exposure, better soil, or fortunate action of the lake on the
temperature, the best potatoes of the region are raised here,
and in some favorable seasons barley will mature.

In all directions over the undulating slope are numberless
mounds of stone heaped together with great regularity, probably the result of ages of labor in clearing the stony ground.
We observed also, lying near our path, many large blocks of
basalt and trachyte, some completely, and others only partially
hewn, and corresponding exactly in material and workmanship
with those of Tiahuanaco.  They were evidently obtained from
the quarries visible at the foot of the rocky eminences on our
left, and had been abandoned midway to the lake.  I have no

doubt that most, if not all, of the stones at Tiahuanaco were procured here, and from the sandstone cliffs south of El Desaguadero, and were transported on balsas to the southern extremity of the bay of Guaque.

All day we enjoyed a magnificent panorama of the great bulk of Illampu and its snow-crowned dependencies, which appeared to rise from the very edge of the bright-blue lake, itself dotted with bold, brown islands. At five o'clock we reached Yunguyo, situated on the narrow isthmus that connects the peninsula of Copacabana with the main-land. It is a considerable town, with two large churches and a great plaza, which we found full of drunken, noisy revellers, who, the night before, had succeeded in setting fire to the thatched roof of a *pulperia*, whence the flames had spread around two sides of the square, leaving only a series of low, black walls, within which still steamed up a choking smoke and a sickening odor of smouldering damp hay and burning feathers. The "conflagration" had not checked the humors of the *fiesta*, and drumming and piping and dancing were going on with an energy only equalled by that displayed at Tiahuanuco. We had some difficulty in getting through the boisterous and rather sinister-looking crowd, and still more in finding any body sober enough to show us the house of the comandante. He was out, attending a grand dinner of the authorities of the place, reënforced by the presence of the district judge from Juli; but he no sooner heard of our arrival than he left his friends, and hastened to welcome us, and then insisted on our returning with him and joining the festive party.

It was in vain we protested that we were unpresentable in polite society, and begged to be allowed to change our coarse and travel-stained clothing. We were literally captured by our new and ardent friend, and followed him submissively to the banquet. The gathering was chiefly of men dressed in black, which is severely *au règle* on grand occasions in Peru; but the styles were various, extending through those of many years. And the stove-pipe hats—well, I could not help thinking that they had been borrowed from some ancient Hebraic recepta-

cle of that wonderful covering for the head.  The ladies were
dressed in a garb less foreign and less pretentious, but much
more tasteful and appropriate.  Chupe, in a variety of shapes,
and different degrees of consistency and nauseousness, formed
the staple of the dinner, while the "flowing bowl" was filled
with sweet Malaga wine with a distinct flavor of treacle and
senna.  Abundant wild-fowl—geese and ducks of many varieties—were disporting within gunshot of our windows, and there
were fish eager to be caught within a hundred paces; yet we
had neither fish nor game—only chupe and lean mutton of the
color and nearly of the consistence of blocks of mahogany.

A DINNER COMPLIMENT IN YUNGUYO.

At Yunguyo the same peculiarly striking habit prevails as at
Lima, already referred to as an act of pleasing condescension on
the part of the gentleman, which is reciprocated by the lady—
namely, of passing morsels of food, the former on his fork, and
the latter with her bare fingers, which convey the tidbits into
the mouth of the gallant.

The lion of the day was the legal luminary and judicial functionary of Juli.  He was misplaced in the Sierra, and only required to have had checks a little more puffy, a voice a trifle
more grum, and a horse-hair wig to have made him an ornament to the English bench.  He was familiar with Roman law

and the "Code Napoléon," but rather weak in geography, and somewhat confused as to the relative positions of London and New York. On his earnest solicitation I promised to stop with him when I reached Juli.

The boundary between Peru and Bolivia—a most arbitrary and inconvenient one—crosses the isthmus leading to the peninsula of Copacabana, a league beyond Yunguyo. Among the guests at our dinner was the Bolivian comandante of the peninsula; and we arranged to leave our baggage-mules behind to recuperate, and to accompany him next morning to the seat of his jurisdiction, where the famous Virgin of Copacabana has her rich and imposing shrine. Thence we proposed to visit the Sacred Islands in Lake Titicaca.

VIEW OF THE BAY OF COPACABANA, LAKE TITICACA.

# CHAPTER XVII.

### THE SACRED ISLANDS OF TITICACA.

A LEAGUE past Yunguyo the traveller ascends a high transverse ridge, which is the boundary between Bolivia and Peru.
Just within the line, and in the territory of the latter, stands
the Calvario of Yunguyo, half church, half fortress, which is the
Peruvian bulwark against Bolivian invasion by way of the peninsula of Copacabana.

Beyond the church militant is a sweet vale, circled in by
rocks of fantastic form, which it requires but little imagination
to shape into rigid and monstrous figures of men and animals.
And I could well understand how the pilgrim in Inca times,
wending his weary way to the Sacred Islands, might have his
simple and superstitious mind impressed and awed by these
stony effigies, which tradition says are the vestiges of impious
men and giants whom an outraged Divinity had congealed into
stone, as a punishment for their iniquities and a warning to
those who might follow them over this holy path without due
preliminary fasting and penitential propitiations.

Climbing another ridge which shoots out abruptly into the lake from the high, rocky, central mass of the peninsula, and passing some fields of oca and patches of lupins, we came to a spot, marked by the ruins of an ancient church, where the Bay of Copacabana is first seen spreading out its blue, tranquil waters framed in by rugged headlands, and lending its liquid perspective to the island of Titicaca, sacred to the Beneficent Sun, and on which first fell the footsteps of his celestial messenger. I am an old traveller, and not given to "sensations," but I must confess that here I experienced an emotion. At least, I was so assured by H——, who felt my pulse for the purpose of ascertaining the fact. "Deducting for a slight irregularity, consequent on walking up the hill rather rapidly, he discovered a percussion in the pulse, such as often attends sudden excitement." And he recommended a tranquillizing glass of chicha from the stores with which Berrios had been supplied by the considerate comandante of Yunguyo. Satisfied with his diagnosis of my case, I walked along the crest of the ridge to the point where it broke off in a sheer cliff, two thousand feet perpendicular, and occupied myself in timing the fall of stones into the water below, while H—— made a sketch of the scene.

Down the steep declivity of the ridge, between substantial stone-walls defining fields just cleared of their barley, or in which quaintly dressed Indians were gathering the bright and tender ocas, we finally turned the point of a promontory, and came in view of the "Ciudad Bendita" of Copacabana—a large and rambling town, built on an eminence at the base of a pyramid of lofty, splintered rocks, with the gray and solemn mass of the Shrine of Nuestra Señora de Copacabana rising grandly in the centre of its low and clustering habitations, just as the Cathedral of Strasburg and the Duomo of Milan project their stately outlines above the haunts of men at their feet.

Minor shrines there were in the suburbs, gaudy in archaic coloring, in which pilgrims, through prayer and penance, prepare themselves to encounter the greater sanctities in store for them in the sacred village. Our comandante did not mind

SHRINE OF NUESTRA SEÑORA DE COPACABANA.

the shrines, but ordered up the first inhabitant he met, who removed his hat, touched his forehead to our stirrups, saluting us with "*Tat-tai Viracocha!*" (Father Viracocha), and directed him, in Aymará, to prepare some house that he designated for our reception, and to get barley for our animals. Clearly the comandante knew how to use his powers in Copacabana.

Nothing could be drearier than the streets of the seat of the famous Virgin. The houses are as close and repulsive as those of Tiahuanaco. The plaza is wide, but the buildings on three sides are dwarfed by the imposing architectural proportions of the shrine occupying the remaining side. The *fiesta* of the church was nearly over, and the candles had flared out and the flowers were withered in the improvised shrines or altars that had been raised under make-shift tents in the corners of the plaza. A line of Aymará women, each with her little store of aji, ocas, dried fish, and lupins, was ranged down the centre of the square, while a vagrant herd of thin, bow-backed dogs sneaked over the vacant space in hopeless search for some fragment of food to satiate their ravenous hunger.  Squalid Indians and lean llamas glided around the corners, and shivering, unkempt Indian women glanced out furtively from behind the hide curtains that answer for doors of their wretched dwellings, as we clattered over the rough stone pavements towards the house of the comandante.  Squalor of life was never more strongly contrasted with splendor in religion than in this remote and almost inaccessible town of Copacabana.

The house of the comandante was by no means imposing, his retinue was not grand, and his *ménage* was scant; but when we rode under the low and crumbling archway that led to the court-yard of his modest residence, his retainers hastened, with uncovered heads, to touch their foreheads to our knees, and to hail us "*Tat-tai Viracocha!*" for Viracocha, reputed to have been born of the sea, and one of the most conspicuous personages of the Inca pantheon, had blue eyes, fair hair, and a light complexion.  They did not salute our dark-browed and sallow host with any such appellation, and he was evidently a little annoyed by the omission, since he asked us to pardon *los tontos* (the idiots)!  We were vain enough not to see the matter in the same light with the comandante, and H—— was at "a loss to know why a blue-eyed Irishman and a fair-haired Yankee should require to have an apology because they happened to be mistaken for demi-gods."  In fact, we only regretted that we did not possess a first-rate *huaca* and a moderate knowledge of Aymará, to enable us to set up an opposition establishment to that of Nuestra Señora, on the hill opposite her gorgeous temple.  For the sanctity of Copacabana is by no means wholly due to Nuestra Señora, but rather to a certain "idol of vast renown among the Gentiles," that preceded her here, to whom, the chroniclers tell us, were raised "sumptuous temples," and who was attended by "a multitude of priests and virgins."

The comandante secured us a vacant house, which, from having been long shut up, was a little close and musty; but as four months had passed since its occupants had died of small-pox, it was considered safe for Viracochas. And he gave us a breakfast as sumptuous as utter disregard of expense and a reckless exercise of unrestricted authority could secure. A pig had been slain and paid for, but there was an Aymará house-hold, like Rachel, comfortless and in tears, for it could not be replaced—there were only four more in all Copacabana! And the comandante exulted in producing a pound of Puno but-ter, golden under its transparent covering. Then we had ocas boiled and ocas roasted to eat with the butter withal. Still, *crescendo*, we had onions, small, it is true, but very strong; and I capped the topmost wave of our morning of enjoyment by producing a box of biscuits, crisp as when they came from the defty hand of the London baker. Chicha was not altogether a successful substitute for Falernian, but, then, all deficiencies were more than made up by a cup of Yungas coffee, fragrant and potential, a fortification and solace to the body, and a stim-ulus to the intelligence.

Any description of the church and shrine of Nuestra Señora of Copacabana would convey but a poor idea of its extent and magnificence. It is built mainly of brick, roofed with glisten-ing green and yellow tiles, and stands within a vast square sur-rounded by heavy walls and planted with quenua-trees and the shrub that produces the brilliant crimson trumpet-shaped flower called "Flor del Inca" (*Cantuta buxifolia*). The entrance is through ponderous iron gates, wrought in Spain, beneath a lofty gate-way. In the enclosure fronting the church is a ma-jestic dome of stone, ninety feet high, rising over three tall and elaborately carved crosses of alabaster, supported on a graduated base of the same material. Sculptured figures of saints and angels bend down from the cornice, and the mystic triangle ap-pears in the midst of a painted glory in the dome. At each corner of the court are square substantial structures of brick, closed by solid iron doors, and without other opening except one or two narrow port-holes. In these are deposited the bones of the pilgrims who have died at Copacabana. The church is high, and the interior so sombre that it is with difficulty one

can make out the elaborate ornaments of the various altars and
the subjects of the numerous pictures that cover its walls.
Connected with it are courts and cloisters, sown with barley or
choked with rubbish, the crazy doors creaking dismally on their
hinges, and all things suggestive of decay and desolation.

The great feature of the edifice, however, is the *camarin*, or
chamber, of the Virgin, which is a large room behind the great
altar. Here is her shrine, and this is the Holy of Holies of
Copacabana. Admittance here must be prefaced by confession
and the payment of a certain sum of money. In this way the
revenues of Nuestra Señora are kept up, and her corps of priests
supported. The guardian of the shrine, a handsome, intelligent
man from La Paz, on whose shoulders the mantle of the priesthood rested lightly, and who appeared better fitted for the
camp and the forum than the services of the altar, received us
in the anteroom of the *camarin*, and, with a smile, made a dis-
pensation of both fee and confession in our favor. The *camarin*
is reached by two stairways—one for ascent, on one side, and
another for descent, on the other, so that the crowds that pay
their devotions here at stated periods may not come to an absolute dead-lock. The *fiesta* had drawn together a considerable
number of Indians from the neighboring towns, and an unbroken
line of them was ascending the stairs, the stone steps of which
were deeply worn by pious knees, guided by a priest who, seated in a niche, drawled out certain chants or prayers in Aymará,
which were responded to by the devotees.

Our conductor peremptorily ordered the dusky pilgrims to
make room for us, and they flattened themselves against the
rough walls on either side, that we might pass. The *camarin*
of the Virgin is judiciously draped so as to secure only that
"dim, religious light" of which poets write. A thick but rather gaudy carpet covered the floor, a cabinet-organ stood in a
niche near the door, and the walls were adorned with votive offerings of every kind and every degree of value. Here were
the diamond-hilted sword and the gold-mounted pistols of General Santa Cruz, and the jewels of his wife, as well as little rude
silver representations of arms, legs, hearts, and eyes, deposited

here by the Indians in token of the wonderful interpositions and cures of Nuestra Señora.

The image of the Virgin is kept in a kind of alcove, behind a heavy curtain of embroidered velvet, and shut off from too close approach by a stout silver railing. At the tinkling of a bell by some unseen acolyte, who next struck up a monotonous strain on the parlor-organ, every body sunk on his knees, the spangled velvet veil was slowly withdrawn, and the *milagrosa imágen* of Nuestra Señora of Copacabana revealed to our heretical eyes. It is an elaborately dressed figure, scarcely three feet high, brilliant in gay satins, and loaded with gold and jewels. Its head is a mite in comparison with the blazing crown that it supports, and its face is delightfully white-and-pink, and as glistening as the average of female busts in the windows of the shops of metropolitan *coiffeurs des dames*. It derives special celebrity, and no doubt much of its popularity among the Indians, from the fact that it was made (so runs the legend) in 1582 by Tito-Yupanqui, a lineal descendant of the ruling Incas, who had had no previous instruction in art, but was inspired by the Virgin herself, who favored him with a special sitting, so that there should be no mistake in her portrait.

This shrine is the resort of pilgrims from almost every part of Catholic America, but especially from the provinces of Brazil and the La Plata. As many as thirty thousand have been known to visit it in a single season. Nor is the renown of Our Lady of Copacabana limited to America. Among the suffering faces of the devotees in the *camarin* I shall never forget that of a fair, pale girl, who was reclining on a mat in front of the shrine, with her great lustrous eyes fixed immovably on the image of the Virgin. Every day for weeks she had been lifted to her place in the sacred chamber by Indians who ascended the stone stairway on their knees. She was from Barcelona, in Spain, and had come here as a last resort, after having visited every shrine of celebrity in the Old World.

Around the neck of the image of the Virgin were several strings of little wooden crosses, one of which the custodian reverently removed, and placed it in my hand as we descended the

stairs. It is supposed to have imbibed special virtues and powers from having been hung around the neck of the Virgin for
a single night. We saw and listened in decorous silence, but
on our way with our conductor to his apartments, under his invitation to join him in a glass of sherry, H—— profanely observed that, except the convent at the foot of Mount Sinai, he
knew of no place that would better repay the sacking than the
shrine of Nuestra Señora of Copacabana. The guardian's eyes
twinkled when I repeated to him the impious observation, and
he gave me an answer which in its ambiguity led me to infer
that the conservators of the shrine had long before taken judi-

SEATS CUT IN THE ROCK, COPACABANA.

cious care of all the real diamonds and rubies that had been deposited there by pious penitents, and that the loot of the robber of the *camarin* would hardly repay him for his risks of
probable detection in this world and of certain damnation in
the next.

The idol that lent its sanctity and fame to Copacabana, before it was supplanted by the handiwork of Tito-Yupanqui,
also gave its name to the place and peninsula; the word signifying, according to the chroniclers, a precious stone from which
one may see, or which gives vision. It was buried by the Indians on the arrival of the Spaniards, but subsequently disin

terred by the latter, and broken into pieces.  It was of a beautiful blue stone, representing the human face.  The temples of
which the early writers speak have entirely disappeared, or left
only few and unsatisfactory traces.  Yet in the suburbs of the
town, near the cemetery, we find a great number of niches,
steps, and what appear to have been intended as seats cut in
the rocks, which may have had some connection with the ancient worship.

THE BATH OF THE INCAS, COPACABANA.

At the hacienda of Cusijata, half a league from the town,
there are some scant remains of what tradition affirms was a
palace of the Incas.  These consist mainly of large and well-
cut blocks of stone; but the sole remaining object of interest
is what is called the "Bath of the Incas."  It may be described
as a huge vase of simple form, cut from a single block of fine-
grained trachyte, having an inner diameter of three feet four
inches, and a depth of five feet two inches.  Its walls are six
inches thick.  It is now sunk in the ground, in a small, dilapidated building of adobes, and is still used as a bath.

Immediately on our arrival in Copacabana, the comandante

had sent an Indian with an order to the alcaldes of the island
of Titicaca to have a balsa in readiness for us on the following day at the embarcadero of Yampupata, four leagues distant.
We started for that point at noon, with the intention of reaching the island the same night. The road descends abruptly
from the rocky eminence on which the town is built into a beautiful level amphitheatre two miles broad, and curves around the
head of a bay that here projects into the land between two high
and rugged capes. The water toyed and sparkled among the
pebbles on the shore, and along it a troop of lively plover was
racing in eager search for the minute mollusks drifted up by
the waves, with the advance and recession of which their line
kept a wavering cadence. Past the little plain is what in Peru
is called a *ladera;* in other words, the road runs high up along
the face of the steep, and in many places absolutely perpendicular, headlands that overhang the lake, and becomes a mere
goat's path, narrow and rugged, half worn, half cut, in the rock.

But neither the difficulty nor the danger of the path could
wholly withdraw our attention from the hundreds of wide and
wonderful views that burst on our sight at every bend and turning. The bold, bare peninsulas; the bluff, panoramic headlands
behind which the lake stole in, through many a rent in their
rocky palisade, and spread out in broad and placid bays; the islands equally abrupt and bold and bare; the ruddy bulk of the
sacred island of Titicaca; the distant shores of Bolivia, with
their silver cincture of the Andes; the blue waters and sparkling waves, with almost every other element of the beautiful
and impressive—went to make up the kaleidoscopic scenes of
the afternoon, and, with the cloudless sky, bright sunlight, and
bracing air, to inspire us with a sense of elevation and repose
inconsistent with the babbling of waters, the rustle of leaves,
and the murmurs of men.

Beyond the *ladera* we came once more to the pebbly shore
of the lake; then, climbing the steep neck of a rocky peninsula,
and skirting the cultivated slopes of a gentle declivity, between
walls of stone enclosing fields of ocas, which, newly dug, shone
like carnelians on the gray earth, we descended to the embarca-

dero of Yampupata, which is now, as it probably always was, the
point of embarkation. Here is a sandy beach between rocky
promontories, and a tambo of stone, windowless, and with but a
single opening into its bare interior, black with smoke, floored
with ashes, and sending forth indescribable and offensive odors.
There was no balsa to convey us to the island, which lay, glowing in the evening sun, temptingly before us, and appearing,
through the moistureless air, as if scarcely at rifle-shot distance.
We hurried to a group of huts clustered round a little church a

VIEW FROM THE "LADERA," THE ISLAND OF TITICACA IN THE DISTANCE.

mile to our left, but most of the population were absent in Copacabana or at work in the oca fields; and we learned little
from the blind, the halt, and the deaf that remained behind, except that balsas would come for us from the island. Through
our glasses we could discover a number of these moored in little rock-girt coves and indentations of its shores, but there was
nobody near them, nor any signs of life whatever. In vain, as
night fell, we lighted fierce and ephemeral fires of quenua stalks;
our signals were unanswered, and we were obliged to dispose

ourselves for the night in the cold and gloomy tambo, a rough stone hut, filthy beyond expression, standing close to the shore.

I was up at daylight, and went down to the shore, where the lake-weed was matted together with ice, and where a group of Indian women were shiveringly awaiting the arrival of a balsa which I discerned just paddling out from under the shadow of the island. Although apparently so near, the balsa was several hours in crossing the strait, and it was ten o'clock before it ranged up along-side and under the protection of some rocks to the left of the tambo. It was small, water-soaked, and its highest part elevated only a few inches above the water. The Indian women endeavored to get aboard, but a personage in a poncho, and evidently in authority (for he carried a tasselled cane), forbade them. He approached us, hat in hand, with the usual salutation of "*Tat-tai Viracocha*," and announced himself as *curaca* of Titicaca, at our service. Berrios declined to embark on the balsa, which, to start with, was a ticklish craft, and with H——, myself, the alcalde, and the two boatmen, barely kept afloat.

Sailing in a balsa is by no means the perfection of navigation, nor is the craft itself one likely to inspire high confidence. It is simply a float or raft, made up of bundles of reeds, tied to-

BALSA NAVIGATION ON LAKE TITICACA.

gether, fagot-like, in the middle of which the voyager poises himself on his knees, while the Indian *marineros* stand, one at each extremity, where they spread their feet apart, and, with small and rather crooked poles for oars, strike the water right and left, and thus slowly and laboriously propel the balsa in the required direction.  Of course this action gives the craft a rocking, rolling motion, and makes the passenger feel very much as if he were afloat on a mammoth cigar, predisposed to turn over on the slightest pretext.  Then, if the water be a little rough, a movement takes place which probably is unequalled in bringing on the pleasant sensation of sea-sickness.  Some of the balsas, however, are large, with sides built up like guards, which can be rigged with a sail for running before the wind, and are capable of carrying as many as sixty people.

Leaving behind the little *playa*, or beach, our Indian boatmen pushed along under a steep, rocky cliff, until they reached the point where the strait between the main-land and the island is narrowest.  The water at the foot of the cliff is very deep, but wonderfully transparent, and we could trace the plunge downwards of the precipitous limestone buttresses until our brains grew dizzy.  We were more than two hours in propelling the balsa across the strait, a distance which an ordinary oarsman in a Whitehall boat would get over in fifteen minutes, and landed on the island under the lee of a projecting ledge of rocks, full in view of the Palace of the Incas and the terraces surrounding it, half a mile to our right.

I do not think I shall find a better place than this for saying a few words about Lake Titicaca, which was for many weeks a conspicuous feature in our landscape, and which is, in many respects, the most extraordinary and interesting body of water in the world.  It is a long, irregular oval in shape, with one-fifth of its area at its southern extremity cut nearly off by the opposing peninsulas of Tiquina and Copacabana.  Its greatest length is about 120 miles, and its greatest width between 50 and 60 miles.  Its mean level is 12,488 feet above the sea. With a line of 100 fathoms I failed to reach bottom, at a distance of a mile to the eastward of the island of Titicaca.  The eastern, or Bolivian, shore is abrupt, the mountains on that side pressing down boldly into the water. The western and southern shores, however, are comparatively low and level, the water shallow and grown up with reeds and rushes, among which myriads of water-fowls find shelter and support.

MAP OF LAKE TITICACA.

The lake is deep, and never freezes over, but ice forms near its shores and where the water is shallow. In fact, it exercises a very important influence on the climate of this high, cold, and desolate region. Its waters, at least during the winter months, are from ten to twelve degrees of Fahrenheit warmer than the atmosphere. The islands and peninsulas feel this influence most perceptibly, and I found barley, pease, and maize, the latter, however, small and not prolific, ripening on these, while they did not mature on what may be called the main-land. The prevailing winds are from the north-east, and they often blow with great force, rendering navigation on the frail balsas, always slow and difficult, exceedingly dangerous. The lake has several considerable bays, of which those of Puno, Huancané, and Achacache are the principal. It has also eight considerable habitable islands, viz.: Amantené, Taqueli, Soto, Titicaca, Coati, Campanario, Toquaré, and Aputo. Of these the largest is that of Titicaca, on which we have just landed; high and bare, rugged in outline as ragged in surface, six miles long by between three and four in width.

This is the sacred island of Peru.* To it the Incas traced their origin, and to this day it is held by their descendants in profound veneration. According to tradition, Manco Capac and his wife and sister, Mama Ocllo, children of the Sun, and commissioned by that luminary, started hence on their errand of beneficence to reduce under government and to instruct in religion and the arts the savage tribes that occupied the country. Manco Capac bore a golden rod, and was instructed to travel northwards until he reached the spot where the rod should sink into the ground, and there fix the seat of his empire. He obeyed the behest, travelled slowly along the western shore of the lake, through the broad, level *puna* lands, up the valley of the Pucura, to the lake of La Raya, where the basin of Titicaca ends, and whence the waters of the river Vilcanota start on their course to swell the Amazon. He advanced down the valley of that river until he reached the spot where Cuzco now stands, when the golden rod disappeared. Here he fixed his seat, and here in time rose the City of the Sun, the capital of the Inca empire.

---

* "It is called sacred," says Pedro Cieza de Leon, " because of a ridiculous story that there was no light for many days, when the sun rose resplendent out of the island; and hence they built here a temple to its glory, which was held in great veneration, and had virgins and priests belonging to it, with mighty treasures."

The most reliable of the chroniclers, Garcilasso, tells us that besides building a temple on the island of Titicaca the Incas sought in all ways to ennoble it, as being the spot where their ancestors, descending from heaven, first planted their feet. They levelled its asperities as far as possible, removing rocks and building terraces, which they covered with rich earth brought from afar, in order that maize might be grown, which, from the cold, might not be otherwise cultivated. The yield was small, but the ears were regarded as sacred, and were distributed among the temples and convents of the empire, one year to one, and the next to another, so that each might have the advantage of a portion of the grain which was brought, as it were, from heaven. This was sown in the gardens of the temples of the Sun, and of the convents of the virgins, and the yield was again distributed among the people of the various provinces. Some grains were scattered among the stores in the public granaries, as sacred things which would augment and preserve from corruption the food of the people. And, such was the superstition, every Indian who had in his store-house a single grain of this maize, or any other grain grown in the sacred island, could never lack bread during his life-time.

The etymology of the name of the island, which has been extended to the lake, is not clear. It has been variously derived from *titi*, signifying "tiger" or "wild-cat," and *kaka*, "rock" or mountain crest: so that it would signify "Tiger Rock," or "Rock of the Tiger," perhaps from some fancied resemblance of the island, or some part of it, to that animal when seen from a distance. The tradition insists, however, that formerly a tiger, or puma, was seen at night on the crest of Titicaca, which carried a great carbuncle or ruby in its head that flashed its light far and wide over the lake, through all the extent of the Collao. Another derivative is from *titi*, "lead" or "tin," and *kaka*, "rock" or "crest," as before; *i. e.*, the "Mountain of Tin." There seems to be no good reason for this characterization, as there are no traces of metal in the island.

Upon this island, the traditional birthplace of the Incas, are still the remains of a temple of the Sun, a convent of priests, a royal palace, and other vestiges of Inca civilization. Not far distant is the island of Coati, which was sacred to the Moon, the wife and sister of the Sun, on which stands the famous palace of the Virgins of the Sun, built around two shrines dedicated to the Sun and the Moon respectively, and which is one of the best-preserved as well as one of the most remarkable remains of aboriginal architecture on this continent. The island of Soto was the Isle of Penitence, to which the Incas of the ruling race were wont to resort for fasting and humiliation, and it has also many remains of ancient architecture.

Two alcaldes of the island, residing in the little village of Challa, were waiting on the rocks to receive us, which they did with uncovered heads and the usual salutation. They told us that they had mules ready for us beyond the rocks, up and through which we clambered by a steep and narrow path, worn in the stone by the feet of myriads of pilgrims. This leads to a platform 73 feet long and 45 broad, faced with rough stones carefully laid and reached by a flight of steps. Above this is another platform, ascended in like manner, on the farther side of which are the remains of two rectangular buildings, each 35 feet long by 27 feet broad, with a narrow passage between them.

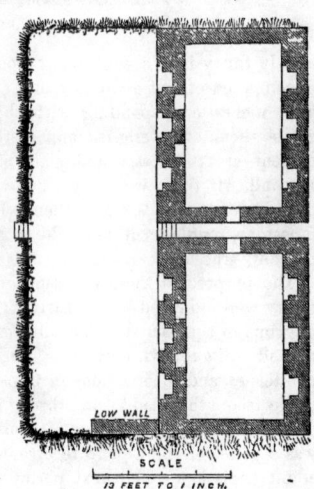

PLAN OF ANCIENT BUILDINGS AT THE LANDING, ISLAND OF TITICACA.

The front of each building is much ruined, but is relieved by reëntering niches of true Inca type, and characteristic of Inca architecture. Midway from the passage between the buildings, which

NICHE IN RUINS AT LANDING, ISLAND OF TITICACA.

is only thirty inches wide, doors open into each edifice, which
is composed of but a single room. The farther sides of these
have niches corresponding with those of the exterior. Opposite them, and designed apparently more for use than ornament, are two lesser and plain niches, like closets sunk in
the wall. If there were any windows, they were in the upper
portions of the walls, now fallen. Both buildings are of blue
limestone, roughly cut, and laid in a tough clay. They were
probably stuccoed.

The purpose of these structures, or rather this structure, is
pretty well indicated by the early writers,* who tell us that the
pilgrims to the sacred island and its shrines were not allowed
to land on its soil without undergoing certain preliminary fasts,
penitences, and purifications in Copacabana; and after landing
on the island they had to pass through certain "portals," the first
of which was called *Pumapunco*, or Door of the Puma, where
was a priest of the Sun to receive confession of their sins and
admit expiation. The next portal was called *Kentipunco*, be-

* We find it thus recorded by the Padre Ramos in his history of the " Sanctuary
of Copacabana," of which church he was a priest, at a period when the traditions of
the natives were comparatively fresh and uncorrupted.

cause it was adorned with the plumage of the bird *kenti*, where other ceremonies had to be performed.  The third was called *Pillcopunco*, or the Gate of Hope, after passing which the pilgrim might continue his journey to the sacred rock of the island, and make his adorations.  But he could not approach the spot within two hundred paces.  Only special priests of exceptional sanctity were allowed to tread the consecrated soil around it.

We can readily conceive that the structure under notice was in some way connected with these rites, and how the pilgrim, on disembarking, was conducted from one terrace to another, and finally made to pass, as through a portal, between the two buildings of which we still find the remains.  In the island of Coati, and in many of the approaches to edifices known to have been temples, we find corresponding buildings, which probably answered a similar purpose.

On the side of the hill overlooking the landing-place, still called Pumapunco, are terraces, with traces of buildings, which Calancha and some of the chroniclers imagine to have been parts of a fortification; but I incline to the belief that they were residences of the priests and *balseros*, or attendants on the landing-place.

After making a rapid plan of these remains, we mounted our mules, and, with an alcalde trotting along in front of us and another behind, we started for the holy *kaka*, or rock, of Manco, and the convent of the ancient priests, at the opposite end of the island.  The path skirts the flanks of the abrupt hills forming the island, apparently on the line of an ancient road supported by terraces of large stones, at an elevation of between two and three hundred feet above the lake, the shores of which are precipitous.  At the distance of half a mile from the landing, we passed a fine ruin called the Palace of the Inca, and farther on passed also the Bath of the Incas, in a beautiful, protected amphitheatre, irrigated by springs, yellow with ripening barley, and full of shrubs and flowers.  Here the path turns to the right over the crest of the island, two thousand feet high, and runs along dizzy eminences, from which, far down, may be discerned little sheltered *ensenadas*, or bays, almost land-locked, where there is a poor thatched hut or two, a balsa riding at her moorings or dragged up to dry on the shore, a few quenua-trees, and whence comes up the sole music of the Sierra, the bark—half yelp, half snarl—of the ill-conditioned, base-tempered, but faithful dogs of the country.   Sometimes our course was on one side of the crest, and sometimes on the other, so that we had alternating views of the Peruvian and Bolivian shores of the lake, and of the bays and promontories of the island.

At almost the very northern end of the island, at its most repulsive and unpromising part, where there is neither inhabitant nor trace of culture, where the soil is rocky and bare, and the cliffs ragged and broken—high up, where the fret of the waves of the lake is scarcely heard, and where the eye ranges over the broad blue waters from one mountain barrier to the other, from the glittering crests of the Andes to those of the Cordillera, is the spot most celebrated and most sacred of Peru.   Here is the rock on which it was believed no bird would light or animal venture, on which no human being dared to place his foot; whence the sun rose to dispel the primal vapors and illume the world; which was plated all over with gold and silver, and covered, except on occasions of the most solemn festivals, with a veil of cloth of richest color and material; which sheltered the favorite children of the Sun, and the pontiff, priest, and king who founded the Inca empire.*

Our guides stopped when it came in view, removed their hats, and bowed low and reverently in its direction, muttering a few words of mystic import.   But this rock to-day—alas for the gods dethroned!—is nothing more than a frayed and weather-worn mass of red sandstone, part of a thick stratum that runs

---

* Calancha and Ramos report, on the authority of the oldest and best-informed Indians of their day, that "the whole concavity of the rock was covered with plates of gold and silver, and that in its various hollows different offerings were placed, according to the festival or the occasion.   The offerings were gold, silver, shells, feathers, and rich cloth of *cumibi*.   The entire rock was covered with a rich mantle of this cloth—the finest and most gorgeous in colors of any ever seen in the empire."

through the island, and which is here disrupted and standing,
with its associated shale and limestone layers, at an angle of forty-five degrees with the horizon. The part uncovered and protruding above the ground is about 225 feet long and 25 feet
high. It presents a rough and broken and slightly projecting
face, but behind subsides in a slope coinciding with the declivity of the eminence of which it is part. In the face are many
shelves and pockets, all apparently natural. Excepting that there
are traces of walls around it of cut stone, and that the ground in

THE SACRED ROCK OF MANCO CAPAC.

front is artificially levelled, there is nothing to distinguish it
from many other projections of the sandstone strata on the isl-
and and the main-land. Calancha, one of the oldest chroniclers
of this region, well observes that it has no special features to arrest the eye or fix the attention.

Its position, however, is remarkable. It is on the crest of a
ridge connecting with a bold promontory—a high, rocky mass,
with precipitous sides and dark, cavernous recesses, which forms
the northern extremity of the island. On every side are bare
rocks, heaped confusedly, except in front of the sacred stone it-

self, where, as I have said, there is a level, artificial terrace, 372 feet long and 125 feet broad, supported by a stone-wall. At each outer corner of this terrace are the remains of small, square structures, probably those referred to by the chroniclers as the shrines of the Thunder and Lightning. According to tradition, the earth of this terrace was brought from the distant rich and fertile valleys of the Amazonian rivers, so that it might nourish a verdure denied by the hard, ungrateful soil of the island.

From the front of this terrace the island falls off to the lake by a steep but smooth declivity, and the eye rests on the small but lovely bay of Chucaripe, in which the clear and sparkling waters ripple gently to a sandy shore, that contrasts pleasingly with the rugged cliffs rising on either hand. Black, rocky islets, frayed and shattered by earthquakes and storms, lift themselves up in the lake beyond; and away in the distance, sharply defined in the clear, rarefied atmosphere, are the hills of Juli and Pomata—the great church of the latter town gleaming out like a point of silver against the umber-tinted background.

Turning around and facing the sacred rock, we find ourselves looking down on another similar bay or indentation, cliff-bound, and in which the waves, driven by the keen, north-east wind, dash and chafe angrily against the rocky shore, in striking contrast with the soft and almost slumberous repose of the opposing bay. This is called the Bay of Kentipunco, in which the Inca landed when he came to visit the spot sacred to the Sun. On a narrow natural platform half-way down to the water are the remains of several structures, which were the residences, it is supposed, of priests and attendants. They are of rough stones, and not architecturally remarkable. From them, leading up to the shrine, is a broad road, partly hewn in the rock. About midway are what are called the "footprints of the Inca," revered among the Indians to this day, as indicating the place where Yupanqui stood when he made his pilgrimage to the island, and removed the imperial *llautu* from his forehead in token of submission and adoration of the divinity whose shrine rose before him. The so-called footprints certainly have a rough resemblance to the impression that might be produced by a sandalled foot; but they are rather large for those of even so mighty a personage as the Inca Yupanqui, being more than three feet long and of corresponding width. They are formed, in outline, by hard, ferruginous veins, around which the rock has been worn away, leaving them in relief.

It was in *adoratorios*, or chapels, here that the chroniclers affirm was placed the triune statue of stone, three figures united in one, which uncritical writers have made to do such large service, as evidence of the existence of the doctrine of the Trinity in Peru. These figures had names, so state the monkish authorities, signifying Great or Lord Sun, the Son of the Sun, and the Brother Sun. Calancha thinks that the making of the third person the brother of the first was a corruption of the mystery as taught by the apostles who had come to America, and was suggested by the devil himself, so as to delude the ignorant natives to their spiritual ruin.

To the front and northward of the sacred rock, and distant about two hundred paces, are the ruins of a large edifice which the chroniclers call the *Despensa*, or Store-house, of the Sun, but which is now called *La Chingana*, or The Labyrinth. It justifies the latter name. It is situated on the slope descending to the little bay of Chucaripe, at a point where the ground falls off very abruptly, so that its lower walls must have been twice or three times as high as those on its upper side. Its leading feature is a court, with terraces cut in the rock, and with a fountain in its centre. The walls facing inwards on the court are all niched, and on each side are masses of buildings, which had evidently been two or three stories in height. Some of the lower rooms or vaults, probably all of them, had been arched after the manner to be observed in the " Palace of the Inca," at the opposite end of the island. The passages leading to the various rooms were narrow and intricate, the door-ways low, and the rooms themselves small and dark, almost precluding the notion that they were intended to be inhabited. From its proximity to the rock, and the identity of its leading features with those of other structures of Peru of known purpose,

I am inclined to regard the Chingana as one of the *Aclahuasas*, or houses of the Virgins of the Sun, one of which existed on the island: and I found no other building that could have served as a retreat for the vestals.

On a promontory, a fourth of a mile to the south-west of the sacred rock, are other ruins, among which treasure-seekers have worked long and diligently, and have left the whole a confused heap, in which we could only trace some foundations of buildings, sections of terraces, and walls, in plain sight of the sacred rock, yet sufficiently removed from it to prevent profane intrusion. This was probably the site of the tambos erected for the accommodation of pilgrims, such as we know were built near every sanctuary of the empire.

The sun had set, casting a fleeting crimson glow on the snows of Illampu, which was followed by a deadly, bluish pallor, and it was beginning to be dark before we got through with our investigation of the rock of Manco Capac. We had arranged to pass the night at the little hacienda of the *Pila*, or Fountain, of the Incas, and retraced our path thither slowly and with difficulty. The hacienda consisted of three small buildings, occupying as many sides of a court. One of these was a kitchen and dormitory, another was a kind of granary or store-house, and in the third was an apartment reserved for the proprietor of the hacienda, a resident of Puno, when he visited the island. The room was neatly whitewashed, the floor was matted, and there were two real chairs from Connecticut, and a table that might be touched without toppling over, and used without falling into pieces. The alcaldes who had us in charge attended faithfully to our wants, and served us in person with chupe, ocas, and eggs. Their authority over the people of the hacienda seemed absolute.

The night was bitterly cold, and we had no covering except our saddle-cloths, having declined the use of some sheepskins, which the alcaldes would have taken from the poor people of the establishment. A sheepskin, or the skin of the vicuña, spread on the mud floor of his hut, is the only bed of the Indian from one year's end to the other. It is always filthy, and frequently full of vermin. Before going to bed we went out into the frosty, starry night, and were surprised to see fires blazing on the topmost peak of the island, on the crest of Coati, and on the headland of Copacabana. Others, many of them hardly discernible in the distance, were also burning on the peninsula of Tiquina and on the bluff Bolivian shores of the lake, their red light darting like golden lances over the water. Our first impression was that some mysterious signalling was going on, connected, perhaps, with our visit. We ascertained, however, that this was the Eve of St. John, which is celebrated in this way throughout the Sierra. On that night fires blaze on the hill-tops in all the inhabited districts of Peru and Bolivia, from the desert of Atacama to the equator.

We were up early, and for the first time ate our chupe with satisfaction, for it was hot. We found the houses of the hacienda seated in the saddle of a ridge projecting into the lake, and terminating in a natural mound or eminence, rounded with great regularity by art, and terraced from the very edge of the water up to its top by concentric walls of stone. Traces of a building, like a belvedere or summer-house, were conspicuous at its summit, from which a fine view of the lake, its islands, and the distant nevados is commanded. At the foot of this eminence, on both sides, are little bays with sandy beaches, that on the right pushing inland towards the terraced Garden of the Incas. Here is the most sheltered nook of the island, and the terraces are covered with barley in the ear, just changing from green to golden, and as we zigzag down we come to patches of pease and little squares of maize, with stalks scarcely three feet high and ears not longer than one's finger, but closely covered with compact vitreous grains.

We go down, down, until we get where we hear the pleasant plash and gurgle of waters; there is an oppressive odor of fading flowers; and in a few minutes we stand before the Pila of the Incas. We are midway down the sloping valley, amidst terraces geometrically laid out and supported by walls of cut stone, niched according to Inca taste, and here forming three sides of a quadrangle, in which there is a pool, forty feet long,

ten wide, and five deep, paved with worked stones.   Into this
pour four *chorros*, or jets of water, each of the size of a man's
arm, from openings cut in the stones behind.   Over the walls
around it droop the tendrils of vines and the stems of plants
that are slowly yielding to the frost, and, what with odors, and
the tinkle and patter of the water, one might imagine himself
in the court of the Alhambra, where the fountains murmur of
the Moors, just as the Pila of the Incas tells its inarticulate tale

PILA, OR FOUNTAIN, OF THE INCAS, TITICACA.

of a race departed, and to whose taste and poetry it bears melo-
dious witness.   The water comes through subterranean passages
from sources now unknown, and never diminishes in volume.
It flows to-day as freely as when the Incas resorted here and
cut the steep hill-sides into terraces, bringing the earth to fill
them — so runs the legend — all the way from the Valley of
Yucay, or Vale of Imperial Delights, four hundred miles distant.   However that may be, this is the garden *par excellence* of

SIDE-VIEW OF PALACE OF THE INCA, ISLAND OF TITICACA.

the Collao, testifying equally to the taste, enterprise, and skill
of those who created it in spite of the most rigorous of climes
and most ungrateful of soils.  Below this reservoir the water is
conducted from terrace to terrace until it is finally discharged
into the lake.

Half-way from the Garden of the Incas to the embarcadero,
standing on a natural shelf or terrace overlooking the lake, but
much smoothed by art, is *El Palacio del Inca*, the Palace (so
called) of the Inca, to which I have already made a brief reference.  Its site is beautiful.  On either side are terraces, some
of them niched, and supporting small dependent structures,
while the steep hill behind, which bends around it like a half-
moon, is also terraced in graceful curves, each defined, not alone
by its stone facing, but by a vigorous growth of the shrub that
yields the Flor del Inca, which blossoms here all the year round.

CHAMBERS IN THE PALACE OF THE INCA.

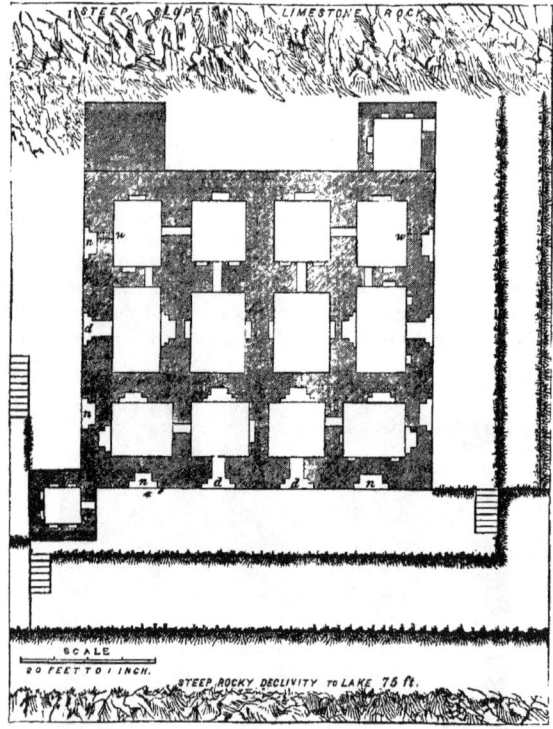

GROUND-PLAN OF THE PALACE OF THE INCA, ISLAND OF TITICACA.

The building is rectangular, 51 by 44 feet, and two stories high. The front on the lake is ornamented or relieved on the lower story by four high niches, the two central ones being door-ways. On each side are three niches, the central one also forming a door-way. It is divided into twelve small rooms, of varying sizes, and connected with each other in a manner that can only be made intelligible by reference to the plan. There are altogether four sets of rooms, two groups of two each, and two of four each. These rooms are about thirteen feet high, their walls inclining slightly inwards, while their ceiling is formed by flat, overlapping stones, laid with great regularity. Every room has its niches, some small and plain, others large and elaborate. The inner as well as the exterior walls were

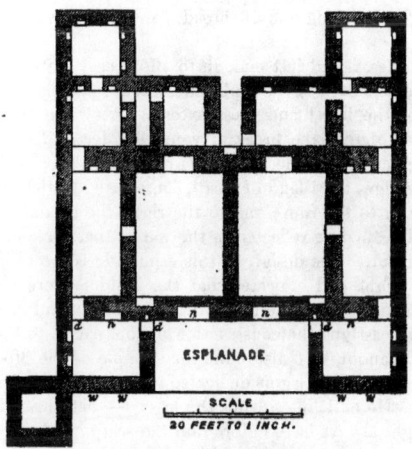

PLAN OF SECOND STORY OF THE PALACE OF THE INCA.

stuccoed with a fine, tenacious clay, possibly mixed with some adhesive substance, and painted. Some patches of this stucco still remain, and indicate that the building was originally yellow, while the inner parts and mouldings of the door-ways and niches were of different shades of red.

The second story does not at all correspond in plan with the first. Its entrance is at the rear, on a level with a terrace extending back to the hill, and spreading out in a noble walk faced with a niched wall, and supporting some minor buildings, or "summer-houses," now greatly ruined. It appears to have had no direct connection with the ground story by stairs or otherwise. The rooms, which are also more or less ornamented with niches, are separated by walls much less massive than those below, and do not seem to have been arched as those are, but to have been roofed with thatch, as were most of the structures of the Incas. The central part of the front of the second story was not enclosed, although probably roofed, but formed an esplanade, 22 feet long and 10 broad, flanked by rooms opening on it.

Two niches, raised just enough to afford easy seats, appear in the wall at the back of the esplanade, whence may be commanded one of the finest and most extensive views in the world. The waves of the lake break at your very feet. To the right is the high and diversified peninsula of Copacabana; in the centre of the view, the island of Coati, consecrated to the Moon, as was Titicaca to the Sun; and to the right, the gleaming Illampu, its white mantle reflected in the waters that spread out like a sea in front. The design of this esplanade is too obvious to admit of doubt, and indicates that the builders were not deficient in taste, or insensible to the grand and beautiful in nature.

Tradition assigns the construction of this palace to the Inca, Tupac Yupanqui, who also built the Temple of the Moon and the Convent of the Virgins dedicated to her service in the island of Coati. He built it—so runs the legend—that during his visits he might always have before him the seat and shrine of the Inti-coya, the sister and wife of his parent, the Sun. The rooms on each side of the esplanade have each two windows, opening on the same view that I have described as to be had from the esplanade itself. There are features, architectural and otherwise, connected with the Palace of the Inca, which are of real interest, but which could only be rendered intelligible by minute plans and drawings.

ISLAND OF COATI AND THE CROWN OF THE ANDES, FROM ESPLANADE OF PALACE OF THE INCA.

# CHAPTER XVIII.

### DÉTOUR TO PUNO.

FINDING that a proper investigation of the remaining monuments of Titicaca and the other islands would require many days, and that it was tedious and difficult to get from one island to another in the clumsy balsas of the natives, I determined to push forward to Puno, the capital of the department, and make that the basis of my future operations in the Titicaca basin. Our return to the main-land was in a more pretentious and comfortable balsa than that in which we had first ventured.

Our ride back to Copacabana was a rapid one, and we found our comandante parading the streets of the town in high choler, shooting indiscriminately all the dogs that he could bring his double-barrelled gun to bear upon. "The miserables," as he characterized the people under his care, "haven't half enough to eat themselves, and yet they will fill the town with these sneaking, snarling, starving, thieving curs. It shall not be so any longer, and I—" Here he caught sight of a dog prowling around a corner of the street, and started in pursuit. A shot and a yelp told us what had happened. The comandante soon returned, apologized for leaving us so suddenly, and conducted us to his house, saying that he knew we must be hungry.

24

Our supper was scant, and the comandante, who was an able eater, rather checked his appetite, we thought, besides appearing a little abstracted and moody. The truth soon came out. Anticipating our arrival, he had procured a kid in Yunguyo, and on it we were to have dined; but the famished dogs had some how got at it, and when the time came for the cook to step in, lo! not even a bone was left. "*Ni un huesito, caballeros!*" said the comandante, with palpable moisture in the corners of his eyes. How many innocent dogs suffered for the sins of their fellows I know not, but they were counted by the score, and next morning not a living specimen of the genus *canis* was to be seen in the place. Those that survived had been carefully secreted by their owners.

I shall not recount the details and incidents of our journey from Copacabana to Puno. Our path was that of the traditionary Manco Capac, along the western shore of the great lake. The disrupted carboniferous strata rise in a thousand contorted and fantastic forms around us, and we see occasionally stretching away over, or rather through, the hills long trap dikes which look like Titanic fortifications. We constantly encounter new and varying views, in which the lake, and its bold, brown islands, and the distant snowy Andes, are the ever-recurring features. Sometimes our path lies along the sandy beach of the lake, on which the waves, driven by the fierce, cold, north-east wind, break with oceanic force. At intervals we reach long, straight, narrow causeways built through the shallows and marshes left by the subsidence of some ancient bay penetrating deep into the land, which were built by the Incas, and have been suffered to fall into ruin by the Spaniards. Some of these are now so ruined as to be untransitable, and we find ourselves compelled to take tedious circuits along the bases of the hills to reach a spot on the other side of the morass not a thousand yards distant in a direct line. Scampering along the broken walls of enclosures, or peeping furtively out of crevices, we notice hundreds of *cues*, or guinea-pigs, indigenous to the country. Marshalled in low meadows are thousands and tens of thousands of aquatic birds, apparently in solemn conclave, which rise, if we approach too near them, with a mighty rush of wings, and a noise like that of a hail-storm in a forest.

At intervals of every four or five leagues we come to considerable towns, the size of which would surprise us if we did not know that in them nearly all the inhabitants of the country are gathered. Those whose occupation lies in the fields go out to their work in the morning and return at night; but during this bitter weather most of them wrap themselves in their ponchos of llama wool, and gather gloomily in their dark, filthy, unventilated cabins at night, or silently bask by day on the sunny sides of their wretched habitations. Nothing more oppresses us than the stupor and gloom of the towns, which appear as if under the pall of a pestilence; and nothing repels us more than the sullen, almost morose, aspect and manners of the inhabitants. A smile is seldom seen, a laugh is never heard. The impassive children never cry. It is only on the occasions of pagan festivals tolerated by the Church or incorporated with its own, and when warmed with chicha or maddened with cañaso, that the apathetic Aymará appears animated; it, however, is a savage, tigerish animation, which causes a shudder, but creates no sympathy.

In these towns are great churches, whose massiveness bids defiance alike to time and neglect. That of Pomata is of stone, inside and out; the very altar is cut in stone, and its roofs and walls and the niches of the saints are covered all over with a lace-work of sculpture, as intricate in design as delicate in execution. The work must have been done by the Indians before they lost the skill in stone-cutting which they possessed at the time of the Conquest, and to which every valley of the Sierra bears enduring witness.

We hear, as we proceed, of fortresses and other works, "*muy disforme*," of "El Rey Inca," but they are always far off, and we know by experience how little dependence we can put on the representations of the ignorant, who so often confound the natural with the artificial, and the trifling with the important. It is only on our third day of journeying that we find any remains of antiquity worthy of notice.

Between Juli and Illave we come upon a mass of sandstone rock, by the roadside, 100 feet or more long, and from 15 to 20 high. It is naturally rounded, but a stairway has been cut to its top, which is levelled artificially. Here is a seat, carved in the rock, resembling a large arm-chair in shape and size; while lower down, in front and around, are other similar but elaborate seats, reached by other flights of steps, also cut in the rock. This, says tradition, was the "resting-place of the Inca," in his journeyings or pilgrimages, where the people came to do him

THE INCA'S CHAIR.

homage, bringing chicha for his delectation and that of his attendants.

Approaching the town of Acora, three days' journey from Copacabana, we come upon a broad plain, high and sandy, covered with ichu-grass, across which the road stretches in a long line. The plain is covered with many rude monuments, small circles and squares of unwrought upright stones, planted in the ground, and sometimes sustaining others, which overlap and form chambers, with openings, generally towards the north.

They are almost identical, in appearance and character, with
the cromlechs of Europe, and might be transferred to Brittany or Wales, and pass for structures contemporaneous with the
thousand rude monuments of antiquity found in those regions.
Subsequent investigation convinced me that they were sepulchral in origin, and that they were rude and early forms of
what subsequently became elaborate and symmetrical chulpas.

Of these towers, unique and characteristic as they are, this
seems the place to give some details, in connection with the
more ancient and ruder works, as we shall find them in abundance all through the ancient Collao.   And here it should, perhaps, be explained that the Collao proper of the Incas appears

ANCIENT SEPULCHRES, ACORA.

to have comprehended only that part of the Titicaca basin of
which the boundary would be defined by an irregular line, circumscribing the sources of the streams falling into the lake,
and not the whole region occupied by the Aymarás, to which
great Andean family the greater part of the inhabitants of the
region called Bolivia belonged.   Before their incorporation
into the Quichuan, or Inca, empire, they seem to have been divided into a number of states or principalities, ruled by chiefs,
or *curacas*, who had their capitals, or seats of power, at wide
distances apart.   One of the most powerful of these had his
seat—so says tradition—on the shore of the rock-girt lake of
Umayo, near the northern extremity of Lake Titicaca, where

we find extensive monumental remains, confirming the tradition. To this chief of Hatuncolla belonged the district on
which we now enter, and where the rude sepulchral monuments I have alluded to are found. A circle or square, composed of stones set in the ground, with other stones placed horizontally upon them, lapping over each other so as to lean together and support each other in the centre, forming a rudely
arched chamber—this is a brief but exhaustive description of
their character. The stones are often large, and imply the use
of considerable power to place them in their present position.

At the base of the hills bounding the plain of Acora on the
west are a number of these chulpas. Some are square, others
round, but all of one plan and style. Their inner mass is of
rough stones laid in clay, but they are faced with hewn limestone blocks. A description of one, with the aid of a view and
section, will sufficiently illustrate the character of all. It is 17
feet square and 24 feet high, and rises from a platform of cut

CHULPAS, OR BURIAL-TOWERS, ACORA.

stones 22 feet on each side, and raised a foot above the ground;
three feet below its top is a projection, or cornice, two feet
deep, protruding about one foot on every side, forming a severe
but effective ornament or finish to the structure. There is a
square opening, 18 inches high and broad, in the eastern face, on

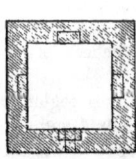

PLAN AND SECTION OF SQUARE CHULPA.

a level with the platform. Crawling into this with difficulty—
for it was obstructed with rubbish—I found myself in a vault,
or chamber, 11 feet square and 13 feet high, the sides of which
rise vertically to the height of eight feet, where the stones begin
to overlap, forming a kind of pointed arch. At the height of

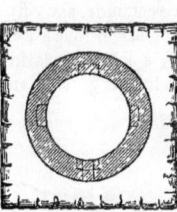

PLAN AND SECTION OF ROUND CHULPA.

three feet from the floor of the vault, in the centre of each of its
four faces, is a niche, $3\frac{1}{2}$ feet high and 18 inches deep, with sides
inclining towards each other at the top. The entrance is immediately under one of these niches. I found nothing in this
dark vault, except some human bones and fragments of pottery,

and the gnawed bones of animals, dragged here, probably, by dogs, for which this had evidently been a favorite retreat.

Chulpa is the Aymará word for tomb; and near that just described is another, 26 feet high, and with a similar niched vault, but round instead of square. Exteriorly, it has a corresponding projection or cornice, and its top is dome-shaped. Its peculiar feature is that, in common with all the round chulpas, it swells outwards or increases in diameter from its base to where the dome begins to spring, where it is sixteen inches more in diameter than at its foundation.

These chulpas are common in the Titicaca region, usually standing in groups of from twenty to a hundred, and almost invariably occupying some rocky ridge or spur of the hills and mountains, or some rugged eminence in the plain. Occasionally they occur singly or in pairs. There is hardly a view to be had in the habitable districts around the head of the lake in which one or more groups do not appear, constituting a singular and interesting feature in the landscape, especially when standing out on their rocky eminences boldly against the sky.

There is a singular monument in the ancient town of Chucuito, once the most important in the Collao, about four leagues from Acora. It is in the form of a rectangle, sixty-five feet on each side, and consists of a series of large, roughly worked blocks of stone, placed closely side by side on a platform, or rather on a foundation of stones, sunk in the ground, and pro-

ANCIENT MONUMENT AT CHUCUITO.

jecting fourteen inches outwards all around. The entrance is from the east, between two blocks of stones higher than the rest. It may be taken as a type of an advanced class of megalithic monuments by no means uncommon in the highlands of Peru.

Almost every traveller in the Sierra is taken for an itinerant vender of *joyas,* or cheap jewellery, and our instruments and iron-clasped photographic boxes seemed to convey the notion that we too were venders of paste and pinchbeck on a magnificent scale. Two leagues before reaching Puno, and just as we struck the bay on which it stands, we observed a man splendidly mounted riding rapidly towards us through the heavy sand. He drew up as we approached, removed his hat, and saluted us in grand style. We responded with equal pomp, and were speculating mentally whether he was a messenger of the prefect of the department, or the prefect himself, who had come to tender us the freedom and the hospitalities of the city of Puno. But he turned out to be the resident vender of trinkets, who, hearing of our approach, had made up his mind that we were pedlers, and had come out to make us an offer for our entire stock, rather than have us open a shop and undersell him in the town. He was slow to be convinced that we were mere travellers, studying the country, but, when satisfied on the point, gave us a contemptuous glance, and, without even an *adios,* spurred his horse into a gallop, and left us to contemplate the flutter of his receding poncho as well as we could through the dust that he raised. I do not think scientific travellers are likely to inspire profound respect, or secure a very high appreciation, among the mixed people of the Sierra. They must content themselves to be taken for Viracochas by the shepherd Indians.

Turning sharp around a high, precipitous headland, on the shelves and among the crevices of which Indian fishermen had established their huts, looking like swallows' nests, we came in sight of Puno, standing on the shores of its bay, half grown up with totora and water-plants, at the foot of the silver-veined hill, or rather mountain, of Cancharani. To the famous mines of the Manto, and others, which have honey-combed the mountain, the town owes its origin. It has about six thousand inhabitants, nine-tenths of whom are pure Indians—the Aymarás occupying the southern, the Quichuas the northern portion.

We had letters to Mr. T——, an American gentleman from Philadelphia, married in the country, and the leading merchant of the place, and rode at once to his house. Here we met a hospitality such as might be expected from an ardent American who but rarely saw the face of a countryman, and here we rested a time from our journeyings.

Puno has an altitude greater than that of any considerable town in Peru, except the mining town of Cerro de Pasco, being 12,550 feet above the sea. No building in the world of anything like equal dimensions with its cathedral occupies so lofty a position, and there are few anywhere better built or more massive. The town is relatively modern, owing its origin to the discovery of rich silver mines in the mountains of Cancharani and Laycaycota, at the feet of which it was built, about the year 1660.

The secret of these mines, it is said, was communicated by an Indian girl to one José de Salcedo, who worked them with immense profit until his wealth excited the cupidity of the avaricious and unscrupulous royal governors. These never lacked for accusations against those of whom they wished to get rid; and under some of these Salcedo was in 1669 seized, taken to Lima, and executed. In vain he offered to pay a thousand marks of silver a day to his judges if they would suspend execution of their sentence during the time it would require to carry an appeal to the crown of Spain. But the triumph of the officers of the crown was short, for as soon as Salcedo's faithful Indians heard of the proceedings against him they stopped the drains of the mine, and it was filled with water. A small lake now covers the spot which tradition assigns to the mine worked by the luckless Salcedo. Numerous other veins, however, were subsequently worked, one of which, the Manto, was carried more than two miles into the mountain. The only mining operations at present consist in extracting the silver from the rejected ores of former days.

Puno no longer depends on her mines, but derives a better support from her trade in wool, from the numerous flocks which now constitute the wealth of the department of which it is the capital. This is mainly sent to Arequipa, whence it finds its way to the world. There is also a limited export of butter.

Puno is a dreary place, with low thatched houses and icy streets, through which glide noiseless llamas, and equally silent Indians in garb as sombre as that of the bare hills that circle round the town, and cut off the view in every direction except towards the lake. Here are the bright waters of the Bay of Puno, bordered all around by a broad belt of totora, and relieved by a few rocky islets, each of which has its Indian tradition, and on one of which the royalist governors confined their patriot captives during the war of the revolution, without shelter from the sun or protection from the cold.

After a few days of rest, we began our preparations for exploring the lake and revisiting the island of Titicaca. I have said that at this time there were no boats on Lake Titicaca. There was one, an ordinary four-oared open boat, fifteen feet long, and, happily, it belonged to our kind host, who introduced us to a person who had been employed in the Chilian navy, Captain Cuadros, to whom I paid instant court. After several "surveys" of the craft, it was finally agreed that if her sides were raised and she were schooner-rigged, we might venture out in her on the broad and often turbulent lake. But to raise the sides (Cuadros called them "bulwarks") was easier said than done. Where were the boards to come from? The last consignment to Puno, consisting of half a dozen planks sawed in Maine, cut in sections, and brought up from the coast on mules, a twenty days' journey, had been exhausted by our host himself in making shutters for the windows of his warehouse. So we were fain to break up some boxes, and build up our "bulwarks" from the pieces. The *Natividad* was a wonderful craft to see when all was done. Her sides were as variegated as a city deadwall under its posters. Here you read "Fragile;" near by, "This side up with care;" and next, "Bitters, X. S. P. 9," in every variety of lettering. The masts were two poles which had been brought all the way from the Amazonian valleys of Carabaya, on the shoulders of Indians, and seemed to have been selected for their marvellous sinuosities. H—— protested that they were "too crooked to lie still." A box that had been lined with tin to hold calicoes, containing a little clay furnace, was firmly fastened in the bow as a kitchen, and, by great good luck, we obtained a bag of charcoal. Captain Cuadros had a little place fenced off for him in the stern, where he acted as captain, mate, and steersman. Professor Raimondi and myself occupied the centre of the craft; while the two *bogadores*, or rowers, and Ignacio, my servant, a consummate rascal, who acted as cook, went "before the mast."

In this frail vessel we started one morning at the early hour of six, with the mercury in the thermometer ranging at zero. We had not even the brisk motion of the boat to warm us by an effort of imagination, for the only channel out of the bay of Puno is shallow and sinuous, the totora, closing in on all sides, never leaving more than five yards clear, and in some places growing completely across. Three hours of patient toil carried us beyond the weeds, and then a good breeze enabled us to make rapid progress towards Coati and Titicaca. Lake though it was, the passengers and cook were soon sea-sick, and paid their tribute to the god of Lake Titicaca as faithfully as they would have done to old Neptune himself, under similar circumstances.

Our sail was by no means a mere pleasure jaunt. The wintry afternoon was closing, when about four o'clock the wind subsided, leaving us becalmed a league from the island of Titicaca. By plying our oars, and with the aid of a few light puffs of wind, we at last succeeded in running into one of the sheltered bays of the island. There were some Indian huts near the shore, and, scattered in these, we managed to pass the night.

Our first thought in the morning was the Intihuai, or Temple of the Sun; but all our inquiries as to its location elicited no information, and we were compelled to defer an attempt at exploring it. We hoisted our sails again for the island of Coati, and by ten o'clock landed on its shores.

## CHAPTER XIX.

THE island of Coati, dedicated to the Moon, as Titicaca was to the Sun, ranks second among the sacred islands of Peru. It is distant about six miles from Titicaca, with which it contrasts strikingly in every respect. While Titicaca is high and rugged, with deeply indented shores and barren soil, Coati is only moderately elevated, with an even surface, regular shores, and capable of cultivation, in every part. It is small, not exceeding two and a half miles in length by, perhaps, three-fourths of a mile in width. It now constitutes a single hacienda, and its population is limited to three or four families of Indians, who raise a little quinoa, maize, and potatoes, and guard a flock of sheep which finds ample pasturage on its slopes, which are terraced up from the water's edge, presenting an appearance of great regularity and beauty when seen from a little distance.

There are two groups of ruins on the island, one on the extremity nearest Titicaca, and close by what was the ancient landing-place for balsas; the other about midway the length of the island, on its northern side. The remains nearest the landing-place correspond in part with those which I have described as being first encountered in landing on Titicaca; that is to say, of buildings placed on terraces, with narrow passages between them, through which the pilgrims had to pass on landing, and where, we have reason to believe, they were compelled to perform certain ceremonies and go through certain lustrations.

Beyond these Gates of Purification, and not far distant, on the crest of the island, are some rather extensive remains of what were probably tambos, or houses for the reception of pilgrims and for the accommodation of the custodians of the island.

The principal monument of antiquity on the island, and which lends to it its chief interest, is the edifice called the Palace of the Virgins of the Sun, but which might probably better be called the Temple of the Moon. It is situated on the northern side of the island, about midway of its length, where the shore curves inwards like the crescent moon, conforming to a similar curve in the high ridge running through the island. In the lap of this natural amphitheatre, its sweep of terraces lined with wild olive or quenua-trees, with their red trunks and dark foliage, stands the shrine of Coati. It occupies the upper of a series of seven terraces supported by retaining-walls of cut and uncut stones. These terraces flanked by others, and ascended by zigzag paths or curiously designed stairways, fall off towards the lake, affording level areas, which seem to have been filled with the richest soil, like the *andenes* of the Temple of the Sun in Titicaca.

The structure itself is built around three sides of an oblong, rectangular court, 183 feet long by 80 broad, and is of complicated but harmonious plan, which no description can make as clear as the accompanying engraving will do. The remains are still in so good preservation that the plan can be made out with little difficulty, and they are among the best and most intelligible illustrations of Inca architecture in Peru. The material of the edifice is stone, roughly broken into shape, laid in tough clay, and, as was the case in the structures of Titicaca, carefully stuccoed. There is but a single apartment—*b* in the plan—of the

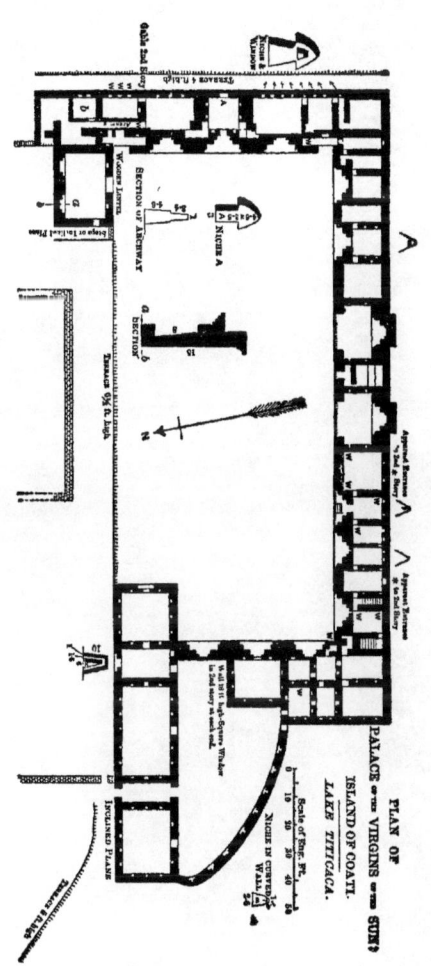

PLAN OF PALACE OF THE VIRGINS OF THE SUN, ISLAND OF COATI, LAKE TITICACA.

thirty-five into which the lower story is divided that is faced
with hewn stones, and this seems to have constituted a kind
of *penetrale*, or secret chamber, approached through a narrow,
arched passage. All the attempts at architectural ornament are
on the façades fronting the court, and consist of lofty and elaborate niches, in which the back in some cases disappears, and
gives an entrance to the inner apartments. Each of these
niches and door-ways is in the centre of a kind of stucco frame-

PALACE OF THE VIRGINS OF THE SUN, COATI.

work, or panel, as shown in the elevation. The niches are uniform throughout, and agreeably and artistically break up the
monotony of the long lines of walls, which are further relieved
by ornaments not easy to describe, but which are shown in the
illustrations, and which are artfully contrived to admit light
into the interior of the building, with no outward indication of
any such purpose. The façade is further diversified by placing
the line of cornice over the entrances higher than elsewhere,
thus distinguishing them from the blind door-ways, or orna-

mental niches. The cornice, which is of three layers of stones, projects eighteen inches. The exterior was painted yellow, with the exception of the niches and the undersides of the graduations of the cornice, which were red.

The building was of two stories, or, rather, had an elevation of a story and a half. The roof was pitched almost as sharply as the roofs of Holland, but it did not extend throughout parallel to the façades. On the contrary, it was broken up by the presentation of gables to the court, so as to produce an effect coincident with that which distinguishes the style of architecture known as Elizabethan.

The floors of the upper apartments have disappeared, having evidently been of wood. The ledges, or sets-off, in the wall which supported them are plainly marked throughout; and there are similar ledges on the inner faces of the gables, with projecting stones on which to rest and fasten the roofs. The places in which the ridge-poles were inserted are still distinct. The upper story probably coincided very nearly in plan with the lower, and was reached by stairways of cut stone, some of which are still perfect.

The apartments were connected with each other by doorways, opening directly through the partitions, or sunk, if I may use the term, in the side-walls. To reach some of the inner apartments it was necessary to pass through several exterior ones. Every door opening on the court led to its special and separate system of chambers. These were variously lighted; some by means of small windows (w) opening on the court where they were masked by the ornaments of the façade, and others by means of windows opening through the exterior and unornamented walls, marked on the inside by niches. Every gable was pierced by one or two large windows, narrow at the top and broad at the bottom. There is, among the remains, a single small apartment, faced with smoothly cut stones, to which access is gained through a vaulted passage 20 feet long and 8 feet high. There is a small opening into this only a few inches square from an outer room or cell, evidently not intended for the admission of light, and which seems to have been designed

to permit verbal communication with the interior.   In fact,
there are many and interesting features connected with the internal arrangements of the structure, obscure cells, strangely-
fashioned niches and masked door-ways, all suggestive of mo-
nastic devices, seclusion, penance, and mystery.   These only become apparent through a careful study of the plan of the buildings.   They baffle description.

The salient features of the buildings, however, are two chambers or rooms, 20 feet long by 12 broad, entered from the centre of the principal façade, not through door-ways such as have
just been described, but through broad openings, 15 feet wide.
The ground or floor within them is raised four feet above the
level of the floors of the building generally, and is reached by
flights of stone steps.   Within, and directly in front of the entrance, there is in each room a great niche, countersunk in the
wall, which is here made very thick.   In style it coincides entirely with those ornamenting the façade.   Two small niches
are seen at each end of the apartment.   These rooms, which
appear to have been much loftier than any of the others, and to
have been surmounted by pyramidal roofs, have no communication with each other, or with any of the other apartments.
Their purpose hardly admits of doubt.   They were the holy
places or shrines of the convent, and contained the statues, or
*simulacra*, of the Sun and the Moon respectively, which, tradition affirms, were, the one of gold, and the other of silver.
The entrances do not appear to have been closed, except, perhaps, with a veil of cloth, such as that which was spread over
the sacred rock of Titicaca.   It is not difficult to imagine the
level court in front of these shrines crowded with reverent pilgrims, who, when the veils were lifted, bowed their heads to
the ground in adoration of the symbols of their divinities, blazing under the splendors of the Sun, alike their father and their
god.

Between the two chambers which I have assumed to be the
shrines of the Sun and the Moon is a smaller apartment, entered by a narrow door.   The view inwards is cut off by a curtain or transverse wall, behind which is a kind of daïs in stone,

with a platform in front of it. We can only conjecture that this was in some way connected with the shrines themselves, and the ceremonies to which they were dedicated.

Facing the convent, we find, behind its right wing, a court bounded by the building itself in part, and in part by a semi-circular, niched retaining-wall, conforming to the sweep of the amphitheatre in which the convent is built. It is entered from the terraces which curve around the heights, by a principal passage between two plain buildings, dependent, however, on the general structure. The probable purpose of this court or enclosure would have been suggested to us on our visit, when we found that it was used as a corral by the Indian shepherds, even if we had not previously known, on the authority of tradition, that it was here that the sacred vicuñas and llamas were kept, from the wool of which the *mama-conas*, or vestals, fashioned their own garments, those of the royal race, and the hangings of the temples.

It were useless to attempt to describe the really beautiful but complicated series of terraces which fall off in harmonious graduations from the court or esplanade of the convent to the lake. Such an attempt would be equally confusing and unsatisfactory, and it need only be said generally that modern taste could hardly suggest a more pleasing disposition of platform and terrace, or modern art carry out more satisfactorily the conceptions of the designer. The retaining-front of the second terrace below the court of the convent is of cut stones, admirably fitted, and along its top runs a wall of stones, breast-high—a kind of parapet or balustrade, pierced at regular intervals with openings, shaped like the niches with which we are getting familiar, through which may be seen the flash and play of the waters of the lake. Two stairways, countersunk, if the term may be used, permit descent to the terrace below, whence curve out flank terraces terminating on rectangular platforms, which perhaps sustained structures as light and temporary, if not as tasteful, as our own summer-houses.

Standing out against the green and gray of the terraced amphitheatre in which it is built, bright with color, and diversified with ornament, boldly and freely designed, with its terraces planted, as we know they were, with flowers, some of which bloom as of yore, the Convent of the Virgins of the Sun, in the fresh little isle of Coati, must have been an object equally impressive and beautiful. It is now sad in its ruin, but not without familiar and home-like features, connecting it with modern life and sympathies. Its gables might be mistaken for those of the ruinous farm-house of some Huguenot exile to North America, such as we see at New Rochelle, near New York; and the stone-work, where the stucco has fallen off, might pass for the work of the same rural architect who built the little stone school-house on the banks of the Hudson in which I learned my alphabet. When we get to Cuzco, in its narrow streets, lined with the high, severe, stony faces of its cold and perhaps more classical walls, almost painful in their geometric precision and regularity, we shall think of the shrine of Coati, and regret its varying tints and diversified outlines.

But if this edifice be picturesque, the view from its terraces is wonderful. It would require some great painter, working in his loftiest and most inspired mood, to give any adequate idea of the majesty of the scene which meets the eye of one who stands on the esplanade of the convent of Coati. Here, as almost everywhere in the Titicaca basin, the great, snowy Sorata, or Illampu, is the centre and dominating feature of the landscape; and nowhere is his mighty mass more plainly visible, or his strange, stern beauties more impressive.

The chroniclers assign both to Huayna Capac and his father, Tupac Yupanqui, the reputed restorer of the shrines of the Sun in Titicaca, the selection of the island of Coati as the sanctuary of the Moon. As the sister and wife of the Inca was called *Coya*, so *Quilla*, the Moon, as the wife and sister of *Inti*, or the Sun, was called by a corresponding name—Inti-Coya. The name of the island is supposed to be derived from this designation, *Coyata*, or *Coata*, the Place of the Coya. One of these Incas—so runs tradition—built here a temple and convent, in which he placed both priests and vestals, with shrines of the Sun and Moon, the first adorned with gold, and the latter with silver. He also assigned two thousand of his subjects, who were free from tribute and other labor, to reside in Copacabana, whose duty it was to guard and cultivate the island, keep its *andenes* in order, and serve the sanctuary. The island was second only to Titicaca as a resort for pilgrims, who brought hither, as offerings, the wool of the vicuña and the alpaca, and the feathers of birds, to be worked up by the vestals, and much chicha to be drunk by the priests, whose prayers were directed to obtaining fine weather and abundant crops.

If this be true, both priests and vestals must have occupied the same building—perhaps the respective portions separated by the shrines to which I have referred. The monkish chroniclers, of course, seek to represent the reputed vestals as rather priestesses of Venus than of Diana, and their religious festivals as lascivious orgies, in which, says Ramos, "they wallowed, like unclean brutes, in the mire of their obscene customs. Which," adds the eulogist and historian of the Virgin of Copacabana, "is the way with all idolatry."

During our stay on the island of Coati we used our photographic tent as our sleeping-quarters; but the splendid moonlight was too attractive to allow us to withdraw to such close quarters, and we remained out far in the night, till the chilling breezes from the snowy Andes sent us, shivering, to our couches.

Three days were devoted to the interesting ruins on this island, and they were marked by one of the few accidents that befell me during my exploration. I had completed my surveys on the third day; and, mounted upon a fragment of wall still rising some ten feet from the ground, I was taking my last look of the island and the lake, when the ancient structure yielded to my weight, and I fell, bringing a mass of ruins with and upon me. I was so much cut and bruised, especially in my right thigh and leg, that I fainted. Recovering consciousness, I endeavored in vain to extricate myself; then, seeing some Indians busied preparing chuño not more than a hundred yards from where I lay, I called to them as loudly as I could; but they would not or could not hear me. All then depended on my own efforts. Removing stones with great difficulty, one by one, I at length succeeded in freeing myself, and scrambled to my feet in great pain. I was able to stand and could walk, though in exquisite suffering. The camp was at least a mile and a half away; but I started for it, and when, with great effort, I reached my companions, it was only to pass the night in intense distress.

The next morning we made sail for Titicaca; but, owing to head winds, the voyage was long and tedious, consuming the whole day. Leaving Professor Raimondi to sketch the Palace of the Inca, which I had explored on my former visit, I climbed the hill to the hacienda, and there passed a most uncomfortable night. The next day I again renewed my inquiries for the Temple of the Sun, but with equally unsatisfactory result. No one seemed to possess the slightest knowledge in regard to it. Failing thus to obtain information, I resolved to begin my labors by examining personally a ruined building at the extreme point of the island, to which some of the natives referred me as the largest ruins they knew. Looking into Calancha's work, I found that, on the authority of Ramos, he actually placed the Temple of the Sun in that spot. With no guide but Calancha's not very definite statements, and the fact that the landing-place of the Incas was a bay called Kintipuca, I skirted the eastern flank of the island, following an ancient winding road for nearly a mile, where I found extensive remains, reputed to be those of the temple I was so anxious to find.

Garcilasso says of this structure that it was only comparable with that of Cuzco, although the remains, as we shall see, are far from justifying the remark of the Inca chronicler. He affirms, on the strength of reports current in his time, that it was plated over with gold, and that all the provinces of the empire made offerings to it every year, of gold, silver, and precious stones, in recognition of the great blessings which in this same island the Sun had conferred on the human race. He adds, on the authority of Blas Valera, that the precious metals which had accumulated in the temple, apart from all that was necessary for making the utensils used in its service, would have built another temple, of like dimensions, from its foundation upwards; but that all of this vast treasure was thrown into the lake when news came of the arrival of the Spaniards.

The Peruvians seem to have had a strong liking for what may be called isthmuses as sites for their palaces and public

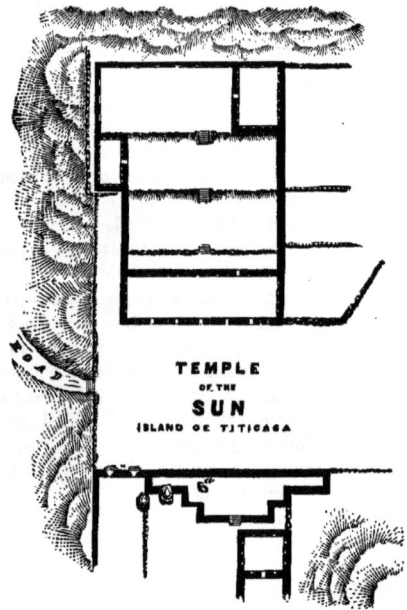

TEMPLE
OF THE
SUN
ISLAND OF TITICACA

structures. I use the term isthmus not only in its strict geographical sense, but as designating also the ridge connecting two hills or mountains—the saddle between two eminences.

The so-called Temple of the Sun occupies the crest of such a ridge, connecting the bulk of the island with a noble promontory rising abruptly from the lake, towards which it presents a

sheer cliff two thousand feet high. This crest has been levelled
so as to form a broad *terre-plein*, sustained by terraces and
reached by flights of steps. On one side, built up against the
slope of the central mass of the island, is the temple, a rectangular structure, 105 feet long by 30 feet wide. Five doors open
on the *terre-plein* at equal distances apart, and each section of
wall between them is pierced with two windows. The interior
presents a series of niches, three feet high, and two feet broad at
bottom, and seems to have consisted of a single apartment. The
walls are much broken down, being at present only from eight
to ten feet high, so that it is impossible to say certainly if the
structure consisted of more than one story. It probably did not.
It is of rough stones, laid in a tough clay, and was stuccoed and
painted inside and out. A single door-way opens to the back
of the edifice upon a series of beautifully levelled rectangular
terraces, rising one above the other, and surrounded by a high
wall. Flights of steps lead from terrace to terrace, and conduct
to two buildings smaller than the temple, but similar in style,
both occupying commanding positions, overlooking the lake on
either hand, and selected with evident appreciation of the wide
and beautiful view that is to be obtained from them. These
terraces still fulfil their probable original purpose as gardens;
and the fineness of the soil and relative luxuriance of their vegetation seem to confirm the story of the chroniclers that rich
earth was brought to the island by the Incas from great distances to redeem its general barrenness.

In front of the temple, on the opposite side of the *terre-plein*,
which is about three hundred feet broad, built up against the
slope of the promontory I have mentioned, are other terraces
and structures, enclosing certain rocks, partly fashioned by hand,
and with which we shall become familiar under the name of
*Intihuatanas*, or places where the Sun was tied up. No description can convey a clear notion of these structures, which
had an obvious dependence on the temple. Behind them the
promontory rises, in conical form, fully a thousand feet, and is
terraced all the way to its top.

It is difficult to imagine a finer site than that of the Tem-

ple of the Sun in Titicaca.  The view from it much resembles
that obtained from the summit of the promontory overlooking
Amalfi and Sorrento, whence the eye commands the bays of
Salerno and Naples, with their islands and rocky shores.  Only
here Nature appears in grander, if less beautiful, aspects, with a
frown on her brow, august and severe.  The Incas sought to
soften her features with their terraces and gardens, but their
efforts were weak against rigors of climate and sterility of
soil; and the sacred island, even when the pilgrims loaded its
shrines with the treasures of a thousand provinces, must have
been almost as harsh and repulsive as in this, the day of its
desecration and abandonment.

There is a little village, with a rude church, on the shore of
the lake, a mile from the temple, called Challa.  In descending
to it, the traveller passes through a little cluster of alder and
molle trees, surrounding a copious spring, which rises in a tank
of Inca masonry, and discharges its waters, by intricate and
artfully contrived channels, over a series of terraces, blushing
with roses and bright with the crimson of the Flor del Inca.
This spot is called the Baths of the Incas, and in the village are
to be seen a number of large stone basins of the size, and very
much the shape, of our modern bathing-tubs.

I have been thus particular in describing the island of Titicaca and its monuments, not only on account of the high veneration in which it was held by the Incas, but as affording an appropriate starting-point in our investigations, in which we shall
trace Inca civilization from the place of its traditional origin
up to that of its highest development in Cuzco.  It will be
seen that none of the remains on the island that have been noticed bear any resemblance to those of Tiahuanaco.  They are
relatively rude and poor, and it would appear that they were
really the first architectural efforts of a young and immature
people.  But such a conclusion would be at variance with well-
authenticated traditions, which rise almost to the dignity of history, and which tell us that most of the structures that existed
on the island were built by the eleventh Inca, Tupac Yupanqui,
grandfather of the ill-fated Atahualpa and the scarcely less un-

fortunate Huascar. Although always held in great veneration, it would seem that the island lost some of its importance with the rapid growth of the empire, until the priests who guarded it represented its decadence to this Inca, who himself resolved to visit it, which he did with great state and ceremony. One of his first acts was to remove all the inhabitants of the island to the main-land at Yunguyo, and to replace them with families of royal blood. He built a palace for the reception of himself and his successors, when making thither their pilgrimages; established a convent for the vestals, at the head of which his successor, Huayna Capac, placed one of his two daughters; founded a temple; and greatly increased the pomp of religion in the island, which was afterwards held as the special domain of the ruler. Assuming the truth of these traditions, most, if not all, the edifices on the island were built some time between 1425 and 1470, which was the period when Tupac Yupanqui reigned.

Having thus briefly described the character of the Inca remains on the two principal and most famous of the sacred islands of Peru, I shall omit reference to the others, as they afford no very different or more striking features.

After thoroughly exploring the ruins of the sacred island, we took a moment when everything seemed to be favorable, and launched the *Natividad* for Puno; but we no sooner got from under the lee of the island than the wind shifted, drove us at right angles to our proper course, and soon increased to a gale, while waves like those of the ocean broke over our little craft. We were tossed and driven before the storm, heartily sick and sore, till the moon rose and the wind subsided somewhat. The next day was not more favorable. Again the gale sprung up, and we pitched and tossed on the waves, seeing storms break on the lake in all directions, while snow set in, with bitter cold. Puno we could not make; we were driven completely across the lake, and when night fell we found ourselves in a little bay just above that of Escoma. Here we thankfully anchored, and began to study our position.

Pentland's map dotted down some ruins in this vicinity, and, as the wind was still unfavorable, I resolved to remain for a day

and examine them. I found some large stone chulpas of comparatively rude construction, one of them standing on a ledge
overlooking the valley of Escoma. It is remarkable as containing two separate chambers, each with a separate entrance, one
above the other, the upper one roughly vaulted. The chambers

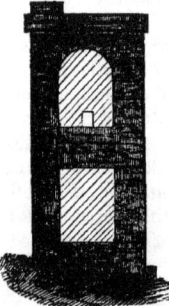

had been long since rifled by treasure-
hunters, and at the time of my visit
nothing remained in them except some
crumbling skeletons and broken pottery.
From the site of this monument, on the
other side of the valley, may be seen one
of the ancient *pucaras*, or hill forts, consisting of a series of five concentric terraces and stone-walls surrounding a conical eminence of great regularity of form.

The wind at last condescended to favor
us, and in our frail vessel we embarked
once again for Puno; but, after a blinding storm of snow and sleet of more than
twenty-four hours' duration, and in which
we could but just keep the *Natividad* afloat by assiduous bail-
ing, a reaction came, and we had pleasant weather, but no wind.
We lay becalmed for five days, during which we exhausted all
our stores, and for two days were without food of any kind. I
hope that that voyage of discovery may be of some use to the
world, for I certainly shall undertake no more in an open boat,
on a stormy lake, two miles above the level of the sea, with the
thermometer perversely inclined to zero.

Our friends in Puno had become greatly concerned on account of our long absence; in fact, they had given us up; and
when we were observed working across the bay, they hastened
down to the little mole, and received us with a cordial welcome.

After our expedition I "assisted" at a grand "function," a
patriotic Festival of Flags, I should call it, symbolical of a
union of all the republics against monarchical intervention in
America. I signed an *acto* on the occasion; and, what was
more, carried an American flag, which the young ladies of the

SECTION OF AYMARÁ CHULPA.

Colejio had improvised for the occasion, getting the number of the stripes wrong, and the azure field a world too little, but making up for all in the size and weight of the staff.  But that was not the worst.  We had to go through a mass and a benediction of the *banderas* in the chill cathedral, with many genuflections and much kneeling on the cold stones, besides enduring a speech from the prefect afterwards, with heads uncovered, in the frosty air.  To the American flag had been given the post

AYMARÁ CHULPA, OR BURIAL-TOWER, AND HILL FORT, AT ESCOMA.

of honor, with those of Chili and Mexico on either hand.  And as, by a remarkable and unprecedented coincidence, two young American engineers had arrived in Puno, so that the Yankee element mustered four strong, and in part recognition of the high honor given to the United States on the occasion of the "function," Mr. T—— determined that the Glorious Fourth, then close at hand, should be celebrated by a dinner, and "with all the honors."

And it was so celebrated.  The brass six-pounder of the place

was fired, a gun for each State, at sunrise; the bells were pealed
at noon; a mass was performed in the cathedral at two o'clock;
the garrison was paraded as an escort to the American flag,
which was carried in triumph through the streets; and, altogether, Puno held high holiday on the 4th of that July. Even
the morose Aymarás seemed to relent, and a few of the more
volatile Quichuas were seen to smile. It was the grand *fiesta*
of St. Jonathan, and chicha could be had gratis in the plaza.

The severe hurt received among the ruins of Coati, and a fever superinduced by exposure on the lake, kept me from taking
an active part in an entertainment and ball given in our hon-
or, which were shared in cordially, and with genuine sympathy,
by all the people of Puno who had ever heard of the United
States, constituting the most respectable, but by no means the
most numerous, class. I regretted this, as it prevented me from
witnessing an incident which, while it illustrates some things in
Peru, is not to be taken as characteristic of the whole people.

It must be premised that in the smaller towns of Spanish
America the populace invite themselves to witness, if not exactly to participate in, any social gathering that may take place.
The style of buildings around a court entered by a single great
door-way precludes much exclusiveness, even if it were attempted. The court of Mr. T——'s house was consequently
filled, not alone while dinner was going on, but afterwards;
and policy, as well as regard for custom, would have induced
him to be extremely liberal of solids as well as liquids to the
"outsiders." Most of these left when the invited and presumably more respectable guests departed; but a few inveterates,
who had got a taste of genuine cognac, persisted in remaining,
in hope of another drink. The great door was closed at midnight, and merely the wicket left open—a hint to leave which
only two or three of the self-invited guests or spectators failed
to understand. Finally, all had departed except a stalwart
mestizo, who wore a long and ample cloak, and lingered and
chatted, and chatted and lingered, until Mr. T——, imagining
that all he wanted was brandy, gave him half a bottle, and, gently crowding him towards the wicket, said,

"Now, my friend, it is past two o'clock. I am very tired; and really you must go!"

"Open the door," responded the man with the cloak.

"Surely you can go out by the wicket. Why should I open the door?"

"To let me out."

This was too much, and our host, in a fit of irritation, gave the persistent intruder a push. Staggering, he dropped a lady's parlor-chair that he had concealed under his cloak, darted through the wicket, and disappeared in the darkness.

## CHAPTER XX.

### SILLUSTANI—ITS CHULPAS AND SUN-CIRCLES.

Lake Umayo.—The Town of Vilque.—Ruins of a Temple.—Sillustani.—Numerous Chulpas.—A Round Chulpa.—Its Construction and Arrangement.—Manner in which the Stones were raised.—A Broken Chulpa at Sillustani.—Chulpas and the Topes of Ceylon.—The Stones cut to Plan before being placed in Position.— Sun-circles. —A Submerged Town and Palace. — Hatuncolla. — Hill-fortress of Quellenata. — Chulpa at Ullulloma compared with Pelasgic Tower in Italy.— Square Chulpas in Bolivia.—The Chulpas evidently Tombs.—Las Casas' Account of Peruvian Modes of Burial.—The Region in which they are found.—Aymará, not Quichua Structures.

BESIDES our long excursion on Lake Titicaca, we made several expeditions to places of interest around Puno. One of these was to the remarkable Lake of Umayo, five leagues to the north-east of Puno, and four from Lake Titicaca. It lies at a higher level than the latter, is about twelve miles in circuit, surrounded on nearly all sides by abrupt cliffs three hundred feet high, and might be taken for a vast, ancient crater, except for a large island in its centre, with its summit level with the plain in which the lake is sunk. The town of Vilque stands near one extremity of the lake, and is celebrated for its annual fair, which is attended by people from a thousand miles' distance—from Cuzco, on the north, to Tucuman and the provinces of the La Plata, on the south-east. Droves of mules are brought from this direction for the supply of the Sierra, where the raising of sheep is more profitable than that of beasts of burden. Beyond Vilque, lying high up among the Cordillera, are other considerable lakes, one of which, called Coallaqui, is not far from seventeen thousand feet above the sea.

The Lake of Umayo, although represented on the maps as discharging into Lake Titicaca, has really no outlet. It nevertheless contains several varieties of fish, some of which, if not

all, are identical with those of the greater lake. It is divided,
with the exception of a narrow strait, into two unequal parts,
by a bold, elevated promontory, rugged and rocky, connected
with the main-land by a narrow and much lower isthmus or
ridge, on which had been built a structure similar to the Palace
of the Inca on the island of Titicaca.

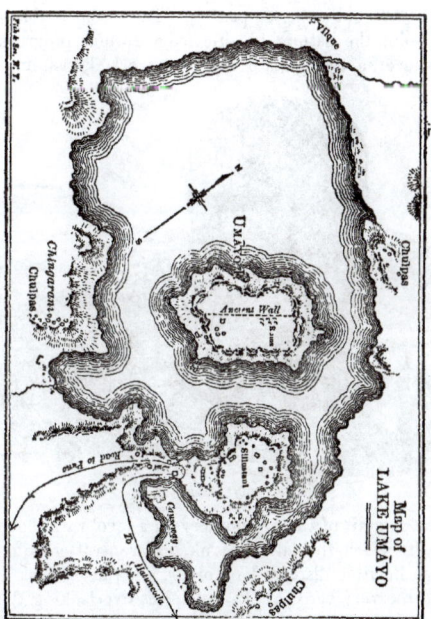

On this peninsula or promontory, which tradition affirms
to have been the cemetery of the chiefs of Hatuncolla, are a
great number of chulpas, of varying size and construction.
Among them are some of the best-preserved and most imposing
of all in the Collao. The headlands of the lake and the hills

around bristle with others, standing singly or in groups of a hundred or more; but few of them rival those of Sillustani in size or workmanship.

Passing the isthmus at its narrowest point, and where the promontory begins to rise, we find the approach obstructed by a series of walls of heavy irregular stones, through each of which there is but a single opening. The ascent is abrupt, and at one point the natural basaltic ledge forbids progress. Up this, however, a zigzag path has been worked, enabling us to

ROUND CHULPAS, SILLUSTANI.

reach the summit of the promontory on a level with the general plateau in which the lake is sunk. Here, scattered in every direction, in utter disregard of order, are the chulpas. Some stand on the very verge of the precipices overlooking the lake, and so near that it is impossible for a man to pass outside of them; others are in the centre of the promontory. Some are in ruins, or partly fallen; others are nearly as perfect as when first built; others seem to have been just commenced, and others still appear to have been but half finished. Great blocks of basalt and trachyte, wholly or partly worked, are scattered pro-

fusely on every side.  No spot could be more favorable for
the study of the design and construction of the chulpas, or for
determining their purpose, than is afforded at Sillustani.

I will take as the first example one of the largest and best preserved.  It stands but a few yards from the edge of the precipice which bounds the peninsula, and close to another unfinished or in ruins.  Like the last of those to which I referred in
Acora, it is round, 16 feet in diameter at the base, and 39 feet
high.  Like that, also, it widens as it rises, until at the spring of
the dome its diameter is thirty-four inches greater than at its
base.  The cornice or band that runs around it, three-fourths of
the distance from base to summit, is about three feet wide, and
projects about three inches.  The material of the structure is a
hard, compact basalt.  The blocks of stone are admirably cut, disposed in nearly even courses, and accurately fitted.  In a few
cases, where an irregularity occurs in the edge of one stone, or
where one of a course projects above another, the stone above is
cut so as to correct the irregularity and preserve the joint and
the succeeding courses perfect.  The lower course, composed of
the largest stones, measured five feet
above the ground.  At what was
probably the original surface of the
ground, these stones are bevelled out,
as are often our stone gate-posts, and
are left rough below, as if designed
to obtain a better hold in the earth.
We have noticed the same feature in
describing the great stones supporting the walls and terraces around
the so-called fortress of Tiahuanaco.
The entrance to this monument is
through a low opening, barely large
enough to admit the body of a man.

FOUNDATION-STONE OF CHULPA.

This is not formed by omitting a stone in the foundation, as
at Acora, but is cut through a single block.  It leads into a
circular vault ten feet in diameter and twelve feet high, arched
as I have already described, with flat, uncut, overlapping stones

laid in clay. It has no niches, but appears to have been stuccoed. Immediately in the centre of the vault or chamber is an opening about two feet in diameter, leading to an upper and smaller vault. In this are still some human bones and fragments of pottery. In common with all the better class of chulpas, this had been ransacked for hidden treasures, and the floor had been dug up in the operation, showing only a rough, mixed mass of stones, broken pottery, and human bones. Among these there remained entire a single skull, which I brought away with me.

The interior arrangements of no two of the chulpas of Sillustani are exactly the same. Some have a single vaulted chamber; some have cists covered with flat stones sunk in the floor of the vault; and others have niches. One has not only a cist, but two series of niches. The cist is octagonal, three feet in diameter, and five feet deep, paved and walled up with stones. The opening was probably closed with a stone slab. The lower niches, four in number, are larger than the second or upper series. These are disposed intermediately, or over the spaces between the lower ones. Between the two series, and projecting several inches from the walls, are a number of flat stones, evidently intended to rest the feet upon in placing any article in the upper niches. On each side of every niche are other thin, flat stones, projecting a few inches, and pierced with holes. These were evidently designed to receive cords to fasten the bodies of the dead in the niches. The chamber in this particular chulpa was not vaulted, but covered with broad, flat, cut stones.

A number of the chulpas of Sillustani were built of rough stones, cast over with clay, stuccoed, and probably painted. There are no square ones here, but the foundations of several; and some are partly finished. These, and some of the unfinished round ones, enlighten us as to the manner in which their builders and those of the other Peruvian monuments contrived to raise heavy stones to considerable heights without the aid of derricks and pulleys. We find, built up against the chulpas, inclined planes of stone and earth, up which the stones were moved, probably with levers, and possibly with the aid of roll-

ers. As the structure rose in height, the plane was raised accordingly; and when the structure was finished, the plane was
dug away.

One of the largest of the chulpas of this group, and that
which was best finished, of fine trachyte, is partly broken down,
or, rather, split apart, probably by an earthquake. It has several stones in it, measuring 12 feet in length on the curve of
the face, 6 feet 8 inches in height, and 5 feet in depth. It
shows perfectly the mode of construction. The ends of the

BROKEN CHULPA, SILLUSTANI.

stones were all cut on a true radius from the centre of the
structure. They entered, to different depths, into the mass of
the chulpa, which in all cases is of rough stones laid in clay,
and were thus more firmly held in place. Another device was
adopted to hold them more securely in position. The ends of
the several stones were hollowed out like a bowl, so that, when
set together, there was a cavity in which a stone was placed, and
the space filled with tough clay. In this manner the stones
were neatly cemented together, without the means by which
it was effected showing on the exterior. For precisely the

same purpose of giving a more even and finished exterior, we sometimes countersink the upper and lower surfaces of the bricks used in facing walls.  The builders of the monuments of Sillustani did not extend this device to the upper and lower sides of the stones, probably depending on the weight of the superincumbent mass of the structure to retain them in position.

Architecturally considered, these chulpas are among the most remarkable monuments of America.  Their domes remind us of the dagobas or topes of Ceylon and India, but the topes never took the form of towers, but consisted simply of domes raised on a platform reached by flights of steps.  Cut off our chulpas below the cornice or band, and the upper part would be very nearly a tope in miniature.  I am by no means seeking for resemblances; for if I were, I should obtain little satisfaction from the topes, which were essentially religious structures, dedicated to Buddha, although often raised over a relic of that teacher; while our chulpas were simple sepulchral monuments, individual or family tombs, corresponding probably in their size and elaboration with the dignity or importance of the dead within them.

Not only were the ends of all the stones forming the exterior walls cut on radii from the centre of the monument, but the gradual swell of the structure as it widened out, as well as the curve of the dome, was preserved in each, and was geometrically accurate.  Those of the dome especially were cut first on the radius, next to conform to the curve or swell of the dome, but finally wedge-shaped on their upper and lower surfaces, so that their thrust or push should be inward.  That the stones were not shaped after having been put in position is proved by the great numbers scattered over the promontory, perfectly cut to conform to their place in structures that were never finished.  It is evident that they were hewn to plans in which every dimension of the structures had been previously fixed.  The intelligent man, as well as the practical stone-cutter, can appreciate the difficulties to be encountered in this kind of work, and be ready to admire the skill with which they were surmounted.

Before leaving Sillustani, and before dismissing the chulpas, attention must be called to some singular remains, unlike any which we have hitherto noticed in Peru. The peninsula of Sillustani has on its eastern side a kind of step or natural terrace, sixty or eighty feet lower than the rocky level on which the greater portion of the chulpas stand. On this we find a number of circles and semicircles of varying diameter, defined by a platform of well-fitted flat stones, inside of which is a line of erect, uncut stones, so nearly coinciding in every respect with what are called the sun-circles, or Druidical circles of England and many parts of Northern Europe and Asia, as to be scarcely distinguishable from them. The stones forming what I have called the platform are roughly cut, and their adjoining edges are on radii from the centre of the circle. The inner ends are highest, and through them runs a groove or gutter, extending all around the circle.

PLATFORM STONE OF SUN-CIRCLE.

Some of these circles are more elaborate than others, and of one of these I give a drawing that will serve to illustrate all. It will be observed that there is, first, a circle of rough, upright stones, of irregular sizes, firmly set in the ground. The circle is one hundred and twenty-four feet in diameter; it has an opening five feet wide on the east, and it encloses two larger upright stones (one of which has fallen), placed one-third of the diameter of the circle apart. The second circle is about ninety feet in diameter. The stones on both sides of the gate-way are pierced with holes. This is the perfected form of the sun-circles of Peru, and it must not be supposed that all of them are equally elaborate, for the greater number are composed of simple upright stones in their natural state.

A few instances have fallen under my notice in the vast region that composed the Inca empire, in which rough upright stones, often of large size, were arranged in the form of squares or rectangles. The ruins of Tiahuanaco, already described, afford a most striking example. Here we find quadrangles defined by great unhewn stones, worn and frayed by time, and having every evidence of the highest antiquity, side by side with other squares of similar plan, but defined by massive stones cut with much elaboration, as if they were the works of later and more advanced generations, which, however, still preserved the notions of their ancestors, bringing only greater skill to the construction of their monuments.

SUN-CIRCLE, SILLUSTANI.

The bay that sweeps behind the peninsula of Sillustani is shallow, grown up with reeds, and with the lake-weed which I have described as affording food for cattle in the dry season, and which is called *llachu*. We observe a line of wall resembling a causeway, running from shore to shore, within which, just traceable above the water, are lines of stone-work, such as might really be left by the sinking or submergence of buildings, and which give some sort of sanction to the tradition, that

here the *Apus* or *Curacas* of Hatuncolla had a palace and a
town, which sunk, and were covered by the waters of the lake
during a great earthquake. I went to the supposed walls in a
balsa, and satisfied myself that they are really the remains of
buildings; but whether originally these were erected on low
grounds, with the supposed causeway as a dike to prevent the
encroachments of the water when the lake rose during heavy

STONE PILLARS OF HATUNCOLLA.

rains, or whether there was a real subsidence of the grounds
during some terrestrial convulsion, I am unprepared to say. I
incline, however, to the former hypothesis.

In the little modern town of Hatuncolla, two leagues from
the lake, are two very remarkable sandstone pillars, 6 or 7 feet
high, 2 feet broad, and 10 inches thick. These monuments are
carved with figures of serpents, lizards, and frogs, and with elab-

orate geometrical ornaments. It is averred that they once formed the jambs of the undoubted Inca structure standing on

ORNAMENTS ON PILLAR.

the isthmus connecting the peninsula of Sillustani with the main-land. According to Garcilasso, the chiefs of Hatuncolla submitted without resistance to Lloque Yupanqui, the third Inca, who reigned from 1091 to 1126.

Chulpa tombs are as varying in their interior arrangement as they are in size and structure. The opening into them is oftenest to the east; but there is no uniformity in this respect, even among those composing the same group. In many cases there is no opening at all. This deficiency is specially noticeable in the hundreds found among the ruins of Quellenata, on the north-eastern shore of Lake Titicaca. Here the inner chamber or vault is formed, as in the case of those already noticed, by a circle of upright stones, across the tops of which flat stones are laid, forming a chamber, which often

FROG ON PILLAR.

has its floor below the general level of the earth. Around this chamber a wall is built, which is carried up to varying heights of from ten to thirty feet. The exterior stones are usually broken to conform to the outer curve of the tower, and the whole is more or less cemented together with a very tenacious clay. Nearly all are built with flaring or diverging walls; that is to say, they are narrower at their bases than at their tops. Sometimes this divergence is on a curved instead of a right line, and gives to the monument a graceful shape. In Quellenata I found only one skeleton in each of the chulpas I examined; and none of these structures had open entrances. Similar remains in shape

HILL FORTRESS OF QUELLENATA.

and construction occur in great numbers among what are called the ruins of Ullulloma, three leagues from the town of Santa Rosa, in the valley of the river Pucura. But here the chulpas have openings into which a man may creep, and all of them contained originally two or more skeletons. For the purpose of comparison, I give a view of a chulpa at Ullulloma and one of the remains of a so-called Pelasgic tower at Alatri, in Italy. There is a very close resemblance in general style and workmanship; but in the Peruvian structure the stones are much more accurately fitted together.

PELASGIC TOWER AT ALATRI, ITALY.          CHULPA AT ULLULLOMA, PERU.

Among the ruins of Tiulmani, on the eastern shore of the lake, all the chulpas are square or rectangular, and many of them have two chambers, one above the other, entirely separated, and reached by different openings from the exterior. In ascending the Cordillera from the coast above Tacna, and in the valley of the little stream that supplies that city with water, a few chulpas (already mentioned) of rough stone are found, stuccoed over, and painted in red, yellow, and white. This preservation of the colors is due to the fact that these structures stand outside the rainy belt. They have the additional and singular feature that the cornice is formed, not by projecting stones, but by a layer of ichu grass, laid with the stems pointing outwards, which had then been trimmed off as if with a shears.

I have assumed throughout that the chulpas were tombs. Of this there cannot be the slightest doubt, albeit a number of travellers, including the eminent Von Tschudi, have supposed them to be the dwelling-places, and even parts of the fortresses, of the ancient inhabitants, from the fact of finding in them traces of fire and broken pottery. But he also mentions having frequently found shelter in these towers for the night, as I have several times done, leaving next day undoubted traces of fire and other evidences of occupation, precisely as hundreds of Indians had done before me. I examined several chulpas which had never been opened, and in all cases found a human skeleton. These seem to have been raised over single individuals, while those that had entrances were family tombs, since we usually find from two to twelve skeletons within them.

In his unpublished "Historia Apologética," Las Casas has given us an account of the burial-rites and the sepulchres of the Peruvians of the coast. Speaking of the people of the mountains, he says:

"They have different tombs, and different modes of burial. In some provinces they have for sepulchres high towers, hollow below to the height of an *estado* (about six feet), built massively of earth or cut stone, all very white. In some parts they are round; in others, square, very high, joining one to another in the fields. Some build them on eminences, a half league or

more from their towns, so that they appear like other and very
populous villages. Each one has a sepulchre of his ancestry
or lineage. The dead are wrapped in skins of the llama, on
which the nose and eyes are indicated, then clothed, and deposited in a sitting posture. The doors of the tombs, which are
all towards the east, are then closed with stone or clay. At the
end of a year, when the body becomes dry, the doors are again
opened. In other places the bodies are enveloped as above described, and then placed along the walls in their own houses.
In some places the bodies are placed in the same houses where
the living eat and sleep. There is no bad odor, because the
skins in which the bodies are placed are sewed up very closely, and, from the cold, they soon become like mummies. The
chiefs or lords place the bodies of their dead in the large or
principal room of their houses, and surround it with the vases,
clothing, jewels, and adornments which were possessed by the
defunct in life."

So far as my observations go, the chulpa is a structure confined to the Collao and Bolivia, in the region occupied by the
Aymarás, or, as Dr. Morton styles them, from the shape of their
skulls, the " long-headed or Titicacan people." I found but a
single group after passing the divide of La Raya into the country proper of the Quichuas. Von Tschudi, nevertheless, found
similar structures in the distant department of Junin, built perhaps by Aymará *mitimaes*, or translated colonies.

# CHAPTER XXI.

### FROM LAKE TITICACA TO CUZCO.

FROM Puno our journey was continued around the upper
end of Lake Titicaca, through the towns of Paucarcolla, Pusi,
and Taraco, to Huancané, near the head of the fine bay of that
name, crossing the considerable rivers Lampa and Ramis, not
far above their mouths. Both these streams are erroneously
laid down in the maps: the former does not flow direct into
the lake, but into the Bay of Puno.

Between Paucarcolla and Pusi we stopped to explore certain
monuments which we discovered wide of our road. We then
sent our baggage ahead, which, darkness supervening, we did not
overtake. Becoming entangled among the hills of Capachica,
we lost the trail, and were obliged to pass the cold night by the
side of a rock, without food or fire, or any covering except our
ponchos. When day dawned we found ourselves less than half

a league from the town to which we were bound, where, in
the firm belief that we had been drowned in crossing the Lampa River, Ignacio had commenced administering on our effects,
and, with the arrieros, at half an hour after daylight, was "drunk
as a lord" on our best cognac. Drunkenness is universal
throughout the Sierra. Nothing that can be made to ferment
is neglected in manufacturing intoxicating beverages. Nearly
all the maize is converted into chicha; even the berries of the
molle-tree are employed in the same way. And as for the cane
grown in the hot valleys, its juice is wholly distilled into cañaso;
so that sugar in Cuzco can only be had at from a dollar to a
dollar and a half a pound!

TURF HOUSE NEAR MOUTH OF THE RIO RAMIS.

The region around the mouth of the Ramis is a kind of del-
ta, very low and level, interspersed with shallow pools, as if but
recently half rescued from the lake by deposits from the river.
These pools are thronged with water-fowl, among which the
scarlet ibis and strong-winged mountain-goose are conspicuous.
The inhabitants here are all shepherds; and as what there is
of solid ground is covered with a thin but tough turf, this is
used exclusively in constructing their dwellings and the corrals,
or pens for their flocks. Quaint and curious structures they
are, looking like tall quadrilateral hay-stacks. In some of them,

attempts had been made at something like architectural adornment ; and these, as well as the chulpas, have a kind of cornice
at the point where the roof begins to converge from the vertical walls—a feature suggested perhaps by the chulpas, or a tradition of style descending from the ancient builders of the
tombs.  In their interior they are, in common with all the
dwellings of the Indian natives, filthy in the extreme.  A few
had been deserted and had fallen down, forming mounds of
more or less regularity and elevation, in which digging would
certainly expose what we generally find in mounds of earth all
over the world — bones, fragments of pottery, some battered
implements not worth removal, and traces of fire.

The town of Huancané is large, and is occupied almost exclusively by Indians of the Aymará family.  It has some hot
springs in its neighborhood, which have a high medicinal reputation, and the place may be regarded as the Saratoga of the
Puno district.  Four leagues beyond, following the shores of
the Bay of Huancané, is the Indian pueblo of Vilquechico, in
the neighborhood of which are other hot springs, the Inca ruins of Acarpa, and the Pre-Incarial monuments of Quellenata.  They consist of a vast number of chulpas, of various sizes,
standing on an eminence that may justly be called a mountain, surrounded by walls of rough or rudely fashioned stones,
pierced with door-ways, indistinguishable from what in the Old
World are called Pelasgic walls.  The ruins of Acarpa stand
on a peninsula projecting far into a shallow bay, and were
reached by the Incas over causeways of stone still visible above
the water.

Leaving Huancané, where, since our visit, the Indians have
risen in open revolt against the whites and committed great
cruelties, we travelled north-west through the town of Chupe
to Azangaro, a famous seat of the ancient inhabitants, and distinguished now as containing one of the most remarkable monuments of antiquity in Peru, the Sondor-huasi, which retains its
original thatched roof after a lapse of over three hundred years,
showing us how much skill and beauty, as well as utility, may
be achieved and displayed even in a roof of thatch.  We know, .

from the concurrent testimony of the chroniclers, that all the
Inca roofs were of thatch—as indeed nine-tenths of the roofs
of all the buildings of the Sierra still are.   From this has been
inferred an incongruity between the skilful workmanship of the
walls and the rude character and meanness of the roofs, which
the Sondor-huasi will go far to correct.   The thin, long, and
tough ichu grass of this mountain region is admirably adapted
for thatch, lying smoothly, besides being readily worked.

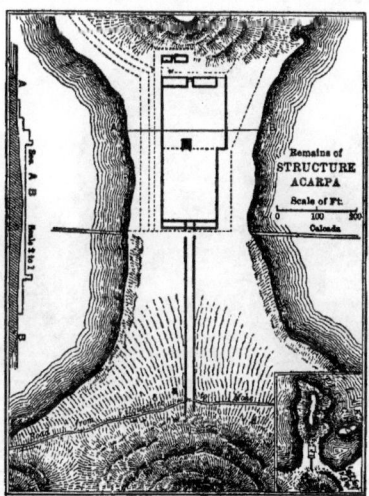

The Sondor-huasi is a circular building, apparently of compacted clay, sixteen feet in exterior diameter.   The walls are
fourteen inches thick and eleven feet high, perfectly smooth
outside and inside, and resting on a foundation of stones.   The
entrance is by a door, opening to the north, twenty-eight inches
wide and six feet high.   Within, extending around the walls, is
a bench of cut stones, except at the point immediately opposite
27

the door, where there is a kind of daïs of stone and compacted clay, with supports for the arms at each end like those of a sofa. Sunk in the walls at about four feet above the floor are two series of niches, and at the height of eight feet are four small windows.

The dome of the Sondor-huasi is perfect, and is formed of a series of bamboos of equal size and taper, their larger ends resting on the top of the walls; bent evenly to a central point, over a series of hoops of the same material and of graduated

THE SONDOR-HUASI.

sizes. At the points where the vertical and horizontal supports cross each other, they are bound together by fine cords of delicately braided grass, which cross and recross each other with admirable skill and taste. Over this skeleton dome is a fine mat of the braided epidermis of the bamboo or rattan, which, as it exposes no seams, almost induces the belief that it was braided on the spot. However that may be, it was worked in different colors, and in panellings conforming in size with the diminishing spaces between the framework, that framework itself being also painted. I shall probably shock my classical readers, and be accounted presumptuous, when I venture a comparison of the Azangaro dome, in style and effect, with that of the cella of the Temple of Venus, facing the Coliseum, in the Eternal City. Over this inner matting is another, open, coarse, and strong, in which was fastened a fleece of finest.ichu; which depends like a heavy fringe outside the walls. Next comes a transverse layer of coarser grass or reeds, to which succeeds ichu, and so on, the whole rising in the centre so as to form a slightly flattened cone. The projecting ends of the ichu layers were cut off sharply and regularly, producing the effect of overlapping tiles.

Cieza de Leon also describes these roofs, as an eye-witness. He says, " They are of straw, but so artfully laid on, that, unless destroyed by fire, they will last many ages."

By referring to Garcilasso we find how closely the roof of the Sondor-huasi coincides with his description of the roofs extant in his day. He says:

" Their roofs were made of poles fastened to each other transversely by strong cords. These supported a layer of grass of the thickness, in some of the houses, of six feet or more, which not only served for a cornice to the walls, but extended beyond them more than a yard, as a pent-roof to keep the rain from the walls, and to shelter people beneath it. The part that projected beyond the walls was clipped very evenly..... I remember a structure in the valley of Yucay, of the kind I have described, more than seventy feet square [around?], which was covered in the form of a pyramid. Although the walls were only three *estados* (eighteen feet) in height, the roof was more than twelve feet."

From this it will appear that the Inca roofs were not really so rude and unsightly as we are apt to imagine from our knowledge of modern thatched buildings, associated as they are with poverty and squalidness. Certain it is, that, if the Sondor-huasi may be taken as an example of how ordinary structures like itself were ornamented interiorly, we can readily conceive that the interiors of the more important buildings and temples were exceedingly beautiful.

From Azangaro our route lay over a high table-land covered
with snow, into the valley of the Rio Pucura, which we ascended through the towns of Pucura and Ayavira, the mountains
closing gradually around as the valley narrows, until we find
ourselves in Santa Rosa, a considerable town, the last of the
Collao, at the foot of the great snowy mountain of Apucumu-
rami, and one hundred miles from the lake.

THE CONDOR AND THE BULL.

Here we witnessed one of those bull-fights, or rather bull-
baitings, which are the delight equally of the people of the
coast and the Sierra.   The plaza of the town was fenced in, and
the bull, with a gaudy crimson cloth fastened over his back,
and his horns loaded with fire-crackers, was let into the enclosure.   Then commenced the process of tormenting the animal.
To mount on the bull's back and ride him round the plaza,
while lighting the fireworks; to prod him with sharp nails set
in the ends of poles, and generally to irritate and vex him,
while dexterously escaping his blind wrath, seem to constitute
the main features of this cherished pastime.

At Santa Rosa the performances were varied by fastening a young condor on the back of one of the bulls, which, when roused by the noise, the motion, and the explosions, began to beat the sides of the bull with his powerful wings, and to lacerate his flesh with his terrible beak.  After both bull and condor had become completely exhausted, and the former, with bleeding flanks and protruding tongue, was standing helplessly in a corner, an Indian approached to unfasten the bird, which, however, seized him by the arm and nearly tore it from its socket.  This condor and another were given me by their owner, and I undertook to send them home as a present to the Central Park, New York.  They, however, never reached the coast, as the following letter from Pedro Lobo, the arriero who undertook to take them there, will, perhaps, sufficiently explain :

"SIR AND GENTLEMAN, VIRACOCHA !—I am ill.  I supplicate your mercy.  I am a poor man, as you know, and my family has had the small-pox.  Manuela died, it is now a long time.  There is little alfalfa to be had in my village.  So I ask your forgiveness.  I could not do otherwise.  It happened so.  It was in the Pampa of Tungasaca.  One of the *pollos* [chickens], he of the bull, tore off the ears of the mule Chepa, which carried him.  You remember the mule Chepa, because of its tail, which was short.  It made strings of my poncho, and grievously hurt me.  I still crave your mercy.  But it got away.

"You know that maize is very high, and, as I said before, poor Manuela died of the small-pox.  They are taking men for the army.  I don't know what may happen to me.  There is measles in my village, and the roads are bad; but when the *pollo* of the *toro* got away, the other got away also.  I know they will say in Santa Rosa that I cut the straps.  And so it may appear.  But, sir, gentleman, and Viracocha, you will not believe them ; for there is little alfalfa and no maize to mention in my village ; and it is now two years since Manuela died, to say nothing of the measles, from which may the Virgin protect your worship !  Hence I ask your mercy."

I should explain that I had on several occasions expressed great sympathy with Pedro Lobo on account of the premature death of his daughter Manuela, and he argued that the reference would soften my heart and avert any anger I might experience on account of the escape of the *pollos*.

At Santa Rosa, the Andes and Cordillera are knotted together, and we soon become involved among their gorges, disputing passage-way with the head-waters of the river Pucura. From Santa Rosa to the divide, a weary distance of five leagues, the scenery is most bold and impressive, resembling that of the valley of the Lauterbrunnen, in Switzerland, or the ascent of the Pass of St. Gothard from Bellanzona. There are no habitations, only here and there, at exposed points, remains of Inca tambos, under whose crumbling walls we find some shivering groups of native travellers, huddled together over a smouldering fire of dung, endeavoring to warm their wretched chupe. The wind forces itself through the gorges with fearful violence, driving before it the sand and gravel of the rough pathway and fine splinters of disintegrating rock, which puncture the chapped and smarting skin like lancets, until the blood starts in drops from every exposed part of the person. Our mules rebel against facing the blast, and obstinately turn their backs towards it, or viciously refuse to leave the shelter of some rock that breaks the force of the wind. The mountains all around us are covered with snow, which occasionally drives down in blinding whirls upon us, when some avalanche precipitates itself from the impending crests that curve over like the combing waves of the ocean before they break on the shore.

We approach a narrow pass ; a frosty stream, curdled with floating snow and icy crystals, frets between the rough rocks on one side, and the cliff rises sheer on the other, with only a narrow shelf for the roadway, so narrow that the animals cannot pass abreast. We have just entered on it, with a hurt cargo-mule now running *de valde*, or free, ahead, when we hear the sound of the warning whistle of some party approaching us from the other end of the pass, and which we had heard before, but, half deaf and blinded, had confounded it with the shriek

of the cruel wind. We make an attempt to turn back the
mule, but she plunges forwards, while we retreat to a wider part
of the shelf, and flatten ourselves against the rock, to permit
the approaching travellers to pass. They prove to be a man
evidently of position, but wearing a thick mask and goggles,
who answers to our inquiry if he had encountered a mule by
pointing down among the rocks at the foot of the precipice.
He had shot the animal as it confronted him in the road : there
was no other alternative.

As we approach the summit, the gorge widens out a little,
and we have a better road. Here we find every rock supporting heaps of stones, and there are hundreds of other heaps on
all sides where there is room enough to build them up, from a
foot to five and more feet high. They have been raised by the
Indians to propitiate the spirits of the mountains, and those
which control the winds and the snows and the bitter frosts.
The river of Pucura, reduced in size to a mere brook, babbles
at our side, and we feel as grateful as the Indians themselves,
albeit we do not rear our little *apachita* in token of having
passed safely the worst part of our road. A mile farther, and
we reach the *cumbre*, or divide—a lap, if I may use the term,
between the two mountain ranges. Here, on one side, is a
great pile of votive stones, and on the other a small lake, or
tarn, welling up among masses of vibrating, half-frozen turf,
edged round with a silvery border of ice, and looking clear but
dark under the cold, steel-like sky.

From this lake, which is only a few hundred feet across, flow
two small, distinct streams — one through the gorge we have
passed southwards, forming in its course the river Pucura, falling into Lake Titicaca, and the other flowing north, constituting the source of the Rio Vilcanota, which, under its successive
names of Vilcamayo, Yucay, Urubamba, and Ucayali, forms the
true parent stream of the Amazon. A cork thrown into the
centre of the lake might be carried into Titicaca or into the
Atlantic, depending probably on the direction of the wind.
The divide which we have reached is in latitude 14° 30' south,
and longitude 70° 50' west, at an elevation of 14,170 feet, domi-

nated by the great snowy peak of Vilcanota, which still rises majestically above us.

Around the lake are the remains of several Inca tambos, some evidently designed for the poorer order of travellers, and one clearly intended for the Inca himself, or those of his blood. The latter has been almost destroyed by the seekers for treasure, and its levelled walls afford no protection from the winds. So we gather for the night under the lee of some standing walls of humbler structures, fasten our mules close beside us, feeding them with raw barley, and, fencing ourselves in with our baggage, huddle around a little fire of sticks of quinoa, which, by a fortunate accident, we were able to buy in Santa Rosa at a little less than their weight in silver. We refresh ourselves with coffee; our arrieros stuff their mouths with coca; we pack ourselves together as closely as possible, and await the dawn, when we shall start down the slopes of the Amazon.

The means of intercommunication in the Inca empire, under the beneficent rule of its aboriginal sovereigns, were infinitely better than they are to-day. Apart from their roads and bridges, they built at all exposed points, at intervals in the *punas* and among the mountains, as well as in the villages, posts for the accommodation of travellers. These were by no means imposing, but large and comfortable, structures, in which not alone the travellers themselves, but their llamas, might find food and shelter. At La Raya, through which all communication between the capital and the Colla-suya, or important region around Lake Titicaca, had to pass, the public requirements were met by the construction of a number of tambos of large size; and there are also traces of a fortification, as if for the maintenance here of a garrison.

I made a plan of one of these tambos, under the crumbling walls of which we found protection for the night, which may be taken as a type of this kind of structures in general, although no two are precisely alike. It is a building with a front of 180 feet in length, with wings extending inwards at either extremity, forming three sides of a court. This court is extended down to the waters of the little lake by rough stone-walls, and the ground falls off by low terraces. The main front has but three rooms, each about sixty feet long; the central one alone having entrances from the outside. The corner rooms open into the court, and each has a smaller inner room that can only be reached through it — designed, perhaps, for the women or persons of distinction.

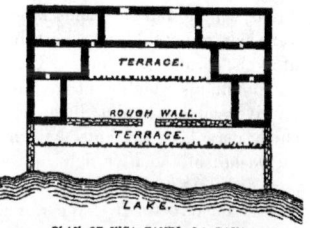

PLAN OF INCA TAMBO, LA RAYA.

The rooms have small niches on their sides, sunk in the walls, which are from two to three feet thick, composed of rough stones laid in clay. Altogether, the tambos seem to have been rough but substantial, common-sense structures, rationally devised to meet the wants of the people for whose use they were built. The courts were, no doubt, designed for the reception of the herds of llamas and alpacas that might accompany travellers, or be sent from the valleys to the plains of the Collao.

We descend now, here between steep mountains, where stream and roadway dispute the passage, with eternal winter enthroned on the heights above us, anon urging our mules over narrow but arable intervals of land, or stopping to rest in quaint villages of Indians, famous in aboriginal history as the Canchus.

From the Pass of La Raya into the valley of the Vilcanota the descent is rapid, and before noon we begin to feel the change in temperature. At the hot springs of Aguas Calientes, a distance of two leagues, we had descended fifteen hundred feet. The waters of these springs are regarded as specifics for certain diseases, and there are near them a few low, rough, stone huts (without windows or doors to close the entrances, and without inhabitants), to which the sick may resort, bringing, of course, their own beds, cooking utensils, and food. The little brook that in the morning trickled, half frozen, from the lake of La Raya, before noon has swollen into a considerable stream, and before night we find it flowing, a scarcely fordable river, through a narrow but fertile and well-cultivated valley.

It is winter, and the fields are dry and sere; but we see on every side the stubble of wheat, barley, and maize, and, at long intervals, a rude grist-mill. The steep gorges that open from the mountains which shut in the valley are terraced up from the river lands, forming little triangular farms or gardens, in which may be seen huts, half hidden by quenua-trees and the bushes of the Flor del Inca. Houses and towns become more frequent, and, in common with the people, have an aspect of relative thrift. We can get food for our animals at some price, and eggs become a luxury within the scope of our exchequer.

The Indians we meet are less swarthy and sullen than those of the Collao, and we extract a grain of satisfaction from that most unpromising of all sources, the cry of a baby. Altogether, we follow the track of Manco Capac, satisfied that he must have found the valley of the Vilcanota a most agreeable change from his cold and barren rock of Titicaca.

We prosecute our journey sixty miles farther, until the stream that trickled from the tarn of La Raya has swollen to be an unfordable river, under the name of Vilcanota. Here we reach the town of Cacha, near which are the remains of the famous Temple of Viracocha. The valley has spread out to the width of a league, and is level and fertile. Beyond the town, on the right bank of the river, and rising nearly in the centre of the valley, is the broad and rather low, irregular volcanic cone of Haratche. It has thrown out its masses of lava on all sides, partly filling up the hollow between it and the mountains, on one hand, and sending off two high dikes to the river, on the other. Between these dikes is a triangular space, nearly a mile in greatest length, literally walled in by ridges of black lava, heaped in wildest confusion to the height of many feet. At the upper end of this space, which has been widened by terracing up against the lava fields, and piling back the rough fragments on each other, is a copious spring, sending out a considerable stream. It has been carefully walled in with cut stones, and surrounded with terraces, over the edges of which it falls, in musical cataracts, into a large artificial pond or reservoir covering several acres, in which grow aquatic plants, and in which water-birds find congenial refuge. From this pond the water discharges itself, partly through numerous *azequias* that irrigate the various terraces lining this lava-bound valley, and partly through a walled channel into the Vilcanota.

Overlooking the reservoir or pond, on a broad terrace, or rather series of terraces, on one side of a great semicircular area, rise the lofty ruins of the Temple of Viracocha, one of the most important ever built by the Incas, and which seems to have been unique in character. Before proceeding to a more minute explanation and description of what remains of this temple, it will not be amiss, and it will certainly aid us in understanding the origin and purport of the structure, to review what Garcilasso has to say about it and its builder.

The Inca Viracocha was the eighth of his line, according to Garcilasso's table, and left the most romantic and brilliant history of his royal race. His father, Yahuar-Huacac, was a mild and somewhat pusillanimous prince, who could poorly tolerate the impetuous and ambitious temper of his son, and whom he sent early into honorable exile from the court, to be custodian of the royal flocks and those of the Sun, on the high, cold plain of Chita, three leagues to the north-east of Cuzco. After three years of banishment, the young prince returned to Cuzco without permission, and forced himself into the presence of his father, asserting that he had that to communicate which concerned the peace and safety of the empire. He related that during a day-dream, or trance, he had been approached by a celestial being, white and bearded, dressed in a long and flowing robe, who said, "I am son of the Sun, brother of Manco Capac. My name is Viracocha, and I am sent by my father to advise the Inca that the provinces of Chinchasuya are in revolt, and that large armies are advancing thence to destroy the sacred capital. The Inca must prepare; I will protect him and his empire." The apparition then disappeared. But the father listened impatiently and with disregard to the supplications of his son, who thenceforward took the name of Viracocha. The Inca made no preparation for the predicted catastrophe. But within three months he was startled by intelligence of the approach, in great force, of the insurgent Chinchasuyas. Appalled by his disregard of the celestial warning, and believing his destruction was inevitable, he abandoned his capital, and went to the fortified town of Muyna—the ruins of which are still marked—where he awaited his fate.

The people, deserted by their prince, were overcome with terror, and were flying in every direction, when the young Inca, Viracocha, appeared among them, with the shepherds of Chita. His courageous bearing, inspiriting words, and lofty spirit rallied and reanimated the fugitives; and he hastened to his father to urge him to return to Cuzco, put himself at the head of his people, and strike a manly blow for his empire. But his entreaties were of no avail; the pusillanimous Inca refused to stir beyond the walls of Muyna.

Viracocha then resolved himself to redeem the honor of his race and preserve the empire. He returned to Cuzco, put himself at the head of such forces as he could collect, and went out and fought the Chinchasuyas with greatly inferior numbers. The white and bearded spirit that had appeared to him at Chita was true to his promise, and the very stones rose up armed, white and bearded men, when the weight of battle pressed hardly on the youthful Inca. He gained a signal victory on the plain which still bears the name, then given it, of Yahuar-pampa, "the Field of Blood."

At the demand of a grateful people, Viracocha afterwards set aside his father, and assumed the imperial *llautu*. In recognition of the power and interference of the divine Viracocha, the young Inca ordered the construction of a sumptuous temple to his worship in Cacha. Why there, in preference to Chita, where the spirit first appeared, or on the plain of Yahuar-pampa, where it fought for the youthful Inca, the chroniclers confess themselves unable to explain. But for some reason he directed that the temple should be built in Cacha, and that in form and structure it should imitate as far as possible the place among the rocks of Chita where, in his noonday dream, the spirit appeared to him.  The temple, accordingly, was to be without roof, with an elevated second story, and in plan and workmanship different from any then in existence. It was to contain a small chapel or shrine, within which was to be placed an image of the celestial Viracocha.

This temple according to Garcilasso, was 120 feet long within the walls, and 80 broad, and was of polished stones.  It had four entrances, opening to the four cardinal points, or rather what appeared to be entrances, for three of them were blind doors, intended only for ornament; and the fourth alone, that opening to the east, gave admittance to the interior.  And as the Indians did not know how to construct arches to support the second story, they built transverse walls which answered as beams, three feet thick and seven feet apart.  Beween these walls were twelve passages ceiled with flat cut stones.  Entering the door-way of the temple, the visitor turned to the right, through the passage opening in that direction, and went on until he reached the wall, when he turned to the left through the second passage, and so on until he reached the twelfth passage or aisle, where there was a stairway leading to the second story and descending on the opposite side.  In front of each aisle were windows resembling port-holes (*falteras*), which admitted sufficient light; and below each window was a niche in the wall for a porter, who could sit there without obstructing the passage.

The floor of the second story was paved with lustrous black stones, brought from afar.  In place of a great altar was a sort of chapel, twelve feet square within the walls, roofed with the same kind of black stones, fitted together, and raised in the form of the capital of a column, with four angles.  This was the finest piece of work in the whole structure.  In this chapel, and sunk in the wall of the temple, was a kind of tabernacle, where was an image of the celestial Viracocha, in honor of whom the temple was built.  On the right and left sides of the chapel were also tabernacles or niches, but they contained nothing, serving only as ornaments. The walls of the structure rose three yards above the second floor, and had no windows. The cornice was of stone on all sides.

In the tabernacle just mentioned, on a great base or pedestal, was a statue of Viracocha, as he appeared to the young Inca in Chita. It represented a man of good stature, with a long beard, and flowing robe like a tunic or cassock, reaching to the feet, where there was the figure of an unknown animal, with the claws of a tiger, and a chain around its neck, one end of which was held in the hands of the statue. All of this was cut in stone; and as the sculptors did not know how to represent the apparition, the Inca was accustomed to dress himself as it appeared to him, so as to give them a model from which to work. "And because," adds Garcilasso, in a tone of reproach, "this temple was such an extraordinary work, the Spaniards should have preserved it for the admiration of future ages; but instead, as if in envy of the works of those who had preceded them, they so destroyed it that now scarcely the foundations are left — a thing much to be regretted. The principal cause of the destruction, however, was the notion that much treasure was concealed beneath it. The first thing thrown down was the statue, because it was said much gold was hidden under it. The statue existed a few years ago, although much disfigured by the stones that had been hurled against it."

Nearly three hundred years have elapsed since Garcilasso wrote, and if the temple was so much ruined in his day as he describes it, what might we expect its present condition to be? The churches of San Pedro and San Pablo Cacha, of Tinta, and other neighboring villages, and more than one of the bridges across the Vilcanota, are built of stones taken from its walls; yet its plan can still be traced, and it is not altogether too late to rescue the pious work of the Inca Viracocha from exaggeration or forgetfulness. The plan does not wholly agree with that described by the chronicler,* who wrote, probably, at sec-

---

* Thus, he describes the temple as being without a roof, while the ruins show that it had a pitched roof. He gives its dimensions as 120 feet by 80, while they really are 330 feet by 87.

ond-hand, from the imperfect descriptions of incompetent observers; but we can easily see that he is describing this very
structure.

The most conspicuous part of the remains of the temple is a
wall 40 feet high, of adobes, or compacted clay, on a foundation of stones, irregularly wrought, but perfectly fitted together. This foundation is 8 feet high, and 5½ feet thick on the
level of the ground, but is "battered in," or decreases slightly
in thickness as it rises, as does also the wall above it. It

RUINS OF TEMPLE OF VIRACOCHA.

may be described as a succession of piers, twelve in number,
each 19½ feet wide, separated by spaces of 8½ feet. These
spaces were carried up (the sides inclining inwards) into the
adobe work above to the height of 14 feet, forming doors of
that altitude, the lintels of which were of wood, now decayed
or removed, but leaving traces in the wall. This wall extended
longitudinally through the centre of the structure, and shows it
to have been about three hundred and thirty feet long. One of
the end-walls is still standing, with a large door, flanked with
niches, opening inwards on each side of the central wall. The

PLAN OF TEMPLE OF VIRACOCHA
AND DEPENDENT STRUCTURES.

Scale of Feet

shape of this end-wall shows that the structure had a pitched roof, and that its total exterior width was 87 feet. The side-walls and one of the gable-walls had disappeared; but, by digging, their foundations may be easily traced.

In the centre of each pier was an opening 3 feet high by 18 inches wide, extending entirely through the wall, the stones being well faced inside as well as outside; and about midway the height of each door-way, or seven feet from the ground, are sockets six inches square, sunk in the stone, as if for the reception of beams or bars. Immediately opposite the openings I have spoken of as penetrating the stone foundation that supports the central wall, and midway between that and the outer walls on each side, are two series of columns, 5½ feet in diameter at the base, twelve on each side, or twenty-four in all. Of these, only one is perfect. Like the central wall, its base, to the height of eight feet or more, is formed of wrought stones, carved on the face, and accurately fitted, above which the pillar is continued of adobes to the height of about twenty-two feet. By digging, the foundations of all these columns may be discovered. On a level with the tops of these columns, and coinciding with their vertical centre, are holes in the central wall, apparently for the reception of the ends of beams, the other ends of which rested on the columns, which may, indeed, have supported other beams extending to the outer walls. This is most likely; for there is no timber within fifty or a hundred leagues long enough to extend from one wall to the other, a distance of thirty-four feet.

I assume that there were no transverse walls, such as Garcilasso describes, but that the second floor of the structure was supported by these columns. We cannot now tell what was the arrangement of the upper story or stories. We only know that the central wall is pierced with a double row of windows or openings, placed immediately over the door-ways of the ground-plan, which diminish in size with their elevation.

Garcilasso describes the outer walls as of cut stones, and the vast numbers that we know have been taken from here seem to justify the statement. The foundations certainly were; but the remaining gable is of adobes, entered by a single door. Whether there were other entrances cannot now be determined : the above-mentioned historian Garcilasso states that there was but one. Of the remaining parts of the structure as described by him — the chapel or sanctuary — there are now no traces whatever.

But neither Garcilasso nor any subsequent writer has noticed the extensive series of remains, scarcely less interesting than those of the temple itself, and connected with it. It is impossible to present a complete plan of them, for it would cover too much space; nor could I hope to convey any very clear idea of them through a description, however minute. I shall confine myself, therefore, to one or two of the more remarkable dependent structures, beginning with a series of edifices surrounding courts, which lie at right angles to the temple, at its southern end. They are built upon a terrace, raised three feet above the general level, and between two parallel walls eight feet high and one hundred and ninety feet apart. There are six series of courts and buildings entire, and one, next to the temple—in fact, immediately in front of its remaining gable—partially destroyed. Each series covers an area about one hun-

28

dred and twenty feet square, and collectively they extend upwards of eight hundred feet in a right line.

In arrangement, every group or series is substantially the
same, and consists of six buildings, two on each of the three
sides of a court, the fourth side, looking towards the artificial
lake, etc., being left open.   The buildings standing transversely to the general line of the range of edifices may be described
as double, that is to say, as divided longitudinally by a party-
wall, every division facing on a separate court.   This middle or

STONE HOUSES NEAR TEMPLE OF VIRACOCHA.

party-wall, like that of the temple, exactly divided the gable,
and rose to the peak of the structure, supporting the upper
ends of the rafters.   The buildings thus divided into two equal
apartments are 46 by 38 feet exterior measurement.   The gables are lofty, and there is ample evidence that each building
consisted of two stories.   The walls are three feet thick, and,
to the height of eight or ten feet, are composed of unhewn
fragments of lava, cemented together with a stiff clay.   Above,
they are continued with adobes, except in one instance, where

the upper part of the central wall of the building was also of lava. The fronts had two entrances, and the interior of every apartment was ornamented with niches—within some of which the fine stucco is still perfect—brilliant with the purple color with which they had been painted. Between the buildings is an alley or passage-way seven feet wide. The two buildings on the third side of the court are not double, like those just described, but consist of a single inner apartment. Their exterior dimensions are 46 by 30 feet, and they also have two doors opening on the court, and are ornamented with niches. Between the line of buildings and the outer wall the space has been divided into enclosures with small buildings, each series corresponding with the principal groups, apparently designed for cooks and attendants.

Exterior to this outer wall are one hundred and twenty circular structures, each twenty-seven feet in diameter, ranged in ten rows of twelve, the streets or passages between them being twelve feet wide. Every building has a door-way opening on the street, but the buildings are so disposed that the doorways do not face each other. These round buildings are comparatively rude, and built throughout of rough blocks of lava. Interiorly, they show very little attempt at ornamentation. To obtain the area on which they are built, the lava has been removed and heaped up outside of them. It would seem as if they were intended for the reception of pilgrims to the shrine of the celestial Viracocha; and if so, they imply that it was held in great esteem, and was much frequented.

The ground in front of the long line of buildings which I have described is a beautiful level, and is terminated by another group of buildings less regular in plan, but very interesting. They are now in part inhabited, and probably present the same general appearance as before the Conquest. Indeed, a considerable part of the lava-encircled, well-watered, and beautiful little plain in which the Temple of Viracocha and its dependent structures are built is now occupied by a village of potters, famed all over the Sierra for their wares. They find a very fine and exceedingly tenacious clay, or kaolein, among the lava,

which, as I have said, was anciently removed from the area
with incredible labor, and heaped up around it.   From the site
of the temple the eye finds no opening in the lava walls, while
on the side towards the crater the lava is piled up in stupendous
masses, as if an ocean of ink had been suddenly congealed during a furious storm.

I cannot refrain from correcting one or two radical errors
which have obtained as regards Inca architecture, and which
have received the support of the great names of Humboldt and
Prescott.   The former, in his account of the fortress of Cannar,
in the northern part of the Inca empire, describes a building
within its walls which, though smaller, was nearly a counterpart
of the double houses found near the Temple of Viracocha.   He
seems to have been surprised to find that the edifice had gables
like those of our own dwellings, and expresses his belief that
they were added after the Conquest.   The fact of the existence
of windows in these gables he regarded as specially favoring
that hypothesis: "for it is certain," he adds, "that in the edifices of Peruvian construction, as in the remains of the houses
of Pompeii and Herculaneum, no windows are to be found."
M. de la Condamine, before him, had expressed some doubts of
the antiquity of the gables, but thought it possible that they
formed part of the ancient structure.   Prescott, probably following Humboldt, denies the existence of windows in Peruvian
architecture.

Humboldt, however, saw but few Inca remains in Northern
Peru.   Had he journeyed in the central or southern part of
the country, he would have found the use of gables and of windows almost universal.   Gables are even to be found among the
ruins of Grand Chimu on the coast, where rain seldom falls.
Everywhere in the interior the ruins of Inca towns are specially
marked by their pointed gables, which have almost always one
window, and frequently two.   These windows were sometimes
used as door-ways for entrance to the upper or half story of the
edifice, and were reached by a succession of flat stones projecting from the walls so as to form a flight of steps.

The gables were not always of equal pitch or shape.   As a

rule, they were nearly as pointed as those of Holland. In
buildings standing on the slopes of hills, which were favorite
situations for villages, inasmuch as the level grounds were thus
saved for cultivation, the slope of the gable nearest the declivity was shortest. We shall find some fine examples of all kinds
of Inca houses—of one, one and a half, and two or more stories,
with windows in the gables and windows in the sides—when we
come to the great and complicated ruins of Ollantaytambo.

I may add that when the Inca ordered the construction of the
Temple of Viracocha on a plan different from that of any other
temple in Peru, he found proper workmen to execute his commands, for it is strictly unique in design. I found no columns
in any other edifice, nor does it appear that any other had so
great a height. The feature of adobes on a base of worked
stone is not, however, peculiar to this building, as I found it in
others, where they were used not only to build up the gables,
but also to form part of the general walls. A notable example
is afforded in the ancient temple, now the church of Guitera,
two days' journey from the coast, in the valley of the river of
Pisco. These brick complements of edifices of stone would naturally be the first to disappear under the action of the weather;
and in many instances they have probably so disappeared, leaving only the stone-work remaining. A wrong inference would
be drawn as to what the chroniclers call the "stateliness" of
some of the Peruvian buildings, from these relatively low stone-
walls.

As ornamental niches constitute a peculiar and constant feature in Inca architecture, a few general remarks may be here
made. Their design, when they appear on the exterior of buildings, is plainly ornamental; and in certain cases, when they appear in interiors, we discover the same purpose. I speak now
of the larger ones, reaching to the floors, or near the floors, of
apartments. There are others which have no smaller reëntering niche, but are mere closets, as it were, without doors, wider
at the bottom than at the top, and of varying depth, which are
found extending round almost every apartment, great or small,
whether built of rough stones or of blocks elaborately cut and

fitted. It is possible that these may have been for use as well as ornament, although always having the latter purpose clearly apparent. The dimensions of these niches vary with the different dimensions of the structures in which they are found; and a line of them running close along the ground is often relieved by smaller and alternating ones. The monotony of long, dull lines of terraces, especially when in connection with public edifices, is nearly always broken up by the introduction of these niches. These terraces are usually formed of irregular stones, fitted together in the style called Cyclopean, in which case the stones around the niches take a more regular shape, and have a finish not to be found in other parts of the wall. In the structures built of rough stones laid in clay, they are always well faced with stucco, and there is reason to believe that they were painted in colors differing from those of the walls they were intended to adorn.

Before we leave this temple, we may remark that the etymology of the name "Viracocha" is variously given. That generally accepted is *vira*, "froth," and *cocha*, "sea"—that is, "Froth of the Sea." And as the spirit that appeared to the young Inca on the high plain of Chita, and gave his name as Viracocha, was white and bearded, and dressed in flowing robes, it is not to be wondered at that the same designation should be applied to the Spaniards, who came from the sea, and who seemed to the simple Indians to be incarnations of the supernatural visitor, holding in their control the lightning and the thunder. Among *Los Indios del campo*, or Indians of the fields, the llama herdsmen of the *punas*, and the fishermen of the lakes, the common salutation to strangers with fair skin and blue eyes is "*Tat-tai Viracocha!*"

It was on the heights of Tungasaca, overlooking the ruins of the Temple of Viracocha, on the opposite bank of the river, that José Gabriel Condorcanqui, better known by the name he ultimately assumed of Tupac Amaru, organized, towards the close of the last century, that uprising of the Indians against the Spaniards which soon spread throughout the Sierra, and threatened the extinction of the Spanish power in Peru. Tu-

pac Amaru was the lineal descendant of the last of the Incas;
and when he gathered his followers in the town of Tinta, on
his way to wrest the capital of his fathers from the hands of
the descendants of Pizarro, he led them first to the ruins of the
Temple of Viracocha, and there, surrounded by black and rugged lava walls, and under the shadow of the crumbling sanctuary, with strange and solemn ceremonies and ancient invoca-
tions, he adjured the aid of the Spirit that had fought by the
side of the young Viracocha on the plain of Yahuar-pampa.
For a time he was successful; the dead gods seemed to live
once more, and the banner of the Incas, glowing anew with its
iris blazon, appeared destined to float again above the massive
walls of the great fortress of Cuzco.  But treachery, more than
force, ruined the cause of the Indian chieftain: he was taken
prisoner, and, after being obliged to witness the execution of
his wife and son, was himself, May 21st, 1781, torn into pieces
by horses in the great square of Cuzco, and under the walls of
its august cathedral, dedicated to the service of a just and mer-
ciful God.

After leaving Cacha we find nothing of special interest until
we reach a point where the mountains close in on both sides of
the Vilcanota, and leave it only a rock-bound cañon wherein to
flow.  At various points we observe extensive remains of ancient towns.  The sites of these were almost invariably some
rocky eminence in the valley, or rugged promontory projecting
from the mountains lining it, among masses of rock and piles
of stones, laboriously heaped up to give room for the houses,
which, in these places, were arranged with little regard to order,
but with the obvious purpose of economizing the arable lands.

As we approach the town of Quijijana, we find a broken
piece of ground in the middle of the valley ; a kind of bluff
overlooking the river, rough and sterile, which was the site of
a large town, with a temple and public square, the whole curiously laid out.  The cliffs facing it and bordering the valley
are thronged with the tombs of the ancient inhabitants.  They
consist of little chambers, faced with stones, built up under
every projecting rock, or against the cliffs, wherever room is

afforded for a wall. Many are in places apparently inaccessible, and it is difficult to understand how they were reached, much more how they were constructed. All appear to have been stuccoed and painted. They produce a striking effect in the sunlight, standing out against the dark, rough background of the cliff.

We leave the narrow valley of the Vilcanota, which has now swollen to a large and powerful stream, with its fallen bridge of masonry, and an existing one of *mimbres*, or twisted branches of shrubs, and, turning sharp to the left, rise by a steep ascent to the town of Urcos, a rambling village, with more chicha shops than respectable habitations. Our destination for the night is Andahuaylillas, which is the musical name of a pueblo twelve miles distant, and we lose no time in Urcos, but climb the intermediate heights to descend into the bolson of Andahuaylillas. This bolson is one of the group of which that of Cuzco is the centre, and is among the most beautiful in Peru.

At the very summit of the ridge, between the valley and the bolson, in a bed like the crater of a volcano, is the small but deep lake of Urcos, which has no outlet. It is most famous because of the tradition that its yellow waters hide the great golden chain of Huayna Capac, which was of the thickness of a man's arm, and extended twice around the great square of Cuzco. It was thrown into the lake to save it from the Spaniards. This tradition was fresh and current in Garcilasso's days, for he gives us the names of the men who undertook to carry a drift through the ridge to drain the lake, and who only desisted, after spending all their money, on striking the *peña viva*, or living rock. The drift is still visible, and, in its extent, shows a very persistent purpose on the part of those who drove it. I shall cheerfully give any information I may possess about the lake, and how to get at it, to the enterprising gentlemen who once organized a company, with five millions of capital, to recover the treasure from the wreck of His Majesty's frigate *Hussar* sunk at Hell Gate, unless, indeed, the searchers for Kidd's ill-gotten gold, at the foot of the Highlands, should make the first application. I leave to those accustomed to deal with large figures to say what should be the capital of the

"Huayna Capac Chain Recovery Company," merely observing that the Square of Huacapata was more than half a mile in circuit, and the chain, "big as a man's arm," went twice around it; and, moreover, the gold of the Incas was pure.

The bolson of Andahuaylillas is an irregular oval, eighteen miles long by from three to six broad; nearly level, and well watered by rills from the surrounding mountains, which are collected in a single stream, that has cut a narrow channel through the intervening ridge, and falls into the Vilcanota. No traveller can resist the conviction that these mountain-girt basins were once lakes, which have been gradually drained by the slow excavation of their outlets; or suddenly, through some convulsion of nature, by the rupture of the barriers confining them. There are some very distinct "lake-terraces" in this bolson, which merit the attention of geologists and other inquirers. I can hardly resist the impression that here is a fragment of Lombardy; and that the Alps, by a masterly flank movement, have circled it in, cut off its retreat, and compelled it to seclusion and quiet.

We pitch down the narrow path that leads into the valley, undismayed by a bellowing bull that tears past us, with a musketed soldier at his heels, who shouts "*Cuidado!*" and, instead of entering the picturesque village before us, bear off to the right to our haven of rest, which bears the cadenced name of Andahuaylillas.

We pass a number of rich and extensive haciendas, heavily walled in, with arched corridors and iron-trellised balconies, speaking of wealth and the arts of home, and take refuge in a deserted house which the wife of the *corregidor* borrows for us for the night. Her husband has gone on a bull-bating "function," or what is known among us as "a spree," to some remote mountain village, where he has a *compadre*, perhaps a *comadre*. We have the house, and the house has a floor, whereon, in the absence of any furniture except a thick carpet of dust, we have the privilege of making ourselves as comfortable as we can. In the morning we waste no time in unnecessary adieus, but hasten on our way.

This bolson is separated from that of Oropesa, which is only an extension of that of Cuzco, by a narrow ridge or pass, which formed the southern limit of the dominions of the first Inca, and where stand the massive remains of the works by which it was defended from aggression from the southward. Before reaching these remains, we come to great projected masses of trachytic and basaltic rock, through which the road or path winds tortuously. Here was one of the principal quarries of the Incas, and hence was taken by far the greater part of the stones used in the construction of the edifices of Cuzco. All around are immense heaps of stone chippings, covering more than half a mile square; and among these are scattered, in all directions, blocks of stone of every size and in every stage of progress, from the rough fragment just broken from the parent mass to the elaborately finished block ready to be put in its assigned place in a building. Here are the rough stone huts of the quarrymen, and also the more pretentious dwelling of the master-workman, or overseer, who built a little wall around his house, and a terrace in front, and otherwise evinced taste and love of comfort.

The whole aspect of things is familiar, and we might readily imagine ourselves in an abandoned quarry at home. Although many of the worked stones have been taken away since the Conquest, yet enough remain to show that the quarries were in full operation at the time of their final interruption, and that the Incas were still actively engaged in enlarging and beautifying their capital. I do not attach much importance to the statements of Cieza de Leon and others, that many of the royal palaces and temples of the empire, as far distant as Quito, were wholly or in part built with stones transported from Cuzco, thereby obtaining some degree of sanctity or reverence, as did the soil of the Campo Santo of Pisa, from the fact that some of it was brought from the Holy Land. The trachytes of which the edifices of Cuzco are mainly built are by no means uncommon throughout Peru; and the coincidence in materials in any given structure with those of another by no means implies that these materials were obtained from a common source.

Although there is no direct evidence remaining in the quarry as to the manner in which the stones were dressed after being extracted from their beds, yet it seems pretty clear that most of them were picked or hammered into shape with a pointed instrument or a hammer before passing under the chisel. Of the manner in which the stones were separated from the natural rock there are here, as in other places, abundant illustrations. Excavations were made, where possible, under the masses of rock, so as to leave some portions of them impending. A groove was then cut in the upper surface on the line of desired fracture, in which oblong holes were worked to a considerable depth, precisely in the manner now practiced. The presumption is strong that wedges of dry wood were driven into these holes, and water turned into the groove. The swelling of the wood would evenly split off the block. This device is probably almost as ancient as the art of stone-cutting itself. I found some disks of hard stone in this quarry, with holes through their centre, as if for the reception of handles, which may have been used in rough-dressing or hammering the stones into shape.

The distance of this quarry from Cuzco is about twenty-two miles. How the stones were transported thither is not easy to say; but as the Incas had no beasts of draught, it must have been done through the direct application of human force. With a redundant and disciplined population, under absolute control, we can understand how the Incas could combine the power of numbers in a most efficient manner.

A mile or so beyond the quarries, the valley still contracting and our path ascending, we come to the Pass of Piquillacta, hemmed in by cliffs, within a width of two thousand feet. Here, rising before us, we find a massive wall of stones, between twenty and thirty feet in height, pierced by two gateways—a wall more massive than that which surrounded Latium. The gate-ways are faced with stones cut with skill, and laid without cement. This is the Fortress of Piquillacta, which was the southern limit of the dominions of the first Inca, whose steps we have followed from the island of Titicaca. The fortress reaches from the mountain, on one side, to a high, rocky eminence on the other. It is popularly called El Acueducto, perhaps from some fancied resemblance to an aqueduct for the purpose of carrying water across the valley; but, as there is no water here to be carried anywhere, the name is evidently misapplied.

The work consists of a single line of massive wall, 750 feet

GATE-WAY OF FORTRESS OF PIQUILLACTA.

long, 34 feet high at its highest part, and 36 feet thick at the base. It is cut through by two passages or roadways, between piers of heavy stones, finely wrought and fitted.

It will be seen by the plan here given of the section embracing the passage-ways, and also a cross-section and elevation, that the wall diminishes by graduations or steps on both sides, which, did it occupy a different position, might appear to conflict with the hypothesis of its being a work of defence or fortification. It would seem to be rather a formidable work for a barrier or toll-gate : but we do not know that the Incas had such establishments. This was the frontier or boundary of the principality of the first Inca, and we may assume that it dates from his reign. With the exception of the ends of the walls facing on the passage-ways, which are of large, cut stones, the remainder of the work is built of rough stones, laid in clay. The top of the wall is throughout of the same level; it consequently becomes less in height as it approaches the hills on either hand, and diminishes proportionally in thickness. Inside the wall are the remains of the guard-houses or barracks wherein dwelt the

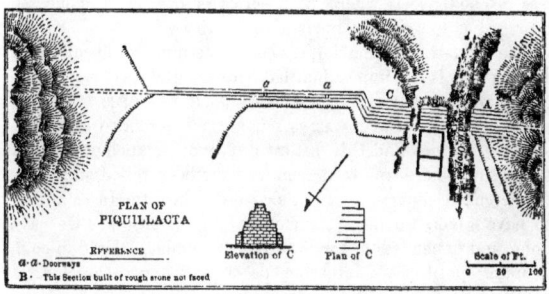

defenders of his narrow domain against the Canchus, who were brought under Inca rule by his successor.

Passing the gate-ways, we strike a well-graded road, which, instead of descending the steep declivity to the lake of Muyna, where the existing road passes, deflects to the right, and skirts the flanks of the hills, to a level promontory, on which we find a collection of ancient buildings, round, square, and oblong, built of rough stones, and with only what may be called the door and window casings of cut stones. A mile farther on, and on a lower shelf, a broad and level area overlooking the lake of Muyna and the valley of Oropesa, we come to the remains of the great Inca town of Muyna, in which the pusillanimous father of Viracocha took refuge when his capital was threatened by the insurgent Chinchas, and where the young Inca confined him in stately bondage, when, after repulsing the Chinchas, he placed on his own brow the imperial *llautu*.[*]

The town of Muyna was large. Its remains cover thickly an area nearly a mile square. The buildings, except one or two near the centre of the town, were of rough stones, laid, as I have already described, in clay. They were arranged regularly, fronting on broad, paved streets, crossing each other at right angles. The whole was surrounded by a high stone-wall, in places still twenty-five to thirty feet high, with a parapet running along the top, and a space behind for its defenders. This was reached, as elsewhere, by a series of projecting stones, so arranged as to serve the purpose of a stairway.

The ruins of Muyna impressed me as among the oldest in Peru, and it is not impossible that here was the early seat of the power which afterwards transferred itself to Cuzco. The position, naturally strong, was, as I have said, defended by a high wall. I did not find this feature in any other ancient town of the Sierra, where true forts seem to have been relied on mainly for defensive purposes. In other words, the later Incas appear to have given up the system of walling in cities, as we have done, and depended on fortifications or citadels, placed in commanding positions, dominating passes and approaches incapable of being flanked, and which required to be forced before an enemy could reach the cities and towns in which the population was concentrated.

Descending from the heights of Muyna, we reach the shallow lake of Muyna or Oropesa, with its surrounding marshes, through which the road follows an ancient causeway of stone,

---

[*] The *llautu*, one of the distinguishing insignia of the Incas, consisted of a band, with a fringe an inch and a half or two inches long, which passed two or three times around the forehead, the fringe depending nearly to the eyebrows. The royal *ayllos*, or families, were privileged to wear the *llautu*, but of black color. The immediate descendants of the Inca were permitted to wear it of yellow color; only that of the Inca was red. He also wore a sort of ball of the same color on his forehead, surmounted by two of the long wing-feathers of the coricanque, or Andean eagle.

probably a part of one of the roads which we are told the Incas built, extending throughout the empire from Quito to Atacama.

I have already described the bolson of Cuzco as the centre of a group of high mountain-encircled valleys, in which the waters are collected from the surrounding elevations, forming considerable streams, which break through the barriers that surround them, and discharge themselves, with many a leap, through dark, narrow, rocky gorges, into the rivers which furrow the Andean plateau.

The white Moorish-looking buildings of numerous haciendas in Oropesa glisten in the sun, at intervals, along the base of the hills on every hand. We press by them all, scarcely heeding their beauties, or those of the lake, for we know the Inca capital is close before us, and we must reach it ere nightfall. The valley contracts; again the passage is disputed by stream and roadway. We are in the Pass of Angostura (the Narrows). A few hundred yards more, the heights all around us crowned with the tall gables of ruined Inca structures, we reach a point where the valley of Cuzco opens on our sight—an oblong valley shut in by treeless mountains, the air shimmering with the seemingly palpable golden bars of the declining sun, underneath which, past the clustering villages of San Sebastian and San Gerónimo, at the head and most elevated part of the valley, reclining in calm repose of shadow against the umber-colored hills, the slant light gleaming on the tops of its threescore towers, whence the low vibration of bells, in whose solid masses are melted the gold and silver idols of an ancient faith, reach our expectant ears. Here we pause, and, in sympathetic action with our muleteers, who remove their hats and bow their heads low to the earth, we too salute reverently the City of the Sun!

We pass through the village of San Sebastian, where the haughtiness of the people might tell us, if we knew it not before, that they are the descendants of the *ayllos* (lineages or families of Inca blood), who, after the Conquest, were assigned this spot as a refuge; and, striking a paved road, we hurry on towards the city of our destination. We enter it at the Plaza of

Rimac-pampa (the Plain of the Oracle); and, between buildings raised on massive ancient foundations, adobes on stone—modern on ancient art—the gutter or open sewer occupying the middle of the street, and by no means redolent of the odors of Araby the Blest, we slowly reach the Inti-pampa, or Square of the Sun, where the serpent-covered walls on every side betray their Inca origin.

Here we inquire for the principal plaza, and are directed through a narrow street, darkened by heavy walls of stones cut with marvellous precision, impressive in their originality, pierced here and there with door-ways, narrowing at the top, which bring back recollections of Egypt; and by-and-by we emerge upon a great square with a central fountain, the Huaca-pata, or Sacred Terrace of the Incas, now flanked by a heavy cathedral on one side, the elaborate church of the Jesuits on another, and surrounded by a low colonnade. It is night, and when we inquire for the residence of the comandante of the forces—there are no hotels in Cuzco—a showily dressed officer undertakes to conduct us thither, points to a heavy archway, beneath which our weary animals, conscious of a refuge at last, dash with unwonted and startling vigor, and we find ourselves the welcome guests of Colonel Francisco Vargas, whose name I shall ever mention with respect and gratitude—a respect and gratitude which all my readers would share had they undergone the privations, the hunger and thirst, the cold, exposure, and annoyances that were really involved in the long and weary journey, of which I have written so lightly, from the distant coast to this lofty eyrie of aboriginal power.

We are finally in Cuzco,* where Manco Capac's magic wand

---

* "Cuzco," wrote Colonel (afterwards Marshal) O'Leary to General Miller, during the war of Peruvian Independence, "interests me greatly. Its history, its fables, its ruins, are enchanting. It may with truth be called the Rome of the New World. The immense fortress, on the north, is the Capitol. The Temple of the Sun is its Coliseum. Manco Capac was its Romulus; Viracocha its Augustus; Huascar its Pompey, and Atahualpa its Cæsar. The Pizarros, Almagros, Valdivias, and Toledos are the Huns, Goths, and Christians who destroyed it. Tupac Amaru is its Belisarius, who gave it a day of hope; Pumacagua its Rienzi, and last patriot"

sunk into the earth, and where he commenced the fulfilment of the high and beneficent mission intrusted to him by his father, the Sun. Here he built his palace, here his successors founded theirs; and here in due time arose that splendid fane, the Temple of the Sun, with the palaces of its ministers and the convents of its vestals. Above it frowns the great fortress of Sacsahuaman, the work of three reigns, the most massive and enduring monument of aboriginal art on the American continent.

29

# CHAPTER XXII.

## CUZCO, THE CITY OF THE SUN.

BEFORE entering upon a description of Cuzco and its objects of interest, I shall notice its position, its climate, and the favorable conditions which contributed to make it the seat of empire. Its very name, which signifies the umbilicus, or navel, was not given to it after the Inca dominion had been widely extended by warlike princes, but at the very period of its foundation, to denote that its position was central and dominating. The bolson, in which it is situated, is the central one of a group or cluster of such valleys, separated from each other by comparatively low passes between the mountains or hills, and is the one most easily defensible. To the north is the valley of Anta or

VIEW OF YEZO AND THE WHARF OF ASINGATA FROM THE BROW OF THE SAUSAHUANAN.

Xaxiguana, where the Pizarros and Almagros decided the rule of Peru, and to the south is that of Andahuaylillas. The rule of the first Inca does not appear to have extended at first beyond this valley of Cuzco.

The city stands at the northern or most elevated end of the valley, on the lower slopes of three high hills, where as many rivulets coming together, like the fingers of an outspread hand, unite to form the Cachimayo, the stream that disputes passage with the narrow roadway, in the Pass of Angostura. These three streams are named, respectively, the Rodadero or Tullamayo, the Huatenay, and Almodena; and within and around the triangles formed by their confluence the city of Cuzco is built. The old city, or that part of it dedicated to the royal family, was the tongue of land falling off from the hill of Sacsahuaman, and lying between the Huatenay and the Rodadero. Here are situated most of the remains of Inca architecture, and to this will our attention be mainly directed.

Cuzco is in latitude 13° 31′ south, and longitude 72° 2′ west of Greenwich, at an elevation of 11,380 feet above the sea. Surrounded by high and snowy mountains, it might be supposed to possess a cold, not to say frigid, climate; but its temperature, though cool, is seldom freezing; and although in what is called the winter season—from May to November—the pastures and fields are sere, and the leaves fall from most of the trees, it is rather from drouth (for the winter is the dry season) than from frost. On the whole, the climate is equable and salubrious. Wheat, barley, maize, and potatoes ripen in the valley, and the strawberry and peach are not unknown. Equalize the extremes of a Pennsylvania summer and winter, or accept the climate of the South of France, and we shall have very nearly that of Cuzco. When we add to these favorable conditions that not more than twenty miles distant are deep and hot valleys, where semi-tropical fruits may be produced abundantly, we may comprehend that Cuzco was not an unfavorable site for a national capital.

From the first the seat of government and the shrine of religion, it ultimately became the centre of a polity more profound than seems to have existed among the other American nations—a polity which subordinated the military arm to the grand object of moulding the scattered tribes and petty nationalities of the Sierra into a homogeneous civil body, and of harmonizing religion, so that the several blocks of the national edifice should form integral parts of a constant and durable whole.

In its very construction and the arrangement of its divisions and wards, it was made to reflect this polity. It was made a microcosm of the empire. In common with the country at large, it was divided into four quarters by four roads leading to the corresponding portions of the empire, which bore the general designation of Tihuantisuya, signifying the "four quarters of the world." These roads do not run exactly in the direction of the cardinal points, as is generally affirmed, but rather intermediately; that is to say, north-east and south-east, and north-west and south-west, their direction being fixed by the conformation of the country. The division to the north-west was named Chinchasuya, and in that direction lay the second city of the empire, Quito. That to the south-west, Cuntisuya, embraced the region of the coast. That to the south-east, in the direction and including the region around Lake Titicaca, Collasuya; and that to the north-east, Antisuya.

The road running north-east and south-west bounded the great square of Cuzco on its south-east side, and divided the city into two very nearly equal parts, the more elevated part in the direction of the hill and fortress of Sacsahuaman being called Hanan, or Upper Cuzco; and the lower part subsiding into the level of the valley, Hurin, or Lower Cuzco. Taking the Huacapata, or central square of the old city, and which is now the Plaza Principal, as a centre, there were grouped around it, in the form of a large oval, no fewer than twelve subdivisions, or wards. These were occupied by inhabitants from the principal provinces of the empire, and the position of each ward was made to conform as nearly as possible to the relative position of the province of which it was the representative. The names of these wards, however, so far as they can be made out, were given entirely with reference to their actual locality

CUZCO;
ANCIENT & MODERN.
From A Survey
BY
E.G.SQUIER.

English Feet
0        500        1500

CHURCHES.—1. San Cristobal; 2. Santa Ana; 3. Los Nazarenos; 4. San Antonio; 5. San Blas; 6.
Beaterio de Arcopata; 7. Jesus Maria; 8. La Catedral; 9. Capilla del Santiago; 10. San Fran-
cisco; 11. La Merced; 12. La Compania; 13. San Agustin; 14. Hospital de Hombras; 15. Santa
Clara; 16. Santa Catalina; 17. Beaterio de San Andrés; 18. Beaterio de Santa Rosa; 19. Santo Domingo; 20. Beaterio de Ahuacpinta; 21. Santiago; 22. Belen; 23. Iglesia del Panteon; 24. University; 25. Prefectura; 26. House of Municipality; 27. Prison.  INCA RUINS.—A. Temple of the
Sun; B. Palace of Virgins of the Sun; C. Palace of Inca Tupac Yupanqui; D. Palace of Inca
Yupanqui; E. Palace of Inca Rocca; F. Palace of Inca Viracocha; G. Palace of Yachahuasi, or
the Schools; H. Palace of Inca Pachacutic; I. Palace of Huayna Capac; J. Palace of Manco Capac; K. House of Garcilasso de la Vega; L. Intahuatana, or Gnomon of the Sun; M. Ruins of
Inca building; N. Chingana chambered rock; O. Carved and chambered rocks; P. Inca graded
road, leading to quarries; Q. Pila, or Bath, of the Incas.  Black lines showing ancient Inca walls.

—such as Cantutpata, the Terrace of Flowers; Pumacanchu, the Place of the Puma—and not with reference to their inhabitants.

As I have said, the most important part of the sacred city was the spur of the hill of the Sacsahuaman, extending down between the rivulets Huatenay and Rodadero — a tongue of land, calculating from the terraces of the Colcompata, where the first Inca built his palace — to the confluence of the two streams, called metaphorically Pumapchupam, or the Tail of the Puma, a mile in length by a quarter of a mile broad in its widest part, and comprising very nearly one hundred and thirty acres. Within this area, on ground sloping to the valley in front, and to the rivulets on either hand, the royal families or lineages had their residences. Here were the palaces of the Incas, the buildings dedicated to instruction, the great structures in which festivals were held, the Convent of the Virgins of the Sun, and, situated far down towards the Pumapchupam, in the district called Coricanchu, or Place of Gold, the gorgeous Temple of the Sun, with its chapels sacred to the Moon, the Stars, the Thunder, and the Lightning. It was here, after the Conquest, that the principal *conquistadores* obtained their *repartimientos* of land, and on the ruins of the Inca palaces reared their own parvenu residences. Over the imposing gateways of the Inca edifices, which they preserved as entrances of their own, we still find, stuccoed in high-relief, the arms of Pizarro, Almagro, Gonzalez, Quiñonez, La Vega, Valdivia, Toledo, and the other adventurers who for a while sought to emulate in pomp and display the nobles of the other, not to say higher, civilization which they had displaced.

By a coincidence perhaps not wholly accidental, the Convent of Santa Catalina was established on the site, retaining in great part the very walls of the Acllahuasa, or Palace of the Virgins of the Sun, and is still sacred to the vestals of another religion. The Temple of the Sun itself became the Convent of the Friars of Santo Domingo, who, in failing numbers, still prolong a sapless life among its gray and classic walls—ruin on ruin, a decadent faith expiring among the cold, dead ashes of a primitive

superstition.   The great cathedral of Cuzco rises on the very
spot where the eighth Inca, Viracocha, erected a building dedicated to the festivals of the people, in which a whole regiment
of men could manœuvre, and where the scant forces of Gonsalvo Pizarro found refuge in the last desperate attempt of the
Peruvians to recover their lost empire and reinstate the vicegerent of the Sun.   Here, according to the legend, authenticated

CHURCH AND CONVENT OF SANTO DOMINGO, CUZCO.

in archaic sculpture over the doors of the Chapel of Santiago,
St. James came down visibly and tangibly on his white charger,
and, with lance in rest, turned the tide of battle in favor of the
Spaniards, and extirpated forever the Inca power.

All over this narrow tongue of land we find still the evidences of Inca greatness, as exhibited in their architecture.
The streets of the new city are almost all of them defined by
long reaches of walls of stones, elaborately cut, and fitting to-

gether with a precision not excelled in any of the structures of
Greece or Rome, and which modern art may emulate, but cannot surpass.   The walls of the Temple of the Sun, of the Convent of the Vestals, of the palaces of the two Yupanquis, of
Viracocha, Huayna Capac, the Inca Rocca, and portions of
those of the palace attributed to the first Inca, are still preserved, and justify the most extravagant praise bestowed by
Garcilasso de la Vega and the early chroniclers on the skill of

VIEW IN THE PLAZA DEL CABILDO, CUZCO.

the ancient builders.   But even where these walls have disappeared, and the stones which composed them have been used
for other structures, we still find the ancient door-ways, which
the modern builders have preserved, and are thus enabled to
define the outlines of the aboriginal city.

   The centre of this city was the Huacapata, or great public
square, now covered in part, as already said, by the modern
principal plaza.   The ancient square, however, extended over
the Huatenay, and embraced also what is now the Plaza del

Cabildo, and the area covered by the block of houses between that plaza and the church and convent of La Merced. And I may here mention that both the rivulets Huatenay and Roda-dero were shut in by walls of cut stone, with stairways descend-ing, at intervals, to the water. and thus confined in narrow beds covered by bridges of a single stone, or by others composed of stones projecting from either side, and a single long stone reach-ing over the space between them.

INCA BRIDGE OVER THE HUATENAY, CUZCO.

Built, as was Cuzco, on declivities more or less abrupt, the ancient architects were obliged to resort to an elaborate system of terracing in order to obtain level areas to receive their edi-fices. These terraces were faced with walls, slightly inclining inwards, and uniformly of the kind called "cyclopean;" that is to say, composed of stones of irregular size and of every con-ceivable shape, but accurately fitted together. Where there are long lines of these walls—as, for instance, those supporting the terraces of the Colcompata—the monotony of the front is gen-

erally broken up by the introduction of countersunk niches,
something like the "blind windows" which our architects introduce to relieve the blank walls of houses.  These niches are
always a little narrower at the top than at the bottom, as were
also nearly all the Inca door-ways and windows.  Inca architecture is peculiar and characteristic.  Wherever it was intro-

CYCLOPEAN WALL, PALACE OF THE INCA ROCCA, CUZCO.

duced among the nations of the coast and other parts of the
empire, it may be at once recognized.  In its massiveness, the
inclination of its walls, the style of its cornices, and in a few
other respects, it certainly bears some resemblance to that of
the ancient Egyptians; but the resemblance is not of a kind
to imply necessarily either connection or intercourse between

Egypt and Peru.  Architectural progress must be made through the same steps and over the same road in all countries; and primitive architecture, as primitive ideas, must have a likeness.

Some of these walls are massive and imposing, composed of hard and heavy stones.  Those sustaining the terrace of the Palace of the Inca Rocca, in the street Triunfo, are of a compact, fine-grained sienite, some of them weighing several tons each, and fitted together with wonderful precision.  Among them is one of large size, which was chronicled by the scribes of the Conquest as "*La piedra famosa de doce angulos,*" or the famous stone of twelve angles, which it has, in fact, each fitting into, or being fitted into by, another stone.

The public buildings of all peoples—their temples, palaces, and schools—are those which are most enduring; and, I think, among the ruins of Cuzco there are none which are not of edifices of these descriptions.  The residences of the people have disappeared here, although they are found abundantly in other places; but enough remains of the palaces and temples of Cuzco to enable us, with the aid of the early descriptions, to make out with tolerable accuracy their original form and character.  It may be said that, as a rule, they were built around a court, presenting exteriorly an unbroken wall, having but a single entrance, and, except in rare instances, no exterior windows.  The entrance in all cases was broad and lofty, permitting a horseman to ride in without difficulty.  The lintel was always a heavy slab of stone, sometimes carved, as well as the jambs, with figures, those of serpents predominating, perhaps from the fact that among the Peruvians, as among some other nations, the serpent was a symbol of the Sun.  It is evident from remains of hinges, and of apparatus for barring, that these entrances were closed by doors of some sort.

The walls of these structures, as well as those supporting the terraces, inclined slightly inwards, and in some instances are narrowed somewhat near the top.  Those of Cuzco are all of cut stone, and of the brown trachyte of Andahuaylillas, the grain of which, being rough, causes greater adhesion between the blocks than would be effected by the use of other kinds of stone. The stones are of various sizes in different structures, ranging in length from one to eight feet, and in thickness from six inches to two feet. They are laid in regular courses, the larger stones generally at the bottom, each course diminishing in thickness towards the top of the wall, thus giving a very pleasing effect of graduation. The joints are all of a precision unknown in our architecture, and not rivalled in the remains of ancient art that had fallen under my notice in Europe. The statement of the old writers, that the accuracy with which the

INCA DOOR-WAY, CUZCO.

stones of some structures were fitted together was such that it was impossible to introduce the thinnest knife-blade or finest needle between them, may be taken as strictly true. The world has nothing to show in the way of stone cutting and fitting to surpass the skill and accuracy displayed in the Inca structures of Cuzco. All modern work of the kind there—and there are some fine examples of skill—looks rude and barbarous in comparison.

In the buildings I am describing there is absolutely no ce-

ment of any kind, nor the remotest evidence of any having
ever been used.  The buildings in which tenacious clay, mixed
perhaps with other adhesive materials, was used to bind together rough stones into one enduring mass of wall are of a character quite different from the edifices of Cuzco.  In dismissing
thus peremptorily the stories and speculations about some wonderfully binding and almost impalpable cement which is said to
have been used by the Incas, and the secret of whose composition has been lost, I am quite aware of the responsibility I assume.  No man has ever investigated, or can more thoroughly
investigate, this mooted question than myself; and I give it as
the result of an inquiry carried on over nearly all the centres of
Peruvian civilization, that in their structures of cut stone the
Inca architects depended, with rare exceptions, on the accuracy
of their stone-fitting without cement for the stability of their
works — works which, unless disturbed by systematic violence,
will endure until the capitol at Washington has sunk into decay, and Macaulay's New Zealander contemplates the ruins of
St. Paul's from the crumbling arches of London Bridge!

The exceptions to which I have referred are those where, as
in Tiahuanuco, the chulpas of Sillustani, and in the Fortress of
Ollantaytambo, the stones were fastened together by bronze
clamps, interfitting grooves and projections, and by other purely mechanical devices, bearing in no way on the question of the
use of mortar.  It is only right that I should say that Humboldt states distinctly that he found a true mortar in the ruins
of Pullal and Cannar, in Northern Peru.

The exteriors of most of the Inca structures of Cuzco present
the appearance of what may be called "rustic work," and of
which the Pitti Palace of Florence, and some other buildings
in that city, afford fair examples, although not nearly so perfect,
as specimens of this style, as those of Cuzco; that is to say,
the outer surfaces or faces of the stones are slightly convex, and
cut slantingly towards the edges, so that the joints form small
flutings.  Humboldt tells us that this cut of the stone is called
"bugnato" by the Italian architects, and adduces the Muro di
Nerva of Rome as an example of similar workmanship.  Some

of the Inca edifices, however, and notably the Temple of the
Sun and the Convent of the Virgins of the Sun, have exterior
surfaces perfectly smooth — the walls having been apparently
"dressed down" after the completion of the structure.

The Inca architects knew as well how to cut their stones for
circular buildings as for quadrangular ones. One portion of
the Temple of the Sun is circular, or, rather, the section of a
flattened circle. The stones must have been cut to conform to
this shape, for their sides of contact are true radii of the double
circle, and the line of general inclination of the wall is perfect
in every block.

To return to the plan of our Inca edifices. As I have already
stated, they were generally built around a court, upon which
all, or nearly all, the rooms opened. As a rule, these had no
connection, and seem to have been dedicated each to a special
purpose. In some cases, nevertheless, there were inner chambers, to be reached only after passing through a number of
outer ones. These were, perhaps, recesses sacred to domestic
or religious rites. or places of refuge for the timid or weak.
Many of the apartments were large. Garcilasso de la Vega describes some of them, of which the remains exist to indicate
his accuracy, as capable of receiving sixty horsemen, with room
enough to exercise with their lances. Three sides of the great
central square, the Huacapata, were occupied by as many grand
*galpones*, or public edifices, in which religious and other ceremonies were observed in bad weather, each of which had the
capacity to receive several thousand people. Garcilasso was
within bounds when he described them as two hundred paces
long and from fifty to sixty broad, and capable of holding three
thousand people each.

Prescott and others have fallen into the error of describing
all the buildings of the ancient Peruvians as of only a single
story, low, and without windows. Now, the walls which remain show that in Cuzco they were from thirty-five to forty
feet high, besides the spring of the roof. They were, perhaps,
all of a single story: on that point it is now impossible to speak;
but elsewhere we know there were edifices, private dwellings

as well as temples, of two and three stories, with windows ade
quate for all purposes of illuminating their interiors; regard
being had to the temperature of the country, which, with a
people unacquainted with glass, would limit the number of
apertures to absolute requirements. Few of the dwellings of
the ruder part of the population of the Sierra of Peru have
even now more than a single opening, and that often so low as
to be entered with difficulty, often on only hands and knees.
A severe climate and absence of fuel will sufficiently account
for deficiencies in door-ways and windows.

Absence of timber will also account for what might appear,
and perhaps was, incongruous in the aspect and character of the
massive buildings I have endeavored to describe. They were
roofed with thatch, as indeed are to-day many of the houses of
the city of Puno, and other towns of the interior. In some
of the two-story structures—as, for instance, the Palace of the
Inca on the island of Titicaca—in the lower rooms, which are
the smallest, the roof or ceiling is an arch formed by overlapping stones, which seems to have been the nearest approach to
the true arch attained by the Mexican and Central American
nations. I found no other kind of arch in the stone edifices
of Peru, but I found the true arch in a structure of adobes at
Pachacamac.

The Temple of the Sun was the principal and probably the
most imposing edifice, not only in Cuzco, but in all Peru, if not
in all America. The accounts of its splendor and riches left by
the conquerors, and in which they have exhausted the superla-
tives of their grandiose language, have been so often reproduced as to be familiar to every intelligent reader. They represent the structure as being 400 paces in circuit, with high
walls of finely cut stones, enclosing a court on which opened a
number of chapels dedicated to the celestial objects of Peruvian worship, and apartments appropriated to the priests and
attendants. The chronicle, erroneously attributed to Sarmiento,
states that he never saw but two edifices in Spain comparable
with it in workmanship; and Garcilasso affirms that all that
was written of it by the Spaniards, and all that he could write

himself, would fail to give a just idea of its greatness. It stood, as I have said, in the lower part of the Inca city, in the district of Coracancha, or Place of Gold, on the high bank of the Huatenay, probably eighty feet above the bed of that stream, towards which the ground fell off, as it still does, by a series of terraces, faced with cut stone, which formed the famous Gardens of the Sun. The temple proper occupied the whole of one side of the court. The principal entrance, says Garcilasso, was to the north. The cornice of the walls, outside and in, was of gold, or plated with gold, as were the inner walls. The roof was high and pointed, and of thatch, but the ceiling was of wood and flat. At the eastern end was a great plate of gold, representing the sun; and ranged beneath it, in royal robes and seated in golden chairs, the desiccated—some say embalmed—bodies of the Inca rulers; the body of Huayna Capac, as the greatest of the Inca line, being alone honored with a place in front of the symbol. This plate, all of one piece, spread from one wall to the other, and was the only object of worship in the building. Surrounding the court were other separate structures dedicated respectively to the Moon, Venus, the Pleiades, the Thunder and Lightning, and the Rainbow. There were also a large saloon for the supreme pontiff, and apartments for attendants. All these are described as having been richly decorated with gold and silver.

The existing remains confirm substantially the descriptions of the chroniclers. The site of the temple, as I have already said, is covered by the church and convent of Santo Domingo. The few ignorant but amiable friars that remain of the once rich and renowned order of Santo Domingo in Cuzco admitted me as an honorary member of their brotherhood, gave me a cell to myself, and permitted me, during the week I spent with them, to ransack every portion of the church, and every nook and corner of the convent, and to measure and sketch and photograph to my fill. Here a long reach of massive wall, yonder a fragment, now a corner, next a door-way, and anon a terrace —through the aid of these I was able to make up a ground-plan of the ancient edifice, substantially, if not entirely, accurate. Its length was 296 feet; its breadth, as nearly as can now be determined, about 52 feet.

The temple proper, as described by Garcilasso, and as my own researches have proved, formed one side of a rectangular court, around which were ranged the dependent structures mentioned by him. It was not built, as has been universally alleged, so that its sides should conform to the cardinal points, but these coincided in direction with the bearings of the ancient streets, which were nearly at an angle of forty-five degrees

COURT OF CONVENT OF SANTO DOMINGO, AND ANCIENT INCA FOUNTAIN, CUZCO.

with those points. Nor was its door at " one end exactly facing the east," so that the rays of the sun, when it rose, "should shine directly on its own golden image placed on the opposite wall of the temple." The entrance was on the north-east side of the building, and opened upon a square, or rather a rectangular area, called now, as anciently, Inti-pampa, or Field of the Sun. This is still surrounded by heavy walls of cut stones, sculptured all over with serpents in relief, on which are raised the houses of the modern inhabitants. This square was dedicated to the more solemn ceremonials of the Inca religion, and within it none dared enter except on sacred occasions, and then only with bare feet and uncovered heads.

The end of the temple next the Rio Huatenay, which is best

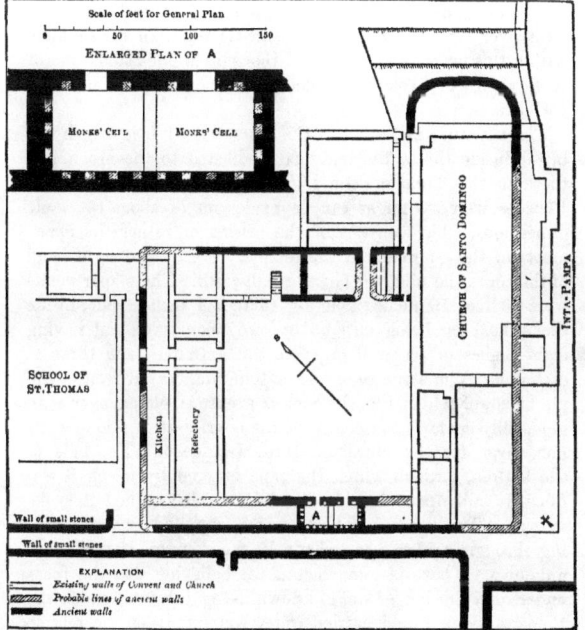

PLAN OF THE TEMPLE AND CONVENT OF THE SUN, CUZCO.

preserved, rose above the famous Gardens of the Sun, and it is now built over by a sort of balcony, not directly connected with the modern church—a belvedere, in short. It was at this end of the temple that the great golden figure of the Sun was placed, which, falling to the lot of the Conquistador Leguizano, was gambled away before morning. I present a view of this extremity of the ancient edifice. It is circular in shape, with walls of beautifully cut and closely fitting stones, sloping gently inwards. The robing-room and store-room for dilapidated effigies of saints, belonging to the Church of Santo Domingo, is built over this wall on a level with its top. In my opinion, within this circular extremity of the temple once stood one of those stones or "columns," which was known by the name of Intihuatani.

The structure dedicated to the Stars was 51 feet long by 26 broad, inside the walls; and that dedicated to the Moon, and those to the Thunder, the Lightning, the Rainbow, and the Pleiades were, so far as can be made out, of about the same dimensions. The convent of the priests, or rather the apartments of the guardians of the temple, were on the right hand of the court, the observer facing northwards. These apartments were 33 feet 10 inches long by 13 feet 4 inches wide, inside the walls, each being entered by two door-ways, and having eight niches in the wall opposite the entrances, and three at each end. The stone reservoir or fountain, carved from a single block, of which the chroniclers speak as plated over with gold, still stands in the centre of the court. It is a long octagon, seven feet by four, and three feet deep. The hole in the bottom, through which the pipe entered by which it was filled, is still open; but the conduit which supplied it is destroyed. The convent, nevertheless, is supplied by water coming through subterranean channels, the sources of which are unknown. There is some reason for believing that the Incas understood the law of fluids known as equilibrium, which the Romans did not, and carried water for supply of the temple and some of their palaces through inverted siphons, and below the bed of the Huatenay.

On the side of the Huatenay the outlook from the Temple of the Sun must have been, as it still is, very fine, bounded only by the mountains that shut in the bolson of Cuzco in that direction. On the opposite side, however, there seems to have been only a narrow street, but nine feet wide, and buildings of a comparatively rude construction. The Inti-pampa in front, entered by three streets leading between lofty walls, still high and solid, from the Huacapata, or Central Square, was, after all,

END WALL OF THE TEMPLE OF THE SUN, CUZCO.

only about four hundred feet long by one hundred wide, and does not realize the grandeur which the early accounts attach to it.

Some of the chronicles speak of the temple as being sur-

rounded by a high wall; whereas nothing is more certain than
that the exterior walls were simply those of the edifice itself.
They tell us also that the terraces which formed the garden of
the temple were covered with golden clods, and supported an
infinite variety of trees and vegetables imitated, in gold and silver, with figures of men, animals, birds, reptiles, and insects, all
in the same precious metals. That the inner walls of the temple were covered with these metals, and that the inner and outer
cornice (a yard broad, as Garcilasso says) were of gold, is not
incredible; but that the gardens of the temple, extending over
an area six hundred feet long by nearly three hundred broad,
were thus covered with gold and silver exceeds belief. Not
that the ancient smiths did not sometimes imitate natural objects with considerable skill, for of this we have abundant evidence, but because the Incas seem to have been a race of remarkably good sense, and eminently practical and utilitarian in
their notions and practices — too much so, I am confident, to
have gold worked up in imitation of fire-wood, and piled away
in the temple! There exist in Cuzco, in some of the private
museums, portions of the golden plates with which the walls of
the Temple of the Sun were covered. There is hardly a doubt
of their authenticity. They are simple sheets of pure gold,
beaten exceedingly thin, not thicker than fine note-paper.

The most conspicuous remains of ancient Cuzco, next to
the Temple of the Sun, are those of the Palace of the Virgins
of the Sun. It was separated from the temple by a block
of buildings occupied by the priesthood, and the existing remains prove it to have been an imposing structure. Through
the favor of the Abbess of Santa Catalina, I was admitted into
the convent which occupies its site. This seems to have been
a long and rather narrow building. One of its side-walls, not
entire, faced on the narrow street of the Cárcel, or Prison, opposite the Amarucancha, or Place of Snakes, where the Inca
Huayna Capac had his palace. This wall is now 750 feet long,
by from 20 to 25 high, and resembles that of the Temple of
the Sun in the size and finish of its stones. One end of this
building fronted on the principal square, and measured about

one hundred and eighty feet.  Altogether the Acllahuasi may
be described as an edifice very nearly 800 feet long by 200
broad.  The existing walls show no entrance or opening; but
that may have been, and probably was, where is the present
entrance to the church and convent of Santa Catalina, which
covers most of the ground occupied by the ancient structure.
There was undoubtedly a court inside, and there are fragments

SIDE WALL OF THE TEMPLE OF THE SUN, AND ANCIENT STREET, CUZCO.

enough of the building remaining to admit of making out its
plan.  The Acllahuasi was dedicated to virgins of royal lineage, who were sent there at the age of eight years, and put under the charge of *mamacunas* (literally, "mother teachers"),
and kept in rigorous seclusion.

Between the Palace of the Virgins and the Huatenay was,
as I have said, the Amarucancha and the palace of Huayna
Capac.  This was an immense structure, nearly or quite eight

hundred feet long, and it is now occupied by the fine church
and convent of the Jesuits, the departmental barracks, and the
prison. This was built of smaller stones, in the style called
rustic work, and had numerous entrances. Over the principal
door, boldly sculptured in relief on the lintel, are two serpents,
allusive, probably, to the name given to the edifice.

On the other side of the Acllahuasi was an immense structure, or series of structures, covering the district called Puca

VIEW ON THE PAMPA MARONI, WITH INCA WALL, CUZCO.

Marca, and containing the palaces of the Yupanquis. One face
of the walls, on the square called Pampa Maroni, is nearly perfect, except where it is pierced with modern door-ways lead.ng
to the edifices that have been built over the ruins. This is
perhaps the finest piece of ancient wall remaining in Cuzco,
and one of the best illustrations of the kind of work most common in Inca architecture. It is 380 feet long and about 18
feet high. The courses of stones are symmetrical and accurate; and, as Humboldt says of some of the walls which he

saw, the joints are so perfect that if the faces of the stones were dressed down smooth they could hardly be discerned. A reach of this wall, more than eight hundred feet long, but more broken up by modern buildings, forming the north-east side of the palaces, faces on the street of San Agustin.

It is said by the chroniclers that every Inca built a new palace, which, on his death, became the residence of his descendants outside of the immediate succession. If so, and if this was rigorously the rule, existing remains go far to confirm the accuracy of Garcilasso's table of rulers, for, apart from public edifices, there do not remain traces of more than fourteen palaces; that being the number of rulers according to this authority. One of the most interesting of these palatial remains is that of the palace of the Inca Rocca, who dedicated himself to the instruction of his people. It was situated on quite high ground overlooking the Rodadero, towards which he had his hanging gardens. The foundations of the structure, or rather the walls which supported the terrace on which the palace was built, are nearly perfect.

The palace itself was of stone, faced after the style of the walls of the great temple. It was about 200 feet long by 150 broad.

"THE SCHOOLS," CUZCO.

Separated from it by a narrow street, now the Calle del Triunfo, were the Yachahuasi, or schools, built by the Inca Rocca, who placed his palace where he did in order to be close to them. They seem to have been rather plainly built, with numerous openings on the terraces of the little stream Rodadero. It was here that the *amautes*, or wise men, taught such knowledge as existed in Inca times: the science of the *quippus*, the historical legends, the songs of the people, and probably also some of the higher mechanic arts.

The site of the cathedral was that of a great *galpon*, or covered hall, and it was within this that the Spaniards had their barracks when they occupied the city. Behind this *galpon* was the Palace of the Inca Viracocha, of which considerable vestiges remain. To the north-west of the great square were other public buildings, or *galpones*, of stones faced like those of the Temple of the Sun, and the Palace of the Inca Pachacutic.

The great central square of the ancient city, now in part occupied by the Plaza Principal, was about 850 feet long by 550 broad. It was divided into very nearly equal parts by the rivulet Huatenay, flowing twenty feet below its level, and which was shut in a channel fifteen feet wide, by walls of cut stone. It was covered over then, as now, by great stone flags.

The area to the north-west side of the stream was called Huacapata, or Sacred Terrace or Shore, and that on the other side of the stream the Cusipata, or Terrace of Joy. A part of the Cusipata is now built over, and there is a block of buildings standing over the stream itself, which flows beneath. On the south-east side of the Cusipata was the house of Garcilasso de la Vega, the chronicler, which may still be recognized from his description. On this side of the Huatenay there were no royal palaces—so say the early writers; but there were some considerable and well-built edifices, as the remains prove. They were probably of the class called *galpones*. Numerous Inca doorways, utilized with sections of adjacent ancient walls by the Spaniards, still exist. It was in the open square of the Huacapata that the great festivals of the Incas were celebrated. Here the Spaniards encamped when they entered the city, and here they sustained the terrible siege which Prescott has so admirably described, and in the course of which Juan Pizarro was slain.

A conspicuous object from every part of Cuzco is the steep, overhanging hill of the Sacsahuaman, rising to the height of 760 feet to the north of the city, and on which the Incas raised that gigantic, cyclopean fortress denominated by the conquerors the ninth great wonder of the world. I shall describe this fortress in another place; but at present refer to it only to say that well up on its *falda*, or slope, just at the point where it becomes so steep as almost to render ascent impossible, is a series of elaborate terraces, supported by cyclopean walls, ornamented with niches, and called the Colcompata, or Terrace of the Granaries. It was here, it is said, that the first Inca, Manco Capac, the founder of Cuzco, built his palace, some fragments of which still remain—a door-way, a window, and a short section of wall, with some portions of foundations, but not enough to enable us to make out a complete plan of the structure. There were fountains here; and the site, now occupied in part by the church and plaza of San Cristobal, not only dominated the whole city,

HOUSE OF GALCILASSO DE LA VEGA, CUZCO.

but the entire valley of Cuzco. The terraces were filled in
with richest soil, still celebrated for its fertility, and altogether
it was, and yet is, almost regal in its position.

The Incas were the heads of a great nation, dependent on
agriculture. To evince their respect for the art lying at the
foundation of their state, to elevate and dignify. labor, they
were wont to initiate here with their own hands the seasons of
planting and of harvest. With pomp and ceremony, when the

VIEW OF THE HILL OF THE SACSAHUAMAN FROM THE PLAZA DEL CABILDO, CUZCO.

season of sowing came around, and the appropriate festivals
had been celebrated, the Inca himself went to the terraces of
the Colcompata, and with a golden pick-axe commenced to
break up the soil; and when the crops of maize and quinoa
had ripened, he again went to the Colcompata and plucked the
first ears of the harvest. The crops gathered here, under the
direct cultivation of the Son of the Sun, were regarded as
sacred, and, like the seeds from the holy Island of Titicaca,
were distributed, to be sown in the lands dedicated to the Sun

throughout the empire.   Thus carefully were the people taught
that the beneficence of their deity was perpetuated through his
children, and thus were they led to look up to him, through the
Incas, as the impersonations of his goodness and mercy as well
as of his power.

I cannot dismiss ancient Cuzco without a few words regarding its pristine state and importance, as inferrible from its monuments.   All students of American early history and archæology are well aware that the Spaniards never understated the
numbers of the enemies they encountered.   It is certain, indeed,

REMAINS OF PALACE OF THE FIRST INCA, CUZCO.

that they very often greatly exaggerated them.   According to
their own accounts, they met and defeated armies exceeding in
numbers any ever brought at once into action upon a single
field in the great wars of modern history; more numerous than
fought on either side at Borodino, Leipsic, or Waterloo; at Ma-
nassas, Chancellorsville, or Gettysburg; at Villafranca, Sadowa,
or Sedan.   But, making all possible allowance for exaggeration,
there can be no doubt that Cortez, Alvarado, and Pizarro, with
their few hundreds of cavaliers and men-at-arms, were confronted by armies vastly superior in numbers, but vastly inferior in
weapons.   The cities of which they took possession are invari-

ably represented as large and populous, and the state of their princes was imposing even in the eyes of men who were familiar with the splendor of European cities and courts, and who knew from history and legend the magnificence of those of the Moors.

In many respects, perhaps in most, Cuzco was certainly the most impressive, if not the most populous, city they had found in all the Americas. That it had barbaric wealth of gold and silver, and stately structures, we can well believe; for this is confirmed by concurrent evidence and existing remains. But that it ever contained much more than its existing population appears to me improbable. The story that it held two hundred thousand inhabitants, and that as many more lived in its suburbs, is simply incredible. The houses of the common people of the Sierra, and in the region around Cuzco, were not built, as are those of Central America and Mexico, of canes and other materials that might disappear in a single season, but of stone or adobes, that could not fail to leave some enduring traces. Such traces do not exist around Cuzco; and, however great may have been the concurrence there on important occasions, when the people gathered from the valleys of Yucay and Paucartambo, from the bolsons of Andahuaylillas and Xaxiguana, the *punas* of Chinchero and Chita, and from all the quarters of a mighty empire, yet it does not seem probable that the city ever possessed a permanent population of more than fifty thousand, while another equal number may have been dispersed through its valley. The department of Cuzco is now the most populous of Peru, its inhabitants numbering upwards of three hundred thousand. These exhaust very nearly all its resources; and even if we concede that the economies of agriculture here are less now than in ancient times, we must, on the other hand, remember that many domestic animals, a number of vegetables, and wheat and barley, have all been introduced since the Conquest, and contribute to the support of the present population.

I cannot agree with those writers who speak of the aspect of ancient Cuzco as bright and shining, and gay with many tints. Its most imposing edifices were, as we have seen, built of trachyte of sombre color. These, clearly, were neither stuccoed nor painted. The residences of the people, built of rough stones laid in clay, were probably stuccoed and painted yellow and red, and may have given some appearance of lightness to the city. The domes and towers of which we sometimes read probably never existed; those architectural terms being oftenest used in loose descriptions, framed on Oriental models, and intended to be impressive rather than accurate. Nor was the city laid out with perfect regularity, the streets crossing each other at right angles. Nor were the banks of the Huatenay faced with stones for a distance of twenty leagues, but simply for the distance it flowed through the city.

Modern Cuzco extends very compactly over the entire space between the Huatenay and Almodena, and even past the latter stream, forming the barrio of Belen. Although considerably reduced in population since the Independence, it still numbers not far from fifty thousand inhabitants, and, as the capital of the department of the same name, is, necessarily, a place of some importance—the seat of a bishopric and a university, a prefecture and a garrison. It is very well built, the edifices being mainly those raised by the conquerors themselves in the height of their wealth and activity, when they had *mitas* and *repartimientos*, before the treasures collected through five centuries had been scattered, and while they had a large, industrious, and skilful population under their absolute control. In style eminently Moorish, the houses are built around courts, with open corridors, supported by delicate columns, into which open the apartments of every story. *Jalousies project from the fronts, and the whole aspect of the place is that of Granada in Spain. The lower or ground floors of the best buildings, facing on the principal streets, are cut up into small, dark rooms, without windows, which are the shops, smitheries, *picanterias*, etc., of the town.

The churches and convents are numerous and extensive. Of the former there are thirty, and of the latter eleven, five of which have been suppressed. They are all remarkably well built. The cathedral, fronting on the principal square, is a

31.

large, massive, and rather heavy structure; but the Church of
the Jesuits, fronting on the same square, is a marvel of architectural beauty—a little too florid, perhaps, but with the finest
façade of any church I have seen in Southern America. The
tower of the Church of La Merced is admirable in proportion
and taste, and the courts of the convent of the same name are
surrounded by colonnades of white stone, elaborately carved, and
which in grace and harmony may challenge comparison with

CHURCH OF LA MERCED, CUZCO.

the finest of Italy. Within this church lie the remains of Juan
and Gonsalvo Pizarro and Almagro. Both churches and convents are crowded with pictures, some of merit and historical
value. Of the latter there is a series in the little church of
Santa Ana, contemporaneous with the Conquest. They illustrate the procession of Corpus Christi, in which the Incarial
family, in regal native costume, take part. Among them is
Paullu, younger son of the great Huayna Capac, and numer-

ous *ñustas*, or princesses, the daughters and nieces of the same monarch. As illustrating the costumes and customs of the period, these paintings have singular interest, and deserve to be faithfully copied.

For many years after the Conquest, and long after Lima was founded, Cuzco continued to be the chief city of Peru, the seat of its wealth and learning, and the residence of its most noble families. But as the roads of the Incas fell into decay, the difficulties of reaching it, always great, were augmented, and the viceregal court established in Lima, more corrupt and luxurious than any other in America, gradually drew away its more enterprising and ambitious inhabitants. In Lima, far less is known of Cuzco than of Berlin; for one native of the capital who has visited Cuzco, a hundred have visited Paris. The journey from Lima to New York is made in less time than it can be made from the same point to the proud but isolated city of the Sierra, and with a fourth part of the trouble and fatigue.

Seven-eighths of the population of Cuzco are pure Indians; and a knowledge of Quichua is almost absolutely necessary for open intercourse with the mass of its inhabitants. The white and foreign population is small, made up chiefly of government officials, a few wealthy *haciendados*, who live a great part of the time on their estates, and a dozen small *comerciantes*, who would be called shop-keepers in any other country. Collectively these are so few as hardly to be appreciable in the streets, and the aspect of the place is, therefore, that of a thoroughly Indian town. There is hardly anything that can be called society, although the better class is hospitable and unaffected, and much more frank and easy in manner than the corresponding class in the towns of the coast, where native manners have been sacrificed in a vain attempt to imitate foreign airs and graces. Some of the old families live in considerable style, and their houses are fitted with real elegance. A few of them retain apartments with heavy damask and embroidered hangings, and the rich and massive furniture and carvings of two hundred years ago, when the nobility and wealth of Peru were concentrated in Cuzco.  Others are furnished in modern, thoroughly French style, with great mirrors, inlaid wardrobes, and grand pianos, that have been brought up, with infinite labor and at almost fabulous cost, from the coast.

I may refer particularly to the residence of the late Señora Zentino, a lady who lived on the Plaza of San Francisco, whose attention to strangers was proverbial, and who established an honorable reputation as the collector of the finest and most valuable museum of antiquities in Peru.  This house would be called a palace even in Venice, if not in architecture, certainly in extent.  In the spaciousness of its apartments, and their rich and varied contents and decorations, it would creditably compare with some of the finest on the Grand Canal.  The señora gave some very amusing accounts of Castelnau and other travellers, and especially of a Frenchman named Lorenzo Saint Criq, who, under the name of " Paul Marcoy," published, after the lapse of many years, a description of Cuzco and other parts of Peru.*  An adequate description of the museum would occupy a volume, and I content myself with engravings of some pieces of pottery selected from many hundreds, illustrating the skill of the ancients in the plastic arts, and their appreciation of humor.

In some respects, the most important relic in Señora Zentino's collection is the frontal bone of a skull, from the Inca cemetery in the valley of Yucay, which exhibits a clear case of trepanning before death.  The señora was kind enough to give it to me for investigation, and it has been submitted to the criticism of the best surgeons of the United States and Europe,

---

* Professor Raimondi, in a paper on the Rivers San Gavan and Ayapata, published in vol. xxxvii. of the Journal of the Royal Geographical Society of London, takes occasion to denounce some of the geographical statements of Señor Pablo Marcoy as "absolutely false," and says that his books, " Voyage à Travers L'Amérique du Sud," and "Scènes et Paysages dans les Andes," " should be looked upon as the product of a vivid imagination rather than truthful composition."  He laments "that one who has had the opportunity of visiting unexplored regions should employ his talents in a work of such a class, deviating so much from the truth, when he could, by faithfully describing countries so new as Peru, have interested the readers much more than by fantastic stories."

and regarded by all as the most remarkable evidence of a
knowledge of surgery among the aborigines yet discovered on
this continent; for trepanning is one of the most difficult of
surgical processes.  The cutting through the bone was not performed with a saw, but evidently with a burin, or tool like that
used by engravers on wood and metal.  The opening is fifty-
eight hundredths of an inch wide and seventy hundredths
long.

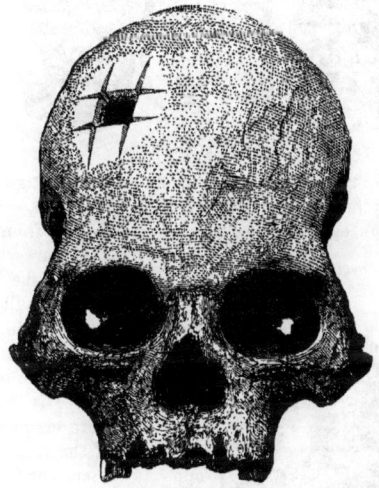

TREPANNED SKULL.

The absence of sculptures in Peru, except of small articles in
stone, is conspicuous, and quite in contrast with what we find in
Central America and Mexico.  A few terra-cottas have been
found at Cuzco; but except figures of serpents in relief on
walls and lintels, and a single group of pumas over the doors of
a house in the Calle de Santa Ana, there are no sculptures to
be seen there.  There are some figures resembling griffins, etc.,
in the court of a house in the Calle del Triunfo, and a so-called

"Siren" built in the terrace wall of the Colcompata; but I regard them as modern. In the collection of the Señora Zentino,

TERRA-COTTAS FROM CUZCO.

however, are two stone figures, rudely resembling tigers, which, it is said, were taken from the Gardens of the Sun, where they stood one on each side the stairway that led up from the ter-

ANCIENT STONE SCULPTURE, CUZCO.

races. The bases are cut in such a way as to favor the hypothesis that they were built in some sort of wall, perhaps in the coping. They are two feet high.

Among the notable objects of interest in Cuzco is the Alameda, to the south of the town, on the banks of the Huatenay, and opposite the ancient Gardens of the Sun. This a long and rather narrow area, planted with willows and alder-trees, laid out with some taste, and having a kind of Grecian temple and a colonnade at its farther extremity. But nobody walks there, and it is grown up with cactuses and weeds, over which the washer-women from the neighboring stream spread their clothes to dry. Public spirit in Peru is spasmodic, and all works of embellishment excite only a mo-

mentary interest, and then succumb under the general apathy
of the people. The sentiment of affection does something to
keep the various *panteones*, or cemeteries, in decent condition,
and that of Cuzco is tasteful and well-ordered. But it strikes
the visitor as strange that, with such a vast expanse of earth
open to receive and protect forever the remains of the dead,
they should be thrust for only a year or two in ovens in the
walls, and then dragged out and burned or buried in a corner.

My first visit to the Panteon of Cuzco was early in the morning, and as I approached the barrio of Belen, outside the city,
in which it stands, I observed a funeral procession in the street
before me, preceded by some men carrying candles, a man play-
ing a violin, and another a clarinet. As they passed the various squalid houses in that quarter, the women rushed out with
dishevelled hair, and, huddling behind the bier, commenced the
loudest and most extravagant wailings of which the human or-
gans are capable. I was astonished at such violence of grief,
and wondered who had died that had so deep a hold on the
popular sympathies. I overtook the procession, or rather huddle, at the bridge of the Almodena, where suddenly the lamentations ceased, and the inconsolables clustered eagerly around a
man, who, standing on a block of stone, distributed *cuartillos*
(three-cent pieces) to them from his hat, whereupon, chatting
and laughing, the afflicted creatures turned back to await another funeral. For a *medio* each, these professional weepers of
the Calle del Hospital will accompany the corpse to the gate of
the cemetery, break their very hearts with grief, and dissolve
themselves in tears.

The Panteon is shut in by high white walls, and entered beneath a lofty stone gate-way, with trellised iron doors, over
which is a deep niche, wherein stands a veritable skeleton, supported by an iron rod, wearing a gilt crown on its bony head,
and holding in its fleshless hands two banners of sheet metal,
one of which bears the inscription, "Yo soy Pablo Biliaca,"
"I am Paul Biliaca;" and the other, "Memento Mori." Pablo
Biliaca was a mason, and had been killed by a fall while repair-
ing the front of the cathedral.

The recreations of Cuzco are religious processions and cock-fighting; the former occurring almost daily, and so frequently that I early ceased to inquire about them. The latter occur only on Sundays. The *cancha*, or cock-pit, is in the court of the old suppressed *beaterio* of San Andres, and consists of a raised ring of mud two feet high and as many thick, surrounded by other rings of graduated height, as seats for the spectators. Around the court are tiers of coops for the cocks, some of which were piled full of skulls and bones of the devout *beatas*, who had died here and been buried in the court, the earth of which, including their own dust, had been dug up to form the walls of the *cancha*. The fights were well attended by the clergy, the judiciary, and the military. I had the good fortune to win an *onza* from the judge of the Supreme Court, who challenged me to bet on the *viscacha*, an imported cock, with a single spur, which had already won two battles. My servant Ignacio had discovered "a bird" of excellent points in Cacha, and had brought him thence wrapped up in his poncho, with a view of matching him in Cuzco. For two weeks he had shared Ignacio's apartment and absorbed most of his care, besides vexing us with his incessant crowing, so that I insisted he should fight soon, be sent away, or decapitated. Ignacio determined on the first alternative, begged a month's pay in advance, matched him for four ounces, won, then sold him for another ounce, got drunk, gambled away every *cuartillo*, absented himself for three days, and then came home with a swollen eye and "very bad in his head."

The dog laws are strict and severely enforced in Cuzco, which would be overrun with mangy curs if they were not rigorously slain. The day of slaughter is Thursday of each week, when decent dogs are confined by their owners in case they do not find out, as many of them do, that the day is a black one for dogs, and stay at home of their own accord. Our host had a fine Newfoundland which understood the danger and the day, and, from his safe position on the balcony, would abuse and malign the dog-killers on their appearance with all the vigor of which the canine language is capable. Woe to any one of them

who undertook to enter the court of his castle on that day or
any other.

The process of slaughter is novel. Two Indians, each holding an end of a rope, station themselves at the mouth of a
street, while two others, armed with clubs, start from its other
extremity, and drive all the vagrant dogs before them. As
these attempt to pass over the rope, which lies harmlessly
enough on the ground, it is suddenly and dexterously straight-
ened out, and the dog thrown high in the air. He is generally
stunned or disabled by his fall, and despatched by the club-
bearers. I am sorry to say that even then he does not always

DOG-KILLING IN FRONT OF THE CONVENT OF SANTA ANA, CUZCO.

cease to be a nuisance, as he is too often thrown into the bed of
the Huatenay, which is the receptacle of all kinds of filth and
rubbish, and there left to poison the air in his decay.

Of the filthiness of Cuzco every visitor must have sickening
recollections. It offends the eye as well as the nose, and reeks
everywhere. The *azequias* in the centre of the streets are
scantily supplied with water during the dry season ; and as they

receive all the slops and wash of the houses, they are often
fetid, and all the more so as that tropical scavenger, the ordinary buzzard, never ventures into this lofty region.  Probably
the world has no more extraordinary spectacle than is afforded
on the banks of these *azequias* in the early morning; certainly
none more startling to the eyes of the stranger accustomed to
the decencies of life.

The Peruvian "Fourth of July" occurs on the 28th, that
being the anniversary of Peruvian Independence, and it came
around on the second day after our arrival in Cuzco.  It was
ushered in by the same sulphurous detonations that we are accustomed to at home on similar occasions; and there were a
review of the garrison and the volunteer militia, and a concurrence of the notables of the city at the Cathedral, with a
discourse from one of the *canónigos*, in which he reflected on
the Government, and was arrested for his pains in the evening.
The students in the university, patriotic as students always are,
were the most active participants in the festivities of the day;
all dressed in black tail-coats, with funny cocked hats, like the
*élèves* of St. Cyr in Paris.  They constituted the leading feature in the procession in the afternoon, dragging with them
through the streets a radiant Goddess of Freedom, in the shape
of a huge doll with flaxen ringlets and a liberty cap, glittering
with tinsel, and mounted on two wheels borrowed for the occasion from the only piece of artillery which a prudent Government entrusted to the rather turbulent citizens of Cuzco.  The
Indians looked on with an indifferent air, as a matter that little
concerned them, and only drank a little more chicha than usual.
The great excitement of the day was the explosion of a keg of
gunpowder in the *cuartel*, or barracks, which are the seques-
tered cloisters of the Jesuits, where a squad of soldiers were
compounding fireworks for the evening, resulting in killing
four or five, and mangling or horribly burning twenty or thirty
more—a practical commentary on the general impolicy of men
smoking cigars in a powder-magazine.  In the centre of the
great plaza was raised a symbolical monument, a sort of Temple
of Liberty, made of canvas, stretched on frames, in which were

portraits of the *beneméritos* of Freedom in all parts of the world—Lincoln and Garibaldi side by side. The students were not satisfied with the performances of the day, but insisted on prolonging them by a procession by moonlight, in which it was proposed that I should carry the Peruvian flag, supported on each side by that of the United States. My Puno experiences were too recent to make me ambitious of the distinction; but the students invaded the court-yard of the comandante's house in a body, dragging the Goddess with them, and refused to credit my assurances of indisposition and Colonel Vargas's more truthful asseveration that we were tired out and wanted rest. Finally, a compromise was effected, and I consented to be a standard-bearer, but only through the plaza and as far as the alameda. The announcement was received with tumultuous *vivas* for the United States, which a single indiscreet individual sought to oppose with some allusion to Mr. Webster's *faux pas* in the Lobos Islands business. This resulted in the dissentient getting so savagely handled that he was obliged to keep his bed for many weeks after.

# CHAPTER XXIII.

### SACSAHUAMAN, THE ANCIENT FORTRESS OF CUZCO.

Import of the Name.—Situation of the Fortress.—The Ravine of the Rodadero.—
Aqueduct and Water-falls.—The Gate of Sand.—The Rock Rodadero.—Character of the Rock.—Garcilasso's Description of the Fortress.—Plan of its Construction. — System of Drainage. — Immense Stones. — Entrances. — The Round
Building, and other Subsidiary Works.—Mistake of Prescott.—How the Stones
were moved. — The Piedra Cansada, or Tired Stone. — El Rodadero, and Von
Tschudi's Error in respect to It.—The Seat of the Inca.—Curiously carved Stones.
—Rock Seats.—Chingana, or the Labyrinth.—Contrasts between Sacsahuaman
and the so-called Fortress at Tiahuanaco.—Date of the Construction of Sacsahuaman.—Modern Cuzco mostly built of its Materials.—Lamentation of a Descendant of the Incas over its Destruction.—Treasure-hunters and their Traditions.—
Legend of Doña María de Esquivel.

THE capital of the Inca empire was not defended by walls,
such as protected some of the ancient Inca cities. Its valley,
surrounded by high mountains, was, in itself, naturally almost
impregnable, and the approaches to it were covered by fortifications. But the city, nevertheless, had its citadel or fortress,
dominating it as the Acropolis did Athens, Ehrenbreitstein the
villages at its foot, the Castle Edinburgh, and "the Rock"
Gibraltar. It was built upon the bold headland projecting into
the valley of Cuzco between the rivulets Huatenay and Rodadero, looking from below like a high abrupt hill, but being really
only the spur of a shelf or plateau, somewhat irregular in surface, which in turn is commanded by higher hills, or apparent
hills or mountains, themselves the escarpments of remoter natural terraces or *puna* lands. This headland is called *Los Altos
del Sacsahuaman*, the latter being a compound word signifying
"Fill thee, falcon!" or, "Gorge thyself, hawk!" Thus metaphorically did the Incas glorify the strength of their fortress.
"Dash thyself against its rocky and impregnable sides, if thou

wilt; the hawks will gather up thy fragments!" Vainglorious
and proud were those ancients, as the nations who to-day call
their war-vessels the *Invincible*, the *Devastation*, and the *Scourge*.

On the side of the city the eminence of the Sacsahuaman
presents a steep front, difficult and almost impossible of ascent.
Up this front, and from the terraces of the Colcompata, led anciently, as now, a zigzag road, ascending in places by stone steps
to a series of terraces on the most projecting and commanding
portion of the headland.
On the uppermost of
these, most conspicuous
of all objects around Cuzco, on the site of an an-
cient building of which
only a part of the foundations remains, stand three
crosses: the Calvario of
the city. These crosses
are 764 feet above the
level of the Huacapata, or
modern plaza.

The usual ascent to the
Sacsahuaman, and which
is practicable by horses, is
through the gorge or ra-
vine of the Rodadero, to
the right of the eminence,
where a road is partly cut

AQUEDUCT OVER THE RODADERO.

out of the hill and partly built up against it—a cliff on one side,
and a precipice on the other. At the bottom of the ravine the
little Rodadero chafes and murmurs; here leaping, a miniature
cataract, from one shelf to another, and there gathering in dark,
shaded, bubble-covered pools, as if recovering courage for another plunge. In ascending the Sacsahuaman we will start
from the foot of the street of El Triunfo, where it rests on
the rivulet Rodadero, or Tullamayo, and then turn to the left.
Leaving the cyclopean terrace of the Inca Rocca behind us,

we pass in front of the Yachahuasi, or school, erected by that patron of learning. It seems to have been a vast building, or series of buildings, several hundred feet in length, with walls of relatively small but perfectly fitting stones, which enter largely into the modern structures. After passing a few blocks we come to the gorge of the Rodadero, where it is traversed by

a modern aqueduct built on arches, between an abutment of rock on one side and of ancient Inca work on the other — a picturesque and pleasing object.

A short, sharp scramble, and we reach one of the lower terraces of the Colcompata, and the road proper to the Sacsahuaman. We pass in succession the upper and lower falls of the Rodadero, which mingle the tinkle and murmur of their waters with the gurgle of the *acequias* that flow in invisible channels above our heads. We must stop frequently in open spaces left for the purpose, either to recover breath or permit our animals to do so, as

LOWER FALL OF THE RODADERO.

well as to allow the troops of llamas, led by their silent owners down the rugged pathway, to pass us. At one point we discover what appears to be a well or square shaft, walled in with cut stones, fourteen feet deep. The wall on the inner side, or that lying next the slope, is also sloping, as if to facilitate the passage of water. The bottom of the shaft is filled with rubbish, and without excavation it is impossible to say whither it leads. It is probably part of one of the subterranean aqueducts through which the Incas conducted water into their capital from distant and often unknown sources.

As we ascend, we observe, high up above us on our left, long lines of walls, which are the faces of the eastern terraces of the fortress. These become heavier as we advance until, when we

finally reach the level of the plateau, up the rugged front of which we have been struggling, they cease to be simply retaining-walls, and rise in massive, independent walls composed of great blocks of limestone. A gate-way, flanked by heavy stones, opens on our left, and we stop while a drove of llamas defile through it. Stone steps formerly existed by which to ascend to the higher grounds within, but they have been broken away, although their traces remain. It was in attempting to force this gate-way, in the last desperate encounter between the Spaniards and the Incas, that Juan Pizar-

UPPER FALL OF THE RODADERO.

ro, the brother of the conqueror, was killed. Passing through this gate-way—the ancient *Tiupuncu,* or "Gate of Sand"—and through the main outer walls of the fortress, we find ourselves in a little open plain, or pampa. On our right we notice a considerable eminence of rock of singular aspect, called El Rodadero, and on the other hand we have our first view of the great cyclopean walls of the Fortress of the Sacsahuaman—the most

PART OF INCA AQUEDUCT.

massive among monuments of similar character, either in the Old or the New World.

Before attempting to describe this vast structure, I should explain that the mass of the headland on which the fortress stands is a metamorphic rock, disintegrating, hard in parts and soft in others, thrust up by igneous action from below, and bearing on its surface huge fragments of limestone from adjacent cliffs of that material—a tumultuous piece of natural workmanship which it would require an accomplished geologist to classify and explain. This headland is highest where it overlooks the city, and behind it is the area or pampa to which I have alluded, perhaps a hundred feet lower than its loftiest point; an area unquestionably much levelled by art, and now smooth as a prairie. Beyond this, and about three hundred feet distant, is the swell of amphibolic rock called the Rodadero, to which I have also alluded, and of which I shall have occasion to speak farther on.

Before going on, let us see what the chroniclers have to say concerning the work within which we are now standing. It elicited from them an admiration scarcely less extravagant than was bestowed on the Temple of the Sun. Garcilasso de la Vega says:

"This was the greatest and most superb of the edifices that the Incas raised to demonstrate their majesty and power. Its greatness is incredible to those who have not seen it; and those who have seen it, and studied it with attention, will be led not alone to imagine, but to believe, that it was reared by enchantment—by demons, and not by men, because of the number and

size of the stones placed in the three walls, which are rather
cliffs than walls, and which it is impossible to believe were cut
out of quarries, since the Indians had neither iron nor steel
wherewith to extract or shape them.   And how they were
brought together is a thing equally wonderful, since the Indians
had neither carts nor oxen nor ropes wherewith to drag them
by main force.   Nor were there level roads over which to transport them, but, on the contrary, steep mountains and abrupt
declivities, to be overcome by the simple force of men.   Many
of the stones were brought from ten to fifteen leagues, and especially the stone, or rather the rock, called Saycusca, or the
'Tired Stone,' because it never reached the structure, and which
it is known was brought a distance of fifteen leagues, from beyond the river of Yucay, which is little less in size than the Gua-
dalquivir at Cordova.   The stones obtained nearest were from
Muyna, five leagues from Cuzco.   It passes the power of imagination to conceive how so many and so great stones could be so accurately fitted together as scarcely to admit the insertion of the
point of a knife between them.   Many are indeed so well fitted
that the joint can hardly be discovered.   And all this is the
more wonderful as they had no squares or levels to place on
the stones and ascertain if they would fit together.   How often
must they have taken up and put down the stones to ascertain
if the joints were perfect !   Nor had they cranes, or pulleys, or
other machinery whatever..... But what is most marvellous
of the edifice is the incredible size of the stones, and the astonishing labor of bringing them together and placing them."

Here Garcilasso proceeds to quote Acosta, "because he had
not received such clear and exact measurements of the stones of
the Fortress of Cuzco as he had asked for."   Acosta says that
he measured stones in Tiahuanaco "30 feet long, 18 broad, and
6 thick;" but that in the Fortress of Cuzco are others much
larger, "and much to be admired, because, although irregular
in size and shape, they were, nevertheless, perfectly joined, each
stone fitting into the other as if made for the place."

The outline of the eminence of the Sacsahuaman, on the side
towards the rocks of the Rodadero, is rather concave than oth-

erwise, and it is along this face that the heaviest works of the fortress were built. They remain substantially perfect, and will remain so—unless disturbed by a violence which is not to be anticipated, and of which the present inhabitants of Cuzco hardly seem capable — as long as the Pyramids shall last, or Stonehenge and the Colosseum shall endure, for it is only with those works that the Fortress of the Sacsahuaman can be properly compared.

The defences consist, on this side, of three lines of massive walls, each supporting a terrace and parapet. The walls are nearly parallel, and have approximately accurate entering and reëntering angles for their total existing length of 1800 feet.

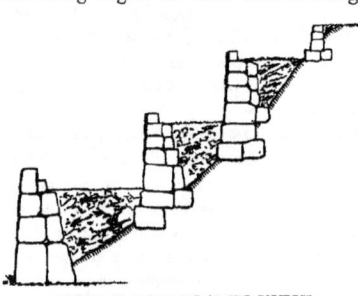

SECTION OF THE WALLS OF THE FORTRESS.

The first, or outer, wall has an average present height of 27 feet; the second wall is 35 feet within it, and is 18 feet high; the third is 18 feet within the second, and is, in its highest part, 14 feet in elevation. The total elevation of the works is therefore 59 feet. I am now speaking strictly of the walls on the northern front of the fortress. Long lines of wall extend along the heights dominating the gorge of the rivulet Rodadero; and there are sections of walls, besides those of the terraces of the Calvario, on the brow of the hill on the side of the city. As these were constructed of regularly squared stones, they have been almost wholly destroyed, the stones having been rolled down the eminence to enter into the walls of the numerous churches and convents of the modern town.

The remarkable feature of the walls of the fortress, on its only assailable side, is the conformation with modern defensive structures in the employment of salients, so that the entire face

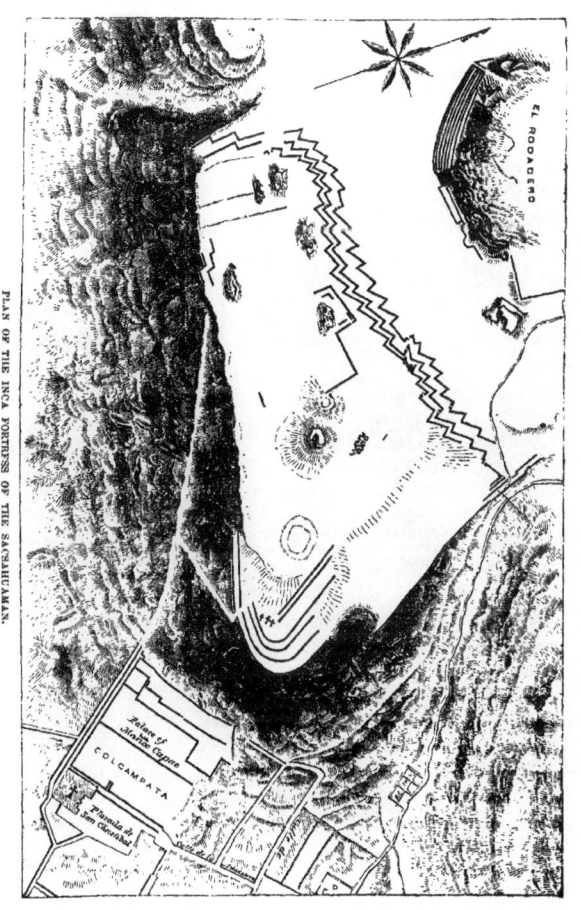

PLAN OF THE INCA FORTRESS OF THE SACSAHUAMAN.

EL RODADERO

Palace of Manco Capac

COLCAMPATA

Parroquia de San Christobal

of the walls could be covered by a parallel fire from the weapons of the defenders. This feature is not the result in any degree of the conformation of the ground, but of a clearly settled plan. The stones composing the walls are massive blocks of blue limestone, irregular in size and shape, and the work is altogether without doubt the grandest specimen of the style called cyclopean extant in America. The outer wall, as I have said, is heaviest. Each salient terminates in an immense block of

SALIENT ANGLE OF THE FORTRESS.

stone, sometimes as high as the level of the terrace which it supports, but generally sustaining one or more great stones only less in size than itself. One of these stones is 27 feet high, 14 broad, and 12 in thickness. Stones of 15 feet length, 12 in width, and 10 in thickness, are common in the outer walls. They are all slightly bevelled on the face, and near the joints chamfered down sharply to the contiguous faces. The joints—what with the lapse of time, and under the effects of violence, earthquakes, and the weather—are not now, if they ever were, so perfect as represented by the chroniclers. They are, nevertheless, wonderfully close, and cut with a precision rarely seen in modern fortifications. The inner walls are composed of smaller and more regular stones, and are less impressive.

Each wall supports a terrace or platform, filled in, as we discovered in the excavations made by treasure-seekers, with large, rough stones and the chippings of those composing the walls. The summit of each wall rose originally from six to eight feet above the level of the terrace, forming a parapet with an interior bench or step whereon the defenders might mount to discharge their missiles against assailants. To prevent accumulations of water behind the walls, the builders cut small drains or conduits through the stones at every second angle near the base of the structure—a common feature in all their terrace and retaining walls. The inner or reëntering angles were not wholly formed by the junction or placing-together of blocks of stone. Here, too, the device common in many of their more regular structures was adopted, of chiselling the angle in the stone so that one end of the block should enter on the face of the next salient, thus "binding" the corner. It is impossible to conceive the variety of shapes of the stones, especially of those of the outer wall, which, as Garcilasso says, "is composed of rocks rather than of stones." In some cases two immense stones, from fourteen to fifteen feet high and ten to twelve broad, will be found placed only one and a half or two feet apart, with a thin slab of corresponding height cut to fit accurately between them. In other cases the upper part of a stone will be concave, and the lower a sharp angle, but each surface matching that which it adjoins.

The extremities of these heavy walls have been much destroyed; but there is evidence that there were entrances or passages at each end, as well as three gate-ways in the main front. The chroniclers speak only of three, called, respectively, Tiupuncu, "the Gate of Sand;" Acahuana-puncu, "the Gate of Acahuana," who was one of the engineers employed in the construction of the work; and the third, Viracocha-puncu, "the

Gate of Viracocha." The main entrance was rather to the
left of the centre of the line of walls, where one salient was
omitted, so as to leave a rectangular space, 63 feet long by 25
broad. In the centre of the left-hand end of this space, between two blocks of stone, the outer one forming the angle
being 15 feet long, 9 feet thick, and 12 high, was left an
opening 4 feet wide. Steps led through this opening to the
level of the inner terrace, the passage being lined with heavy
stones. The chroniclers affirm that these openings, in times of
danger, were closed by great blocks of stone, which are yet to
be found near some of them, and for the reception of which
one step was omitted on the inner side of the wall. The entrance through the second wall at this point is more intricate,
and opens against a transverse wall, where the steps turn at
right angles, and thus reach the second terrace. The third wall
has two entrances, one plain, like that through the first, and the
second corresponding with that through the intermediate wall.
The lesser entrances to the right and left of the principal ones
just described are simple openings, occurring not opposite each
other, but in the alternating salients. The easternmost gate-
way of all, through the parallel walls running at right angles
to the general line of fortifications, is very nearly perfect, and
shows the stairway very clearly. It has ten steps, each 10 inches
high and 12 inches broad.

The ground within the walls rises to a further elevation of
about sixty feet, and is rocky. Several masses of metamorphic
rock and limestone project above the soil or are scattered over it.
In one of these a cavern forty feet deep has been excavated, and
others are cut into steps and seats. Here are fragments of the
foundations of considerable structures, of regularly cut stones,
but of which the plans cannot now be made out. These are
probably the remnants of what the chroniclers describe as three
small fortresses, or citadels, within the greater work. Two of
these are said to have been square and one round. The latter
was the largest and in the centre, and was called Muyuc-Marca,
or "Round Building," and was designed to receive the Inca and
his family in case of danger, together with the wealth of his

palaces and the treasures of the Sun.  It is said to have been
rich in decoration, and lined with gold and silver.  This is also
said to have communicated by subterranean passages with the
two square towers, destined for the reception of the garrison
of the fortress, and with the royal palaces and the Temple of
the Sun.  I can credit the former part of the statement, for
there are remains of such passages; but that any of these descended, as they must have done, almost vertically for seven
hundred and sixty-four feet, and then horizontally into the city,
is a presumption altogether improbable.

Prescott has given the name of "the Fortress" to the three
towers or citadels, and mistakes in supposing that there were
but two lines of walls protecting approach to them from the
side opposite the city.  This is the more surprising, as Garcilasso and others distinctly state that there were three walls, and
that these constituted "the Fortress," which they regarded as
the eighth wonder of the world.  As I have said, it was in a
desperate attempt to recover this fortress from the revolted
Indians that Juan Pizarro was mortally wounded; and it was
from the battlements of the Muyuc-Marca that the Inca commander hurled himself to the ground when the issue of battle was decided against him.  His was the last blow struck in
behalf of the Inca power.

The stones composing the Fortress of the Sacsahuaman are
limestone, and masses of the same still lie within the walls of
the fortress, and are scattered over the plateau behind it.  That
some of these in the wall were taken from their natural positions near the place where they now stand is most probable;
but that others were brought from the limestone cliffs that edge
the plateau, three-fourths of a mile to a mile distant, is certain.
Two distinct, well-graded roads still remain leading to these
ledges, where the evidences of quarrying are as clear as they
are at Quincy, in Massachusetts.  The rock is the cliff limestone, evidently considerably changed and fissured by igneous
action, splitting off in great, irregular blocks, in turn much
seamed and furrowed by the elements.  The earth and débris
were excavated away beneath these; and when they fell by

their own gravity, they were partly hewn on the spot, dragged
to the fortress, and there fitted. Blocks half hewn still lie in
the quarries, and some in nearly perfect condition by the side
of the roads to which I have referred. How they were thus
dragged we can only infer from the undoubted fact that the
Incas had no draught animals. They must, therefore, have been
moved by combined human force on rollers of wood or stone,
and forced up inclined planes to the positions they were to occupy. If the force of a thousand men was insufficient to move
them, it was quite within the power of the Incas to bring ten
times that number to the task. The Incas, Garcilasso to the
contrary notwithstanding, had both ropes and cables, and I have
seen nothing in the size of the stones here or elsewhere not
amenable to the power of numbers. It is not to be supposed
for an instant that limestone masses should be brought from beyond the Yucay, fifteen leagues distant, when precisely the same
stone was to be had near at hand in inexhaustible quantities.

The great *Piedra Cansada* ("Tired Stone"), or Sayacusca, of
which Garcilasso and others speak as having occupied 20,000
men in moving it, and which, rolling over, killed 300 workmen,
is an enormous mass of a thousand tons or more, and certainly
was never moved ever so slightly by human power. Its top,
like the tops of hundreds of other rocks on the plateau of the
Rodadero, is cut into what appear to be seats and reservoirs
of every shape; its sides are cut into niches and stairways—the
whole a maze of incomprehensible sculpture and of apparently
idle although elaborate workmanship. The largest stone in the
fortress has a computed weight of 361 tons.

Water was conducted into the fortress by *azequias* from the
Rodadero, and from streams falling into the Huatenay, high up
towards its sources. The channels of these *azequias* are in
part subterranean, and the origin of the water flowing through
some of them is unknown. Two of the national engineers
were employed for several days during my stay in Cuzco in
trying to find where one of these channels had been obstructed
or tapped by some Indian having traditionary knowledge of its
course, but without result.

Three hundred feet in front of the fortress is the dome-shaped mass of trachytic rock, the Rodadero—which, on the side towards the fortress, was faced up in terraces with large and beautifully cut stones, which have been removed and rolled down into the city. This rock is also called *La Piedra Lisa*, inasmuch as its convex surface is grooved, as if the rock had been squeezed up in a plastic state between irregular and un-yielding walls, and then hardened into shape with a smooth and glassy surface. A mass of dough forced up under the outspread hands would give something of the same appearance in min-iature. It is said that the Inca youth amused themselves in coursing through these polished grooves on festival days—a custom which the youth of Cuzco have not allowed to fall into disuse. And here I may allude to a very comical mistake into which Rivero and Von Tschudi, together with their translators, have fallen regarding this rock. Misled by the designation "Rodadero," they have described this eminence, which is more than half a mile in circumference and at least eighty feet high, as follows: "A short distance from the fortress is a large piece of amphibolic rock, known by the name of the Smooth Rolling Stone, which served, and still serves, for diversion to the in-habitants, by rolling like a garden-roller, having a sort of hollow formed in the middle through friction!"

On the very summit of the rock of the Rodadero there are a series of broad seats, rising one above the other in front and laterally, like a stairway, cut with unsurpassable precision in the hard rock. This is called "The Seat of the Inca;" and tradi-tion relates that it was here the Incas came at intervals, through three reigns, to watch the progress of constructing the fortress. There are other smaller seats lower down, which, the same au-thority relates, were occupied by the attendants on the Inca.

As I have said, the rocks all over the plateau back of the fortress, chiefly limestone, are cut and carved in a thousand forms. Here is a niche, or a series of them; anon a broad seat like a sofa, or a series of small seats; next a flight of steps; then a cluster of square, round, and octagonal basins; long lines of grooves; occasional holes drilled down to reservoirs in some

PART OF THE FORTRESS OF THE SACSAHUAMAN, FROM "THE SEAT OF THE INCA."

fissure in the rock, widened artificially into a chamber—and all
these cut with the accuracy and finish of the most skilful work-
er in marble.   In one or two instances these rocks had walls of
.cut stones built up around or in part against them, and have
traces of small edifices on their summits, conveying the impression that they were shrines, from within the hollowed chambers
of which the wily priest
uttered oracles in response
to offerings of chicha or
maize.

One part of a low lime-
stone cliff, not far from
the Rodadero, is called the
*Chingana*, or " Labyrinth,"
and it well deserves the
name.  It is much fissured
naturally.   These fissures
have been enlarged by art,
and new passages opened,
with low corridors, small
apartments, niches, seats,
etc., forming a maze in
which it requires great care
not to be entangled and
lost.   The interior and remoter ramifications cannot
now be followed, since General San Roman, when Pre-
fect of Cuzco, had some of
the passages walled up, in

NICHE IN TERRACE WALLS OF THE COLCOMPATA.

consequence of the recurrence of accidents—the last accident
happening to three boys, who were lost and starved to death in
the recesses of the Chingana.   There is a story current of two
students who, many years ago, undertook the exploration of the
Chingana, and followed its passage until they found themselves
beneath the Temple of the Sun, and could distinctly hear the
chanting of mass in the Church of Santo Domingo, which occu-

cupies its site. "All of which," in the phrase with which committees end their reports, "is respectfully submitted."

I have thus described, as it is, the great fortress of the Sacsahuaman from the modern stand-point. It is a mistake of our old chronicler, Garcilasso, that the fortress could not be commanded even by artillery. It is commanded in great part by the Rodadero at short musket-shot; and from the heights of Cantutpata, on the left of the rivulet Rodadero, it is completely commanded by the lightest artillery, and a portion of it by arrows. Still, it was no doubt an impregnable fortress, under the system of warfare practised in ancient times, when slings and arrows were the longest-reaching of offensive arms.

ROCK SEATS, NEAR FORTRESS.

I have alluded to the tradition preserved by the chroniclers, that the structure called "the Fortress" at Tiahuanaco was the model on which the Fortress of the Sacsahuaman was constructed. It is very clear that the slopes of the former were supported by three at least, perhaps more, retaining-walls, each with a terrace between, and each, perhaps, terminating in a parapet. But there the resemblance ceases. The walls of one were in right lines; those of the other were broken into salients. One was regular in shape; the defences of the other coincided with the formation of the ground. One occupied a strong strategic position, and was a true fortress, while the other commanded nothing, and could, at best, be only a temporary refuge.

The old authors differ as to the date of the construction of the Fortress of Cuzco. Garcilasso assigns it principally to Yupanqui, the tenth Inca, who came to power about the year 1400, and reigned thirty-nine years. He says that Pachacutic, ninth Inca, and father of Yupanqui, conceived the design, and left the plan, with a great quantity of the stones prepared for building it; but that it was not finished until during the reign of Huayna Capac, the father of Atahualpa and Huascar, and but a short time before the arrival of the Spaniards. We can sympathize with the lament of the old descendant of the Incas, who writes thus:

"The Spaniards, flushed with their victories, might well have spared this fortress, and kept it up for their own glory, to show to future generations the grandeur of their own achievements, and make their deeds eternal. But, instead of this, they deliberately destroyed it, to save the cost of cutting stones for their buildings, and tumbled down all the squared stones into the city, so that there is not a house in it that is not built of them, or from other superb monuments of the Incas. So that this majestic structure was almost ruined, to the eternal grief of those who may hereafter look upon its sad remains. The three walls of rock the Spaniards left standing because they could not throw them down; but they have, nevertheless, injured a part of these in vain search for the golden chain of Huayna Capac, which some supposed to have been buried here."

Three hundred years have not sufficed to eradicate the notion that enormous treasures are concealed within the fortress; nor have three hundred years of excavation, more or less constant, entirely discouraged the searchers for *tapadas*. In making our surveys of the fortress and of the Rodadero, often have we found, upon returning to our work in the mornings, the ground deeply excavated overnight where we had planted our little peg to determine the limit of our day's survey, and as a guide for resumption of our work.

I doubt if, among all the people, high and low, whom I met in the Sierra, half a dozen could be found who, when questioned apart, would not testify to a belief that the investigation of ancient monuments was rather a clumsy pretext under which to carry on search for the chain of Huayna Capac or some other *tapada* of equal value. I presume there are not a few who would take a distinct oath that my rather precipitate retreat to the coast, when the rains began to fall, was the immediate

consequence of having been successful in my search; and it
is not impossible that the stones that were rolled down on us
in the defiles of Andahuaylas were intended to create a confusion, wherein the mules laden with supposed Inca treasure
could be "stampeded," and the strangers and heretics spoiled.
What a disappointment it would have been to the evil-minded
assailants if they had succeeded in obtaining the coveted pack-
ages, only to find them filled with skulls and all uncleanness!

In a manuscript in the British Museum, a copy of which is in
my possession, I find recorded a curious story touching the supposed treasures of the Sacsahuaman, told by Felipe de Pomanes,
who says:

"It is a well-known and acknowledged thing that in this
Fortress of Cuzco there is a secret vault, in which is a vast
treasure, since there were placed in it all the statues of the
Incas, wrought in gold.  And there is living to-day a lady who
has been in this vault, named Doña María de Esquivel, wife of
the last Inca, and whom I have heard describe how she came to
go there, and what she saw there.  It was thus: This lady had
married Don Carlos Inca, who had not the means to keep up
the state of the great personage that he really was, and the
Doña María neglected him [the chronicler says something
worse], because she had been deceived into marrying a poor
Indian under the pretence that he was a great lord and Inca;
and she so often repeated this reproach that Don Carlos one
night said to her: 'Do you wish to know if I am the miserable
pauper and wretch you accuse me of being?  Do you wish to
know if I am poor or rich?  If so, come with me, and you shall
see that I possess more wealth than any lord or king in the universe.'  And Doña María, overcome by curiosity, consented to
have her eyes bandaged — so unlike a woman — and to follow
her indignant lord, who led her a number of turns, and then
took her hand and conducted her down into a room, when he
removed the bandage from her eyes, and she saw herself surrounded by unbounded treasures.  In niches in the walls were
many statues of all the Incas, as large as youths of twelve years
old, all of finest gold, besides numberless vases of gold and sil-

ver, and blocks of the same, and altogether a wealth that convinced the lady that here was the grandest treasure of the world."

How she behaved to her lord afterwards the chronicler does not tell us; and as to whether she wheedled Don Carlos Inca out of a statue of his fathers, or a block of gold, we are unfortunately left in ignorance. But the chronicler does say that it is not to be presumed that an author of such judgment and character as Felipe de Pomanes would tell an untruth, even if it were possible that a lady of the character and known virtue of Doña María de Esquivel could be guilty of such a thing.

All I can say is, that if the secret chamber that she entered has not yet been found and despoiled, it has not been for default of digging, for I doubt if a foot of the soil of the Sacsahuaman has escaped being turned a dozen times over. Men were constantly busy there during the whole time of our stay. Perhaps our visit gave a new impulse to money-digging, or treasure-hunting, which, if called on to say, I should declare to be the principal occupation of the people of Peru. The time, labor, and money that have been spent in digging and dismantling ancient edifices would have built a railway from one end of the country to the other, given wharves to the ports, and, what is far more needed, sewers to the cities.

# CHAPTER XXIV.

### THE VALLEY OF YUCAY.—OLLANTAYTAMBO.

THE valley of Yucay, probably the most beautiful in Peru, is formed by the river Vilcanota, which we saw trickling from the dark tarn of La Raya, now swollen into a large stream, bearing the names, according to locality, of Vilcamayo, Urubamba, and Yucay; it is truly the Ucayali, and the parent stream of the Amazon. The valley is separated from the bolson of Cuzco by a high, irregular table-land, or *puna*, a hard day's journey across, although the distance in a right line can hardly exceed twenty miles. The Incas had two roads over this high, bleak ridge; one leading direct from Cuzco to Yucay, with the intermediate establishment of Chinchero, where they had a palace; and the other more circuitous, by way of the plain of Chita, where the young Inca, Viracocha, chafed in exile, watching the flocks of his irate father, until the Brother of the Sun called him to victory and power. The roads, of which fragments remain, were formed of rough stones set in the ground, and were raised in the centre, with a row of larger stones set on edge on each side, through which at intervals there was an opening to pass off the water. The road was supported by terrace-walls of cut stone in some places, where, zigzagging up declivities, it evinces in plan and execution capable design and much skill.

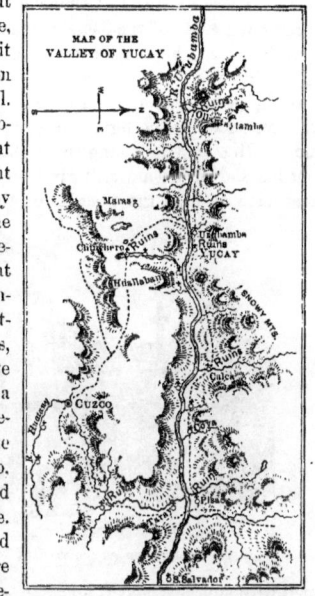

In Chinchero are very elaborate remains. The present plaza of the town is an ancient square, flanked on one side by a terrace, supported by the most beautiful and elaborately niched retaining-wall that I saw in Peru, several hundred feet long. The structures, probably Inca palaces, built on this terrace have mainly disappeared, but a portion of the walls, corresponding with those of the Temple of the Sun in Cuzco, still form part of the vast and quaint church of the village. The ancient edifices stood back a little from the edge of the terrace, which is remarkable, but by no means peculiar, in being crowned with a cornice or coping of large stones. The terrace is 12 feet high: most of the niches 7 feet high by 3 feet 10 inches wide at bottom, 3 feet 3 inches at top, and 2 feet 7 inches deep. Some years ago, a portion of this fine terrace wall was torn down, and excavations made behind it by seekers for *tapadas;* and I must stop to applaud the deed of the then prefect of the department. Señor Guarmendia, who obliged the iconoclasts to replace the work they had destroyed. The restoration is shabby, for the wretches were unable to put together the

stones they had torn apart, so much easier is it to destroy than
to build up.

In the neighborhood of Chinchero are great sculptured rocks
resembling those of the Sacsahuaman, but if possible more elaborately cut and quite as enigmatical.  The most interesting one
is of limestone, cut in gradients, and with a bold projection,
like the pedestal of a statue, on which, sculptured in relief from
the same rock, is the figure of a puma or tiger reclining on its
side, with one of its young in its embrace, as if suckling.  The
outline and action are well given, but the finer details are lost, `
inasmuch as it is the practice of the youth of the village to

COPED AND NICHED TERRACE WALLS, CHINCHERO.

pelt with stones *el gato de los gentiles* (" the cat of the gentiles ").
The work probably suffered greatly from the hands of the early
priests.

Two leagues beyond Chinchero we come to the abrupt edge
of the table-land on which it stands, and look almost sheer down
on the valley of Yucay, four thousand feet below.  Here the
traveller pauses instinctively, for the view before him is unsurpassed for beauty or grandeur by any on which his eyes have
rested.  In front rises that gigantic spur of the Andes which
separates the valleys of the Vilcamayo and Paucartambo, with
rugged escarpments of bare rock, lofty snowy peaks, and silvery

glaciers, sharp, bright, and distinct, except when the clouds surge up its eastern side, to dissolve and disappear in flurries of snow on its summit. The great peaks of Chicon, Huacahuasi, and Calca tower up with a majesty scarcely second to that of the mighty Sorata, and with the abruptness of the Alpine Jungfrau, Eiger, and Matterhorn. The glaciers that lie between them have a sweep, as compared with those of the Alps, like that of a Western prairie as compared with a meadow valley of New England.

From the glittering crests of these vast mountains the eye ranges down, through every graduation of color and depth of shadow, past cleft and cliff, ravine and precipice, until it rests on

SECTION OF TERRACE OF CHINCHERO.

the graceful *andenes*, or terraces, of the far-famed Gardens of Yucay. These sweep in curves around the feet of mountains, or project into the narrow valley through which steals the Rio Vilcamayo, in every combination of geometrical outline. Though now midwinter, and the crops are gathered in, yet the valley is gay with clumps of trees, gardens, and green hedge-rows, which define the outlines of fields laid out by the Incas themselves, and with that regularity which distinguishes all the works of their hands. Although only about two thousand five hundred feet lower than the bolson of Cuzco, the valley of Yucay, sheltered on every side, enjoys a climate much milder, corresponding very closely with that of Nismes and of other parts of the South of France.

Equally salubrious and fertile, easily accessible from the capital, and with a vegetation exceptional in the Sierra, this sweet, calm valley, framed in by the loftiest mountains of the continent, became early the favorite resort of the Incas. Here they constructed those marvellous hanging-gardens which, while they astonish by their extent, and charm with their beauty, bear constant witness to the skill and the taste of their builders. Here, too, they built their palaces, and on every pass leading to their retreat they raised immense and impregnable fortresses. Borne

hither in their golden palanquins, with a ceremony and pomp
becoming the heads of a vast empire, surrounded by followers
who revered them as embodying the power of the State and
the majesty and sanctity of Religion, the Incas must often have
paused on the heights of Chinchero to gaze with awe and admiration on the grand panorama that here opened before them,
and which the pencil may faintly portray, but which the pen
cannot adequately describe. Before them were the mighty
mountain barriers they never could pass; at their feet the smiling valley of which their poets were never weary of singing,
filled with the enduring works of their hands, and bright beneath the clear rays of the parent Sun. Under the inspiration
of scenes like these, and in constant contact with Nature in her
grandest forms, it would have been wonderful indeed if the
Incas had not risen to conceptions higher and ideas more ex-
panded than those of the dwellers in the gloom of the dense
forests and among the jungles of the Amazon, where the sun
only penetrates to quicken deadly vapors, and where life is a
vain warfare against an unconquerable vegetation, fierce animals, venomous reptiles, and insects scarcely less poisonous.

I fear that I have dwelt too long on the Gardens of the
Inca, since I feel that I have failed to convey any adequate notion of their beauty, or of the art and taste displayed in their
construction. Among the profoundest regrets connected with
my journey through Peru, is that I failed to obtain photographs
of the lovely valley of Yucay and its wonderful *andenes* from
the heights of Chinchero. The rains set in before we could
complete our explorations, and we were obliged to retreat without securing the form and features of many objects of interest
and beauty.

The descent from the *altos* of Chinchero into the valley is
long, laborious, and dangerous. Fragments of the zigzag road
of the Incas still remain, supported by heavy walls of masonry,
broad enough for six persons to pass abreast, and of easy gradients. Although its careful preservation would seem to have
been dictated by the commonest prudence—for there are few
points where the escarpment of the plateau can be overcome—

yet this artfully constructed road has been allowed to fall into utter ruin by the wretched successors of the provident Incas.

What at once arrests the attention of the visitor to the valley of Yucay is the vast system of terraces that lines it on both sides, wherever the conformation of the ground admits of their construction, and of which the so-called *andenes*, or Gardens of the Inca, form part. These terraces, rising from the broader ones at the edge of the level grounds, climb the circumscribing mountains to the height of from one thousand to one thousand five hundred feet, narrowing as they rise, until the topmost ones are scarcely two feet broad. The terrace-walls are of rough stones, well laid, slightly inclining inwards, and varying in height from three to fifteen feet. Very often an *azequia*, or artificial aqueduct, starting high up some narrow ravine, at the very verge of the snow, is carried along the mountain-sides, above or through the *andenes*, from which water is taken for irrigation, running from one terrace to the next, and carefully distributed over all. Access from one terrace to another is variously effected; sometimes by zigzag paths, sometimes by regular stairs, but oftenest through the device to which I have had occasion to refer, of projecting stones. This description will apply to the ordinary mountain terraces, of which the whole

TERRACE WALL AND AZEQUIA, YUCAY.

country is full, and which were built to retain the earth on the steep mountain and hill sides, which would otherwise be washed away.

The more elaborate *andenes* are built, as are those of Yucay, the most extensive, most regular, and most beautiful of all Peru. They are raised at the mouth of a gorge, which has a rapid fall from among the splintered summits of the Nevada of Calca, and which enters the valley at its widest part, and nearly at right angles to it. Through this leaps out from the rocky entrance to the mountains a bright, clear stream, fed from the drip of the impending glaciers and snowy peaks, which, in the course of ages, has brought down a great mass of débris, rock, and earth, that, until smoothed down and made symmetrical by the Incas, must have been a rude and disfiguring heap in the valley.

The first step seems to have been to confine the stream in a single channel, between walls of stone; next, to construct a series of semicircular terraces, supported by rude but durable walls, over which the stream leaps in a series of cataracts. As the declivity lessens, these terraces become broader, and the stream is diverted into several channels, each feeding a new series of terraces, falling off in front and flank of the central one in almost every possible combination, in outline, of the square and the circle; in gradients, like the Pyramids, and so artfully that the water from the stream is evenly distributed over them all, and then carried off to irrigate the wide wings that sweep in grand lines of beauty around the bases of the mountains up and down the valley. The central and most elevated series of terraces, which pushes out boldly in the plain, is made up chiefly of square areas, with flanking aprons, filled with richest soil, from which the stones have been carefully removed, and which nurtures that noblest of native cereals, the *maiz blanco*, or white maize of Yucay.

Upon one of these areas, with broad terraces on every side or circling away in graceful perspective, with the white glaciers of Calca impending behind, and the mural face of the plateau of Chinchero rising in front—high up among the *andenes*, where the eye commands long reaches of teeming valley and of the river, with its burnished pools and swirling rapids, surrounded by lofty pisote-trees, clothed in unfading green, and glowing like sunset with their orange-colored flowers, amidst baths and fountains and the murmur of falling waters—stood the Summer Palace of the Incas. Only a few sad remnants attest its site and intimate its finished architecture. The delicately cut stones of which it was built went early to construct the churches of the neighboring villages of Huaylabamba, Calca, Urquillos,

Urubamba, and the convents which the warrior priests of the Conquest were not slow to raise in the genial and fertile valley of Yucay. Every foot of ground is utilized; every part is artfully irrigated. The soil is rich, and the climate, notwithstanding the valley is shut in by lofty and snowy mountains, is mild and agreeable. A more beautiful spot than this does not smile among the rigors of the Andes.

I commenced my explorations in the valley from the town of Urubamba ("Plain of the Spider"), the capital of the district, which is entered over a lofty stone bridge of ninety feet span, and between two rows of gigantic willows. The town itself is like all other towns of the Sierra, but its position can hardly be surpassed in beauty—a beauty enhanced, to our eyes, by the reappearance of a verdure to which we had long been strangers. Apart from great willows and gigantic pisotes, we found other familiar varieties of trees. Hundreds of wild cherry-trees lined the roads, some in blossom and some in fruit, while peaches and apples, oranges and lemons, hung temptingly in the gardens. Our host, Señor Umeres, the sub-prefect of the district, was a very enterprising and intelligent man, who provided us with mules for our visit to Ollantaytambo, and a letter of recommendation to the *gobernador* of that frontier town, lying eight leagues distant, down the valley of the river.

The ride to this point is extremely varied and interesting, amidst scenery alternately grand and picturesque. At a distance of three leagues, the road running between stone-walls and rows of cherry and peach trees, and lined with rude stone-houses, we came to where a broad gorge opened between lofty mountains on our right. This gorge extends high up into a region of mist and snow, to a great glacier, or a series of glaciers, which appear to unite in it from different directions. A very considerable stream emerges from these, which, however, distributes itself into several channels over a vast mass of rocks and stones and gravel, with scrubby bushes interspersed, that has been swept or crowded down through the gorge, filling up the valley for miles, and pressing close on the river, where, owing to the wash of the stream, it presents a perpendicular face of indurated material at least two hundred feet high, cut into fantastic, castellated forms, like an aggregation of old Gothic cathedrals. To descend this escarpment was no easy matter, the path being both narrow and precipitous and full of rolling stones; and, when once down, the road was a ticklish one, between cliff and river.

VIEW IN THE VALLEY OF YUCAY FROM CORRIDOR OF THE HACIENDA UMERES.

Farther on, beyond this mass of débris, the valley widens out into a sort of marshy pampa, on the farther edge of which we discerned an ancient Inca edifice, connected with a series of extensive terraces and other complicated works, too much ruined to be intelligible. Immediately back of the structure, however, rises a high cliff, the face of which is full of ancient tombs; that is to say, of excavations, natural and artificial, in the rock, within which the dead were placed, and then walled up with stones, stuccoed over, and painted. Many of these seemed absolutely inaccessible, or to be reached only by ropes let down from above. We contrived, however, to clamber up to several of them, from which I obtained a number of interesting skulls. The fronts of some of the least protected tombs had fallen away, and the bones of their former inmates were scattered at the foot of the cliff, or lay in full view on the narrow shelves of rock.

ROCK TOMBS, OLLANTAYTAMBO.

Beyond this Golgotha the valley narrows again between bare cliffs from two to three thousand feet high, leaving just room enough for the roadway and river—the latter deep and swift, and of a bright-green color. Our view was limited to a strip of blue sky above, and to the snowy mountain of Chicon, which rose, white and sepulchral, directly in front, as if blocking up the valley and prohibiting further passage. Again the valley widened, and we rode through a forest of Spanish broom, which here becomes really arborescent, covered thickly with brilliantly yellow and oppressively fragrant flowers, among which darted a great variety of humming-birds, some of them as large as swallows. The mountains now fall farther back from the river, which becomes less rapid, and on the opposite or left bank the ground spreads out into broad meadows and cultivated grounds.

Descending through these, at right angles to the river, from a dark and rugged gorge, we noticed a considerable stream, the Rio Guarconda, draining the high bolson of Antis.    There is a rough and dangerous pathway through this gorge to the plain above, which the Incas protected by works of considerable extent at its mouth.    But their principal works were built farther down the stream, at a point where a low ridge extends nearly across the valley.    This ridge had been terraced up with high, vertical walls, rising from the very bed of the stream, on every side, to the height of nearly one hundred feet.    Held by any considerable body of men, it commanded completely the passage of the valley.    The river pours with arrow-like rapidity between these terraces and the rocky escarpment opposite, along the face of which runs the narrow and dizzy pathway over which all travellers to Ollantaytambo are obliged to pass.

From this point forward for a league, the valley is narrowed to a mere cleft between mountains rising in rugged masses, but with almost vertical fronts, to enormous elevations.    The brain reels, in straining to discern their splintered summits.    Dark and chill, this is one of the grand *portadas*, or mountain gateways, of the Andes, leading to the plains of the Amazon, of which the early chroniclers write with undissembled awe.    The river looks black and sinister in the subdued light, and its murmur subsides into a hollow roar.    The shrubs of broom become scant and small, and their flowers are few and mean.    In front rises forever the white, ghastly Chicon.    We hasten through this gloomy gorge as fast as our mules can travel, and rejoice when the valley again commences to spread out, and we can see patches of sunlight in the open space that invites us onwards.    Still the river presses us close to the mountain, at the base of which is a series of narrow, ruined *andenes*, while on the opposite bank of the river, again confined between heavy artificial walls, we notice a long building of two stories, with turrets and loop-holes, hanging against the mountain, and dominating a narrow pathway that runs between it and the rapid, compressed river.    It more resembles the castles of the Rhine and the Lower Rhone than anything we have yet seen, and

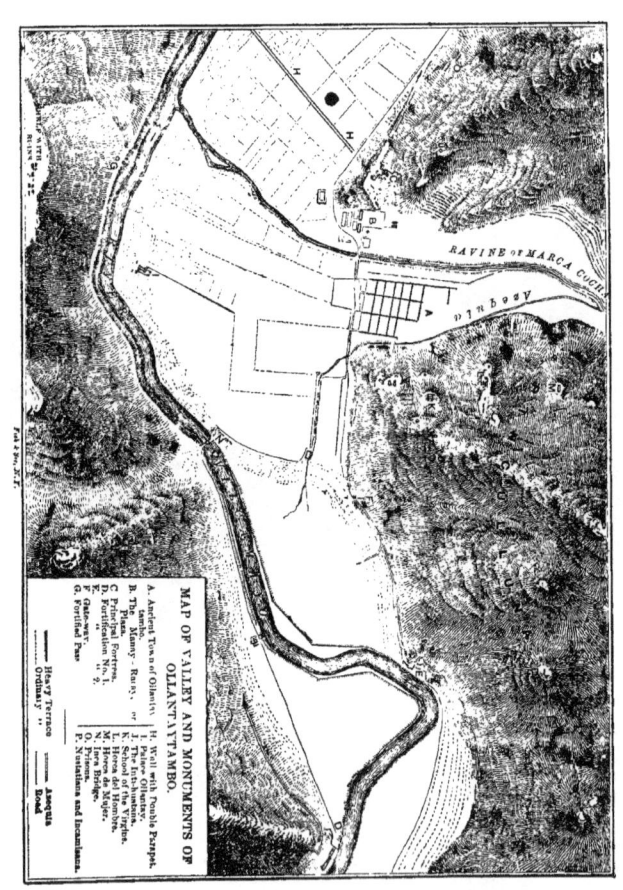

MAP OF VALLEY AND MONUMENTS OF
OLLANTAYTAMBO.

A. Ancient Town of Ollantay-    H. Wall with Double Parapet.
    tambo.                      I. Palace—Ollantay.
B. The Many-Rains.             J. The Inti-huatana.
C. Principal Fortress.         K. School of the Virgins.
D. Fortification No. 1.        L. Horca del Hombre.
E.       "        No. 2.       M. Horca de Mujer.
F. Gateway.                    N. Inca Bridge.
G. Fortified Pass.             O. Prison.
                               P. Nustallana and Incamisana.

——— Heavy Terrace        ——— Acequia
·········· Ordinary "     ——— Road

would be regarded as a most striking and picturesque object in any part of the world.

A little farther the mountains on our right send out a high spur of bare rock directly in front and across our path, deflecting the river across the valley, which now widens out in broad and beautiful intervals, as level as a table, in which we discover men with oxen ploughing. At the extremity of this rocky barrier, and between it and the wall against which the river frets

THE FORT, OLLANTAYTAMBO.

and swirls, is a narrow roadway, overshadowed by the cyclopean walls of another fortress or outwork, above which, perched on the cliffs, at every elevation, we see round towers of stone of varying sizes, with port-holes opening on our line of approach, and from which stones might be precipitated on our very heads. The roadway is partially blocked with the débris of one of these towers and many tons of the rock on which it once stood, all of which had fallen down during the heavy rains of the preceding summer. These rockslips are frequent among the Andes, sometimes rendering the so-called roads impassable, and occasionally damming up the rivers, when the water, setting back, forms deep, narrow lakes, until it breaks through all obstructions in a devastating flood below.

Passing around this salient outwork, our path ascends a series of terraces, underneath niched and crenated walls, until the upper terrace is reached, on which the road runs. An ancient *azequia* is high above on the rock's side, in which we hear the gurgle of invisible waters. Here, still clinging to the foot of the mountains, we look down past the *andenes* upon level fields, which in the proper season must afford a wealth of grain. But directly in front, extending, as before, transversely across the valleys and at right angles to our path, their edges defined by tall willows and flowering shrubs, with water leaping brightly in mimic cataracts from one to the other, we discover the famous terraces of Ollantaytambo.

Standing on the edge of the topmost, in strong relief, is a group of buildings which our guide points out as the house of the Governor of Ollantaytambo, to whom we are recommended. It was getting late; we were hungry, certainly, and tired withal; and we spurred our mules forward towards our resting-place. Soon we came to a massive crenated wall, pierced by two gate-ways with grooves in their piers, as if to receive a sliding portcullis, and flanked on the beetling ledges of the mountain by round, loop-holed towers, like those already mentioned. Beyond, the road led between two ancient stone buildings, still inhabited, which fill the space between the edge of the terrace and the cliffs, apparently designed as guard-houses, and between which the visitor to Ollantaytambo had to pass in the olden, as he has to do in the modern time. Past these the road continues between a high niched wall, on one hand, and the cliff with its gurgling *azequia*, on the other. Thus shut in betwixt wall and mountain, and our view circumscribed, we jog on for half a mile. Then the wall ends. A lane leads off to our left at right angles for a few hundred yards between stone-walls and hedges of flowering shrubs, when we come to a sort of shrine, in which is a crumbling cross covered with faded ribbons and withered

flowers.   Here we turn again, and again at right angles, and at
the end of another long lane, with an *azequia* running through
its centre, we discover the house or group of houses belonging
to the governor.   They are low and mean enough in reality,
but in the purple shadow of the mountains, over whose tops the
setting sun casts a crimson glow, they look a blissful haven of
rest.   Our mules pricked up their ears, and, with visions of in-

PRINCIPAL FORTRESS OF OLLANTAYTAMBO.

finite alfalfa before them, broke into a lively trot, carrying us
through the gate-way and into the paved court of the govern-
or's house with a spirited clang and clatter that made us feel
that we were *caballeros*, if not conquerors.

Señor Benavente, the governor, was a man of some wealth as
well as of consequence, hospitable and reasonably intelligent.
His house is built around a court, in which the horses are teth-

34

ered, the cattle fed, the pigs allowed to roam without restraint, in company with the dogs, the geese, the ducks, the chickens, and the little indigenous guinea-pigs that go squeaking in and

DOOR-WAY TO CORRIDOR, OLLANTAYTAMBO.

out every crevice in the walls. For the delight of all of these, the *aze-quia* runs through the centre of the court into a paved pool, whence it is conducted over the terraces to help irrigate the level lands below. From this pool the cattle drink; in it the pigs wallow, and the geese and ducks disport themselves. From it the water you drink and wash in is ladled up; in it the dishes you ate from are cleansed; and if, when the modest night drops its curtain, you peep through the cracks of your door, you may discern the servants of the establishment bathing in it. Not too often, however. But the water flows in rapidly at one extremity, and is discharged with equal rapidity at the other, and you take it for granted that it carries all impurities with it.

Señor Benavente gave us an apartment about twelve feet square, next to the close den in which the servants slept. It had the advantage of a small unglazed window under the eaves, and a door which would shut, and remain shut, if only braced with a stick from the inside. Dinner he served us in his own *sala*, which had a mud floor, an unsteady table, and a long bench whereon to sit. There was a hide bed in the corner, with saddles and bridles draped over it, improvised, the governor said, because the señora, his wife, whose suppressed moans we could hear through a thin partition of cotton cloth, was ill of fever.

I administered, after due solicitation : Blue pills, two at night ; grains of quinine, fifteen in the morning; chicken broth, light, in the interval. To be repeated daily. Cure complete in three days.

We had some difficulty in disposing our mattresses in our narrow quarters, when Señor Benavente came and shared our coffee and cognac. I inquired minutely about the antiquities, the fortress, the Tarpeian Rock, the great "Tired Stones," the quarries, the Inca Bridge, and about all the marvellous things

NICHED CORRIDOR, OLLANTAYTAMBO.

we had been told existed here, and about all of which the governor was much confused, and, as we thought, very ignorant. Finally, wearied by my questions, he said he had a book which explained every thing concerning *los reyes Incas,* which he would fetch. He did so. It was a translation of Prescott's "Peru."

We were up and out early ; and, although a little chill, the morning was clear and glorious. Not a ray of sunlight fell in the valley, but the clouds that clung to the summits of the high mountains rising on either hand were a mass of gold and crim-

son.   No light, however, seemed to touch the giant bulk of
Chicon, that still rose before us, as calm and pale as death, and
as remote as ever.   The mountains on all sides, as I have said,
are steep, even precipitous, but yet we discerned at elevations
of thousands of feet on their rocky flanks, where it seemed that
only the condor could reach, large and regular edifices.   One
in particular appeared to impend over the governor's rude
but hospitable dwelling.   It had never been visited, he said, by
human being in modern times, whereupon Mr. C—— made a
vow that he would climb up to it, and measure it withal; which
he did, to the amazement not of the governor alone, but of all
the chocolate-colored denizens of Ollantaytambo.

Between coffee and breakfast time we were conducted past
long reaches of terrace-walls, and through the village of Ollantaytambo—which in plan and structure is little changed from
what it was under Inca rule—across a turbulent, icy, glacier-fed
stream, milky in color from the ground rock held in suspension,
which descends from the transverse ravine of Patacancha to
the fortress—a work less imposing than that of the Sacsahuaman, but more complicated and with equal evidence of skill.

I went there often during our stay of two weeks in Ollantaytambo, surveyed it carefully, and made drawings and photographs of its more important features.   It is built on the spur
of a great snowy mountain that projects between the two valleys of Patacancha and the river of which I have so often
spoken, each side of which, except where it presents a sheer escarpment of rock, is built up with terraces, ascended on one
side by steps, and on the other by an inclined plane over half
a mile long.   This plane, up which the gigantic stones for the
fortress had been moved, and on which many of them still rest,
is protected at intervals by square buildings of stone, looped,
something like our block-houses, and is supported by a wall of
stones, inclining inwards, and in places upwards of sixty feet
high.

The exterior walls of the fortress zigzag up the mountain-
side, and, turning at right angles, extend to where a precipice,
more than a thousand feet high, makes their prolongation im-

possible and unnecessary. They are about twenty-five feet high, built of rough stones stuccoed outside and inside, crenated, and have an inner shelf for the convenience of defenders. They might easily be mistaken for the work of Robert Guiscard, and

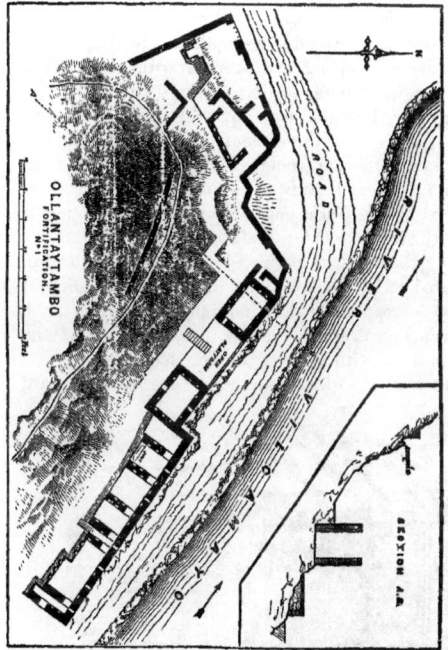

are not unlike the Middle-age fortifications of that chief that hang on the brow of the hills above Salerno, in Italy. Within the walls, and on the projecting rocky point which they isolate from the mountain, is a confused mass of buildings and walls, great porphyritic blocks, closely fitted in place or lying isolated, rock-cut seats, door-ways of beautifully hewn stones with jambs inclining inwards, long ranges of niches in cyclopean walls, stair-ways and terraces, with a shabby and tottering wooden cross at the extremity of all, bending over the village which lies like a map beneath.

It would require far more space than I can afford properly to describe the fortress, nor would a description be intelligible; so I refer the reader to the plans and cuts herewith given. The stones composing it, or lying scattered over its area, are of a hard red porphyry, brought from quarries more than two leagues distant, upwards of three thousand feet above the valley, and on the opposite side from the fortress. They are nearly all hewn into shape and ready to be fitted, and among them I noticed several having places cut in them for the reception of the **T** clamp, which I have mentioned in describing the remains of Tiahuanaco. One of these porphyry blocks, built in the wall of what appeared to be the beginning of a square building, is 18 feet long by 5 broad and 4 deep, not only perfectly squared, but finely polished on every face, as are also the stones adjoining it, to which it fits with scarcely perceptible joints.

The most interesting series of stones, however, are six great

PORPHYRY SLABS, FORTRESS OF OLLANTAYTAMBO.

upright slabs of porphyry supporting a terrace, against which they slightly incline. It will be observed that they stand a little apart, and that the spaces between them are accurately filled in with other thin stones, in sections. The sides of these, as well as of the larger slabs which they adjoin, are polished. The following table gives the dimensions of the slabs in feet and tenths, commencing with the one at the left:

| | No. 1. | No. 2. | No. 3. | No. 4. | No. 5. | No. 6. |
|---|---|---|---|---|---|---|
| Height.............. | 11.5 | 10.7 | 12.8 | 12.1 | 12.4 | 13.3 |
| Width at base ...... | 6.2 | 4.7 | 3.7 | 5 7 | 7.0 | 7.1 |
| Width at top ....... | 5.4 | 4.4 | 4.2 | 6.0 | 6.8 | 6.4 |
| Thickness.......... | 4.0 | 3.5 | 2.3 | 2.6 | 2.5 | 5.9 |

The faces of these slabs are not hewn entirely smooth, but have several projections, indicating that the work of accurately facing them was never completed. No. 4 shows traces of the same kind of ornamentation observed on some of the blocks at Tiahuanuco, only here the ornament is in relief. But gigantic as are these blocks, they are small in comparison with the "Tired Stones" lying on the inclined plane leading to the fortress or at its foot, as if abandoned there by the ancient workmen. One of these is 21 feet 6 inches long, by 15 feet broad. It is partly embedded in the ground, but shows a thickness of five feet above the soil.

The view from the fortress in every direction is wonderful in variety, in contrast, in beauty, and grandeur. The whole valley of Ollantaytambo is laid out like a garden, in a system of terraces, one below the other, falling off step by step to the river, each terrace level as a billiard-table, or with just enough of declivity to permit of easy irrigation. The river flows at the very feet of the bare majestic mountains on its farther side, and falling into it at right angles is the chafing, turbulent, mountain, snow-fed torrent to which I have alluded, descending from the steep valley or gorge of Patacancha or Marcacocha, in which rise, one above another, a long vista of green terraces like the seats in a Roman amphitheatre. The *portada* through which we entered this wonderful vale looks dark and

forbidding, and the turreted fortress that defends it appears
stern and threatening under the shadow of the mountains that
close in around it.   Looking down the valley, there stands always the death-white, silent Chicon, apparently barring all passage, and repelling all approach.   Facing us, most remarkable
and impressive of all, is the Mountain of Pinculluna, or " Hill

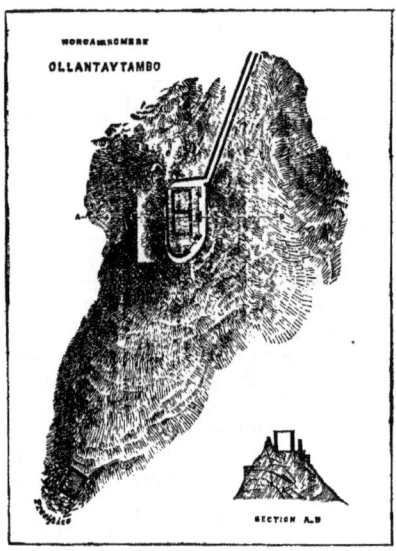

of Flutes," an abrupt, splintered mass of rock, thousands of feet
high, cutting the sky sharply with its jagged crest.   Hanging
against its sides, in positions apparently, and in some places really, inaccessible, are numerous buildings.   One group—a series
of five long edifices, one above the other, on corresponding narrow terraces—is the "School of the Virgins."   On a bold, projecting rock, with a vertical descent of upwards of nine hun-

dred feet, stands a small building, with a door-way opening on the very edge of the precipice; it is the Horca del Hombre, the Tarpeian Rock of Ollantaytambo, over which male criminals were thrown, in the severe Draconian days of the Incas. Above it, at a little distance, on a narrow shelf, are the prisons in which the criminals awaited their doom. To the left of these again, separated by a great chasm in the mountain, but at the same giddy height, and overlooking another precipice not less appalling, is the Horca de Mujer, or place of execution for women—vestals false to their vows, or ñustas faithless to their Inca lords. These airy spots I subsequently visited, obtaining drawings and plans of them all.

I have said that the village of Ollantaytambo is little changed from Inca times. The old central square of the town, the Mañay - racay, or "Court of Peti- tions," is nearly perfect, and one of the Inca build- ings, near it and at the feet of the precipices of the fortress, is com- pletely so, lack- ing only the roof. It is a story and a half high, built of rough stones

INCA BUILDINGS, OLLANTAYTAMBO.

laid in clay, and originally stuccoed, with a solid central wall reaching to the apex of the gables, dividing it into two apartments of equal size. The corners of the building, the jambs, and lintels of the lower doors are of cut stones. There seems to have been no access to the upper story from the interior, but there are two entrances to it through one of the gables, where four flat projecting stones seem to have supported a kind of balcony or platform, reached probably by ladders.

Nothing can exceed the regularity and taste with which the

ancient town was laid out, the streets running parallel to the stream that watered it, which was, and is, confined between walls of stone.  Regular terraces of richest soil, with flights of steps at intervals, rise from the stream to the level *terre-plein* on which the town stands, and which extends back to the cliffs of the Pinculluna.  The longitudinal streets are about fourteen feet broad; the transverse ones nine feet.  Each block is surrounded by a high wall, itself forming part of the walls of a double series of buildings, as shown in the plan; and each series has a central court and three dependent ones.  What may be called the central or principal building, facing the entrances, is half in one group and half in the other, divided longi-

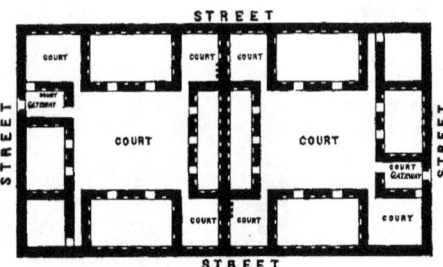

AN ANCIENT BLOCK IN OLLANTAYTAMBO.

tudinally by a wall continued up to the apex of the gables. Like the building just described, the upper half story was entered through a door in the gable, the sill of which was a broad, flat, projecting stone, reached by a series of flat stones set, stairwise, in the wall dividing the two groups of buildings forming the "block."

These ancient houses, substantially perfect, are still inhabited, and in their arrangement and other respects give us an accurate notion of the mode in which the ancients lived.  We detect a rigid system and order such as might be supposed to exist in a Fourier establishment, or a penitentiary, and suggesting a probable division and subdivision of the people into ranks and orders. Of course the long, dull lines of walls, with no other openings than a single, heavily jambed door-way in each block, give the cramped streets a gloomy, monotonous appearance, and the eye turns from them, with a sense of relief, to the bright sky above, and to the lofty, splintered, and snowy mountains that terminate the view in every direction through their narrow vistas.

If the town of Ollantaytambo is substantially what it was four hundred years ago, so, too, are the inhabitants—of whom none that I encountered spoke any language except the Quichua. They are a quiet, saturnine, and industrious people, not specially addicted to the Catholic religion, I should think, in view of the ruinous condition of their little church; although I must give them the credit of having followed my photographic boxes through the plaza with uncovered heads, kissing them devoutly, under the mistaken notion that they contained relics of the saints.

A few days after our arrival the governor arranged to conduct us to the great porphyry quarries of the ancients, high up on the shoulders of the mountains on the other side of the river, at the foot of a lofty and impressive peak, almost always enveloped in clouds. We crossed the river on a bridge of *mimbres*, or braided withes—a suspension-bridge, in fact, but of the rudest description—a perpetuation of those in universal use at the time of the Conquest. There are thousands of such bridges to this day in Peru. This particular bridge is distinguished as being in two spans, of about forty feet each, reaching from the opposite shores of the river to a pier of heavy stones, of unmistakable Inca workmanship, in the centre of the stream.

A great rock lies just above the pier, which tradition affirms was placed there for its protection against the force of the current; but we thought more likely that this natural protection suggested the feasibility of erecting the pier, which would have to be massive indeed to resist the rush of the Vilcamayo at certain seasons. As I have said, the bridge consists of several great cables of braided withes or branches, chiefly of a tough kind of shrub called "ioke," placed side by side and firmly

anchored by a variety of clumsy devices to buttresses on the
banks of the river. Sticks are placed transversely across these,
and fastened to the cables with thongs of raw hide or with
vines, forming a road-way about four feet wide. Above this
rude roadway, and less for support of the bridge than as a protection against falling off the yielding, swaying, and apparently
unstable structure, are two smaller cables, elevated a few feet,

INCA BRIDGE, OLLANTAYTAMBO.

one on each side, with vines or cords reaching down to the
bridge at intervals, forming a kind of netting, but with openings so far apart as to afford slight security against danger.
Not long before our visit, a drunken Indian and his wife and
mule stumbled from the bridge and were lost. Mr. D——,
however, rode his horse across with the utmost nonchalance.
These bridges are seldom level, and, besides sagging greatly,
often get lop-sided, when, in wet weather, the sticks corresponding to plankings become so slippery that it is no easy
matter to retain one's footing. There is another and greater

danger in passing the long bridges of this kind, like the famous ones over the rivers Apurimac and Pampas; namely, their swaying to and fro, like hammocks, when the wind sweeps through the deep gorges, across which they are suspended at heights so great that they appear as light and airy as cobwebs. It often happens that they become impassable, and that travellers are detained for days from this cause.

Past the bridge of Ollantaytambo, our road ran along a narrow shelf between the foot of the desolate mountain and the river; here partly cut in the rock, and yonder supported by a retaining-wall built up from the edge of the water. Indeed, the river throughout, except where a sheer precipice closes in on it from one side or the other, is confined between ancient artificial walls of such excellent workmanship that its impetuous waters have failed to dislodge them in the lapse of centuries. Nothing could be more beautiful than the system of terraces supporting the rich, level fields and meadows of Ollantaytambo on the opposite bank. They bend in and out with the sinuosities of the river, in graceful curves, their stony faces relieved by the vines and shrubs that cling up against them or droop in festoons over their edges. No visitor can see them without being amazed at the skill, patience, and power to which they bear, and will bear for ages, a silent but impressive testimony.

At the distance of half a league, a high, rocky spur of the mountain projected itself boldly before us, presenting a vertical front to the river. Around its feet the waters swirled and fretted in impotent rage. The path over it is narrow—so narrow that two animals can not pass each other—besides being steep and stony. On the summit itself stand two towers, flanked by an impassable rock towards the river, little smaller than those that crown the headlands of the Mediterranean, with openings like port-holes to complete the resemblance. The way lies between them, in a deep notch in the rock, through which a loaded mule can barely pass. At the base of the towers, on the other side, we noticed the remains of buildings, the quarters, probably, of the garrison that held this almost impregnable position in the days of yore.

Farther on, the mountain-slope is less abrupt, and its face is terraced up for many hundreds of feet, to a comparatively broad shelf on the mountain-side, where are the remains of an ancient village. We ascend through these *andenes* by a steep, rough path, to a headland also dominating the river in front. The path is narrow enough to flutter most nerves, and a false step would send man and mule whirling into the rocky bed of the river, brawling, now almost inaudibly, below. Clambering over the headland, we descended rapidly to a broad and beautiful road, with gentle grade, winding along the flank of the ridge, and reaching far back towards the head of a mighty ravine intervening between the buttress on which we stand and another, equally bold, a mile or two distant. This is the old Inca road leading to the porphyry quarries, whence the giant stones of the Fortress of Ollantaytambo were obtained. We follow this to the very extremity and brow of the headland, over which they were toppled, sliding down two thousand feet into the valley. The plane worn in their descent is distinct, and lying around us are blocks more or less shaped artificially, which the apparition of the Spaniards prevented the ancient workmen from launching down to their destination. How these blocks were got across the swift and turbulent river, in the bed of which some still remain, I do not attempt to explain. Starting back along the ancient quarry-road, we constantly encountered blocks of porphyry, entirely or partly hewn, some in the middle of the road, and others lying by its sides. Traces of rude cottages, and evidences of attempts at cultivation in little areas between the rocks, are visible at intervals.

Two miles from this, and we see rising before us, and extending across the head of the ravine, two vast walls of stone, more than a fourth of a mile long, and from thirty to fifty feet high— the retaining-walls of terraces designed to receive the great rocks that man, or time, or the earthquakes may wrench or splinter off from the impending porphyry cliffs, and prevent their tearing down the steep declivity of the ravine into the valley, where, apparently at our very feet, we discern the tile roofs and clustering huts of the richest hacienda of Ollantaytambo.

Piled on the terraces supported by these massive walls, which incline inwards towards the mountain to secure greater strength, are confused masses of porphyry blocks, thousands on thousands, as if a glacier had been converted into stone. Some of these, in their descent, have torn away portions of the retaining-walls designed to stay their headlong course. A few have passed both barriers, and are heaped below the lowest in threatening readiness to take a final plunge into the smiling vale three thousand feet below.

Perched on some of the largest of these rocks are dozens of little buildings, somewhat resembling the chulpas of the Collao, but scarcely bigger than the toy-houses that children build. They are of rough stones laid in clay, and roofed, or rather arched, with other flat stones overlapping each other like the tiles of modern dwellings, and projecting over the walls so as to form a rude cornice. Some of these curious structures are square, but most of them are round, from four to five feet high, with about the same di-

SMALL HOUSES, OLLANTAYTAMBO.

ameter, and all have little door-ways, opening, for the most part, towards the ragged, threatening cliffs. A few show traces of having been stuccoed and painted inside. Our first impression was that they were the tombs of the ancient quarry-men; but we found no human bones in any of them, and finally came to the conclusion that they were shrines, like those around Vesuvius; but instead of containing a figure of St. Januarius or other saint, had held some *huaca*, or sacred object, placed there to arrest the danger of the mighty rock avalanches that had piled up their porphyritic masses in a ragged wilderness above and around them.

Most of the ancient stone-cutting had been done on the lower terrace, as evinced by heaps of chippings on every side. Here the ancient road ends. Our host insisted that the real quarry was some hundreds of feet higher up. To reach the spot we had to climb a lateral ridge that no one but a traveller among the Andes would dream of being accessible, and up which we scrambled with infinite labor and no little risk. The summit of the ridge presented quite a broad area, in great part covered with porphyritic rocks heaped up in the same dire confusion that I have already described, at the foot of a bare peak of the same material, from which they had splintered off, and which presented towards us an absolutely precipitous face. The point where we stood was 3240 feet above the valley, and this rocky warder must tower up to treble that height. I have said that its summit is usually lost in clouds; but this day it stood out sharp and clear against the sky, revealing all its rugged features. A few condors were circling in front of it and around its lofty head, the only things of life to be seen. Yet here the patient, persevering Incas had cleared the cold soil of stones, and built up little *andenes*, to gain scant areas for the hardy mountain grasses on which the llamas feed.

We found no wrought stones here, but many which appeared to have been split into regular blocks, chiefly parallelopipeds, of varying dimensions. The greater number were from eight inches to a foot square at the ends, and from six to ten feet long; but there were others much longer, and which, tradition insists, were intended to be girders for the bridge which we had passed in the morning. I measured one of these, and found it to be 20 feet 6 inches long, by 2 feet 1 inch broad, and 1 foot 9 inches thick. I can hardly believe that these were produced by natural cleavage; yet, as before said, there are no traces of tools on them.

Our descent to the valley was rapid enough, but not composing to the nerves.  At the hacienda we found the *cura* of the
village, who had just returned from Cuzco, and was anxiously
awaiting *los Franceses*.  All foreigners in the Sierra are supposed by the mixed population to be French by nationality, and
peddlers of jewellery by occupation.  He advised us not to go
down the valley to Santa Ana, adding, significantly, that the
peones had ascertained the real value of the glittering wares
which the last *Franceses* had disposed of there.  And then he
wanted to see what trinkets we had with us, and intimated the
possibility of making a purchase.  It was with difficulty that I
convinced him that we were not peddlers, when he inquired,
what, in the name of the Most Holy Trinity, had brought us
to Ollantaytambo?  "*Antigüedades!*" he repeated after me,
with unfeigned astonishment, became suddenly silent, and left
the room.  Directly after this, he returned to the door, and
beckoned me to come out to a remote corner of the court
among the horses.  Like the *cura* of Tiahuanaco, he, too, was
weary of life in an Indian village ; he knew the soil was stuffed
with treasure, and understood perfectly the object of our visit.
It was well enough to disguise it from the people generally
and the governor in particular ; but now we might just as well
take him into our confidence, and divide the spoils we had come
so far to obtain.  Like the *cura* of Tiahuanaco—and, for that
matter, like all the *curas* in the Sierra—he was maudlin, and
wept.  I respected his tears, and, thinking from my silence that
my heart was touched and the seals of my confidence melted,
he became finally composed ; and then I shocked him by insisting that *antigüedades*, and only *antigüedades*, had brought us
to Ollantaytambo.  This was too much ; the face of the Lord's
minister became livid under the starlight, and he strode away
with the ominous suggestion, " All the roads are bad that lead
from Ollantaytambo!"
I described our interview to the governor, who did not seem
to regard it as a laughing matter, and was not at all reassuring
when he said that the *cura* was a great scoundrel, and quite
capable of attempting harm.  It was good for that priest that

we did not meet him in any of the narrow passes on our road back to Urubamba, for we very likely would have shot him before inquiring the reason of his being there.

After what I have said and intimated about the priesthood in Peru, it is perhaps supererogatory to add a paragraph concerning them from the "Apuntes y Observaciones" of Don Juan Bustamente, a native and resident of the Sierra. "It is sixty years," says Don Juan, "since the Department of Puno has seen a bishop, and, as a consequence of this strange abandonment, the *curas* live according to their fancies, gratifying their passions without restraint or fear of any kind, carrying their scandals to the extent of living publicly with their concubines and bastards." The reason assigned by Don Juan for the demoralization of the clergy of Puno certainly can not apply in the Department of Cuzco, where there have been bishops enough, but where about the same lax condition of things prevails that he so loudly deplores.

No portion of my stay in Peru was more pleasant or profitable than that passed in Ollantaytambo. It was in the season called winter, and the winds that swept through the valley were fierce, yet most of the trees retained their foliage, and the bushes along the *azequias* were green and blooming with flowers, among which toyed at morn and even-tide such numbers of humming-birds as I have rarely seen, even in the tangled thickets of Nicaragua, where prolific Nature exhausts her energies in swelling the sum of animal and vegetable life. Doves and pigeons of many kinds cooed among the branches, and little *cues* skurried along the terrace-walls, or in a tame condition nestled around our feet, inspiring constant fear that an unlucky step might crush out their innocent and busy lives. On every hand were traces and monuments of ancient art, industry, and intelligence. Enigmatical buildings, towers, and terraces impended on the mountain-sides; fortresses in positions skilfully selected, and themselves artfully designed, closed every approach and frowned from every crag; while in the centre, overhanging the ancient town, rose the stately citadel. In the valley, art had levelled every inequality, and raised hundreds of miles of terraces, filled with earth scraped from hill-slopes and mountain-side, and watered by *azequias* whose channels were carried along the faces of inaccessible cliffs, or tunnelled through rocky projections which it was impossible to turn. And high over all, a square building, in which was the Inti-huatana, or Gnomon of the Sun, by means of which the solstices and equinoxes, the seasons of planting and harvests, and the periods of the great festivals, were determined and their arrival proclaimed.

Ollantaytambo was the frontier town and fortress of the Incas in the valley of the Ucayale, as it is to-day of their conquerors. There were outlying works some leagues lower down the river at Havaspampa, but the bulwark of the empire against the savage Antis in this direction was here. It is around Ollantaytambo also that cling the traditions of Ollantay, the lovelorn chieftain, whose thwarted affections drove him into rebellion against the Vicegerent of the Sun, and whose suffering and adventures form the basis of the nearest perfect and the best of all the dramas of Ancient America that have descended to our days.

Cusi-Coyllur, the Joyful Star, was the daughter of the Inca Pachacutic. Ollantay was a brave and handsome chieftain of the Inca's army, who had carried the Inca power farther down towards the Amazonian plains than any other of the Inca generals. But he was not of royal blood. Returning in triumph to Cuzco, he was received with unprecedented honors in the Huacapata; but in the very hour when his fame was highest and his ambition most elated, he caught sight of the Joyful Star, and became the prey of a passion guilty alike in the eyes of religion and the law. None but Incas could ally themselves with those of Inca lineage, and whoever outside of the royal line should aspire to such distinction was adjudged guilty of sacrilege, and visited with the severest punishment. I scarcely need tell the rest of it—the old, old story. Thwarted in his suit ignominiously, where any one less distinguished would have been slain, the young chieftain, mad with disappointment and burning for revenge, returns to his army, and in passionate words recounts his wrongs, and asks his soldiers to assist in avenging them. In flying from the capital, however, he pauses on the heights above it, and exclaims :

> " Ah, Cuzco! ah, beautiful city!
> Thou art filled with my enemies.
> Thy perverse bosom will I tear;
> Thy heart give to the condors!
> Ah, haughty enemy! ah, proud Inca!
> I will seek the ranks of mine Antis;
> I will review my victorious soldiers;
> I will give them arrows!
> And when on the heights of Sacsahuaman
> My men shall gather like a cloud,
> There shall they light a flame,
> Thence shall descend as a torrent!
> Thou shalt fall at my feet, proud Inca!
> You will ask me, 'Take my daughter!
> On my knees I implore my life!'"

The army responds to his fiery appeals, and hails him Inca. He places on his own head the imperial scarlet *llautu,* and marches on Cuzco. Midway, however, he hears of the approach of the old, astute, and invincible Inca General Ruminani, whose name of "Stony-eye" fairly indicates his cold, implacable character. Ollantay, impetuous, but cautious, does not undervalue his powerful and wary antagonist, but seizes on the important position destined to bear his name in future times, fortifies himself, and establishes a firm base for his operations against his sovereign. For ten years he maintains himself here, until, by a wonderful act of treachery, he is made prisoner, and brought to Cuzco to suffer death. But meantime the stern old Inca has died, and his son, whose younger heart can better appreciate the tender passion, touched by the rebel warrior's story, not only pardons him, but consents to his marriage with the Joyful Star, who had all this time been confined in the Acllahuasi, or Convent of the Vestals. And they lived to a good old age, and were as happy and prolific as the hero and heroine of any modern novel.

And such, according to the old Quichua drama, was the origin of Ollantaytambo. The site of Ollantay's palace is not only

pointed out, standing on a series of charming terraces overlooking the smiling valley, but its remains are still distinct, and
some parts of it almost entire.   It was elaborate in plan, as the

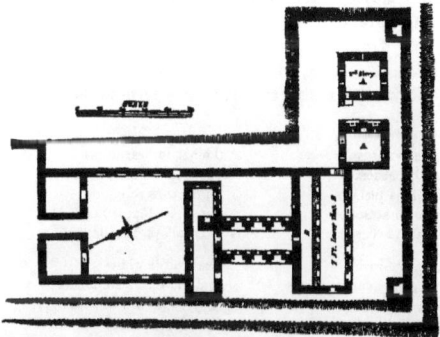

PLAN OF PALACE OF OLLANTAY.

reader will see; and it shows also that Inca architecture did
not, as has been alleged, balk at the task of raising buildings of
more than a single story.

VIEW OF PART OF PALACE OF OLLANTAY.

Apropos of the drama of Ollantay, I may add that the Quichua langua.. is one of remarkable beauty and scope, plaintive and soft to the ear. As the language of the Incas, it was spread wherever they carried their arms from Quito to Chili, and is still the ruling tongue of the Sierra. As an example, I subjoin a harvest-song from the drama referred to, with Mr. Markham's translation. It is addressed to the mischievous little black-and-yellow tuya, a bird that robs the corn-fields.

| QUICHUA. | ENGLISH. |
|---|---|
| "Ama pisco micuychu | "O bird! forbear to eat |
| Ñustallipa chacranta | The crops of my princess: |
| Manan hina tucuichu | Do not thus rob |
| Hillacunan saranta. | The maize that is her food! |
| Tuyallay! Tuyallay! | Tuyallay! Tuyallay! |
| | |
| Panaccaymi rurumi | The fruit is white, |
| Ancha ceuni munispa | And the leaves are tender; |
| Nucmunaccmi uccumi | As yet they are delicate: |
| Llullunacmi raphinpa | I fear your perching on them. |
| Tuyallay! Tuyallay! | Tuyallay! Tuyallay! |
| | |
| Phurantatac mascariy | Your wings shall be cut, |
| Cuchusaccmi silluta | Your nails shall be torn, |
| Puppaseccayquin ccantapas | And you shall be taken |
| Happiscayquin ccantapas. | And closely encaged. |
| Tuyallay! Tuyallay! | Tuyallay! Tuyallay! |
| | |
| Hinasccatan ricunqui | This shall be done to you, |
| Huc rurunta chapchacctin | When you eat a grain: |
| Hinac taccmi ricunqui | This shall be done to you |
| Huc llallapas chincacctin. | When a grain is lost. |
| Tuyallay! Tuyallay!" | Tuyallay! Tuyallay!" |

It was with a pang that I bade farewell forever to Ollantay-tambo, equally garden and fortress, with its climate of endless spring, framed in by the mightiest mountains of our continent, as bare and stern as the valley itself is bright and verdant.

# CHAPTER XXV.

## THE VALLEY OF YUCAY.—PISAC.

Excursion to Pisac.—The Sacred Rock at Calca.—The Circular Building.—Serpentine Channel in the Rock.—Its Design.—Worship of Isolated Rocks.—The Boundary of the Inca Dominion.—The Great Frontier Fortress of Pisac.—Its Commanding Position.—The Approaches to it.—The Inti-huatana, or Solstitial Turret, the best preserved in Peru.—Other Inti-huatanas.—Garcilasso's Account of them.—Ascent to the Fortress of Pisac.—Complex and Elaborate Character of the Works.—Auxiliary Fortifications.—The Burial-place.—Desiccated Corpses.—Character of Peruvian Defensive Works.

OUR return from Ollantaytambo to Urubamba was rapid, and we spent several days there in examining the remains of the palaces and baths of the Incas in and around the picturesque little village of Yucay. Thence up the rich and beautiful valley to the town of Pisac, over which impends the wonderful fortress of the same name.

Almost every step in the valley is marked by monuments of the ancient inhabitants; but I should exhaust the patience of my readers were I to undertake even to enumerate them. I cannot omit, however, to notice some remarkable remains near the village of Calca, which illustrate the craft of the Inca priesthood, while giving us a peculiar form of Inca architecture. They occupy that favorite site to which I have had occasion before to allude, the neck of a promontory whence extensive views may be commanded, and over which the roads of a valley like that of Yucay would naturally pass.

The most conspicuous structure is a round building, too low to be called, strictly speaking, a tower. It stands upon a rocky knoll, is 24 feet in diameter, and its walls are 18 feet high to the cornice, which has an exterior projection of 10 inches, and an interior one of 8 inches. The walls are 2 feet 4 inches in thickness at their base. It is built of rough stones, or stones only partly broken into shape, laid in the same tenacious material which I have called clay, and which seems to me to be nothing else. Originally it was stuccoed inside and out. The doorway, 3 feet 8 inches wide, opens fifteen degrees west of south;

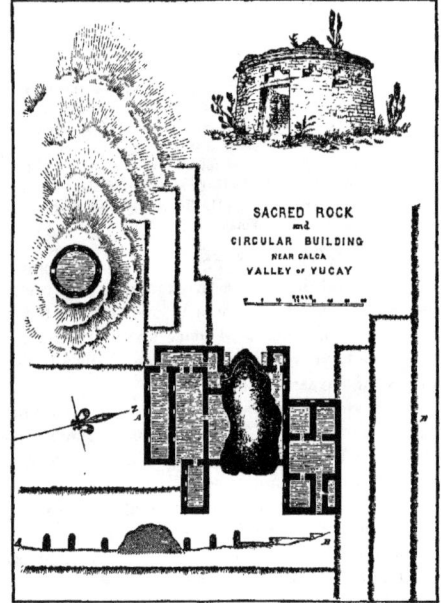

SACRED ROCK
and
CIRCULAR BUILDING
NEAR CALCA
VALLEY of YUCAY

and there are false doors or niches corresponding with it in dimensions at every quadrature of the circle formed by the plan, through each of which opens a small window. Over each of these, as well as over the door, are inverted T's, like the Egyptian *Tau* (⊥), of which there are also three in each section between the principal niches. These are entirely peculiar to this structure.  In the interior, within reach of the hand, and symmetrically distributed, are eight oblong niches, as shown in the plan.   The lintels of the doors and niches still remain.   They are composed of sticks of wood about the size of a man's arm, closely wound with coarse ropes of *pita*, or the fibre of the agave, evidently for the purpose of securing an adhesive surface for the smooth coating of stucco that was applied as a finish. This was a common device in buildings of rough stones, concrete, and adobes.   We resort substantially to the same thing in our lathing.   The height of this structure was probably not much greater than now, and it may be assumed that it was roofed in similar manner with the Sondor-huasi in Azangero.

Its purposes can only be inferred from the character of the adjacent, and apparently dependent, remains, which are both sufficiently singular and suggestive.   They are situated 60 feet distant from the tower or circular building, and consist of a number of rectangular structures covering an area of about 100 feet square, raised around a great limestone boulder, 60 feet long, 30 broad, and 25 feet high above the ground.   The walls of the buildings come up to the rock, and are built against it. Indeed, near the extremities they were carried over it, so as to leave only the ends of the rock exposed.   These present their natural surfaces, excepting the northern end, in which is cut a groove, or channel, of from three to four inches wide, and about three inches deep.   This winds around and down the rock in serpentine form for a length of twenty feet, and disappears through one of the transverse walls built against the rock, reappearing in one of the side-buildings or rooms where the rock projects something like the eaves of a house, and there terminates in a kind of spout, carved rudely in the form of a serpent's head. Any liquid poured into the channel at any part would run to this point, and be discharged into whatever vessel might be placed here.   That the groove was designed to represent a serpent is obvious from the manner in which it tapers to the tail and widens elsewhere, and from its sinuosities as well as from its sculptured head.

That isolated rocks were held in great veneration by the an-

cient Peruvians, were often strangely carved, and frequently
had structures of some sort raised around them, and had offerings made to them or the spirit supposed to dwell in them, admits of no dispute.  I saw hundreds of such rocks in the country; and, to this day, there is hardly one at all remarkable for
shape or position on any of the highways of the Sierra, to which
the Indians do not take off their hats and bow with reverence,
uttering in a low voice some words of adjuration.  Often this
ceremony is accompanied by removing the quid of coca from
the mouth and casting it against the rock.  Occasionally the
Indian searches for a little pebble, which he throws against the
· rock, generally at one point, so that, in the course of ages, considerable cavities have been worn in the stone by this process.

The boulder under notice, from its position and size, is a
conspicuous object, and, surrounded as it was by so considerable a pile of edifices, was clearly an object of much sanctity.
And as we know sacrifices by libations were common in all
parts of Peru, we can readily believe that the serpentine groove
around this rock was intended to receive the offerings of chicha
that might be made by the travellers obliged to pass this spot
in their journeys through the valley.  It was cut at a judicious
height above the ground, about breast-high, so as to facilitate
the contributions of the faithful, who probably were never told
what became of their offerings after they had flowed away into
the recesses of the adjacent buildings to inspire the oracle that
spoke to them from the sacred rock.  Among the remains of
ancient Greece and Rome the antiquarian has often smiled to
find the convenient chamber of the priest behind the statues of
the dead gods, and the cunningly devised tubes connecting with
their marble lips, through which came words oracular and po-
tent to the trembling questioner who had duly made his offering at their shrines.

I have said that the Incas, with all their power, were unable
to extend their empire far to the eastward, or very far down the
Amazonian valleys, into the regions of the savage Chunchas or
Antis.  They stopped short when they reached the thick forests, and at those points raised great fortresses to protect them-

selves against insult and to resist invasion. One of the most
severely contested of the valleys was that of Paucartambo, lying
parallel to that of Yucay, only eight leagues distant, but separated from it by an impassable snowy range of the Andes.
Through this range there is but a single pass, formed by the interlocking valleys, or rather gorges, of two considerable streams,
one flowing into the Rio Paucartambo, and the other into the
Vilcamayo or Yucay, at a point where stands the town of Pisac.

VIEW OF POINT OF FORTRESS, PISAC.

At both ends of this pass were gigantic forts; that dominating
Pisac being most formidable, and, taken as a whole, quite as remarkable as that of the Sacsahuaman, and only to be paralleled
in the Old World by the great hill forts of India.

Let us imagine a bold headland of mountain, projecting out
from the great snowy masses of the Andes, an irregular oval
in shape, three miles long, and at its most elevated point four
thousand feet high. It is separated by gorge and valley from
the parent mountains, except at one point, where it subsides

into a relatively low and narrow ridge, scarcely a hundred paces broad. It is rough and forbidding in outline, here running up into splintered peaks, yonder presenting to the valley enormous beetling cliffs, and here and there holding open, level spaces and gentle slopes in its rocky embrace. Except at three points it is absolutely inaccessible. Two of these are on the side towards the valley of Yucay, which it was mainly designed to defend; and the third is at the narrow neck or ridge connecting

STAIRWAY, PISAC.

it with the parent mountain. Wherever, while in its natural condition, it might have been possible for a bold mountaineer to clamber up, there the Incas built up lofty walls of stone against the rock, so as to leave neither foothold nor support for adventurer or assailant. The ascent on the side of the town is by a stairway partly cut in the rock and partly composed of large stones, which winds and zigzags along the face of the rocky escarpment, in places hanging over dizzy precipices, next turning sharp around projecting bastions of rock, on every one of which are towers for soldiers, with their magazines of stones ready to be hurled down on an advancing assailant. At long intervals up the laborious ascent, and where some friendly shelf gives room, are resting-places—paved or rocky areas, fifteen to twenty feet square, surrounded by stone seats, but always dominated by some sinister tower, with a door-way opening to its foundation, just within which, or projecting out ominously, you may see the great stone that requires only to be moved a little to crash down upon your head.

At about half-way up the mountain the lower series of cliffs are surmounted, and there are some considerable slopes, which are artificially terraced up with great skill and beauty. These terraces extend to the very edge of the precipices. They are ascended by flights of steps, through the centre of which run narrow conduits, or *azequias*, down which the water was conducted, not only for irrigating the terraces, but to supply the reservoirs connected with the lower series of fortifications. But here also we find every projection or escarpment of rock, not only faced up artificially with stones so as to be inaccessible, but crowned with towers, generally round, with openings for looking out, and others through which weapons might be discharged and stones hurled down. On occasional natural shelves, reached in some instances only by stairways, are clusters of buildings, long and narrow, with tall gables, placed close together, with characteristic economy of space.

FORTIFIED PASS, PISAC.

In a word, every rood of surface that can be propped up by terraces and cultivated is carefully dedicated to agriculture; every avenue of ascent, except such as the engineers determined to leave open, is closed, and every commanding and strategic spot is elaborately fortified. There is not a point to the very summit of the first peak of the mountain which is not somewhere commanded or somehow protected by a maze of works which almost defy the skill of the engineer to plan, and which baffle description.

Between the first and second peaks there is, of course, a depression or saddle—a crest, rather narrow, but so terraced up and levelled as to afford space for a group of structures of beautifully cut stones, and which were undoubtedly religious—for the great mountain fortress of Pisac was almost a province, supporting not only a garrison, but a considerable population. I estimate that the terraces sustaining its *andenes*, supplied with water by aqueducts carried along the face of the cliffs, through passages excavated in the rock, and artfully from slope to slope of the mountain, would, if extended, reach more than one hundred miles. It had its minor fortifications—forts within forts, its isolated buildings, villages, and, it would appear, its temple, and its priests, warriors, and laborers, and was impregnable and self-sustaining.

The most interesting feature of this group of remains is the Inti-huatana; and as it is best preserved of any of the similar contrivances of Peru—thanks to its almost inaccessible position—I will endeavor to explain it. Etymologically, Inti-huatana resolves itself into *Inti*, sun, *huatana*, the place where, or thing with which, anything is tied up. It also signifies a halter. The whole, therefore, is equivalent to "place where the sun is tied up." These Inti-huatana seem to have always been formed out of a rock, the summit of which was carefully levelled or chiselled away, leaving only in its centre a projection very nearly of the shape and size of a truncated sugar-loaf. These rocks were not only almost always in conspicuous positions, but also within the courts of temples or buildings plainly religious in origin, or else standing near such structures, within separate enclosures of stone, open to the sky, and clearly such as were never covered by roofs.

In this instance the principal bulk and most elevated part of the rock is enclosed by a wall of finely cut and accurately fitted stones, resembling in outline the letter D. (See A in the plan, p. 527.) The rock fills what may be called the curved side of the letter, and here the wall is built close up against it, the inner faces of the stones being cut to fit the irregularities of the rock, while the outer face of the wall is regular and smooth.

On this side the wall is about twenty feet high. On the straight
side of the letter the wall is prolonged in one direction, and
then bends around on itself so as to form a second enclosure—an irregular triangle in outline, covering a lower portion
of the rock already mentioned. Within this are several interesting features, connected, perhaps, with the astronomy of the
Incas, but which it is not necessary to my purpose to describe.
The entrance to the principal and most elevated enclosure is
through a door-way of the usual form, which is reached from
the outside by a flight of stone steps. Passing this, the ex-
plorer finds himself in an irregular, oblong area, with the rock,

THE INTI-HUATANA OF PISAC.

hewn with some regularity on his right, and rising to the level
of the outer walls. Steps in the rock lead to its summit, which
is cut perfectly smooth and level, affording an area 18 feet long
by 16 broad. In the centre of this area, and rising from the
living rock, of which it is part, is the Inti-huatana of Pisac. It
is in the form of a cone, sharply cut and perfectly symmetrical,
11 inches in diameter at its base, 9 at its summit, and 16 inches
high. I was told by the Governor of Pisac, who accompanied
me on my visit, that this column, or gnomon, was formerly
surrounded by a flat ring of *chumpe*, or Peruvian bronze, several inches wide, which he had often seen when a boy.

Near the Temple of Guitera, in the upper valley of the river Pisco, occupying the summit of a ridge projecting at right angles into the valley, and commanding an extensive view both up and down it, as well as dominating the temple, is another Inti-huatana, but in a ruined condition. Instead of being surrounded by artificial walls, it is encircled by a parapet formed by digging away the solid rock around it, so as to leave an area of about fifteen feet in diameter. Another, somewhat similar to that at Pisac, enclosed in a square of cut stones, overlooks the great fortress and ancient town of Ollantaytambo. Still another, cut from a limestone rock, which had also been built in, exists on the banks of the Rodadero or Tullamayo, near the foot of the terraces of the Colcompata, in Cuzco; and I am confident that a similar rock existed within the circular part of the great Temple of the Sun itself, in the imperial city. That part is now filled in solid behind the great altar of the Church of Santo Domingo, which occupies the place assigned to the golden effigy of the Sun. On an eminence in front of the original Temple of the Sun, in the sacred island of Titicaca, is an Inti-huatana, which appears to have been a natural formation of the limestone rock, which has itself been considerably modified artificially. I need not recur to other examples. Almost every place of importance in the more ancient parts of the Inca empire seems to have had its Inti-huatana.

Garcilasso says, "*Huata* is a word which signifies a year, and the same word, without change in its pronunciation or accent, is a verb signifying *to tie.*" Inti-huata would thus become "Sun-year;" and according to De Velasco, who wrote towards the close of the last century, the solar year was distinguished in Quito by precisely this name, as distinguished from the lunar year, or Quilla-huata. It is possible that the name was in part accepted because of a concurrent double, and therefore, to superstitious minds, mysterious, significance.

Of the public, and probably sacred, character of the edifices surrounding the Inti-huatana, there can be but little doubt. It is evidenced by their position and peculiarities of structure. Now, in all references to the astronomical ideas and achieve-

ments of the Incas of Peru, we read of certain devices and contrivances by means of which they determined the solstices and
equinoxes.  We are told by the early chroniclers—Garcilasso de
la Vega, Cieza de Leon, Acosta, Betanzos, Gemelli, and others
—that on the eminences around Cuzco and Quito were built
what Garcilasso calls towers and Betanzos pyramids, so placed
that by noting their shadows, or by taking observations between
them, the periods of the solstices and the length of the solar
year could be accurately determined.  Garcilasso states that at

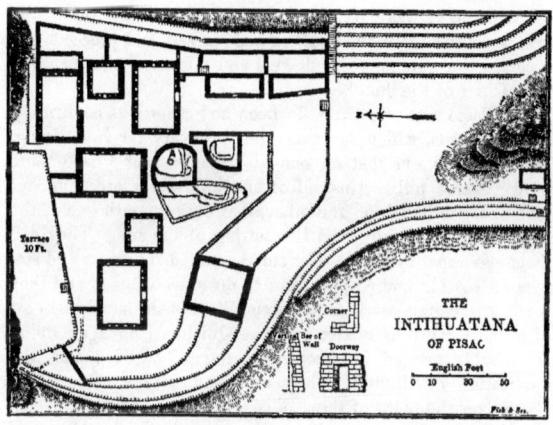

Cuzco there were sixteen of these towers, the largest equal in
size to the watch-towers of Spain, eight to the east and eight
to the west of the city: Acosta says there were twelve; and
Betanzos, four.  Their site, so far as it is fixed by any of these
authorities, was on the hill of Carmenca, dominating Cuzco on
the north-west, where Garcilasso says they were standing in
1560.  I was unable, however, to find any traces of them on
that eminence.

Besides these solstitial towers, reference is made by the

chroniclers to certain single columns or pillars " for determining the equinoxes." These, Garcilasso tells us, were of sculptured stones, richly worked, and placed in the open courts of the temples of the Sun. It was the duty of the priests, on the approach of the equinox, to watch the shadows of these columns, which were in the centre of circles embracing the whole area of the courts of the temples. Through the centre of each circle (and its column) was drawn a line due east and west. On the day when the centre of the shadow followed this line from sunrise to sunset, and when, at noon, the rays of the sun fell full on the column, and it was "bathed in light," casting no shadow, the priests declared that the equinox had arrived, and proceeded to decorate the gnomon with flowers and offerings, placing on it "the Chair of the Sun."

Garcilasso refers to Cieza de Leon and Acosta as confirming his statements, which, however, they are very far from doing. The latter tells us that on one of the hills near Cuzco there were "twelve pillars [instead of sixteen], set in order, and at such distance one from the other, that every month one of the pillars noted the rising and the setting of the sun. They call them *succanga*, by means whereof they fixed the feasts and seasons for sowing and reaping, and to do other things; and they performed certain sacrifices to these pillars of the sun." I know of no such word as *succanga* in the Quichua language; and it is probably printed for *rucana*, "a finger," which makes the application intelligible. They were sun-fingers, or pointers. Cieza fixes the place of these pillars, columns, or towers, which he calls *torricelli*, on the hill of Carmenca, to the north-west of Cuzco, and merely observes that they "served to show the motion of the sun."*

---

* Velasco, in his history of Quito, affirms that the year was determined in that city by twelve pillars, which served as gnomons to mark the commencement of each month, and that the priests ornamented the pillar with flowers on the day when it indicated the commencement of each month. He quotes Acosta as his authority for saying that in Cuzco there were twelve towers for the same purpose. He states that in Quito there were two columns instead of four, as at Cuzco, which marked the solstices, when they gave no shadow. Of course he means the equinox.

Making due allowance for the probable exaggerations and misinformation of Garcilasso, we may readily believe that the towers of which he speaks—the pillars mentioned by Acosta, and the *torricelli* of Cieza—were simply Inti-huatanas. This conclusion is supported by the negative fact that no remains of such structures as he describes now exist on the hill of Carmenca or any of the others around Cuzco, while there are many carved and hewn rocks, some of which might have served, and some of which certainly did serve, as Inti-huatanas, or sun-fingers, where the sun might appear to be stopped, or tied up for a moment in his course; and on which, in his passage through the zenith, he might sit down in all his glory.

We have here the undoubtedly correct explanation of the purposes of the Inti-huatana of Pisac, which is no doubt a true type of the "columns" of which the chroniclers speak, and through the aid of which the Peruvians were able to ascertain the periods of the solstices and the arrival of the sun in the zenith. The Mexicans and Central Americans seem to have made greater advances in astronomy and the computation of time than the Peruvians.

From the undoubtedly religious structures of which the Inti-huatana of Pisac forms part, we climb the great central peak of the fortress. The path is steep and devious, under constantly recurring towers, and along narrow paths, skirting the faces of cliffs a thousand feet sheer down on one side, and five hundred feet straight up on the other; where the brain grows dizzy, and where it is impossible for two men to pass abreast. Along such narrow pathways, where the condor sails level with you above the abyss below, and where you lean inwards till your shoulder grazes the rock, along such paths as these, which from the valley do not form even a line on the face of the precipice, the visitor to Pisac must make his perilous way.

My companions absolutely refused to attempt the passage, and I was left to undertake it accompanied by a single silent alguazil. At the end of a quarter of a mile, I breathed freer, as the shelf, in most parts artificial, widened a little, and we came to a flight of steps, ascending, perhaps, one hundred and

fifty feet, to a small tower, standing like a sentinel by the side
of one of the great rocky ribs of the mountain, past which we
could not see.  Just beyond this tower, and perfectly commanded from its port-holes, the path is excavated through the comb
of rock, so as to allow but one person to pass at a time, and
then only in a crouching position.  It is only by this difficult
and perilous route that access can be had from the central to
the eastern peak or division of the mountain fortress.  This
central peak or division is accessible only from the two other
divisions, and is consequently less elaborately fortified.  Its
summit, or extreme topmost point, is a level area of about a
quarter of an acre, supported by walls of cut stones, and is, by
the barometer, 4250 feet above the river in the valley of Yucay.
Here are numerous traces of fire, and from this commanding
point it is probable signal-fires telegraphed important intelligence from the heights over Paucartambo to those overlooking
the capital.

Another narrow and fortified crest connects this central bulk
of the fortress with the lower or western one, which adjoins
the snowy spur of the Andes.  This is, perhaps, the most elaborately fortified of all.  Not only is there carried across the
crest connecting it with the mother-mountain a great cyclopean
wall of limestone, only second to that of the Sacsahuaman in dimensions, but there are inner walls and fortified barracks, with
outlooks and port-holes, all admirably situated for defence, with
covered parades and granaries, abodes for servants, and the material protection for a garrison of two thousand men.  Quaint
symbols cut on the rocks, needless stairways built up against
them, *dilettante* elaboration of door-ways, and a hundred other
evidences exist here of the unforced occupations of an idle and
*ennuyé* garrison.  But the designers of this great fortress were
not content with its obvious and absolute strength.  They built
outworks on the opposing mountain, which modern warfare,
with all its appliances, would find it difficult to force.  They
carried subterranean aqueducts from the rivulets formed by
the melting snows throughout the length and breadth of the
fortress, not merely to supply its defenders, but to water the

gardens they had reared in mid-air on the flanks of the mountain.

On the opposite side of the deep and rugged ravine which isolated them from the mother-mountain and cut them off from it, on a vast promontory, or headland, in many a niche and crevice, under projecting strata of sandstone and limestone, tier on tier, in solitary cells or populous chambers, plastered up like the nests of the mud-swallows, they buried their dead. The cliff, which, for the length of a mile, and for the height of hundreds

ROCK TOMBS, PISAC.

of feet, is literally speckled with the white faces of tombs, is called Tantana Marca ("the Steeps of Lamentation"). Some of the tombs were elaborately built up of cut stones, the rock being dug away behind them, so as to form large chambers; but these have all been broken into and rifled. Many of the others have also been desecrated, but most remain intact. They contain the desiccated, or dried, bodies of the dead, bent in a sitting posture, with their heads resting on their hands, and their hands on their knees, wrapped in coarse cotton cloth or mats of rushes, with a few rude household or other utensils and implements surrounding them.   The dry, rarefied air of this elevation acts on the dead body very much as do the dry air and sandy and nitrous soil of the coast.   Protected from the rain when rain falls, all flesh here dries up and hardens, and, enclosed in tombs like those of the Steeps of Lamentations, bodies may be preserved for many centuries.

I might endeavor to describe at any length the various singular and interesting features of the gigantic mountain fortress of Pisac, and yet fail to give an adequate idea of its extent and strength, or of the skill in design and ability in execution displayed by its builders.   The purpose is similar to that of the fortresses of Sacsahuaman and Piquillacta, which I have already described, but the plan is different.   Taken together, all of them will illustrate the general system of defence practiced by the ancient Peruvians.

# CHAPTER XXVI.

## OVER THE CORDILLERA, FROM CUZCO TO THE COAST.

THE morning broke bright and pleasant on which I was to bid a final adieu to imperial Cuzco, where I had passed many weeks with the same unabated interest with which I had first commenced my explorations, the day after my arrival. But my work here was now done, and imperative duty called me to other fields and to my far-distant home. There were lofty mountains to climb, great rivers to cross, and then the almost endless waters of two oceans stretched between me and that home.

Although the morning was bright and beautiful, it was twelve o'clock before we finally started. We were accompanied for a league by a large cavalcade of friends who wished to see us well on our way. They brought out with them a plentiful supply of ale, with which some of the party became so exhilarated that we were not sorry to bid them all a final good-bye, and commence our journey in dead earnest.

Besides H—— and myself, there were D—— and C——, government engineers, who had been sent out upon surveying duty and were returning to Lima. Before leaving Cuzco, Colonel Várgas, the comandante, had supplied D—— and myself with two extra horses, selected from his own stock. They were valuable as having already twice made the difficult and trying descent to the coast, a hazardous experiment for animals bred in the Sierra. Mine was a dark bay, his back sprinkled over with white spots, like snow-flakes, and hence called " El Nevado." He was a gentle, intelligent, and hardy animal, to whom I became deeply attached. The other was a gray, not so good-tempered, but equally hardy, and, for some whimsical reason, named "Napoleon." Both had been brought up together on the same estate, and were inseparable when free, and unhappy when apart. My wonderful breech-loading rifle, which had excited the astonishment and admiration of all Peru, was to be sent back to Colonel Vargas from Lima.

The road for four leagues was down a small valley leading into the plain of Anta. The town of that name stands upon a promontory, or headland, projecting into the plain, which is broad, low, and in some parts swampy. It was on this plain, also called Xa Xa, that young Almagro was defeated and taken prisoner; and hence he was carried to the place of his execution in the great square of Cuzco. We reached Surita, three leagues from Anta, over the plain, towards noon, and found the master of the post drunk and in ill-humor; and although we were accompanied by a special messenger from the sub-prefect, we were unable to do anything with him. I left D—— and

C—— behind with the boys and baggage, and with H——
pushed on ahead towards Limatambo to examine the ancient
remains at that spot, while the others were coming up.

On the divide between the waters flowing into the Vilcamayo and those of the Apurimac, a magnificent view is obtained of the Andes, including the great snowy peaks of Sal-
jantai and Umantai. The descent for two leagues from this
point was very steep, and it was quite dark when we reached
the hacienda of Tarahuasa, where we passed the night. In the
morning we rode on to the village to obtain post-mules, but
were told the old story grown familiar to our ears, for we had
heard it in every part of Peru—"*Mañana!*" (to-morrow). We
tried the effect of a little harsh language, but it fell on impassive hearers.

We then proceeded to examine the ruins of Limatambo.
These consist entirely of terraces, built up in the manner of others which have been described. They are cyclopean in style,
faced with finely cut stone, admirably fitted together; the surface even with the terrace being accurately cut and levelled.
What has been spoken of by some travellers as a palace or temple is really only a terrace, with a niched wall; though a temple or structure of some kind may once have been built upon
it; but of this there are now no traces. The outer terrace is 20
feet high and 800 feet long, commanding the valley, which is
here very narrow, so that it was probably intended for a fortification.

Pursuing our route down the narrow valley, we came at
nightfall to the village of Mollepata. It is a collection of
wretched huts, on a high shelf of the mountain, with a tumble-
down church, a drunken governor, who is also keeper of the
hovel called a post-house, and a priest as dissolute as the governor  The country around the village is bare, and we had
great difficulty in procuring a little water and a bushel of maize
for our animals for which we paid the modest sum of three
dollars. There was to be a bull baiting the next day, and the
village was full of drunken, sinister-looking vagabonds from far
and near, most of them in a state of beastly intoxication. They

crowded around us, stared at our mules and equipments, and arranged among themselves, in Quichua, which of our animals they should severally steal — so at least Ignacio, who understood their language, informed us.  As the *patio* of the house in which we stopped was open on two sides, we determined to stand guard all night, keeping regular watches, armed to the teeth.  It was well we did so, for several attempts were made to steal or stampede our animals.  We left early, glad to escape from a place unsurpassed in evil repute by any in Peru.

Our road now wound around the high, rocky peak of Mollepata, and ran up each ravine that seamed its sides to its head, then wound back again almost to the place of divergence, so that in a ride of two miles we accomplished an actual advance of but a few hundred yards.  The mountain became steeper and steeper, and we found ourselves at last on a narrow shelf worn by the feet of mules in the mountain-side, and away down below us we discovered the river Apurimac, appearing, in the distance, no larger than a meadow-brook.

Describing half the circumference of the mountain of Mollepata, we came upon a profound ravine, separating the mountain from a high ridge on the other side, on the flanks of which we could discern the red-tile roofs of the extensive hacienda of Bellavista, surrounded by emerald fields of lucern and great yellow patches of sugar-cane.  A league to the right of the hacienda, extending across a depression in the crest of the ridge, appeared a line of arches, something like those stretching across the Campagna of Rome, and a cluster of huts, which our arriero pronounced to be the post-houses of La Banca, to which we were bound.  Accustomed as we had already become to the wonderful ins and outs of mountain travel in Peru, it was nevertheless a question in our minds how we were to cross the deep, dark chasm, with its steep, rocky, and in some places absolutely precipitous sides, which separated us from La Banca.  It certainly was a long and tedious process.  Our course was by a plunging path, skirting the side of the ravine, here and there turning back on itself, and, by a series of sharp zigzags, achieving a descent of a hundred or more feet at points where a child might toss a pebble over the heads of the entire cavalcade into the abyss below. Thus descending, and gradually working our way towards the head of the ravine, we finally came within hearing of the noise of running waters, shut out from view, however, by a vigorous growth of wild olive-trees, canes, and other shrubbery. We soon entered these, and, still plunging downwards under the cool shadows, and among damp and mossy rocks, reached the Rio de la Banca, a strong and rapid torrent, chilled by the melting snows. At the ford it spread out into a broad and quiet pool, and there was a level, trodden space on its banks, showing that this was a favorite resting-place for travellers and muleteers. Only a few yards below, the stream makes a bold leap down a sheer precipice of great height, and falls in a series of cataracts through the black ravine into the Apurimac. Birds were numerous among the trees in this deep gorge, and joined their music to the rough melody of the stream. Our arriero told us that bears were sometimes found in the shrubbery higher up; but we saw no animals except a grayish-yellow fox, which thrust its snout around a neighboring rock for an instant, and then disappeared. A shaded spot like this is so rarely to be found in Peru, that we were loath to leave it to encounter the long and painful ascent to La Banca.

The ascent was, nevertheless, achieved, not without much trouble from our cargo-mules, some of which gave out in the attempt. Before reaching the post-houses, on a sort of shelf of the great ridge, we came upon a few molle and some other trees, sustained by a small, trickling spring. Here, gray and ruined, were the crumbling walls of an Inca tambo, with its well-made adobes and its Egyptian-like doors and windows. These remains indicated, apart from the physical conformation of the country, that we were still on the great route of communication between Cuzco and the northern provinces of the Inca empire. A rough scramble up a steep bank brought us to the huts of La Banca, and beneath the shadow of the arches which had looked so Romanesque from the other side of the great barranca. We found them belonging to a grand *azequia*,

which extended from the foot of the snow-line in the great
mountains of Vilcaconga, and which irrigated the hacienda of
Bellavista, whose owners had restored it, on the line adopted by
its original Inca builders.  By carrying the *azequia* on arches
over a depression in the ridge, they were able to distribute the
water at a higher elevation than the Incas had done, and thus
render productive a larger area of ground.

At this point the ridge was narrowed to a knife-like crest,
and the huts of La Banca, crowded for room, were built partly
against and partly under the arches.  The ravines on either
side were thousands of feet deep, and, standing here, one experienced a sensation akin to that which a man must feel when
perched on the ridge of a narrow-gabled house.  There was
barely room for our animals in the little corral of the post-
house.  The keeper of the post was away at Mollepata, swelling the crowd of drunkards in that village, and his representative, whose personal attractions were not heightened by an
enormous goitre, was in a state of blear-eyed intoxication.  He
responded to all our inquiries by insisting that we should take
a gourdful of turbid chicha, which, so far as we could make
out, was "*muy bueno*," because made from the berries of the
molle-tree.  The condition of the lieutenant postmaster was
that of the remaining few inhabitants of La Banca, male and
female, goitre included, with the exception of one matron, who
advised us not to stop there, where, she said, there was nothing
for man or beast except chicha, and that of the poorest kind,
but to go to the hacienda.

We endeavored to secure from the acting master of the post,
who by law is obliged to have mules always ready, some animals with which to pursue our journey; and showed him the
express and special orders of the Government in our favor.
These he disdained to look at; and, with that contempt of Government which is universal in Peru, except when its authority
is visibly manifested in the shape of an armed force, he con-
signed us to the bottomless pit, and staggered off to his den, in
which a couple of filthy sheepskins served him for a bed.  We
were compelled to temporize; and, finally, on the promise of

double pay, he agreed to have the necessary cargo-mules at the
hacienda early on the following morning.

With this assurance, drawn rather incoherently from the fellow, we started for Bellavista, following the embankment of the
*azequia*, which for most of its length was lined with willows.
These, nourished by the water, had struck their roots deep in
the ground, and formed the principal support of the embankment in places where it seemed next to impossible to carry an
aqueduct except sustained by high and expensive walls of masonry. A rapid ride of half an hour brought us to Bellavista,
a great, low building surrounding a quadrangular court, and containing within its single wide and heavily built gate-way the
apartments of the family, a church, the stables, and the offices
of an establishment, itself the nucleus of a considerable village
of adobe and cane-built huts, the residences of the laborers on
the estate.

Here we met a welcome which anywhere would be generous
as well as cordial, but which in Peru has a higher appreciation
from its rarity. The proprietress is a widow, somewhat advanced in years, and suffering (if the term may be used in reference to an affection which is painless) from the goitre, which
afflicts all the women, young and old, at Bellavista as well as at
La Banca, and gives warrant to the hypothesis that it is sometimes, if not generally, superinduced by the use of snow-water.
Her husband had been a man of enterprise, and had established
a sugar and aguardiente estate here, after first restoring and im-
proving upon the old Inca works for irrigating the previously
barren lands of the hacienda. This covers the whole of a broad
headland, connected with the Vilcaconga Mountains by the narrow crest of La Banca, and slopes down, through almost every
degree of temperature, to the deep, narrow bed of the Apurimac, where the fervid sun creates a more than tropical climate.

Here, wherever there is a patch of soil, tropical products
flourish with more than tropical luxuriance. The water is judiciously distributed over this slope, which looks like a green gem
in a setting of dull, amber-colored mountains. Connected with
the dwelling is a garden, somewhat neglected, but full of peach

and apple trees, and gay with flowers. On one side of the court
is a series of well-furnished apartments, but closed and unoccu-
pied, which our good hostess told us, with moist eyes, belonged
to her children, now absent in Lima, where a son was Deputy
and a son-in-law Senator.

The admirable lady of Bellavista conducted all the complicated business of a large estate with a promptitude, clearness,
and composure that would do credit to the highest administra-
tive talent of any country. In the morning, seated at her window, separated by a screen from the corridor, she called together all the young people of the hacienda to recite their morning
lessons; and the quaint little church, which occupied one corner of the court, never failed to open its rude doors at fixed
hours, to admit her humble dependents to worship before the
dimly lighted but chaste altar supporting the symbols of their
faith.

Of course, the mules promised by the deputy-postman at La
Banca did not make their appearance in the morning; and it
was resolved that the engineers should improve the inevitable
delay in examining a point on the Apurimac supposed to be
favorable for building a bridge, and which was accessible from
the hacienda, while I undertook to return to La Banca armed
with our Government letters, and secure mules for the following days.

H——, our artist, went with the engineers. While in Cuzco
he had expressed his belief that he would be unable to cross the
great swinging bridge over the Apurimac, and the extravagant
stories which he heard there of the difficulties and dangers attending the passage had so excited his apprehensions, that he
declared, in advance, his determination not to make the attempt.
It was in vain we urged him to wait until he reached the
bridge before committing himself so decisively, representing
that the stories about it were doubtless exaggerations, and that
this difficulty, like many others which had been held up to us
by way of terror, would probably disappear on being confronted.
He adhered to his purpose, and announced that if he could not
cross the river by swimming, at Huaynarima, he could go no

farther.  To determine this, he accompanied the engineers in
their expedition.  After a long and difficult descent, in which
they passed a cliff of variously colored salt, the party reached
the Apurimac, where the ravine through which it flows widened
out a little, affording a narrow interval, covered with scrubby
acacias and spiny cactuses, hot as an oven, and swarming with
sand-flies.  The river was low, and C—— swam across it without difficulty, carrying a line wherewith to determine its width.
The town of Curahuasi, on the other side of the river, but
perched some thousands of feet above, and distant little more
than three leagues, was visible from this point.  It would have
been easy for H—— to have crossed, with the aid of his companions; and it would not have been difficult for him to have
reached Curahuasi before nightfall, where we would have overtaken him on the following day.  But for some inexplicable
reason he declined to cross then, and returned with the party
to the hacienda.

My visit to La Banca, meanwhile, was a provoking one.  All
there were drunk, as on the previous day, and, as usual, the deputy-postman was incoherent, and I could extract neither information nor promises from him.  His blear eyes lighted up mo-
mentarily with a gleam of malignant contempt when I produced the letters of the Government, instructing all prefects
and sub-prefects and local governors incontinently to seize on
and imprison all contumacious masters of the posts, or those
who failed to furnish us with horses or mules as provided for
by law.  From the by-standers, male and female, I failed equally to get any satisfactory information.  One declared that there
were no animals; another that they were "*muy arriba*" (high
up), projecting his lips in the direction of the overhanging
mountains; another that they were "*muy léjos*" (very distant),
and he projected his lips down the valley.  Instead of pointing
out an object with the hand or finger, these people use their
lips, puckering them up and pouting them out with a forward
jerk of the head in the direction they wish to indicate.  Half
an hour of alternate expostulation, threats, and entreaty failed
to elicit anything satisfactory, and I returned to the hacienda

with the unpleasant conviction that we might be detained there
for an indefinite period; perhaps, indeed, until the rains had
fairly set in, when it would be impossible to cross the swollen
torrents in our route.   Our good hostess, however, came to our
rescue, and sent her *mayordomo* with a party of stout young
fellows, accompanied by Ignacio, to La Banca, instructed to find
the post-mules, and bring them to us that night; which they
did by main force.

In the morning the postman made his appearance, looking
remarkably seedy; but he was very officious and obsequious.
We gave him but little attention, rejected all his offers of as-
sistance, and scouted his demand for double pay, based upon
our promise of two days before.   We paid him the least the
law allowed, and comforted him with the assurance that he
should be faithfully reported to the sub-prefect at Abancay.

H—— declined to accompany us, and insisted on going afoot
to Huaynarima, and there swim the river.   He also declined
our proffer of a guide and assistant.   I gave him an India-
rubber life-preserver, and, with a cheerful assurance that he
would reach Curahuasi first, he went his way.   We saw him
no more.

The great and elaborate highways, or public roads, which the
chroniclers, and the historians, following their authority, tell us
were constructed by the Incas throughout their vast empire, all
radiating, north, east, south, and west, from the imperial city of
Cuzco, if they existed at all in Central and Southern Peru, have
disappeared, leaving here and there only short sections or fragments, hardly justifying the extravagant praise that has been
bestowed on them.   The modern mule-paths, miscalled roads,
must, necessarily, follow nearly, if not exactly, the routes of the
Indians under the Empire.   The physical conformation of the
country is such that communication between *puna* and *puna*,
and from valley to valley, must always be made by the same
passes.   All these passes over the mountains are marked, by
huge piles of stone raised like the cairns of Scotland and Wales,
by the contribution of a single stone from each traveller as an
offering to the spirits of the mountains, and as an invocation

for their aid in sustaining the fatigues of travel.  These great
stone-heaps still exist, and will remain to the end of time, monuments marking forever the routes of travel in the days of the
Incas.

We know, therefore, from these rude monuments very nearly
what were the ancient lines of communication.  These are also
further indicated by remains of the tambos, which occur at intervals all through the country, and oftenest in places remote
from supplies, in cold and desert districts, where the traveller
stands most in need of food and shelter.

The modern voyager would consider himself supremely fortunate were he to find one in a hundred of these tambos now
in existence; for travelling in Peru is infinitely more difficult
and dangerous than it was in the days of the Incas: more difficult, because the facilities are less; more dangerous, because
the laws are more lax, and the moral standard of the people
lower.  The influence of Spain in Peru has been every way del-
eterious; the civilization of the country was far higher before
the Conquest than now.

As I have said, few traces of the Inca roads, such as are described by the early writers, and such as Humboldt saw in Northern Peru, are now to be found in the southern part of that
country; and as the modern pathways must follow the ancient
lines, I infer that they never existed here, for there is no reason why they should have suffered more from time and the elements in one part of the country than in another.

Between Cuzco and the sweet valley of Yucay, there are numerous traces of an ancient road, some sections of which are
perfect.  These sections coincide in character with the long
reaches in the direction of Quito.  They consist of a pathway
from ten to twelve feet wide, raised slightly in the centre, paved
with stones, and the edges defined by lines of larger stones sunk
firmly in the ground.  Where this road descends from the elevated *puna*—a sheer descent of almost four thousand feet into
the valley of Yucay — it zigzags on a narrow shelf cut in the
face of the declivity, and supported here and there, where foothold could not otherwise be obtained, by high retaining-walls

37.

of cut stone, looking as perfect and firm as when first built centuries ago.

High mountain-ranges and broad and frigid deserts, swept
by fierce, cold winds, are not the sole obstacles to intercommunication in the Altos of Peru, and among those snow-crowned
monarchs of the Andes and Cordilleras.    There are deep valleys, gorges, and ravines among these mountains, or cut deep
in the plains that alternate with them, in which flow swelling
rivers or rapid torrents, fed by the melting snows in the dry
season, and swollen by the rains in the wet season.    They are
often unfordable; but still they must somehow be passed by
the traveller.    A few bridges of stone were constructed by the
Spaniards soon after the Conquest, and a few others have been
erected by their descendants; but, as a rule, the rivers and mountain torrents are passed to-day by the aid of devices the same as
were resorted to by the Incas, and at points which they selected.
Had the principle of the arch been well understood by the ancient inhabitants, who have left some of the finest stone-cutting
and masonry to be found in the world, there is no doubt the
interior of Peru would have abounded in bridges rivalling those
of Rome in extent and beauty.    As it was, occupying a country destitute of timber, they resorted to suspension-bridges, no
doubt precisely like those now constructed by their descendants and successors—bridges formed of cables of braided withes,
stretched from bank to bank, and called *puentes de mimbres*
(bridges of withes).    Where the banks are high, or where the
streams are compressed between steep or precipitous rocks, these
cables are anchored to piers of stone.    In other places they are
approached by inclined causeways, raised to give them the necessary elevation above the water.    Three or four cables form
the floor and the principal support of the bridge, over which
small sticks, sometimes only sections of cane or bamboo, are
laid transversely, and fastened to the cables by vines, cords, or
thongs of raw hide.    Two smaller cables are sometimes stretched
on each side, as a guard or hand-rail.    Over these frail and swaying structures pass men and animals, the latter frequently with
their loads on their backs.

BRIDGE OF THE APURIMAC.

Each bridge is usually kept up by the municipality of the nearest village; and as it requires renewal every two or three years, the Indians are obliged at stated periods to bring to the spot a certain number of withes of peculiar kinds of tough wood, generally of that variety called ioke, which are braided by experts, and then stretched across the stream or river by the united exertions of the inhabitants. Some of the larger and most important structures of this kind are kept up by the Government, and all passengers and merchandise pay a fixed toll. Such is the case with the great bridge over the Apurimac, on the main road from the ancient Guamanga (now Ayacucho) to Cuzco.

The Apurimac is one of the head-waters of the Amazon, a large and rapid stream, flowing in a deep valley, or, rather, gigantic ravine, shut in by high and precipitous mountains. Throughout its length it is crossed at only a single point, between two enormous cliffs, which rise dizzily on both sides, and from the summits of which the traveller looks down into a dark gulf. At the bottom gleams a white line of water, whence struggles up a dull but heavy roar, giving to the river its name, *Apu-rimac*, signifying, in the Quichua tongue, "the great speaker." From above, the bridge, looking like a mere thread, is reached by a path which on one side traces a thin, white line on the face of the mountain, and down which the boldest traveller may hesitate to venture. This path, on the other side, at once disappears from a rocky shelf, where there is just room enough to hold the hut of the bridge-keeper, and then runs through a dark tunnel cut in the rock, from which it emerges to trace its line of many a steep and weary zigzag up the face of the mountain. It is usual for the traveller to time his day's journey so as to reach this bridge in the morning, before the strong wind sets in; for, during the greater part of the day, it sweeps up the cañon of the Apurimac with great force, and then the bridge sways like a gigantic hammock, and crossing is next to impossible.

It was a memorable incident in my travelling experiences, the crossing of this great swinging bridge of the Apurimac. I shall never forget it, even if it were not associated with a circumstance which, for the time, gave me much uneasiness and pain. The fame of the bridge over the Apurimac is coextensive with Peru, and every one we met who had crossed it was full of frightful reminiscences of his passage: how the frail structure swayed at a dizzy height between gigantic cliffs over a dark abyss, filled with the deep, hoarse roar of the river, and how his eyes grew dim, his heart grew faint, and his feet unsteady as he struggled across it, not daring to cast a look on either hand.

Our road to the bridge was circuitous and precipitous, leading down the steeper side of the ridge of La Banca, where it seemed hardly possible for a goat to find foothold. It was a succession of abrupt zigzags, here and there interrupted by a stretch of horizontal pathway. To see our cavalcade it was necessary to look up or down, not before or behind. It was like descending the coils of a flattened corkscrew. In places the rocks encroached on the trail, so that it was necessary to crouch low on the saddle-bow to pass beneath them, or else throw the weight of the body upon the stirrup overhanging the declivity of the mountain, to avoid a collision. The most dangerous parts, however, were where land-slips had occurred, and where it was impossible to construct a pathway not liable at any moment to glide away beneath the feet of our animals. The gorge narrowed as we descended, until it was literally shut in by precipices of stratified rock strangely contorted; while huge masses of stone, rent and splintered as from some terrible convulsion of nature, rose sheer before us, apparently preventing all exit from the sunless and threatening ravine, at the bottom of which a considerable stream struggled, with a hoarse roar, among the black boulders.

There was foothold for neither tree nor shrub; and our mules picked their way warily, with head and ears pointed downwards, among the broken and angular masses. The occasional shouts of the arrieros sounded here sharp and percussive, and seemed to smite themselves to death against the adamantine walls. There was no room for echo. Finally the ravine became so narrowed between the precipitous mountain-sides as barely to afford room for the stream and our scant party. Here a roar, deeper, stronger, and sterner than that of the stream which we had followed, reached our ears, and we knew it was the voice of "the Great Speaker." A little farther on, we came in view of the river and two or three low huts built on the circumscribed space, where the two streams come together. Our muleteers were already busy in unloading the baggage, preparatory to its being carried across the bridge on the cicatrized backs of the occupants of the huts.

To the left of the huts, swinging high in a graceful curve, between the precipices on either side, looking wonderfully frail and gossamer-like, was the famed bridge of the Apurimac. A steep, narrow path, following for some distance a natural shelf, formed by the stratification of the rock, and for the rest of the way hewn in its face, led up, for a hundred feet, to a little platform, also cut in the rock, where were fastened the cables supporting the bridge. On the opposite bank was another and rather larger platform partly roofed by the rock, where was the windlass for making the cables taut, and where, perched like goats on some mountain shelf, lived the custodians of the bridge. The path could barely be discovered, turning sharp around a rocky projection to the left of this perch, then reappearing high above it, and then, after many a zigzag, losing itself in the dark mouth of a tunnel.

My companions and myself lost no time in extracting the measuring-tapes and sounding-lines from our *alforjas*, and hurriedly scrambled up the rocky pathway to the bridge. It was in bad condition. The cables had slacked so that the centre of the bridge hung from twelve to fifteen feet lower than its ends, and, then, the cables had not stretched evenly, so that one side was considerably lower than the other. The cables on either hand, intended to answer the double purpose of stays and parapets, had not sunk with the bridge, and were so high up that they could not be reached without difficulty; and many of the lines dropping from them to the floor, originally placed widely apart, had been broken, so that practically they were useful neither for security nor for inspiring confidence.

Travelling in the Andes soon cures one of any nervousness about heights and depths, and is a specific against dizziness. Nevertheless, we all gave a rather apprehensive glance at the frail structure before us, but we had no difficulty in crossing and recrossing—as we did several times—except on approaching the ends, to which our weight transferred the sag of the cables, and made the last few yards rather steep. A stiff breeze swept up the cañon of the river, and caused a vibration of the bridge from side to side of at least six feet. The motion, however, inspired no sense of danger.

We carefully measured the length and altitude of the bridge, and found it to be, from fastening to fastening, 148 feet long, and at its lowest part 118 feet above the river. Mr. Markham, who crossed it in 1855, estimated the length at 90 feet and the height at 300 feet. Lieutenant Gibbon, who crossed it in 1857, estimated the length 324 feet and the height 150 feet. Our measurements, however, are exact. The height may be increased perhaps ten feet when the cables are made taut. They are five in number, twisted from the fibres of the cabuya, or maguey plant, and are about four inches thick. The floor is of small sticks and canes, fastened transversely with raw-hide strings. The Indians coming from Andahuaylas and other districts, where the cabuya grows, generally bring a quantity of leaves with them, wherewith to pay their toll. These are prepared and made into rope by the custodians of the bridge, who must be glad of some occupation in their lone and lofty eyrie.

Our baggage was carried over the bridge, and the animals were then led across one by one, loaded and started up the mountain. The space is too limited to receive more than two loaded mules at a time, and instances are known of their having been toppled off the precipice from overcrowding. We led our horses over without difficulty, except in getting them on the bridge. But once fairly on the swaying structure, they were as composed as if moving on the solid ground. Perhaps even to the lowest animal intelligence it must be apparent that the centre of the bridge of the Apurimac is not the place for antics, equine or asinine.

Mounted once more, we commenced our steep and difficult ascent. At one place the sheer precipice presented itself on one side, and a vertical wall on the other; next it was a scramble up a ladder or stairs, partly cut in the rock and partly built up with stones against it; then a sudden turn, with a parapet built around it in a semicircle, to prevent descending animals from being carried into the abyss below by their own momentum. Our cargo-mules toiled up painfully above us, stopping every few steps to breathe, while the muleteers braced themselves against their haunches to afford them some support and rest.

We had scarcely reached half-way to the mouth of the tunnel, which enters the mountain at the base of a vast, vertical mass of rock, when our attention was arrested by the shouts of our men, and a commotion among the animals above us. It was occasioned by a descending train of loaded mules, just plunging out of the black throat of the tunnel. The mountain mule always seeks to take the wall of the animal it meets, being perfectly aware of the danger of trying to pass on the outer side of the pathway; and it sometimes happens that neither will give way under any amount of persuasion or blows. The muleteers have to unload the animals, which may then be got past each other. A similar difficulty occurred now, and the conductor of the advancing train hurried down to warn us to dismount and seek the widest part of the path, or some nook by its side, and there await the passage of his mules. He had hardly done speaking when we saw one of our own mules, loaded with our trunks, come plunging down the narrow zigzagging way, evidently in fright, followed wildly by its driver. Just before reaching the place where we stood the animal fell, going literally heels over head, and would have been carried over the little platform of rock into the river, had not the master of the descending train caught the falling mule by its fore-leg, and in this way saved it from tumbling over. He at once placed his whole weight on its ears, thus preventing it from struggling, and thus obviating its destruction, while we detached its cargo. A foot farther, and the mule would inevitably have been lost.

It was with no little satisfaction that we saw the last mule of the train pass us, and resumed our ascent. We found the tunnel a roomy one, two or three hundred yards in length, with openings from the face of the precipice for the admission of light and air. Through these we caught brief glimpses of the grand and solemn mountains on the opposite side of the cañon, and through them came in also, hoarse and sullen, the deep voice of the river. I am uncertain as to how far this tunnel may be ascribed to the Incas, but feel sure that their bridge across the Apurimac was at precisely the same point with the present one.

We were fully two hours in ascending the steeps, and reaching the high mountain-circled plain in which stands the straggling town of Curahuasi, a well-watered village buried among the trees and shrubbery. Although more than eight thousand feet above the sea-level, we noticed several fields of sugar-cane near the village. We had no letters to Curahuasi, and went straight to the post-house, a squalid hut indeed, with but two rooms, one of which was kitchen and dormitory, shared equally by the family, dogs, hens, and guinea-pigs. The other, or guests' room, had a rickety table as its complement of furniture, and its mud floor was piled with rubbish of all descriptions, dust-covered and repulsive, showing that no one had occupied it for a long time.

Our men cleared a space wide enough for our beds, and here we awaited the arrival of H——. That he had not reached the *posta* did not surprise us, as it was still early, and it was not impossible that he had found some better stopping-place in the village. So we rambled out inquiring of every body we met whether he had been seen, but heard nothing of him. Night came, and we recklessly burned our last candle, and kept alternate watch for him in the street. It was past midnight before we gave up our expectations of his arrival, and went to bed, counting on seeing him early in the morning. Towards daylight, but while it was still dark, we were startled by a loud pounding at the door. Supposing that it proceeded from our missing companion, I rose hastily, struck a light, and removed the brace against the door, when the strangest figure entered that I ever saw in my life. It was that of a man, tall and skeleton-like. His limbs were bare and deeply scarred, and his long, tangled hair was bleached by sun and weather. Beneath his left arm he carried a miscellaneous collection of sticks, bones, pieces of rope, and other rubbish, and in his right hand a long and gnarled stick. Altogether, with his deeply sunken eyes and parchment skin, he might have passed for one of Macbeth's witches, and was not a pleasant object for one to encounter when just awaking from sleep. I perceived at once that he was insane, but, as insane men have disagreeable freaks, I was not sorry to find that my friends were also awake and at my side. Our visitor, however, showed no violence, but commenced talking rapidly and incoherently.

We thought for a while that he intended to communicate something to us about H——, but we could extract nothing coherent from him. He seemed to comprehend that we were foreigners, and repeated frequently the word "*Ingleses*" (Englishmen). We gave him the fragments of our supper, and he left. Next day we ascertained that he was a Spaniard, who had been at one time largely engaged in mining in the vicinity, but had become completely demented some years ago in consequence of death in his family and financial troubles.

Morning brought no news of the missing artist. We climbed the hills back of the town in a vain effort to discover some approaching figure in the direction whence he was expected. At ten o'clock, after great difficulty, we succeeded in finding the syndic, and in despatching Indian couriers to Huaynarimac, where H—— had proposed to cross the river, with instructions to scour the banks as far as they could be followed, and to explore every hut on the way. Another courier was sent back to Bellavista, to ascertain if, failing in his attempt, he had returned thither.

It was useless for my friends to remain waiting in our wretched quarters, and it was arranged that they should leave at noon, and wait for me in Abancay, nine leagues distant. I passed the day anxiously, my apprehensions increasing hourly; and when some of the couriers returned at night without bringing any news of our missing friend, I felt deep alarm. The night, in the filthy little *posta*, was long and dreary, and my feelings were in no degree soothed by the circumstance that my servant, Ignacio, had improved the idle day in getting dead-drunk.

Morning came, and still no intelligence.  By ten o'clock the Indians had all come in, having failed to obtain the slightest news or trace of the missing man, and the belief was reluctantly forced upon me that he had been swept down by the current of the river into the deep cañon through which it flows, and where it would be impossible to follow, even with boats.  The syndic agreed with me that I could do no more; and, arranging with him to send a courier to me at Abancay, if he succeeded in obtaining any information as to the fate of our friend, I determined to start for that place, and enlist the power of the sub-prefect in making further investigations.  I found myself almost powerless in Curahuasi, even with the aid of the syndic, and could excite no kind of interest among the stolid and sullen Indians, in the object of my solicitude.

At Abancay the sub-prefect took up the matter with zeal, and issued imperative orders to all the authorities within his jurisdiction to spare no efforts to ascertain the fate of the missing artist.  We remained for several days in Abancay; but, hearing nothing relating to the lost man, we were compelled to pursue our journey over the mountains to the coast, in the full conviction that the worst had happened.

Some time after my return to the United States, I received the following letter from Professor Raimondi, who had been my fellow-voyager in the open-boat exploration of Lake Titicaca.  It is dated from Cuzco:

"As regards our friend, Mr. H——, I have received the most extraordinary story.  It seems that he did swim the Apurimac in safety, and, finding the water pleasant, under the great heat of the valley, he placed his clothes on a rock overhanging the stream, and amused himself by taking a longer bath.  Unfortu-

nately, a sudden gust of wind tumbled his bundle of clothing,
containing also his shoes, into the river. His efforts to recover
it were fruitless, and, after receiving several severe bruises
among the rocks in the attempt, he was glad to get ashore
again, naked as our father Adam. Here, on the arid, treeless
bank, among sharp rocks, spiny cactuses, and thorny acacias, under a fervid sun, and swarmed all over by venomous sand-flies,
he commenced his search for some inhabited place. His feet,
however, soon became cut up by the sharp stones, and his person blistered by the heat. His only relief consisted in throwing water from time to time over his body, until night, with its
dews, came on, and sheltered his nakedness. The heat in the
close *quebrada* of the Apurimac, although intense by day, gives
place to rather severe cold after sundown, and Mr. H——, to
protect himself from this, was obliged to dig a bed in the
warm sand, where he passed the night. The next day he resumed his painful journey, but night again came on without
his being able to reach any human habitation. For three whole
days he wandered about in this primitive condition, without
nourishment of any kind. His feet were cut in pieces, and his
body raw with the heat, bites of insects, and the scratches of
shrubbery. Finally he reached a wretched hut, but his mis-
eries did not end here.

"It should be premised that this *quebrada* is notorious for
its insalubrity. Fever here reigns supreme, and has inspired
the few Indians who live here with the greatest dread. Having little conception of things not material, they have come to
give even to diseases a physical form, and the fever is embodied in a human figure. Consequently, when Mr. H—— approached the hut, its occupants imagined that the dreaded fever
had made its palpable appearance. Some of them fled in terror; but others, more valiant, caught up stones wherewith to
attack and drive off the horrible apparition, so that he had a
narrow escape with his life. After much delay and trouble,
the fears of the Indians were allayed, and the sufferer was admitted to such shelter and food as the wretched hut could afford. Here he was subsequently found by the men in search

of him, taken to Curahuasi, and thence to Abancay, where he
was hospitably treated. It was, however, some months before
he became able to move about. I venture the prediction that
he will never again flinch from the imaginary dangers of the
swinging bridges of Peru."

As I have said, I never saw H—— after our parting at the
Hacienda Bellavista; but many months after my return to the
United States, he forwarded to me from Lima many drawings
and sketches which he had made after our separation. One of
these is here reproduced.

THE ARTIST AND THE INDIANS.

The road from Curahuasi led us still upwards for three
leagues, till we reached the highest point since leaving Cuzco.
Then we commenced our descent to the small but industrious
town of Abancay, which we reached about dark, just at the
commencement of a heavy thunder-storm, which continued un-
interruptedly during the night.

At the elevated and retired point known as Concacha, near Abancay, is one of the many remarkable sculptured rocks of Peru. It is of limestone, about twenty feet long, fourteen broad, and twelve high. The top is cut into what appears to be a series of seats, reached by a broad flight of steps, at the side of which is a flight of smaller but narrower steps, which could hardly have been intended for purpose of ascent, since that purpose is fully answered by the larger and broader stairs.

THE ROCK OF CONCACHA—FRONT AND BACK.

The upper surface of the smaller, or southern, end of the rock is raised a few inches above the general level of the summit. and has sunk in it a number of round and oval bowl-shaped cavities, varying from four to nine inches in diameter, and from three to six inches deep. From one of these nearest the edge of the rock leads off a little canal, which conducts over the side of the rock, where it branches, leading into four reservoirs cut in the stone, in the style of pockets, the two larger ones capable of holding half a gallon each. Water poured into the upper receptacle would flow out and find its way into these singular side receptacles. M. Desjardins, having before him a sketch and description of this rock, does not hesitate to connect it with human sacrifices, and seems satisfied that the blood of the victims was shed on the top of the rock, and that the manner in which it flowed into one receptacle or another, or over the sides into the side reservoirs, in some way decided the divinations of the priests. He, however, wholly begs the question concerning human sacrifices, the existence of which in Peru is certainly not yet proved. I am more inclined to think that the purpose of the rock was not far different from that of the one which we saw in the valley of Yucay; and that here, as there, were poured out libations of chicha, which thirsty priests thriftily collected in the various receptacles, while those who made the offering devoutly believed that it was absorbed by the oracle which dwelt in the rock. That one dwelt there on occasion is pretty clear, since we find, on the side of the rock opposite the stairway or ascent a deep niche cut in the stone, large enough to receive a man. The stone slab with which the niche was closed when requisite lies to-day before it. Traces of a building of stone, surrounding the rock, still remain, and there are many other rocks in the neighborhood cut in the forms of enormous seats. We see that the Inca priests were nearly as skilful and crafty as their more polished ancient brethren beyond the seas, and that the great trade of imposing on the credulity and weaknesses of humanity has flourished in all times, is indigenous to all climes, and is confined to no age or family of men.

About a mile north of the town of Abancay is a high limestone rock, faced round with masonry to the height of twenty-five feet on two terraces. It has been called an Inca fort, but in fact is an inti-huatana. There is a graded way or steps leading up the north-west side, and from the top there is a fine view of the valley in all directions. There are traces of a small building upon the top, about fifty feet square.

From Abancay the road descends rapidly, through sugar-estates, to the river Pachachaca, which we crossed on a fine stone bridge of a single arch, and bearing the date of 1564. By its side are some remains of a suspension-bridge, probably of Inca origin. We spent a day in Andahuaylas, for the simple reason that there were no mules to be had to enable us to get away. We succeeded with difficulty in getting a promise of those necessary animals for the following day, Sunday. We were entertained by the sub-prefect during the night.

Though it rained in the morning, when he at last obtained the mules, we had lost too much time to make any further stay, and we started on our way, noticing, as we passed along, the yellow Flor del Inca. We rode through the town of Talavera, and, if physiognomy is any test, the looks of its inhabitants fully justified their bad reputation. Again our route ascended, and then, at a distance of four leagues, we reached Moyobamba, a post station, consisting of a couple of rude buildings of rough stone, entirely untenanted. No time was lost in making a fire and in sending out some of the party to obtain necessary fodder for our jaded animals. Every thing around us was cold and desolate, and, though we seemed in absolute solitude, we prudently fastened up the entrance as well as we could with ropes, and then sought our couches. Considering our accommodations, we passed a very comfortable night, thankful to be even thus sheltered from the rain, which poured incessantly. Nor had it ceased in the morning, when we had to resume our journey over a road that was scarcely in a condition for travel, even by our experienced animals. As we made our toilsome way up to the high, bleak *puna*, the rain changed to sleet, hail, and snow, which seemed to envelop us, and to come from all directions. It was all our poor beasts could do to make head against the storm; they slipped fearfully, but toiled patiently on to the *puna* above. Here, for the first time since leaving the plain of Tiahuanaco, we saw flocks of vicuñas.

From this elevated point, our road now ran down, steep and slippery, to the Rio Pampas; and, late in the afternoon, we entered the tumble-down town of Chinchero. The governor, to whom the sub-prefect had written, was, of course, absent; but we were directed to a house on the plaza. This, however,

38

proved to be carefully locked, and we had to wait with what
patience we could command.   Two hours exhausted all we possessed.   We then picked the lock and entered, but deemed it
most prudent to keep watch over our beasts, which we did in
turn, all the long, rainy night.

HANGING BRIDGE OVER THE RIO PAMPAS.

The weather clearing late in the morning, we started and descended a long and difficult crest to the Rio Pampas, which
flows through a somewhat wider valley than we usually met in
the mountains.   We rode through the uninhabited valley for a
league, between perpendicular, conglomerate cliffs, to the suspension-bridge of the Rio Pampas, after crossing which we

camped for the night.  This bridge is next in interest to that
over the Apurimac.  The surrounding scenery, if less grand, is
still magnificent.  The bridge is picturesquely situated, and is
135 feet in length, and 45 feet high, in the centre, above the
rapid and broken waters of the river.  At the time of our visit
the bridge had sagged somewhat to one side, but not to an ex-

LOOKING ACROSS THE BRIDGE.

tent that made it at all dangerous, and our animals crossed without giving us any difficulty.

The morning enabled us to take some fine views, though carrying the photographic apparatus across this frail structure
swaying in the wind was by no means an easy matter.  At ten
o'clock we were again in the saddle, and toiled upwards a long

and tiresome four-league way, over a desolate and parched country, nothing appearing to remind us of human existence except a

few traces of former Inca occupancy. The miserable little town of Ocras, when we reached it, offered us a post-house alive with fleas innumerable. The rain without compelled us to keep them company, but I cannot say that we passed a comfortable night. Yet it was decidedly superior to the night following, when we tried to sleep under the

THE POST-HOUSE AT OCRAS.

lee of a hut which was reputed to be a post-house, but which was too repulsive for us to think of entering, and could afford no food for man or beast.

The next day's ride was over a dreary, barren country of steep ascents and headlong descents. It was by far the most miserable that we had yet passed in Peru, but at its close, eighteen days after our start from Cuzco—days of adventure as well as fatigue—we entered Ayacucho, a considerable town of ten thousand inhabitants. Letters were to have reached us here; but we were sadly disappointed at failing to receive them.

Near this town is the battle-field of Ayacucho, where the viceroy Laterna, with the royalists of Spain under his command, met the so-called patriot army, under General Sucre. The battle took place December 9th, 1824, and ended in the capitulation of the royalists, eleven thousand in number, to the patriot army of seven thousand. This overthrow put an end to the power of Spain in South America. When they first came to Peru, the Spaniards called this city Guamanga; but the republicans changed its name to Ayacucho, in honor of their decisive victory. The houses are of two stories, with court-yards and large rooms. The whole city, indeed, is laid out and built on a grand scale, but there are unmistakable signs of a

gradual decline in wealth and population. Ayacucho boasts of
a cathedral and twenty-two churches; but that which interested
me most was the Church of San Cristobal, in which were laid
the remains of the Corregidor Holguin, who captured Guate-
mozin, on the Lake of Mexico. In the plaza, where you can
buy of the Indians barley, wheat, maize, and fruits brought
from the farther side of the eastern ridge, is a fountain, with
a statue of Liberty, which to me was emblematic of the country, as it stood there, without a head to direct or an arm to en-
force or defend.

In regard to some of the remains in the vicinity of Ayacucho,
we find the following account, by one of the early native writers.
I did not have the time to investigate the truth of the statement if I had had the inclination, and only give it as a literary
curiosity, and for what it may be worth:

"In the year 1637, in the town of Guinoa, two leagues from
the ancient Guamanga, was accidentally discovered a subterranean palace, with grand portals of stone and sumptuous edifices. In this was found a stone, with an inscription that could
not be read; and there were statues of men, also in stone,
which, after the style of pilgrims, carried their hats suspended
to their shoulders. Among them was one mounted on a horse,
with lance in rest, and a shield on his left arm. These remains
were examined by the aid of torches, a thread being carried in
from the entrance as a guide by which to return. I do not
affirm the existence of this palace, because I have not seen it:
the witness thereof is Señor Pinelo, who assures us of the fact.
If this author did not see what he describes, or was imposed on
by others, it must be easy to find out, in the town of Guinoa,
if such famous monuments really exist."

We recruited a week at Ayacucho before starting over the
Despoblado intervening between this ancient and historical
town and the coast — a region in no place less than fourteen
thousand, and generally not less than eighteen thousand, feet
above the sea. The journey is a long, tedious, and exhaustive
one, and for several days after leaving Ayacucho lies over the
broad, lofty mountain billow, distinguished from the Andes

proper by the name of the Cordillera de la Costa.  There are
neither towns nor refuges, except caverns, in this cold, arid, desolate region—no wood, and, for long distances, neither grass nor
water.  To be overtaken here by storms, or to have your animals succumb to fatigue or the dreaded *soroche*, involves, as its
least consequence, great suffering, and often loss of life, as the
thousands of skeletons and desiccated bodies of men and animals scattered over the savage *punas* and among the lofty
passes of the mountains too plainly suggest to the adventurous
traveller.

For five days we struggled over the bleak hills and barren
plains, through a savage scenery which only the pencil of Doré
could depict, with no shelter except such as our little photographic tent afforded, and without food, except such as we carried with us, or was afforded by the flesh of a few biscachas,
vicuñas, and huanacos, the only animals to be found here.  The
rainy season was commencing, and the bitter winds howled
in our ears, and drove the sand, like needles, into our tumid
faces, while the snow flurried around the high, rugged peaks
that lifted their splintered crests on every hand.

On the sixth day after leaving Ayacucho, our arriero halted
us on the brow of a tremendous ravine, up the walls of which
we had scrambled for two weary hours, with imminent peril to
life and limb.  It was only two o'clock ; and although the animals drooped their heads and breathed heavily—for we were
nearly sixteen thousand feet above the sea—I felt impatient at
the halt, especially as I saw that he had commenced unloading
the mules with the evident intent of going into camp.

"Why," I asked, "are we stopping here at this hour?"

He did not answer in words, but waved his hand in the direction of the vast, open, but most dreary and desolate broken
plain, that seemed to spread out interminably before us.   A
plain without a blade of grass or sign of life, bare, bleak, and
looking as if furrowed by the searching winds that had swept
out every grain of sand from between the jagged edges of the
rocks that projected, like decaying fangs, above its surface.
"But we have got to cross it—why not now?"

"*No hay agua—nada!*" (There is no water—nothing).

We succeeded, however, in carrying our point.  Our arriero, with unconcealed disgust and some muttered words in Quichua, which we did not understand, but which were significant enough, repacked the animals and started them off, at a rapid pace, over the rough and repulsive *puna*.

How he kept our already weary animals at the tremendous pace across the *puna* that he did, I do not know.  I only know that we had a brief race on the edge of the plain after a wounded vicuña, and that we halted only once or twice to bag a stray biscacha.  Yet, long before dark, we could barely detect our baggage-animals, looking like ants in the distance.  C—— had gone on with them.  As it grew darker we changed our saddles, and took a bearing upon our friends before they were out of sight.

It was well that we did so; for a minute afterward they had disappeared behind a swell in the land.  I had been riding "El Nevado" all the day, leaving my mule to run free, while D—— had left "Napoleon" to do the same—the free animals running with their halters fastened to our cruppers.  But as this was a rather unnecessary precaution, and, when moving rapidly, an obstruction, we packed the slaughtered vicuña and biscachas on the liberated animals, and cast them loose, and then started at a round pace to overhaul our train.  "El Nevado" and his companion fell a little behind, but not to such a distance as to alarm us, especially as we soon struck the trail.  Sometimes we lost sight of our followers behind some inequality of the ground, but always discovered them pacing after us when we ascended the swells of the land.

It was getting dark, and we could with difficulty make out the track, at best but lightly marked in the flinty soil.  Our chief guides were the white skeletons of animals that had succumbed, and had been left by the side of the path as prey for the condors.

We did not doubt that "El Nevado" would follow us, especially as his foster-brother was ahead.  As soon as it became absolutely dark, we slackened our pace, and peered ahead to discover our companions, and behind to discern our horses, but equally without result. All trace of our road disappeared. We dismounted, and literally felt our way. I resorted to the Indian expedient of putting my ear to the ground, to detect the step of man or animal, but in vain. There was but one thing left to do; so I fired a round from my rifle. A second or so afterwards a faint response, so faint that we thought it an exhausted echo, seemed to rise from some place deep down to our left. I fired another round, and we listened intently. A moment more, and a faint report struggled up, as from the bottom of a well.

We found that our arriero had plunged into a ravine that might be called an abyss, because there was a little water there, a few tufts of coarse ichu grass, and, what was of no little importance, some heaps of vicuña dung, which answered for fuel. D—— and myself, after a sumptuous supper of charqui and coffee, scrambled up to the plain again in a vain search for our missing animals. We went to bed (if stretching one's self on the bare ground may be called going to bed) under hopeful assurance from our arriero that the *bestias* would find us before morning.

Morning came, raw and damp, and the animals had not made their appearance. While breakfast was preparing, D—— and myself climbed the steep sides of the ravine again, only wondering how we ever got up or down in the dark.

We mounted the rocks and ranged our glasses around the horizon, in vain effort to discover the animals. Scrambling down again, we instructed the train to push ahead, unburdened ourselves of our *alforjas* and water-proof over-garments, retaining only our pistols: in short, put ourselves in light-marching order, and, telling our friends that we would overtake them before night, started off again to scour the plain in search of "El Nevado" and his errant companion.

We rode for two hours, back over the dreary plain, looking for the trail of our missing animals, and were about giving them up, when we came suddenly upon their tracks. It was past noon, but to give up now, on the very threshold of success, was not to be thought of a second time. Up, up for half a mile, where foot of man or horse had perhaps never gone before, to the rough crest of a rocky peak that seemed to dominate the forest of similar eminences around it, and which broke off in an absolute precipice on the other side.

We followed a narrow, lightly worn path, the merest trace in the steep declivities of the barren hills, winding out and in, now around the heads of lateral ravines, and then down into the dry, stony beds of torrents. Suddenly, on turning a sharp bend, some object started from the path in front, and began with deer-like fleetness to ascend the mountain. It only needed a second glance to perceive that the object was an Indian dressed in vicuña skins, and with a head-dress of flossy alpaca, which drooped behind him in the form of the conventional fool's cap. We shouted for him to stop, but he paid no attention to our command, until D—— threw up the loose dirt a few yards in advance of him with a bullet from his revolver. Then he came down, meekly enough, holding his alpaca cap in both trembling hands.

We reassured him as well as we could, and were delighted that he knew a few words of Spanish, in virtue of which we made out that the stray animals were just around a projecting ledge in another *barranca*. He led the way, and, after a tough scramble, we came in sight of a poor hut of stones sunk in the earth, with the exception of its conical roof of ichu grass, and hardly distinguishable from the hard and barren soil. On the instant "Napoleon" set up a shrill, interrogative neigh, which was responded to by an affirmative winnow from "El Nevado," safely tethered behind the Indian hut, whose occupants, an unkempt woman with two equally unkempt children, suddenly projected their heads, like rabbits, from a low orifice at the base of the hut, and as suddenly withdrew them.

The Indian, who was the shepherd of some llama and alpaca flocks that found a scanty support in a neighboring valley, had encountered the animals that morning, struggling on the blind path to his hut, and had tethered them there, not knowing what else to do with them. We found that his wages were eight dollars a year, and his means of support such llamas and alpacas as might die, and a little quinoa that he was able to cultivate in a distant *quebrada*. The vicuña and biscachas that he had found still strapped on the backs of our mules were a bountiful and unexpected addition to his scanty stores; and I have no doubt he had already made sacrifice of a quid of coca to the Indian god corresponding to the genius of Good Fortune. We rewarded our new acquaintance as we were able, and he undertook to guide us back to the trail we had left, a good league and a half distant.

We recovered our horses, but we nearly lost our lives. It was late in the afternoon when we struck out again on the horrible waste which we had traversed twice before. The sky was sullen and threatening, and every portent was of cold and storm. The prospect was not provocative of conversation; and we urged our animals, which seemed to comprehend the situation, at the top of their powers over the stony *puna*. Directly rain began to fall, changing rapidly to sleet, which fell in blinding sheets, and froze on our garments. Every indication of the trail soon disappeared, and an icy waste spread around us as far as we could see. To stand still was to freeze; to go on was to wander off in an unknown desert.

We gave ourselves up to the guidance of our horses, "Napoleon" heroically leading the way. On, on we trudged, the icy crust crackling under our tread, until it became pitch-dark, when we discovered, by the zigzagging course and downward plunge of our animals, that we were descending rapidly. They ultimately stopped, and we supposed that we had reached the place of our previous night's bivouac. But by the light of a twisted roll of paper, ignited by the solitary match that had escaped being wetted in D——'s pocket, we found that we were in a ravine full of great rocks, and that the animals were at a dead fault as to how to get on farther. They huddled close to us, and we stood leaning on their rimy necks all that long and dreary night—oh, how long and dreary!—until the sun struggled through the clouds, surcharged with snow, and thawed our stiff, unyielding garments. It was nearly noon before we could find the trail, which we followed until late in the afternoon, when we were met by an Indian, carrying charqui and bread, one of several messengers whom C—— had sent back from his camp under the friendly rock which our arriero described with grim irony as the "Posada de San Antonio." We found C—— in great distress on account of our absence. He had kept awake all night, and had repeatedly fired his gun to guide us to camp.

We were now upon the banks of a small rivulet, the source of the river Pisco, and from a high point, the highest in the Western Cordilleras, caught our first view of the Pacific. The descent was now very rapid, and in a few hours we were among some fine alfalfa estates. At 7 P.M. we reached the estate of La Quinya, where we were hospitably permitted to sleep in the corridor.

The next day, at an early hour, we arrived at Pisco, after experiencing an earthquake in the morning, which lasted a few seconds, and to which I have already referred. We were thirty days in making the journey from Cuzco to Pisco, which includes five days' stoppage at Ayacucho. At Pisco we met the welcome letters and papers from home.

After two years, spent in exploring the country, during which we crossed and recrossed the Cordillera and the Andes, from the Pacific to the Amazonian rivers, sleeping in rude Indian huts or on bleak *punas*, in the open air, in hot valleys, or among eternal snows, gathering with eager zeal all classes of facts relating to the country, its people, its present and its past, I found myself surrounded with my trophies of travel, on the deck of a steamer in the harbor of Callao, homeward-bound, brown in color and firm in muscle.

## CHAPTER XXVII.

### CONCLUSION.

Inca Civilization.—The People, as found by the Spaniards.—Rapidity of their Conquest.—The Civilization of Peru Indigenous.—Nature of Inca Superiority.—Originally Several Tribes.—Quichuas and Aymarás.—Their Differences not solely owing to Physical Conditions.—Probable Course of Union and Development.—Growth of Separate Historical Legends, merging into each other.—Legends as transmitted by Garcilasso and Montesinos.—How the Traditions were perpetuated.—Their Quippus very Imperfect Means of Record.—Consequent Importance of the Monuments.—What we may learn from them.—Probable Course of the Inca Empire, without the Spanish Conquest.—Date of the Peruvian Monuments wholly Uncertain.—Some of them among the Oldest existing.—Reasons why they are not more Numerous.—No Evidence that the Peruvians came originally from Abroad.

In this chapter I shall present a rapid *résumé* of some of the conclusions to which I have been led as to the ancient civilization of Peru, and especially of the Incas, from my examination of their works which still remain. The Spanish conquerors found in America nations far advanced in the arts, who had constructed great works of public utility, and who had founded imposing systems of government and religion. Among these there were two, far in advance of all the others: the Mexicans, who occupied the lofty table-land of Anahuac; and the Peruvians, who had spread themselves among the valleys and down the slopes of the Andes. Prescott, following the Spanish chroniclers, has traced the story of the overthrow of these empires; but this overthrow was so sudden and complete that the chroniclers had hardly time to set down the events which took place before their own eyes, and had little leisure, or perhaps inclination, to make a careful investigation into the principles of their civil and religious polity. This work has devolved upon the laborious students and archæologists of a later time.

That the civilization of the ancient Peruvians was indigenous admits of no reasonable doubt. Wherever we find its traces, whether in the bolsones of the mountains or in the valleys running down to the coast, it presents everywhere peculiar and distinct traces. I have endeavored to show how far, and in what manner, these peculiarities were induced by the physical character of the region. Up to the time when the Incas were able to commence that system of aggrandizement which resulted in the establishment of their great empire, civilization seems to have gone on, with almost equal steps, in all those parts of South America in which the natural conditions were favorable to its development. The superiority of the Incas was more apparent than real; or, rather, their superior traits were more the outgrowth of their new condition and relationships than of any innate superiority in themselves. Warfare never produces military capacity which has not before existed in times of peace; and the Incas did not commence to be conquerors until they had first shown themselves to be statesmen: and when they were fairly brought into contact with the other families, they showed that they had already become strong.

There can be no doubt that, in very remote times, there were numerous petty tribes isolated—locked up, as it were—in the narrow valleys and secluded bolsones. Some writers have undertaken to group these numerous families into the Chinchas of the coast, and the Quichuas, Huancas, and Aymarás in the interior. D'Orbigny, one of the best of these writers, divides the indigenous population of what was the Inca empire into the Quichuas and the Aymarás; the former occupying the region from the river Andasmayo, above Quito, to the Rio Maure in Chili, with the exception of a transverse section extending from the western base of the Andes, overlooking the great basin of Lake Titicaca, and reaching to the coast, thus completely cutting in two the territory which he assigns to the Quichuas. But even while making this division, he tells us that, "considered in their physical and moral character," the Quichuas and Aymarás were evidently of the same stock, and that their languages were only dialects of a common tongue.

I am not prepared to admit the accuracy of these generaliza-
tions, even while recognizing the great differences which certainly existed among them. These differences are too great
to be referred wholly to the influence of climate and physical
conditions, and may be fairly considered as amounting to distinctions of race. The Quichuas and Aymarás were, indeed,
Indians, and both South American Indians, as distinguished
from the aborigines of North America. But they differed from
each other as widely as the Germans differ from the French;
and both differed widely from the present degenerate natives
of the coast. There was, indeed, a certain blending of the various families, or races, and a certain predominance of the Quichua language, which was that of the Incas; but this was less
than can be reconciled with the accounts which we have of the
persistent and energetic efforts of the Incas to assimilate all the
peoples who fell under their sway.

If we recognize the full weight of all the conditions which
I have indicated, and presuppose that the different portions of
what ultimately became the Inca empire had reached indepen-
dently certain degrees of development, which, in course of time,
acted and reacted upon each other, we can perceive how it happened that their various historical legends grew to be contradictory and apparently irreconcilable. Let us suppose, for example, that a family or group, established in the bolson of Cuzco,
attained a preponderance of power under local chiefs, and that
they finally broke over their ancient narrow bounds, reduced
other families under their rule, and assumed the supremacy
over them. Evidently, then, two sets of traditions would grow
up among a people so constituted; and these traditions would
also group themselves into two distinct epochs. These, in time,
would naturally tend to merge together; for the predominant
race would seek to attribute to themselves the great achievements of the others, and at length it would be hard to say where
the history of one race ended and that of the other began. In
this way, we may account, at least partially, for the contradic-
tions in legendary Peruvian history, and for the differences in
the tables of Inca lineage, as given by Garcilasso de la Vega

and by Montesinos, the former of whom gives fourteen Inca sovereigns, whose dynasty commenced in the eleventh century; while the latter mentions one hundred and one wearers of the imperial *llautu*, whose reign goes back to within five hundred years of the Deluge. In other words, it seems evident that the legendary history of the various principalities, if we may so style them, which went to make up the Inca empire is one thing, and that of the empire itself is quite another. The former is very ancient, going back, probably, as far into antiquity as that of any other people on the globe, while the latter is comparatively modern.

Perhaps the traditions of the Incas were preserved with as much care as those of any other nation which depended solely upon oral means of preservation. They were confided to the keeping of the *amautes*, or wise men, who taught them in the schools of Quito. Probably, so far as they related to the comparatively modern history of the Incas and their empire, properly so called—the succession of the princes and their conquests —they were substantially correct. But it is by no means certain that they were faithfully reported to the Spanish chroniclers, through whom they come to us, or that these chroniclers even took the pains faithfully to set them down as they were given to them. We have no means, for example, of knowing certainly that Garcilasso, who is our principal authority, had good foundation for the genuineness of the accounts which he has transmitted; for it must be borne in mind that the *quippus*, or knotted cords, which were used to continue the records, were a very clumsy and inadequate contrivance for perpetuating dates and numbers. They were, at best, only aids to memory, about on a par with Robinson Crusoe's notched calendar, or the chalked tally of an illiterate tapster. Even if they had a proper numerical significance (and this is by no means certain), they were in every other respect inferior to the rudest pictured symbols of our North American Indians, and still far inferior to the painted records of the Mexicans, or the probably syllabo-phonetic writings of the aborigines of Central America.

In this virtual absence of all written documents, the study of the architectural monuments of the Peruvians becomes of the highest importance in the investigation of their history and civilization. These are, indeed, of the greatest value. They show clearly the state of their arts in almost every department. We have evident remains of what they could do in architecture. Their reservoirs and aqueducts give us a clear insight into their agricultural system. Their bridges, roads, and tambos tell us of their means of intercommunication. Their great fortresses and other public works show that the rulers had at their disposal the labor of a numerous and industrious population. And the very absence of any remains of the habitations of the common people shows us conclusively what must have been the condition of the masses. These monuments also illustrate the proficiency to which they had attained in what may be called the sciences. We have, for instance, the very means which they used for determining the solstices and the passage of the sun through the heavens. From the position and character of the great fortresses, as at Ollantaytambo and Pisac, we can learn much of the military condition of the empire. Events vaguely recited by tradition assume a historical character when we find the ruins of such and such a town, which such and such an Inca is said to have built or destroyed, or of works which he is said to have constructed. Fortifications, if on a grand scale, naturally occur near the frontiers of an empire, and in the direction from which an attack might be anticipated. These ruins also throw much light upon customs, modes of life, and political, social, and domestic organization. We know how crimes were punished, from the elaborate prisons; how executions were performed, from the ruins of structures which unmistakably indicate the purpose of their construction. The sites of their villages, and the indications of the quarters of the cities, show how closely the people must have been crowded together in their narrow homes. We have remains which indicate the general character of their household implements and the texture of their garments. Their chulpas and tombs give evidence of their belief in a future life. The field thus, and in a thousand other ways, opened to us is a wide one; and I may confidently trust that my researches and explorations furnish many valuable aids for its further investigation. It is not too much to hope that patient labor in this department will enable some future student to reconstruct for us the vanished empire of the Incas. What we already know is enough to awaken the desire to know more.

It would be a curious, possibly an unprofitable, speculation to consider what might have been the future of Peru had not the empire been subverted by the Spanish Conquest. The monuments show that fortresses and towns, roads and bridges, were in course of erection when that untoward event occurred. I call it untoward because there was, under the Incas, a better government, better protection for life, and better facilities for the pursuit of happiness than have existed since the Conquest, or do exist to-day. The material prosperity of the country was far in advance of what it is now. There were greater facilities of intercourse, a wider agriculture, more manufacture, less pauperism and vice, and—shall I say it?—a purer and more useful religion. But one sinister fact darkened the future of the empire. Under Huayna Capac it had spread to its grandest proportions. He could have said, with more truth than Alexander, "Alas, there are no more worlds to conquer!" But his unhappy departure from the prescriptions of his fathers had given him one son by the daughter of the conquered chief of Quito, and he had another by his wife and sister, in the sacred city and capital. His vain attempt to divide the administration of the government of the empire between the son of his love and the true heir to the crimson *llautu*, between Atahualpa and Huascar, brought on civil war, and facilitated a conquest that not even the apparition of horses and the apparent control of the thunder and lightning could have effected otherwise.

How far this civil war, without the Spanish intrusion, would have changed the political and social condition of the empire, we can hardly conjecture. It seems probable that it would have ended in nothing worse than a division of the long and narrow country; the establishment of two great principalities, each of which would have followed its own career of development—a development which, if commensurate with that of the preceding three hundred years, would have carried Peruvian civilization to the highest point of aboriginal American development. The only requisite would have been a written language to place the Peruvians on a level with the best of Oriental nations.

That the empire would, under any circumstances, have greatly extended beyond what it was under Huayna Capac is not probable, unless, indeed, the rulers of Cuzco might have chained the Chibchas or Muyscas of Columbia to their car of conquest; for they never seem to have been able to fight successfully against the savages who inhabited the forests at the foot of the Andes, or to extend their dominions into the broad fertile plains below their mountain homes. The narrow-bladed American axe, victorious over the forests of a continent, was an implement to which they had not attained. How a people who had grown up to existence in regions where every foot of ground which could be made to produce a stalk of maize or a handful of quinoa would have developed in the boundless plains so near to them and yet so far, is a problem which will never have a solution.

It may fairly be asked, What approximate date should be assigned to the remains and monuments which have been described? Here are vast and elaborate structures, ruined, it is true, but still evidencing great skill and labor. From what epoch do they date? They were, of course, the results of gradual development; they are the later mile-stones of progress. But where are the anterior mile-stones — where the antecedent monuments marking the stages of development? And in default of these, it may be asked with apparent, if not with real triumph, "Were not these the works erected, inspired, or suggested by a matured and exotic people; by emigrants or teachers from older and distant centres of civilization—of a civilization of which this is a copy, a reflex, or a caricature?"

To this I may answer, without even advancing an hypothesis, much less propounding a theory, and certainly without dogmatism, that there are some, not to say many, evidences in Peru of an early and comparatively rude past. Combined with the

stupendous and elaborate remains of Tiahuanuco—remains as
elaborate and admirable as those of Assyria, of Egypt, Greece,
or Rome—there are others that are almost exact counterparts of
those of Stonehenge, and Carnac in Brittany, to which is assigned the remotest place in monumental history.  The rude
sun-circles of Sillustani, under the very shadow of some of the
most elaborate, and architecturally the most wonderful, works
of aboriginal America, are indistinguishable counterparts of
the sun-circles of England, Denmark, and Tartary.  Place them
in Scandinavia, and close indeed would be the criticism that
would detect the slightest difference between them.

It is true there are but few and slight traces of early Peruvian towns and buildings, and we might generalize that Inca
civilization, or that out of which it grew, was young or im-
planted.  But we must remember that the habitable and arable area of Peru was, as it is, small, and that under the beneficent rule of the Incas the population became redundant.  The
utmost wisdom of the rulers was exercised to find room and
support for their numerous and increasing subjects; and, as
we have already seen, they in every way economized the precious earth.  Profound indeed must have been the reverence,
deep indeed the superstition, that would have prevented this,
the most practical and utilitarian of American nations as well
as the most progressive, from sweeping away the remains, rude
and uncouth, of an earlier people, albeit their own progenitors,
to give room and scope for their people, to whom they acknowledged their obligation to supply water and food, as their
parent, the Sun, furnished light and warmth.  The only modern
nation that, in its polity, its aggressiveness, its adaptation, and,
above all, its powers of assimilation, as well as in its utter disregard of traditions and of monuments, at all comparable to
the Incas is our own.  Does the most ancient of cemeteries
stand in our way?  Do we respect monuments if they inter-
fere with our notions of utility?  Let us suppose, then, that
we were rapid or even gradual in growth, but circumscribed by
deserts and mountains; would we respect the rude structures,
public or private, of our fathers?  It is only wonderful that so

many remains of a remote antiquity survive in Peru, where, more than in any country in the world, the necessities of the people required the utilization of every inch of ground on which grain or grass could grow or a human habitation be built.

I shall make no attempt to assign dates, or even eras, for Peruvian civilization, much less a date for Peruvian origin. But I do assert the existence in Peru of monuments coincident in character, if not in time, with those which the unanimous verdict of science gives to the earliest of what we call the Old World; and I claim that if more of these do not remain to this day, it is because the limits of the country available for population were so small that their removal, and the substitution of other structures more fitted for a later and more numerous people, became a rigorous necessity. All that can now be safely said is that these monuments are old, very old; but how old we cannot, at least at present, ascertain. And, further, that there is no valid evidence that within any period known to human records the progenitors of the Peruvians reached their country from abroad, or that their civilization was imparted to them by any other race. Even if it be assumed that the whole human family sprung from a single pair, and that their original seat was in the highlands of Armenia, whence they have overspread the globe, still it remains true that the period of their advent in Peru antedates all human record. The attempt to make them Hindoos because *inta* is the Quichua name for the sun, and *Indía* has the same meaning in Hindostanee, is simply absurd.

# APPENDIX.

## A.

THE trepanned skull mentioned on page 457 was taken from an Inca cemetery in the valley of Yucay, within one mile of the "Baths of the Incas." There is no doubt of its ante-Columbian date.

M. Broca presented to the Anthropological Society of Paris the following paper, after a critical examination of the trepanned skull. He says:

"The walls of the skull are very thick, and it presents characteristics which could only belong to an Indian of Peru. And I shall proceed to show that the trepanning was practised during life.

"Upon the left side of the external plate of the frontal bone there is a large white spot, quite regular, almost round, or rather slightly elliptical, forty-two millimetres long and forty-seven broad. The outlines of this spot are not irregular or sinuous. The surface is smooth, and presents the appearance of an entirely normal bone. Around this, to the edges, the general color of the skull is notably browner, and is perforated with a great number of small holes, caused by dilatation of the canaliculi. The line of demarkation between the smooth and cribriform surfaces is abrupt, and it is perfectly certain that the smooth surface had been denuded of its periosteum several days before death. It is thus, in truth, that denudations of the cranium behave. In the denuded points, the superficial layer of the external table, deprived of vessels, and thus deprived of life, undergoes no change, and preserves its normal structure; while the surrounding parts, in undergoing the effects of traumatic inflammation, become the seat of the ostitis.

"After considering the development of these perforations (*porosités*) of the external table of the denuded surface, it seems to me impossible to admit that the subject could have survived the denudation less than seven or eight days. M. Nélaton, who examined the specimen, thinks he may have survived fifteen days.

"The trepanning was performed in the centre of the denuded part; but the four incisions, which circumscribe the removed portion, extend at their extremities to the very limits of the denudation. It is, from this, certain that the separ... on of the periosteum was produced by the surgeon who performed the operation; for the denudation, more regular than it could be as the result of an accident, presents exactly, neither more nor less, the dimensions and form necessitated by the operation done upon the bone.

"This operation consists of four linear incisions, two of which are horizontal and two perpendicular — the horizontal lines cutting the vertical ones at right angles, and sufficiently separated to include a rectangular portion of the bone fifteen millimetres long and seventeen wide; the rectangular portion of bone included by the lines was entirely removed down to the dura mater, and the result is a loss of bone. whose absolute extent corresponds very nearly to that produced by our circular trephines of ordinary size.

"At their middle part the four incisions in the bone occupy its entire thickness, which at this point is six millimetres; and beyond the limits of the removed portion they become more and more superficial, and terminate in a slight depression on the surface of the bone at the limits of the denudation. The width of the incisions is about two millimetres in their middle and superficial part. This width diminishes in the deep parts, so that the bottoms of the cuts become linear: it diminishes in the same way in approximating the extremities of the incisions. * * *

"There is evidently no resemblance between this mode of trepanning and that which has been known from time immemorial in Indo-European surgery. This is not, however, the first time that we have shown how very different in America and the Old World were the first sources of industry, of sciences, and arts.

"In conclusion. I call attention to another question. For what motive has this trepanning been performed? There is no fracture or fissure of either external or internal table. We notice, it is true, on the internal table several very delicate linear cracks, but these present all the ordinary characters of those produced by time, and which are found in the majority of old crania. There was, then, no fracture; and the surgeon who performed the operation could consequently only be governed by the functional troubles in diagnosing the existence of an intra-cranial lesion. Was this diagnosis correct? Did the operation succeed in evacuating a fluid poured into the cranium? I am far from affirming this, but am tempted to believe it. In truth, the internal table around the opening is the seat of a very different alteration from that which existed on the external table around the denudation. It is in patches, the seat of little perforations (*porosités*), which attest the existence of an ostitis; but this does not seem to have been the result of the trepanning, because it is not at all regularly distributed around the opening. It is entirely wanting above the opening, it is slight below, a little better marked on the outside, and is only really well pronounced about a centimetre and a half on the inner side of the internal border of the opening. These peculiarities and several others, which would take too long to detail, are well explained, if we suppose that there had been for some days before the operation an effusion of blood under the dura mater.

"What astonishes me is not the boldness of the operation, as ignorance is often the mother of boldness. To trepan on an apparent fracture at the bottom of a wound is a sufficiently simple conception, and does not necessitate the existence of advanced surgical art; but here the trepanning was performed on a point where there was no fracture, or probably even no wound, so that the surgical act was preceded by a diagnosis. That this diagnosis was exact, as is probable, or that it was false, we are in either case authorized to conclude that there was in Peru, before the European epoch, an advanced surgery; and this idea, an entirely new one, is not without interest in American anthropology."

Note 1.—"After examining carefully this interesting skull, and reading the able opinion of M. Broca, an idea occurred to me, which may afford an explanation of the nature of the injury that led to the operation, and the reasons for which it was performed. According to the account of M. Broca, there is no satisfactory reason for the performance of so bold an operation. He has made no allusion to the probability of a *punctured wound*, one made with a small sharp-pointed instrument. Very small perforations of a skull are sometimes made by a bayonet, dirk, etc., without fracture. They, however, often cause extravasation of blood within the cranium, violent inflammation, suppuration, delirium, coma, etc. A punctured wound, followed by such symptoms, would clearly indicate trepanning to a surgeon of our day. The operation, too, would remove the whole of the injured bone, and leave no trace behind of fracture or other bone injury.

"Such, to my mind, is the rational explanation of the kind of injury inflicted, and of the symptoms, which justified the operation.—Dr. J. C. Nott."

Note 2.—The spear, lance, and arrow-heads of the ancient Peruvians were generally of bronze, sharply pointed. I have in my collection a bronze lance-head, with a socket at one end for the reception of a staff or handle. At this point it is round, measuring a trifle over half an inch in diameter. The socket extends inwards five and a half inches, and from the point where it terminates the solid portion of the lance gradually assumes a square form, and tapers regularly to a point. The whole length of this lance-head is twenty-three inches. What may be called spear-heads are heavier, thicker, and not so long. The arrow-heads are of similar form with the lance-heads, usually about five inches long; also fitted with a socket for receiving the shaft of the arrow. Among the ruins of Grand Chimu, where, according to tradition, was fought the final decisive battle between the Chimus (Yuncas) and the Incas, I found a vast number of skeletons, the skulls of most of which showed evidence of violence. Some were crushed in, as if from the blows of a club; others were cleft, as if by the stroke of a battle-axe, and others perforated, as if by lances or arrows, exhibiting a small square hole corresponding precisely with what would probably be made by the weapons I have described. In fact, I found a skull thus perforated, with a bronze arrow still sticking in it. The orifice was a clear one, with no radiating fissures. I regret that this interesting specimen was lost, with other valuable relics, on its way to the United States. These facts, it appears to me, tend to sustain the hypothesis of Dr. Nott in regard to the wound or injury leading to the operation of trepanning in the skull from Yucay.—E. G. S.

## B.

In the fourth annual report of the Peabody Museum of American Archæology and Ethnology, at Cambridge, Massachusetts, the late Professor Wyman, the curator, gives some "Observations on Crania," with comparative measurements of fifty-six skulls from Peru, presented by Mr. Squier. He remarks:

"The Peruvian crania present the two modes of artificial distortion commonly seen; those from chulpas, or burial-towers, and other places in the neighborhood of Lake Titicaca, being lengthened, while those from nearly all the other localities are broadened and shortened by the flattening of the occiput. They are, on the whole, massive and heavy. Many of the measurements usually recorded in describing ordinary crania have been omitted, since they would, in those under consideration, depend upon the degree to which the distortion has been carried, and would therefore give artificial and not natural dimensions.

"We find nothing in these crania which sustains the view once admitted, but afterwards abandoned, by Dr. Morton, and more recently revived by Mr. John H. Blake and Dr. Daniel Wilson, in regard to the existence of naturally long (dolichocephalic) Peruvian skulls. Dr. Wilson bases his belief in the existence of such upon some crania in the collection of the late Dr. J. C. Warren, which Mr. Blake brought from Peru. He thinks their forms must be natural, because, in crania artificially distorted to the extent that these are, 'the retention of anything like the normal symmetrical proportions is impossible.' We find, however, that the lengthened Peruvian crania in our collection showing unequivocal marks of circular pressure are, contrary to Dr. Wilson's opinion, quite symmetrical. Circular pressure could hardly produce any other than a symmetrical change of form. Through the kindness of Dr. John Collins Warren, we have been able personally to examine the crania above referred to in Dr. Warren's collection, and have been led to adopt the view of Dr. J. Barnard Davis, based on Dr. Wilson's figures, viz., that the lengthening in the alleged dolichocephalic Peruvians is artificial, since the indications of circular pressure are obvious.

"Although the crania from the several localities, as seen in Tables I.-VII., show some differences as regards capacity—*e. g.*, those from Casma, Cajamarquilla, and Truxillo, as compared with those from Grand Chimu, Amacavilca, and Pachacamac—yet in most other respects they are alike. The average capacity of the fifty-six crania measured agrees very closely with that indicated by Morton and Meigs, viz., 1230 c. c., or 75 cubic inches, which is considerably less than that of the barbarous tribes of America, and almost exactly that of the Australians and Hottentots as given by Morton and Meigs, and smaller than that derived from a larger number of measurements by Davis. Thus we have, in this particular, a race which has established a complex civil and religious polity, and made great progress in the useful and fine arts - as its pottery, textile fabrics, wrought metals, highways and aqueducts, colossal architectural structures, and court of almost imperial splendor, prove—on the same level, as regards the quantity of brain, with a race whose social and religious conditions are among the most degraded exhibited by the human race.

"All this goes to show, and cannot be too much insisted upon, that the relative capacity of the skull is to be considered merely as an anatomical, and not as a physiological, characteristic; and unless the quality of the brain can be represented at the same time as the quantity, brain-measurement cannot be assumed as an indication of the intellectual position of races any more than of individuals. From such results, the question is very naturally forced upon us whether comparisons based upon cranial measurements of capacity, as generally made, are entitled to the value usually assigned them. Confined within narrower limits, they may perhaps be of more importance. But even in this case the results are often contradictory. If the brains of Cuvier and Schiller were of the maximum size, so were those of three unknown individuals from the common cemeteries of Paris; while that of Dante was but slightly above the mean, and Byron's was probably even below it."

The tables given on the four following pages are those alluded to by Professor Wyman in his report:

## TABLE I.

SIX CRANIA OF AYMARAS FROM BURIAL-TOWERS, OR CHULPAS, NEAR LAKE TITICACA.

|  | Maximum. | Mean. | Minimum. | Range. |
|---|---|---|---|---|
| Capacity......................... | 1445 | 1292 | 1155 | 290 |
| Circumference................... | 490 | 460.3 | 432 | 58 |
| Length........................... | 178 | 160 | 148 | 25 |
| Breadth ......................... | 136 | 128.5 | 125 | 11 |
| Height........................... | 154 | 138.7 | 130 | 24 |
| Breadth of frontal............... | 93 | 87 2 | 81 | 12 |
| Index of breadth................. | .... | 807 | .... | .... |
| Index of height.................. | .... | 868 | .... | .... |
| Index of foramen magnum........ | .... | ...... | .... | .... |
| Frontal arch..................... | 284 | 206.85 | 257 | 27 |
| Parietal arch.................... | 358 | 309 | 326 | 32 |
| Longitudinal arch................ | 386 | 368 | 348 | 38 |
| Length of frontal ............... | 130 | 126.5 | 120 | 10 |
| Length of parietal............... | 128 | 118.8 | 108 | 20 |
| Length of occipital............... | 127 | 118 | 106 | 21 |
| Zygomatic diameter ............. | 144 | 129.5 | 124 | 20 |

## TABLE II.

FOURTEEN CRANIA FROM CASMA.

|  | Maximum. | Mean | Minimum. | Range. |
|---|---|---|---|---|
| Capacity......................... | 1455 | 1254 | 1050 | 405 |
| Circumference................... | 482 | 471.8 | 450 | 32 |
| Length........................... | 171 | 154 | 143 | 28 |
| Breadth ......................... | 156 | 146 | 130 | 26 |
| Height........................... | 140 | 128.6 | 118 | 22 |
| Breadth of frontal............... | 97 | 91.4 | 82 | 15 |
| Index of breadth................. | .... | 948 | .... | .... |
| Index of height.................. | .... | 835 | .... | .... |
| Index of foramen magnum........ | .... | ...... | .... | .... |
| Frontal arch..................... | 295 | 276.3 | 265 | 30 |
| Parietal arch.................... | 352 | 336.2 | 305 | 47 |
| Longitudinal arch ............... | 362 | 337 | 308 | 54 |
| Length of frontal................ | 123 | 116 | 105 | 18 |
| Length of parietal ............... | 129 | 112.3 | 90 | 39 |
| Length of occipital ............... | 145 | 107.5 | 93 | 52 |
| Zygomatic diameter ............. | 143 | 130.3 | 121 | 22 |

## TABLE III.

SIXTEEN CRANIA FROM AMACAVILCA.

| | Maximum. | Mean. | Minimum. | Range. |
|---|---|---|---|---|
| Capacity............................ | 1320 | 1176.2 | 1055 | 265 |
| Circumference.................... | 491 | 460.3 | 440 | 51 |
| Length............................ | 159 | 149.7 | 144 | 15 |
| Breadth .......................... | 149 | 144.1 | 136 | 13 |
| Height............................ | 134 | 129 | 118 | 16 |
| Breadth of frontal................. | 100 | 92.4 | 88 | 12 |
| Index of breadth.................. | .... | 962 | .... | .... |
| Index of height.................... | .... | 861 | .... | .... |
| Index of foramen magnum ........ | .... | ...... | .... | .... |
| Frontal arch...................... | 296 | 276.4 | 255 | 41 |
| Parietal arch...................... | 338 | 324.5 | 303 | 35 |
| Longitudinal arch ................ | 344 | 321 7 | 300 | 44 |
| Length of frontal ................. | 122 | 111.5 | 102 | 20 |
| Length of parietal ................ | 112 | 105.1 | 87 | 25 |
| Length of occipital ............... | 124 | 106.6 | 97 | 27 |
| Zygomatic diameter............... | 141 | 127.5 | 99 | 42 |

## TABLE IV.

SEVEN CRANIA FROM GRAND CHIMU.

| | Maximum. | Mean. | Minimum. | Range. |
|---|---|---|---|---|
| Capacity............................ | 1460 | 1094.28 | 1065 | 395 |
| Circumference.................... | 512 | 474.85 | 440 | 72 |
| Length............................ | 165 | 153.71 | 137 | 28 |
| Breadth .......................... | 168 | 149.28 | 131 | 37 |
| Height............................ | 126 | 123.85 | 117 | 9 |
| Breadth of frontal................. | 107 | 94 | 83 | 24 |
| Index of breadth.................. | .... | 964 | .... | .... |
| Index of height.................... | .... | 805 | .... | .... |
| Index of foramen magnum ........ | .... | ...... | .... | .... |
| Frontal arch...................... | 305 | 279.71 | 261 | 44 |
| Parietal arch...................... | 357 | 331 | 305 | 56 |
| Longitudinal arch................. | 350 | 316.57 | 309 | 14 |
| Length of frontal ................. | 128 | 114.57 | 105 | 23 |
| Length of parietal................. | 119 | 108 | 94 | 25 |
| Length of occipital ............... | 115 | 108.14 | 95 | 20 |
| Zygomatic diameter ............. | 143 | 131 | 104 | 39 |

### TABLE V.

FOUR CRANIA FROM PACHACAMAC.

|                          | Maximum. | Mean.   | Minimum. | Range. |
|--------------------------|----------|---------|----------|--------|
| Capacity.................| 1365     | 1195    | 1035     | 330    |
| Circumference............| 500      | 484     | 472      | 28     |
| Length...................| 164      | 158.5   | 155      | 9      |
| Breadth .................| 150      | 145.4   | 142      | 8      |
| Height ..................| 131      | 127.5   | 119      | 12     |
| Breadth of frontal.......| 98       | 92.5    | 83       | 15     |
| Index of breadth.........| ....     | 923     | ....     | ....   |
| Index of height..........| ....     | 804     | ....     | ....   |
| Index of foramen magnum .| ....     | ....... | ....     | ....   |
| Frontal arch.............| 294      | 281.5   | 267      | 27     |
| Parietal arch ...........| 331      | 326.75  | 315      | 16     |
| Longitudinal arch .......| 342      | 336.5   | 327      | 15     |
| Length of frontal .......| 120      | 118     | 114      | 6      |
| Length of parietal ......| 117      | 111.25  | 109      | 8      |
| Length of occipital......| 126      | 113     | 103      | 23     |
| Zygomatic diameter.......| 140      | 136.33  | 129      | 11     |

### TABLE VI.

FIVE CRANIA FROM CAJAMARQUILLA.

|                          | Maximum. | Mean.   | Minimum. | Range. |
|--------------------------|----------|---------|----------|--------|
| Capacity.................| 1410     | 1268.75 | 1155     | 255    |
| Circumference............| 490      | 478.6   | 459      | 31     |
| Length...................| 170      | 161.4   | 150      | 20     |
| Breadth .................| 142      | 138.2   | 136      | 6      |
| Height ..................| 131      | 127     | 125      | 6      |
| Breadth of frontal.......| 93       | 91      | 88       | 5      |
| Index of breadth.........| ....     | 556     | ....     | ....   |
| Index of height..........| ....     | 786     | ....     | ....   |
| Index of foramen magnum .| ....     | ....... | ....     | ....   |
| Frontal arch.............| 287      | 278     | 268      | 19     |
| Parietal arch ...........| 332      | 322.6   | 315      | 17     |
| Longitudinal arch........| 361      | 347     | 330      | 31     |
| Length of frontal .......| 125      | 117.4   | 109      | 16     |
| Length of parietal.......| 120      | 115.4   | 111      | 9      |
| Length of occipital......| 119      | 113     | 98       | 21     |
| Zygomatic diameter ......| 139      | 122.8   | 91       | 48     |

## TABLE VII.

FOUR CRANIA FROM TRUXILLO.

| | Maximum. | Mean. | Minimum. | Range. |
|---|---|---|---|---|
| Capacity........................... | 1325 | 1236 | 1135 | 190 |
| Circumference.................... | 500 | 482.7 | 473 | 27 |
| Length........................... | 177 | 158.5 | 150 | 27 |
| Breadth.......................... | 146 | 141.7 | 132 | 14 |
| Height.... ...................... | 135 | 126.7 | 117 | 18 |
| Breadth of frontal ............... | 95 | 93 | 90 | 5 |
| Index of breadth................. | .... | 890 | .... | .... |
| Index of height.................. | .... | 793 | .... | .... |
| Index of foramen magnum ........ | .... | ........ | .... | .... |
| Frontal arch..................... | 294 | 280 | 275 | 19 |
| Parietal arch.................... | 330 | 326.2 | 321 | 9 |
| Occipital arch ................... | .... | ........ | .... | .... |
| Longitudinal arch................ | 359 | 341.25 | 324 | 35 |
| Length of frontal................ | 119 | 116.75 | 114 | 5 |
| Length of parietal............... | 123 | 116 | 110 | 13 |
| Length of occipital .............. | 125 | 106.25 | 195 | 20 |
| Zygomatic diameter .............. | .... | ........ | .... | .... |

## C.

A LARGE share of the attention of the world that has lately been attracted to Peru has been directed to the marvellous railway schemes that have been devised in the country, some of which have been carried into execution, while others remain incomplete. It may be well to mention a few of these, and the course of events that has brought them about and made them possible. I find that I have left but little space for what, at the best, could be only an outline of the present material resources of Peru.

It is true that at the time of the Conquest the Spaniards drew large amounts of gold and silver from the country, so that its name became almost a synonyme for boundless riches. The harvest, however, swept off by Pizarro and his followers left the country bare of the precious metals. The mines and washings whence the Indians drew their supplies were gradually discovered, and made wonderfully productive. Potosi, for its yield of silver, became as celebrated as Golconda for its diamonds; but its glory, like that of Golconda, has departed. Cerro de Pasco is now the great silver-mining centre, and affords the principal supply of silver to Peru. These mines are 13,800 feet above the sea, and 200 miles from the coast. Coal has been discovered in the vicinity, which affords some amelioration to the dwellers in that desolate region.

The mines on the shores of Lake Titicaca, near Puno, which at one time yielded quite a million and a half ounces annually, have for many years produced little or nothing. The opening of the railway to Puno will, no doubt, put them in operation once more. There is no lack of mines in other parts of Peru; but they mostly lie beyond the vast barriers of the Cordilleras, in desolate regions, where their development is almost impossible. The great quicksilver mines of Huancavelica, which formerly yielded, in seven years, 600,000 pounds of mercury, are now practically abandoned, and mercury from California is carried by the mines to work the silver veins beyond.

Gold does not seem to be liberally distributed in Peru. It is reported to be abundant in the remote province of Carabaya, lying beyond Lake Titicaca, where the Indians have some washings. No roads lead to them, and the region is destitute of labor. Tin and copper ores of great purity are found in Southern Peru and Bolivia, between the ranges of the Cordilleras and the Andes. They occur in the singular form of little nodules in the drift strata, are obtained by washing, and are mostly, if not entirely, shipped to England for reduction there.

The principal wealth of Peru, or rather that which was its principal wealth and which was most available, and which has contributed more towards the corruption of the country than any other one thing, is its guano. Deposits of guano are found on the Chincha Islands on the South, and on the Guanajos and Lobas on the North, not to mention some smaller ones on other islands and on the mainland. As it could be rapidly shipped and at low cost, it has been always available as a source of revenue and as good as gold in the treasury. And it has formed the basis of extensive loans which were only limited in amount by the demand and supply of guano.

Guano is the excrement of sea fowl, intermixed with their eggs and decomposed bodies and the remains of seals. It was known to the Incas as a valuable manure, and the birds were protected by them during the breeding season. The guano which is now accumulating slowly at the various islands is deposited almost entirely by birds. The seals have been so much hunted in years past that they are now mostly exterminated, and those which remain venture but a short distance inland. They frequent the shores, caves and low rocks which are washed by the waves and where they can quickly secure safety by taking to the water. Formerly they travelled to the very centre and climbed to the highest points of land, as is shown by the deposits of their skins and bones. At the Lobas Islands and the Macabis the birds are still increasing the deposits rapidly.

There are several species of these birds that inhabit the land, but they do not all contribute in like degree to the formation of the guano Sea birds of the size of the Peynero (little smaller than a goose) will deposit from four to six ounces of excrement daily, and in the space of ten weeks, which is the length of their breeding season, from eighteen to twenty-eight pounds.

The guano which was found in Bahia de Ferrol was formed exclusively by seals, and is so filled with seals' skins and bones as to be almost worthless for exportation.

Among the many other valuable productions of Peru may be mentioned the Alpaca wool. The supply of the whole world is obtained here. Also sugar and cotton.

Perhaps the most useful to mankind of all the natural productions of Peru is the cinchona or Peruvian bark from which the drug quinine is extracted. This tree can be found in the most inaccessible spots in all the mountain wildernesses, towering above all other trees, at an elevation of from three to five thousand feet above the sea. The bark is sent down to the coast on the backs of mules and llamas, and shipped to Europe and parts of America to be manufactured into quinine. Owing to the destructive methods employed in collecting the bark practised by the native collectors, and the constantly increasing demand for quinine, it looked at one time as if the source of supply for the world would be soon exhausted; but, owing to the action of the British Government, who succeeded in transplanting the tree in India and other of her colonies having a climate similar to that in which the tree flourishes in Peru, the importance of the Peruvian bark was greatly diminished; while under the intelligent and careful cultivation in the English colonies, there has been a large increase of the world's supply, the price of quinine has been brought down to a point which is within the reach of all suffering humanity, and a future supply has been guaranteed.

With the large accessions of revenue from the sale of guano and nitrate of soda, vast projects of public works were started. With a judicious administration of this income, the difficulties of communication between the coast and the interior should have been overcome and the country should have been put into a condition to be permanently prosperous when these sources of wealth were exhausted.

To this end, it was proposed to construct lines of railways to scale the Cordilleras and the Andes. The plan of any such work must of necessity be a bold one. No other country in the world has greater need of roads, and if any mistake has been made, it has been in building railways where there should have been good mule-paths and carriage-roads. Over one hundred and fifty millions of dollars have been invested in these enterprises and they are still incomplete. Some of the roads are finished and in working order, and others but partially completed. An idea can be formed of the immense expense and labor of building these roads, when we are told that it was necessary for all the supplies to be brought from abroad. The ties came from the United States, and the rails from England. To penetrate very far into the interior, the Cordilleras must be overcome with the necessary heavy grades and many tunnels and bridges.

The Oroya road, a line seventy-eight miles long, obtains an altitude of 15,645 feet and passes the divide through a tunnel. There are on this single road no fewer than sixty-three tunnels with an aggregate length of 21,000 feet. The road from Ariquipa to Puno crosses the Andes at an elevation of 14,660 feet, and it is proposed to continue the road to La Paz and with a branch of two hundred and ten miles in length to Cuzco.

Whether or not any of these railroads will directly pay the smallest percentage on cost is more than doubtful ; one thing is quite certain, they do not pay at present.

Whether these many roads and great expenditures of treasure will bring a large agricultural people to the high tablelands of Peru, the Thibet of America, and to the immense and interesting basin of Titicaca, of which we have had so many occasions to speak ; whether they will make the deserts of the coast bloom and blossom like the rose ; whether they will develop new life in the people and will be a new source of wealth in the country, remains to be seen. This much, however, we do know, that the wastage of the vast wealth of Peru in railroads and other so-called improvements left the country in such a condition as to fall an easy prey to an ever-jealous, overbearing and restless neighbor, who, seeing the vast accumulations of nitrate of soda lying next to her territory, conceived and carried out the plan of taking it all to herself. Under various pretexts Chili made war upon Peru, but there would have been no war if there had been no guano lands and no nitrate embedded in the desert coast of Peru.

The first battle of the war was fought among the nitrate beds, and at Iquique the great sea-fight took place, and from there the invading army overran the whole country, not even stopping at the gates of Lima. And then when the whole nation of Peru lay prostrate at the feet of the

Chilian conquerors, they only retired upon the concession to them of the whole country lying south of Arica and which contained the nitrate beds, the prize for which the war was instigated. But Chili, after obtaining the prize, found that her title was not as clear as it should have been, and that there were many embarrassments arising from the claims of the foreign bondholders to whom most of this vast wealth had been hypothecated to furnish money whereby the railroads of Peru might be built. She has at last been compelled to make a compromise with the creditors, and recognize the principle, in the annexation of conquered territory, that the rights of neutral creditors must be respected.

---

# D

The coat of arms appearing on the title-page of this book is copied from Mr. C. R. Markham's " Peru and India," and is the one granted to the royal Inca family by Charles V. of Spain, after the Conquest.

# INDEX.

40

CPSIA information can be obtained
at www.ICGtesting.com
Printed in the USA
LVHW080239280621
691267LV00026B/384